Issues in Race and Ethnicity

FOURTH EDITION

CQ PRESS

A Division of SAGE
Washington, D.C.

SELECTIONS FROM **CQ RESEARCHER**

CQ Press
2300 N Street, NW, Suite 800
Washington, DC 20037

Phone: 202-729-1900; toll-free, 1-866-4CQ-PRESS (1-866-427-7737)

Web: www.cqpress.com

Cover design: Kimberly Glyder
Cover photo: AP Images/Steve Klaver

∞ The paper used in this publication exceeds the requirements of the American National Standard for Information Sciences—Permanence of Paper for Printed Library Materials, ANSI Z39.48-1992.

Printed and bound in the United States of America

12 11 10 09 08   1 2 3 4 5

A CQ Press College Publishing Group Publication

Executive director	Brenda Carter
Chief acquisitions editor	Charisse Kiino
Development editor	Dwain Smith
Marketing manager	Christopher O'Brien
Production editor	Anna Socrates
Compositor	Olu Davis
Managing editor	Stephen Pazdan
Electronic production manager	Paul Pressau
Print and design manager	Cynthia Richardson
Sales manager	Linda Trygar

Library of Congress Cataloging-in-Publication Data

Issues in race and ethnicity. — 4th ed.
    p. cm.
  "Selections from the CQ [Congressional Quarterly] Researcher"— ECIP galley.
  Includes bibliographical references.
  ISBN 978-0-87289-614-7 (alk. paper)
  1. United States—Race relations. 2. United States—Ethnic relations. I. Congressional Quarterly, Inc. II. Title.

E184.A1I843 2008
305.800973—dc22

2008049204

Contents

ETHNICITY AND IMMIGRATION

Annotated Contents

The 12 *CQ Researcher* reports reprinted in this book have been reproduced essentially as they appeared when first published. In the few cases in which important new developments have since occurred, updates are provided in the overviews highlighting the principal issues examined.

RACE

Race and Politics

The once unthinkable has happened this November: A black man won the presidency in what many are calling a game-changing election. When freshman Illinois Senator Barack Obama was born in 1961, African Americans couldn't vote in parts of the United States. First dogged by questions of whether he was "black enough," Obama faced doubts during his campaign battle with Arizona Senator John McCain, a 71-year-old Vietnam War hero, about whether racial prejudice would prove a major obstacle to his historic campaign, especially among white working-class voters. Nonetheless, Obama won a decisive majority and benefited from changes in the country's demographic makeup, which is growing less white as immigration diversifies. At the same time, younger voters showed notably less racial prejudice than older generations. Meanwhile, some top Republicans acknowledged that the GOP failed to appeal to a broader range of voters in this election, instead courting its conservative base.

Changing U.S. Electorate

Demographics have played nearly as large a role in this year's presidential race as health care, war and the economy. The Democratic primary contest came down to an African American man dominating voting among blacks, the young and highly educated voters and a white woman winning older voters, Hispanics and the white working class. Barack Obama, as the Democratic nominee, faced a formidable task during the campaign to reunite the party against Republican John McCain. Election results showed that Democrats increased support among Latinos and voters under 30. But states that have traditionally supported Republican candidates are gaining in population and will gain electoral votes by 2012. One sign of changing voter dynamics is the white working class, which made up a majority of all voters not so long ago and is now the key "swing" group of voters, courted by both parties, as evidenced by the Republican attempts to court "Joe the Plumber"and both parties' campaign pitches to working and middle-class voters in battleground states such as Ohio and Pennsylvania. As the American electorate changes shape, the big question is which party stands to gain the most in the long term.

Affirmative Action

Since the 1970s, affirmative action has played a key role in helping minorities get ahead. But many Americans say school and job candidates should be chosen on merit, not race. In November 2008, voters considered ballot initiatives in Colorado and Nebraska to eliminate race as a selection criterion for job or school candidates but would allow preferences for those trying to struggle out of poverty, regardless of their race — an approach endorsed by foes of racial affirmative action. Voters narrowly rejected the ban in Colorado; however, the initiative passed in Nebraska, though the legitimacy of the signatures on the ballot petition has been challenged in court. Big states, meanwhile, including California and Texas, are still struggling to reconcile restrictions on the use of race in college admissions designed to promote diversity. Progress toward that goal has been slowed by a major obstacle: affirmative action hasn't lessened the stunning racial disparities in academic performance plaguing elementary and high school education. Still, the once open hostility to affirmative action of decades ago

has faded. Even some race-preference critics don't want to eliminate it entirely but seek ways to keep diversity without eroding admissions and hiring standards.

Black Colleges

Before the 1950s, most black Americans had little choice but to attend colleges and universities founded for blacks. The outlawing of segregation in 1954 gave black students more higher education options, and many took them. But the nation's 103 historically black colleges and universities (HBCUs) still enroll about 14 percent of African American students. Supporters say black colleges offer important educational and social benefits over predominantly white institutions. Some critics, however, say many HBCUs are academically inferior institutions and do not prepare students for living in a diverse society. Still, in the past few years enrollment has increased at black colleges and universities, following a period of decline, but finances at many remain precariously shaky.

Racial Diversity in Public Schools

Fifty years after the Supreme Court outlawed racial segregation in public schools, a new ruling has raised doubts about how far local school boards can go to integrate classrooms. The Court's 5-4 ruling in cases from Seattle and Louisville bars school districts from using race as a factor in individual pupil assignments. Like many other school districts, the two school systems used racial classifications to promote diversity in the face of segregated housing patterns. But parents argued the plans improperly denied their children their school of choice because of race. Dissenting justices said the ruling was a setback for racial equality. In a pivotal concurrence, however, Justice Anthony M. Kennedy said schools still have some leeway to pursue racial diversity. Meanwhile, some experts argue that socioeconomic integration — bringing low-income and middle-class students together — is a more effective way to pursue educational equity.

Hate Speech

When Don Imus labeled the Rutgers University women's basketball team "nappy-headed hos" in April 2007, it first sounded like just one more insult hurled in his long career as a shock jock. Imus was penalized initially with a two-week suspension. But when a clip of the incident appeared on the Internet site YouTube.com, organizations ranging from the National Association of Black Journalists to the liberal media watchdog group Media Matters for America urged a tougher stance against racial stereotyping on public airwaves. Advertisers began pulling their sponsorship from Imus's show, and both networks that carried it — CBS Radio and MSNBC TV — fired him. The outcome was hailed by some as a long-needed response to an increasingly uncivil culture in which shock jocks, comedians, rappers and other media figures traffic in name-calling, racism and misogyny. However, other analysts say silencing Imus was unfair and could begin a purge of outspoken conservative radio hosts, including political commentators like Rush Limbaugh.

Debating Hip-Hop

Since exploding from the streets of New York in the 1970s, the cultural phenomenon known as hip-hop has morphed from hard-driving dance numbers into sex- and violence-filled "gangsta rap" — and a record-label goldmine. Gangsta lyrics have sparked periodic outbreaks of indignation, but the outrage intensified after white shock jock Don Imus was fired in April 2007 for describing black female athletes in the degrading terms used commonly by hip-hop performers. African American leaders, including Bill Cosby, Oprah Winfrey and the Rev. Al Sharpton, claim the genre's glorification of thug culture — often for the entertainment of white youths — drags down the black community. In response, a few top hip-hop figures have called for cleaning up gangsta content. Meanwhile, a school of socially conscious hip-hop remains vibrant, embraced by political activists, school reformers and artistic innovators who call it an inspiration no matter what happens to the gangsta style.

Reparations Movement

After the Civil War, efforts to compensate former slaves were blocked. Calls for reparations to the ancestors of slaves, to help the nation come to terms with a gross historical injustice, have softened since the start of this decade. But they have helped trigger formal apologies from businesses, universities, states and the U.S. House of Representatives. Other mistreated groups, such as survivors of the Nazi Holocaust, World War II "comfort women" and Australian aborigines, have had mixed success in obtaining financial restitution, but many have also recently been comforted by governmental acknowledgment of the wrongs they have suffered. Some have argued that historic reconciliation is necessary to prevent future atrocities. But others argue that reconciliation efforts are distractions from present-day concerns.

ETHNICITY AND IMMIGRATION

Immigration Debate

The number of illegal immigrants in the country has topped 12 million, making immigration once again a central topic of debate. Moreover, with undocumented workers spreading far beyond traditional "gatekeeper" states such as California and Texas, complaints about illegal immigrants have become a daily staple of talk radio. Enacting tougher enforcement policies was a dominant theme in the early stages of the 2008 presidential campaign, particularly on the Republican side. Just in the past year, states and localities have passed hundreds of bills to crack down on employers and illegal immigrants seeking public benefits. But Congress has been unable to act, despite a bipartisan deal brokered in 2007 by the Bush administration. A new administration and the next Congress will likely face what has proved so far an impossible task — curbing the number of immigrants without causing labor shortages in key economic sectors such as agriculture and hospitality.

America's Border Fence

America is rushing to build 670 miles of fencing along the U.S.–Mexican border by the end of 2008. The fence — or wall, as critics along the border call it — is to include 370 miles of fencing intended to stop illegal immigrants on foot and 300 miles of vehicle barriers. To speed construction, the Bush administration is using unprecedented authority granted by Congress to waive environmental, historic and cultural protection laws. No one claims that building physical barriers along roughly a third of America's 2,000-mile southern border will stem illegal immigration by itself, but supporters believe it is an essential first step in "securing the border," providing a critical line of defense against illegal immigration, drug smugglers and even terrorists. Opponents see it as a multi-billion dollar waste that will only shift illegal immigrants toward more dangerous and difficult routes into the country, while doing environmental, cultural and economic damage.

American Indians

Winds of change signal improved prospects for many of the nation's 4.4 million American Indians. The number of tribes managing their own affairs has increased dramatically, and an urban Indian middle class is quietly taking root. The booming revenues of many Indian-owned casinos seem the ultimate proof that Indians are overcoming a history of mistreatment, poverty and exclusion. Yet most of the gambling houses don't rake in stratospheric revenues. And despite statistical upticks in socioeconomic indicators, American Indians are still poorer, more illness-prone and less likely to be employed than their fellow citizens. Meanwhile, tribal governments remain largely dependent on direct federal funding of basic services — funding that Indian leaders and congressional supporters decry as inadequate. But government officials say they are still providing essential services despite budget cuts.

Gang Crisis

Once an urban problem, street gangs have now infiltrated U.S. communities large and small. Gang experts say at least 21,500 gangs — with more than 731,000 members — are active nationwide. Long-established domestic gangs like the Bloods and the Crips remain powerful, but the problem has worsened dramatically in recent years. Heavy immigration, particularly from Latin America and Asia, has introduced highly violent gangs like Mara Salvatrucha and the Almighty Latin Kings Nation. Bound by tight ethnic and racial ties, they often stymie police investigations by assaulting or killing potential witnesses. Having already diversified from illegal drugs into auto theft, extortion, property crimes and home invasion, some East Coast gangs have begun trafficking in fraudulent identification papers that could be used by terrorists. While experts agree gangs are more pervasive than ever, few agree on a remedy. Proposed legislation would increase penalties for gang membership and gang crimes, but critics say it won't solve the problem.

Preface

As we go to press with this edition, America prepares for its first African American president. At the same time, minority populations continue to grow, and concerns intensify about U.S. border security and immigration. It is during such dynamic times that issues in race and ethnicity resonate ever more profoundly with Americans. These topics confound even well-informed citizens and often lead to cultural and political conflicts because they raise formidable public policy questions: Are whites losing political clout? Has affirmative action outlived its usefulness? Would blocking all illegal immigrants hurt or benefit the U.S. economy? To promote change and hopefully reach viable resolution, scholars, students and policymakers must understand the context and content of each of these issues, as well as how these debates play out in the public sphere.

Based on the premise that only an objective examination that synthesizes all competing viewpoints can lead to sound analysis, this fourth edition of *Issues in Race and Ethnicity* provides comprehensive and unbiased coverage of some of today's most pressing policy problems. It enables instructors to fairly and comprehensively uncover opposing sides of each issue and illustrate just how significantly they impact citizens and the leaders they elect. This book is a compilation of twelve recent reports from *CQ Researcher*, a weekly policy backgrounder that brings into focus key issues on the public agenda. *CQ Researcher* fully explains complex concepts in plain English. Each article chronicles and analyzes past legislative and judicial action as well as current and possible future maneuvering. Each report addresses how issues affect all levels of government —

whether at local, state or federal — and also the lives and futures of all citizens. *Issues in Race and Ethnicity* is designed to promote in-depth discussion, facilitate further research and help readers think critically and formulate their own positions on these crucial issues.

This collection is organized into two sections: "Race" and "Ethnicity and Immigration." Each section spans a range of important public policy concerns. The reports in this volume were chosen to expose students to a wide range of issues, from affirmative action to illegal immigration. Eight of the twelve reports are new to this edition, and two reports, "Black Colleges" and "Reparations Movement," have been updated. We are gratified to know that *Issues in Race and Ethnicity* has found a following in a wide range of departments in political science and sociology.

CQ RESEARCHER

CQ Researcher was founded in 1923 as *Editorial Research Reports* and was sold primarily to newspapers as a research tool. The magazine was renamed and redesigned in 1991 as *CQ Researcher*. Today, students are its primary audience. While still used by hundreds of journalists and newspapers, many of which reprint portions of the reports, *Researcher*'s main subscribers are now high school, college and public libraries. In 2002, *Researcher* won the American Bar Association's coveted Silver Gavel Award for magazine excellence for a series of nine reports on civil liberties and other legal issues.

Researcher staff writers — all highly experienced journalists — sometimes compare the experience of writing a *Researcher* report to drafting a college term paper. Indeed, there are many similarities. Each report is as long as many term papers — about 11,000 words — and is written by one person without any significant outside help. One of the key differences is that the writers interview leading experts, scholars and government officials for each issue.

Like students, staff writers begin the creative process by choosing a topic. Working with *Researcher*'s editors, the writer identifies a controversial subject that has important public policy implications. After a topic is selected, the writer embarks on one to two weeks of intense research. Newspaper and magazine articles are clipped or downloaded, books are ordered and informa-tion is gathered from a wide variety of sources, including interest groups, universities and the government. Once the writers are well informed, they develop a detailed outline and begin the interview process. Each report requires a minimum of ten to fifteen interviews with academics, officials, lobbyists and people working in the field. Only after all interviews are completed does the writing begin.

CHAPTER FORMAT

Each issue of *CQ Researcher*, and therefore each selection in this book, is structured in the same way. A selection begins with an introductory overview, which is briefly explored in greater detail in the rest of the report.

The second section chronicles the most important and current debates in the field. It is structured around a number of key issue questions, such as "Should school systems promote racial diversity in individual schools?" and "Should the government do more to restrain hate speech?" This section is the core of each selection. The questions raised are often highly controversial and usually the object of much argument among scholars and practitioners. Hence, the answers provided are never conclusive, but rather detail the range of opinion within the field.

Following those issue questions is the "Background" section, which provides a history of the issue being examined. This retrospective includes important legislative and executive actions and court decisions to inform readers on how current policy evolved.

Next, the "Current Situation" section examines important contemporary policy issues, legislation under consideration and action being taken. Each selection ends with an "Outlook" section that gives a sense of what new regulations, court rulings and possible policy initiatives might be put into place in the next five to ten years.

Each report contains features that augment the main text: sidebars that examine issues related to the topic, a pro/con debate by two outside experts, a chronology of key dates and events and an annotated bibliography that details the major sources used by the writer.

ACKNOWLEDGMENTS

We wish to thank many people for helping to make this collection a reality. Thomas J. Colin, managing editor of

CQ Researcher, gave us his enthusiastic support and cooperation as we developed this edition. He and his talented staff of editors and writers have amassed a first-class collection of *Researcher* articles, and we are fortunate to have access to this rich cache. We also thankfully acknowledge the advice and feedback from current readers and are gratified by their satisfaction with the book.

Some readers may be learning about *CQ Researcher* for the first time. We expect that many readers will want regular access to this excellent weekly research tool. For subscription information or a no-obligation free trial of *Researcher*, please contact CQ Press at www.cqpress.com or toll-free at 1-866-4CQ-PRESS (1-866-427-7737).

We hope that you will be pleased by the fourth edition of *Issues in Race and Ethnicity.* We welcome your feedback and suggestions for future editions. Please direct comments to Charisse Kiino, Chief Acquisitions Editor, College Publishing Group, CQ Press, 2300 N St, NW, Suite 800, Washington, DC 20037, or send e-mail to ckiino@cqpress.com.

— *The Editors of CQ Press*

Contributors

Thomas J. Colin, managing editor of *CQ Researcher*, has been a magazine and newspaper journalist for more than 30 years. Before joining Congressional Quarterly in 1991, he was a reporter and editor at the *Miami Herald* and *National Geographic* and editor in chief of *Historic Preservation*. He holds a bachelor's degree in English from the College of William and Mary and in journalism from the University of Missouri.

Marcia Clemmitt is a veteran social-policy reporter who joined *CQ Researcher* after serving as editor in chief of *Medicine and Health*, a Washington-based industry newsletter, and staff writer for *The Scientist*. She has also been a high school math and physics teacher. She holds a bachelor's degree in arts and sciences from St. John's College, Annapolis, and a master's degree in English from Georgetown University.

Alan Greenblatt is a staff writer for Congressional Quarterly's *Governing* magazine, and he previously covered elections and military and agricultural policy for *CQ Weekly*. A recipient of the National Press Club's Sandy Hume Memorial Award for political reporting, he holds a bachelor's degree from San Francisco State University and a master's degree in English literature from the University of Virginia.

Kenneth Jost, associate editor of *CQ Researcher*, graduated from Harvard College and Georgetown University Law Center, where he is an adjunct professor. He is the author of *The Supreme Court*

Yearbook and editor of *The Supreme Court A to Z* (both published by CQ Press). He was a member of the *CQ Researcher* team that won the 2002 American Bar Association Silver Gavel Award.

Reed Karaim, a freelance writer living in Tucson, Arizona, has written for *The Washington Post, U.S. News & World Report, Smithsonian, American Scholar, USA Weekend* and other publications. He is the author of the novel, *If Men Were Angels*, which was selected for the Barnes & Noble Discover Great New Writers series. He is also the winner of the Robin Goldstein Award for Outstanding Regional Reporting, as well as other journalism awards. Karaim is a graduate of North Dakota State University in Fargo, North Dakota.

Peter Katel is a veteran journalist who previously served as Latin America bureau chief for *Time* magazine in Mexico City and as a Miami-based correspondent for *Newsweek* and the *Miami Herald*'s *El Nuevo Herald*. He also worked as a reporter in New Mexico for eleven years and wrote for several nongovernmental organizations, including International Social Service and the World Bank. He has won several awards, including the Interamerican Press Association's Bartolome Mitre Award. He is a graduate of the University of New Mexico with a degree in university studies.

David Masci is a senior research fellow at the Pew Forum on Religion & Public Life, where he is the in-house expert on church-state issues. He is a former *CQ Researcher* staff writer and was a reporter at CQ's *Daily Monitor* and *CQ Weekly.* He holds a bachelor's degree in medieval history from Syracuse University and a law degree from The George Washington University.

William Triplett is a veteran writer who is now Washington correspondent for *Variety.* A former *CQ Researcher* staff writer, he previously covered science and the arts for such publications as *Smithsonian, Air & Space, Washingtonian, Nature* and *The Washington Post.* He holds a bachelor's degree in journalism from Ohio University and a master's degree in English literature from Georgetown University.

1

Race and Politics

Peter Katel

Republican presidential candidate Sen. John McCain greets supporters at a primary night party in Alexandria, Va., last Feb. 5. Some Republicans say the GOP must attract more Latinos and blacks to remain competitive with the Democrats.

From *CQ Researcher*, July 18, 2008.

When the Rev. Martin Luther King Jr. delivered his famous "I Have a Dream" speech at the Lincoln Memorial, capping the historic 1963 March on Washington, he was talking about only the most basic rights. "I have a dream," he thundered, "that one day this nation will rise up and live out the true meaning of its creed: 'We hold these truths to be self-evident: that all men are created equal.' "

Perhaps only in King's inner-most, private dreams did he even entertain the possibility of an African American running for president, let alone being elected. At the time, standing up for voting rights for black people often meant laying your life on the line.

Yet, 45 years later, to the day, Sen. Barack Obama — a black man — accepted the Democratic Party nomination for president. The freshman U.S. senator from Illinois boasts a relatively slim résumé for a major-party presidential candidate: before his Senate stint, eight years in the Illinois legislature and three years of community organizing. Where he most obviously differs from his predecessors, though, is his skin color, the result of having a black Kenyan father and white Kansan mother.

"A lot of black folks, myself included, occasionally pinch ourselves to see if this is really real," says James Rucker of San Francisco, co-founder of ColorOfChange.org, a Web-based network that aims to boost the political presence of African Americans.

Perhaps adding to the dreamlike quality of the moment, Obama's almost-certain Republican opponent, four-term Sen. John McCain of Arizona, a white, 71-year-old war hero — is running slightly behind in some polls. But even if McCain later moves to the lead, Obama, 46, already has upset expectations

Hispanic Population Grew Fastest

The number of Hispanics in the United States has grown by nearly a third since 2000. By contrast, blacks and whites have only grown by 9 and 2 percent, respectively.

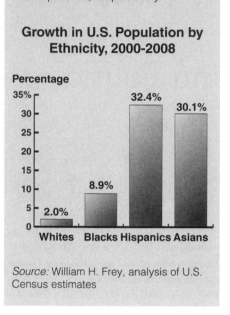

Growth in U.S. Population by Ethnicity, 2000-2008

Source: William H. Frey, analysis of U.S. Census estimates

rooted in America's complicated and violent racial history.

Obama's strong showing may be as much generational as racial. "We have more racially conservative people being replaced by younger people coming into adulthood who are much more comfortable with the racial and ethnic diversity that characterizes the country today," says Scott Keeter, director of survey research for the nonpartisan Pew Research Center.

Even so, most recent poll results still show a close race. In June, a *Washington Post*-ABC News survey showed Obama with 48 percent support, against 42 percent for McCain. Estimates of electoral votes showed McCain ahead, but by only six votes. [1]

Arguably, Obama should be leaving McCain in the dust. A Republican affiliation is a ticket to the political graveyard these days, as any number of GOP politicians are saying. Former House Speaker Newt Gingrich sees a "catastrophic collapse in trust for Republicans." Yet Obama and McCain are in "a very competitive race for president," Democratic pollster Peter Hart told *The Wall Street Journal.* [2]

Is Obama's race — as opposed to his relative inexperience or his policy proposals or his personality — holding his numbers down?

A national poll in early July found that Americans disagree on some — but not all — race-related issues. Twenty-nine percent of blacks thought race relations in the U.S. were generally good compared to 55 percent of whites. Yet 70 percent of whites and 65 percent of blacks thought America is ready to elect a black president. As to the candidates themselves, 83 percent of black voters had favorable opinions of Obama compared with 31 percent of whites. And only 5 percent of blacks had favorable opinions of McCain vs. 35 percent of whites. [3]

Obama supporters and the candidate himself are predicting that Republicans inevitably will resort to race. "They're going to try to make you afraid of me. 'He's young and inexperienced and he's got a funny name. And did I mention he's black?' " Obama told a fundraiser in Jacksonville, Fla., in late June. [4]

Republican officials and activists reject the notion that race will be the deciding issue. "I don't believe this presidential election is going to be determined by the race of the candidates," says Minnesota Gov. Tim Pawlenty, a Republican who had been frequently mentioned as a potential vice-presidential running mate for McCain.

Republicans predict, however, that Obama's camp will treat legitimate political challenges as racial attacks. "Every word will be twisted to make it about race," said Sen. Lindsey Graham, R-S.C., a McCain friend and adviser. But GOP attacks on Obama on issues such as national security and the economy, he said, will have "nothing to do with him being an African American." [5]

Still, no one disputes that race inevitably will affect the election. Race has been intertwined with American history even before nationhood, and racial issues have figured in virtually all past presidential elections for the past half-century — before a major party had a black candidate.

In the politically crucial South — a Republican bastion since 1980 — most white and black voters (when blacks could even register) have always joined opposed parties. When the Democratic Party carried the banner of segregation, blacks tended to be Republicans. After the Democrats aligned themselves with the civil rights movement of the 1960s, the races switched parties.

"The majority [of Southerners] define themselves as conservative," says political scientist Merle Black, a specialist in Southern politics at Emory University in Atlanta. "White moderates have tended to be more Republican than Democratic; that isolates the Democrats with white liberals and African Americans, who are not a majority in any Southern state."

Democrats Al Gore in 2000 and John Kerry in 2004 each failed to win a single Southern state. But some experts give Obama a strong chance in Virginia — and outside possibilities in North Carolina and Florida. As if to underline the point, Obama opened his post-primary campaign in Virginia on June 5.

Obama's bold move exemplified the approach that has taken him further than any African American politician in U.S. history.

Indeed, Shelby Steele, a conservative writer of black and white parentage, is disavowing the last part of the subtitle of his recent book, *A Bound Man: Why We Are Excited About Obama and Why He Can't Win.* Steele, a senior fellow at the Hoover Institution at Stanford University in Palo Alto, Calif., says: "I underestimated the hunger in America for what Obama represents — racial transcendence, redemption. He's this wonderful opportunity to prove that we're not a racist society. I thought that would take him a very long way, but I didn't think it would take him all the way, but it may."

However strong that hunger may be, it's not universal. Hard-core race prejudice remains a factor in American life. If Obama wins, "We'll end up slaves. We'll be made slaves just like they was once slaves," Johnny Telvor of Williamson, W. Va., told *The Observer*, a British newspaper. And Victoria Spitzer, an Obama campaign volunteer from Pennsylvania, told *The Washington Post* of even uglier comments. "Hang that darky from a tree," she said she was told once as she made phone calls to dozens of prospective primary voters. [6]

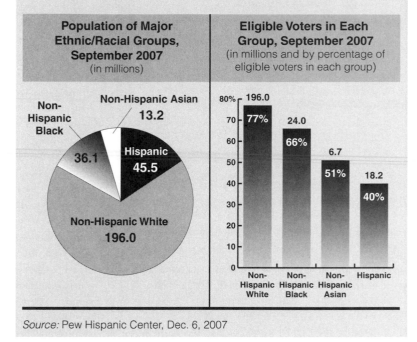

Hispanics Lag in Percentage of Eligible Voters

Hispanics are the largest minority group in the U.S. (left) but have the lowest percentage of eligible voters (right) because so many Hispanics don't have U.S. citizenship or are under age 18.

Population of Major Ethnic/Racial Groups, September 2007 (in millions)

Non-Hispanic Asian 13.2
Non-Hispanic Black 36.1
Hispanic 45.5
Non-Hispanic White 196.0

Eligible Voters in Each Group, September 2007 (in millions and by percentage of eligible voters in each group)

Non-Hispanic White: 196.0 — 77%
Non-Hispanic Black: 24.0 — 66%
Non-Hispanic Asian: 6.7 — 51%
Hispanic: 18.2 — 40%

Source: Pew Hispanic Center, Dec. 6, 2007

Obama argues that the country is indeed ready to rise above America's centuries-old racial divide. "In the history of African American politics in this country there has always been some tension between speaking in universal terms and speaking in very race-specific terms about the plight of the African American community," Obama said during a National Public Radio interview in 2007. "By virtue of my background, you know, I am more likely to speak in universal terms." [7]

"Universal" now describes a far more diverse population than the white-majority/black-minority paradigm that prevailed only a few decades ago.

The U.S. Census Bureau calculates the nation's entire minority population — of whom Latinos make up the biggest single component — at 34 percent. (*See sidebar, p. 14.*) "In a single lifetime, we will have gone from a country made up largely of white Europeans to one that looks much more like the rest of the world," writes Simon Rosenberg, president of NDN (formerly New Democratic Network), a liberal think tank and advocacy organization. [8]

AFP/Getty Images/Emmanuel Dunand

Sen. Barack Obama talks with construction workers at Indiana's University of Evansville on May 5, 2008. Although Obama has encountered resistance from white, working-class voters, 90 percent of the white respondents to a recent survey said they would be comfortable, in principle, with a black president.

Still, old-school racial issues persist. The "post-racial" aura of Obama's candidacy suffered some erosion after a video clip surfaced in March of a fiery black nationalist sermon by Obama's pastor, the Rev. Jeremiah A. Wright Jr. of Trinity United Church of Christ in Chicago, ending with the unforgettable: "God damn America." [9]

After cable news channels put the clip in round-the-clock rotation, Obama disassociated himself from Wright's remarks. When that didn't calm the waters, the Indonesia- and Hawaii-bred candidate gave a major speech on March 18 in Philadelphia, in which he confronted suggestions that his childhood outside the continental United States, and his Ivy League education had sheltered him from the U.S racial drama: "I have never been so naïve as to believe that we can get beyond our racial divisions in a single election cycle, or with a single candidacy — particularly a candidacy as imperfect as my own." [10]

The primary contest was winding to a close. Inevitably, the Wright affair and its aftermath permeated news coverage of the final elections.

In a *Newsweek* poll in May, 21 percent of white registered voters said they didn't think America was ready to elect an African American president, and 18 percent of non-whites agreed. But pollsters also tried gauging the extent of prejudice, asking white voters only if "we have gone too far in pushing equal rights in this country." Thirty-nine percent said yes. [11]

And in Democratic primary elections in the politically critical states of Ohio and Pennsylvania, as well as in West Virginia and Kentucky, exit polls showed that Obama faced clear resistance among white voters with no more than high-school educations — the standard definition of "working class."

But a Roanoke, Va.-based political consultant who specializes in rural voters argues that Obama's race is a dealbreaker only with a small minority of voters in the Appalachian region that includes Pennsylvania, Ohio and Virginia. "There's one thing that could kill him — his gun record," says David "Mudcat" Saunders. "He's got to come to Jesus on guns. You start taking peoples' handguns, which is how the National Rifle Association right now is defining him — if he gets branded with that, he's done." [12]

Obama may have weakened his case with rural gun owners with his widely reported comments at a San Francisco fundraising event shortly before the Pennsylvania primary. "You go into some of these small towns in Pennsylvania, and like a lot of small towns in the Midwest, the jobs have been gone now for 25 years, and nothing's replaced them," he told prospective donors. "Each successive administration has said that somehow these communities are gonna regenerate, and they have not. So it's not surprising then that they get bitter, they cling to guns or religion or antipathy to people who aren't like them or anti-immigrant sentiment or anti-trade sentiment as a way to explain their frustrations." [13]

To Obama's foes, the comments confirmed their depiction of him as an arrogant and condescending Ivy Leaguer — someone who aroused class-based suspicion more than racial hostility.

Whether Obama, who grew up fatherless and whose family at one point relied on food stamps, fits the standard definition of "elite" is one question. Another, say some scholars, is whether depictions of negative personal reactions to Obama as working-class pride are a cover. "I don't buy the argument that the racial argument is just a class discussion," says Paula McClain, a specialist in racial politics at Duke University. "For blacks, it doesn't matter how high you get. Millions of middle-class blacks still experience slights."

Obama lost Pennsylvania. But a *Washington Post* reporter traveling through its small towns found voters who agreed with Obama's basic assessment, if not with his wording. "People are sort of bitter, but they're not carrying around guns and causing crimes like he specified," said retired factory worker George Guzzi. "Everyone makes mistakes." Guzzi plans to vote for Obama. [14]

American voters may be more nuanced in their judgments than some pundits think they are. And Obama's influence is undeniable. "No one up until this point has been able to change the dynamics like he has," says Hanes Walton Jr., a political scientist at the Center for Afroamerican and African Studies at the University of Michigan. "Some people would call it a sea change."

As voters debate the impact of race on this year's election, here are some of the key issues being discussed:

Has Republican Party identification with white Southerners cost it support in other regions?

Beginning in the late 1960s, Republican strategists focused on cultivating white Southerners. By the time Ronald Reagan opened his post-nomination presidential campaign in Philadelphia, Miss., in 1980 the Republicans' "Southern strategy" had virtually locked up the white South.

The massive shift of white Democrats to the GOP followed Democratic President Lyndon B. Johnson's victory in passing the Civil Rights Act of 1964 and the Voting Rights Act of 1965, even though some Republicans say opposition to ending segregation played virtually no part in their party's takeover of former Confederate states.

Whites and Non-Whites Share Attitudes on Race

About three-quarters of whites and non-whites believe the United States is ready to elect an African-American president. Two-thirds of both groups think Barack Obama would not favor any specific racial group if he were elected president.

Do you think America is ready to elect an African-American president, or not?

Whites: No 21%, Yes 72%
Non-whites: No 18%, Yes 75%

If the choices for president in November are Barack Obama, the Democrat, and John McCain, the Republican, how important will the candidates' race be to your voting decision?

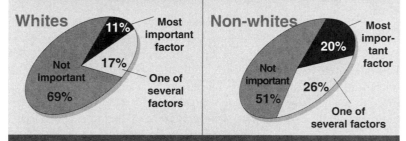

Whites: Most important factor 11%, One of several factors 17%, Not important 69%
Non-whites: Most important factor 20%, One of several factors 26%, Not important 51%

If Barack Obama were to become president, do you think his administration's policies would favor African-Americans and other minorities, would favor whites, or would not favor any group in particular?

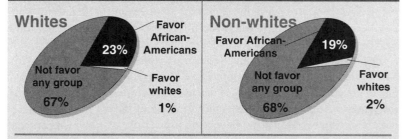

Whites: Favor African-Americans 23%, Favor whites 1%, Not favor any group 67%
Non-whites: Favor African-Americans 19%, Favor whites 2%, Not favor any group 68%

Note: Percentages do not add to 100 because "Don't know" answers are omitted.

Source: Princeton Survey Research Associates International, "Obama and the Race Factor," poll for *Newsweek*, May 23, 2008

Number of Black Elected Officials Skyrocketed

The number of elected black officials in the United States rose to more than 9,000 in 2000 — the most recent available data — up from less than 1,500 in 1970 (graph at left). The biggest gains were in county and municipal offices (bar graph at right).

Elected Black Officials in the U.S.

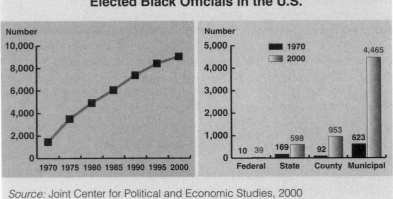

Source: Joint Center for Political and Economic Studies, 2000

But twin brothers Earl and Merle Black, white political scientists who've spent their careers studying the South, argue that the timing of the rise of Southern Republicanism was no coincidence. Citing data from a long-running research project, "American National Election Studies," the Blacks note that college-educated Southern white Protestants — the backbone of the Republican South — largely reject affirmative action and court-ordered busing to achieve racial balance in schools and say equality has been overemphasized as a goal. [15]

These findings don't point to a vast pool of unreconstructed racism in the South. But they do lend credence to the view that post-civil-rights-era unease among white Southerners fits easily into the modern low-tax, small-government, strong-military ideological package that Reagan assembled and that his Republican successors have continued. "On matters of race, religion, philosophy of government, taxes, national defense and culture," the Blacks write, "[Reagan] gave voice to many of their most cherished conservative values and aspirations as well as their most practical and material interests." [16]

Conservative Republicanism remains the dominant Southern doctrine. But some political analysts argue that its appeal is waning elsewhere. "The political views and social views of white Southerners are so out of step with the rest of the country," says Ruy Teixeira, a political analyst and senior fellow at the Center for American Progress, a think tank founded by former Clinton administration officials. "Voters of similar demographics outside the South tend to be a lot less conservative."

McCain, Teixeira says, "would like to move to the center," but most high-level Republicans are in sync, ideologically, with the views of their party's Southern base.

Minnesota Gov. Pawlenty argues that the GOP's nearly all-white demographics reflect no ideological or strategic intent. Rather, he says, "We had success on the traditional formula. Maybe we've gotten a little complacent; maybe we're living a little in the past."

Still, Pawlenty says, Republicans have become "purposeful about reaching out to include candidates who are women and from more diverse backgrounds." This tactic can be more successful than most people realize, he argues. "Areas where socioeconomic challenges exist tend to be heavily represented by Democratic officeholders, but they also happen to be areas that are not doing very well. I always say, 'How is that working out for you? Over time, if we show results, are you willing to at least be open-minded?' It's at least an icebreaker."

Outside the Republican orbit, however, some analysts argue that the party's chances of broadening its base are limited by dependence on its Southern base. "These people are anti-immigration," says David Bositis of the Joint Center for Political and Economic Studies, "which is not the greatest thing in the world to be when the country is exploding with an immigrant population. As soon as they become citizens, they're registering to vote in record numbers. So the Republicans are putting themselves in a position where they're seriously alienating the fastest-growing population group in the country."

Some Republicans agree. Grover Norquist, a conservative activist and president of Americans for Tax Reform, advocates a more energetic GOP effort to attract Latino support and says anti-immigration Republicans aren't helping the cause.

"Some of the smart restrictionists, or 'deportationists,' say, 'Three out of four Hispanics are in the country legally,' " Norquist says. " 'They won't care if you deport the fourth one.' " But, he adds, the fourth one is "their relative or their neighbor or their friend. When you scare the one out of four, you irritate the three out of four."

But Norquist disputes the view that the anti-immigration campaign waged by Rep. Tom Tancredo, R-Colo., and supported by other top Republicans grows out of the party's Southern history. Nor is the party's poor record in attracting African Americans the result of any institutional GOP prejudice, he says. "The party has allowed Democrats to make that case," Norquist told a recent conference at the New America Foundation, a liberal think tank. "The modern black church became an organizing tool for the Democratic Party. The Republican Party needs to spend more time doing outreach and pointing out that the Democratic Party is the party that historically has played racial politics. As Bill Clinton and Hillary Clinton have shown, they're perfectly capable of playing racial politics when she's running against Obama."

Can the Democrats attract white, working-class votes outside the South?

Near the end of her contest with Obama for the Democratic nomination, Sen. Clinton suggested that her race gave her an advantage with white, working-class voters in Pennsylvania and Ohio. "I have a much broader base to build a winning coalition on," she said, citing an Associated Press article "that found how Sen. Obama's support among working, hard-working Americans, white Americans, is weakening again, and how whites in both states who had not completed college were supporting me." [17]

Rep. Charles Rangel, D-N.Y., a Clinton backer and an African American, later called the remark "the dumbest thing she ever could have said." Clinton herself agreed.

Still, the comment had some basis in exit poll data. Among Ohio and Pennsylvania Democrats with no more than a high-school education, Clinton won 6 in 10 votes. And in Pennsylvania, of the 13 percent of white voters who said race mattered to them, three-quarters voted for Clinton. [18]

Near the end of the primary race in Kentucky, exit polls showed a high level of race-based opposition to Obama. Of the 20 percent of white voters who said race played a part in their decisions, 90 percent voted for Clinton. [19]

White and black Democrats have diverged politically in the past, though not consistently. Since the civil rights era of the 1950s and '60s, the Democratic Party has become the political home for African Americans. But even before blacks became a national political presence, the Democratic Party identified itself as the voice of working folk. But it also had widespread support from highly educated professionals, such as plaintiffs' lawyers, plus many Hollywood stars and Wall Street financiers. [20]

Links between the party's well-heeled members and its working-class base began unraveling in the late 1960s. In his winning 1980 presidential campaign, Reagan further deepened the divide, cultivating white working-class voters who became known as "Reagan Democrats."

The extent to which race played a role in these defections to the GOP has been debated for decades. But there is no question the Republican Party played up resentment over affirmative action and school busing that was simmering among some whites. By the late 1990s — after three landmark Supreme Court decisions limiting the federal government's role in ordering school desegregation — some of that anger was dying away.

And President Bill Clinton's support for welfare-reform legislation eliminated another racially charged issue from the political agenda.

Today, sensitive to the possibility that affirmative action could reappear as an issue, Obama took care to say last year that he doesn't think his daughters would be good candidates for race-based preferences, given the advantages they're enjoying. Race-based affirmative action should become a "diminishing tool," he said, adding that white students from poor households should get some special consideration in school applications. [21]

Democratic analysts who specialize in working-class issues agree that race can influence voting decisions, but not overwhelmingly.

"There are going to be people who vote against Barack Obama because they're racists — but I don't give a damn about those people," says Saunders, the Virginia-based political strategist. "We ain't going to get the racist vote." He adds, "I'm not saying that if you're a Republican, you're a racist."

Fundamentally, Saunders says, rural and urban working people — white or black — are subject to the same economic and social forces. "We both have problems with education, health care, drug abuse — they've got crack, we've got crystal meth," Saunders says. "None of us can keep our children in our neighborhoods, because there are no jobs." Obama can win votes, Saunders argues, by uniting blacks and whites around these shared problems.

But other trends run counter to the populist vision of a city-rural alliance, say some Republicans with expertise on the subject of working-class Republicans. Minnesota Gov. Pawlenty's four siblings are all "classic Reagan Democrats," he says, including two longtime union members. "They've morphed over the decades in their political views — they're independent and lean Republican," he says. "They don't want their taxes raised, they don't care for too much of a liberal agenda socially or economically. They don't want the government taking over the healthcare system. My brothers like to hunt and don't like anyone messing with their guns."

The Center for American Progress' Teixeira, who has written extensively from a Democratic perspective about working-class voting, argues that Obama will be trying to get past that standard Republican argument. "His candidacy could revive issues about giveaways to the undeserving poor," Teixeira acknowledges. "But what he mostly wants to talk about is the economy, the war and health care."

Republican activist Norquist, meanwhile, argues against the conventional wisdom that white, working-class voters will respond to fears of further economic decline by peeling away from the GOP. Democrats, Norquist says, are the ones bearing the burden of political disadvantage. "They have a problem with the people they're expecting to pay for their trial lawyer-labor coalition," he says. "And a cultural problem, if you want to count stealing peoples' guns."

Obama has made clear how wide a gulf divides him from working people outside big cities, Norquist says. He cites Obama's widely reported and widely criticized remark that rural voters "cling" to guns and religion. That was, Norquist says, a "snobbish comment."

Is race a major factor in the presidential election?

Early in Obama's run for the nomination his mixed racial heritage, his upbringing outside the continental United States, even his speaking manner, situated him outside the "black politician" profile. The term "post-racial" floated through news coverage and the blogosphere to describe Obama's candidacy.

NPR commentator Juan Williams, a journalist specializing in racial matters, saluted Obama's effort to move political culture into a new era in which back-grounds such as his have become common. "If black and white voters alike react to Mr. Obama's values, then he will really have taken the nation into post-racial politics," Williams wrote. "Whether he and America will get there is still an open question." [22]

Williams' skepticism turned out to be well-founded. In March, the video of the Rev. Wright's "God damn America" sermon surfaced. The condemnation followed a passage in which Wright enumerated the sins of past colonial powers, leading to a denunciation of the drug war and its effects on African Americans: "The government gives them the drugs, builds bigger prisons, passes a three-strike law and then wants us to sing 'God Bless America.' No, no, no, not God Bless America. God damn America — that's in the Bible — for killing innocent people."

Obama's Philadelphia speech, in which he said that he couldn't break with Wright even when he disagreed with him, seemed to put the matter to rest. But six weeks later, Wright reappeared on the scene. Speaking at the National Press Club, he stood by another sermon, given after Sept. 11, in which he had declared that the terrorist attack amounted to retribution. "You cannot do terrorism on other people and expect it never to come back on you," Wright said. [23]

As Republican politicians and political commentators kept those remarks in circulation, a Catholic clergyman and longtime Obama supporter, the Rev. Michael Pfelger of Chicago, poked fun in racial terms at Sen. Hillary Rodham Clinton during an appearance at Trinity.

That episode led Obama to break with Wright and resign from Trinity. Both preachers' views echoed Black Nationalist views — concerning the drug war, for instance — that became commonplace in the 1970s and '80s.

Even so, proclaiming that America is suffering God's righteous wrath has never been a monopoly of black preachers. "I called down damnation on America as 'fallen away from God' at . . . national meetings where I was keynote speaker, including the annual meeting of the ultra-conservative Southern Baptist Convention," Frank Schaeffer — an ex-evangelist and son of Francis Schaeffer, a founder of the Christian right — wrote in the wake of the Wright affair. "The top Republican leadership depended on preachers and agitators like us to energize their rank and file. No one called us un-American." [24]

The argument by Schaeffer and others that the wave of condemnation of Wright grew out of a double standard may have encouraged McCain to break ties with two right-wing ministers — the Rev. John C. Hagee and the Rev. Rod Parsley — who had endorsed him. Hagee is a Christian backer of Zionism who called the Holocaust a divine tool for creating Israel, and Parsley called Islam a "false religion." [25]

But McCain's moves didn't seem to take much weight off Obama. For his foes, the entire sequence of events served to link the candidate to old-school racial challenge. "This is a huge story because it contradicts the whole persona and appeal of Obama as a man who transcends race," columnist Charles Krauthammer told *USA Today*. "I think it ought to be explored a lot more deeply." [26]

How openly Republicans might explore the race issue remains uncertain. Bill Clinton still hasn't recovered from the aftershocks of remarks he made after Obama's victory in the South Carolina primary. The ex-president noted, in what sounded like a dismissive tone, that Jesse Jackson had won that state as well. African Americans accused him of deliberately lumping Obama in with traditional black politicians who never succeeded in gaining major footholds among white voters. Clinton denied any such intent. [27]

Even so, Krauthammer's comments, and others, tell Democratic analysts that Obama will have to openly take on the issue of race once again. "I think he will have to give another speech, as in Philadelphia," says Thomas Schaller, a political scientist at the University of Maryland at Baltimore who specializes in the interplay between race and voting patterns.

Moreover, Schaller acknowledges that race played a role in the extent to which Hillary Clinton beat Obama in the Appalachian region — while he outperformed her among whites in the upper Midwest. Those results don't necessarily predict the course of the general election, he adds. Still, from a political-geography perspective, he says, "It's amazing how they really did slice the Democratic Party right in half."

American history may demonstrate the power of race as a political weapon, but Gov. Pawlenty says the Republican Party has no need for it. A majority of voters will reject Obama's "classic liberal philosophy," he says.

Obama's rhetorical skills give him an advantage over McCain, but McCain trumps him in accomplishments, Pawlenty says. "Everyone says they'll work across party lines; McCain has actually done so," the governor says. "Barack Obama has nothing in his record to suggest that his rhetoric of being a uniting force is consistent with his record."

Former Rep. J. C. Watts, R-Okla., who in 1995-2003, served as the lone black Republican in the House, is skeptical that race won't enter into the campaign. Speaking of a hypothetical match between himself and a white opponent, Watts says, "Operatives and consultants will say, 'You have to drive his numbers down.' Man will always do what is best for man. If it's a matter of making [the opponent] look like he's anti-faith, that's good, or making him look like a racist, that's good."

Consequently, Watts says of Obama, "If the political establishment doesn't try to put him in that box of being a black candidate running for president, as opposed to a Democratic candidate who happens to be black, he has a decent chance."

Democratic analyst Teixeira, however, warns against overplaying race as a factor. "I don't think race is an obstacle in nearly the sense it once would have been. Public opinion data show dramatic liberalization of attitudes."

Teixeira doesn't buy the argument by many academics and political analysts that explicit racist attitudes have been replaced by "symbolic racism" on issues such as public safety. "It's a different breed of cat than old-time racism, and probably should not even be called racist," he says. "If you oppose affirmative action, that doesn't mean you're a racist. If you believe blacks should try harder to get ahead, does that make you a racist?"

BACKGROUND

Change in the South

Race runs through the history of the entire United States, but the drama began in the South. [28]

Following the Civil War, the Republican Party's identification with Abraham Lincoln, who ended slavery, turned Republicans into pariahs among white Southerners, while Democrats became the political mainstays of the system of racial segregation.

The ground under this political arrangement began slowly shifting during the New Deal era, which began with the election of President Franklin D. Roosevelt in 1932. Roosevelt's overwhelming popularity lessened the Democratic Party's reliance on Southern votes in presidential elections.

After World War II, Democrats began openly embracing black voters — that is, black voters outside of the South, where they weren't prevented from voting by

CHRONOLOGY

1948-1965 *Calls for desegregation and civil rights escalate.*

1948 Democrats pass a resolution supporting civil rights. . . . Leading Southern Democrats bolt party to form States' Rights Democratic Party (Dixiecrats).

1952 Only 20 percent of eligible blacks are registered to vote in the South because of Jim Crow restrictions.

1954 U.S. Supreme Court's *Brown v. Board of Education* ruling outlaws segregation in public schools.

1963 President John F. Kennedy agrees to call for a national civil rights law. . . . Assassination of Kennedy and black civil rights activist Medgar Evers and brutal police repression in Birmingham, Ala., shock nation. . . . The Rev. Martin Luther King Jr. delivers "I Have a Dream" speech.

1964 President Lyndon B. Johnson wins passage of Civil Rights Act. . . . Republican presidential candidate Barry M. Goldwater touts his "no" vote on the legislation while campaigning in the South.

1965 Johnson pushes Congress to pass Voting Rights Act, initiating a vast increase in black voter registration

1968-1992 *Major political realignment along racial lines occurs in South as racial episodes surface regularly in presidential campaigns.*

1968 Republican presidential candidate Richard M. Nixon appeals to Southern resentment about desegregation but doesn't flatly oppose it.

1976 Democratic Georgia Gov. Jimmy Carter wins White House with overwhelming support from black Southerners, who offset his low support among white Southerners.

1980 Ronald Reagan opens his post-convention campaign for president by calling for "states' rights" in Neshoba County, Miss., where three civil rights workers were murdered. . . . Reagan wins 72 percent of white Southern vote.

1988 Independent groups supporting Republican George H. W. Bush for president televise ads featuring black murderer William "Willie" Horton Jr., who raped a white woman while on furlough; Democrats attack the ads as racially inflammatory. . . . Bush wins 67 percent of white Southern voters.

1992-1996 *Gov. Bill Clinton, D-Ark., shakes up racial politics during his presidential campaign, temporarily eroding Republican hold on the South.*

1992 Clinton criticizes rapper Sister Souljah for what he calls racist comments. . . . Clinton carries four Southern states in presidential election.

1996 Republican presidential candidate Sen. Bob Dole of Kansas attacks affirmative action, prompting Clinton's vow to "mend it, not end it.". . . Clinton wins reelection thanks in part to 84 percent support by black voters.

2000-2008 *Racial politics shift as Republican President George W. Bush ends his second term; Barack Obama launches winning campaign for Democratic nomination.*

2000 Republican primary foes Bush and John McCain support South Carolina Legislature's decision to keep Confederate flag flying over statehouse; McCain later retracts decision. . . . Presidential election vote-counting marked by controversy over disqualification of some black voters in Florida listed as ex-felons. . . . Democrat Al Gore loses every Southern state.

2004 Senate candidate Obama electrifies Democratic National Convention with a speech citing his life story.

2008 Questions about whether Obama is "black enough" give way to skepticism about his appeal to whites. . . . Stung by the Rev. Jeremiah Wright episode, Obama gives major speech on race and history. . . . Republican officials fear political criticism of Obama will be called racist. . . . Obama cuts ties to Wright after provocative new comments. . . . Rumor that Michelle Obama condemned "whitey" proves fraudulent. . . . McCain bids for votes of mostly white women furious at Sen. Hillary Rodham Clinton's primary loss to Obama.

poll taxes and other barriers. In 1948, the Democratic presidential nominating convention passed a resolution supporting civil rights instead of states' rights — code words for "Jim Crow" laws mandating racial segregation.

In response, several high-profile Southerners founded the States Rights' Democratic Party — the Dixiecrats. They aimed to defeat Harry S. Truman's bid for the presidency in 1948. Dixiecrat co-founder J. Strom Thurmond, then South Carolina's governor, became the new party's presidential candidate.

Support for Jim Crow was entrenched in the South, but so was loyalty to the Democrats, and the Dixiecrats won only about 25 percent of white Southerners' votes.

The Dixiecrats' defeat gave the Democrats' Southern monopoly a temporary reprieve. Thus, in 1950, every one of the region's 22 senators were Democrats, as were all but two of its 105 House members. Similarly all Southern governors and other statewide elected officials and nearly all state legislators were Democrats, and 80 percent of the registered voters were Democrats. [29]

But in 1952, only 20 percent of eligible Southern black voters were registered. [30]

Civil Rights

The social revolution that would change the Southern political map took shape following the landmark 1954 U.S. Supreme Court's *Brown v. Board of Education* decision outlawing segregation in public schools.

By the early 1960s, pro-civil rights demonstrations — and retaliatory violence — had spread throughout the South. In 1963 alone, Medgar Evers, the Mississippi field secretary of the National Association for the Advancement of Colored People (NAACP), was assassinated outside his home in Jackson, Miss.; four young black girls were killed in the bombing of a church in Birmingham, Ala.; and peaceful marches by ministers and young people demanding desegregation were met with police clubs, dogs and high-pressure water hoses.

In August of that year, the Rev. King made his "I Have a Dream" speech at the March on Washington for Jobs and Freedom, which attracted some 250,000 people to demand federal civil rights legislation. By then, President John F. Kennedy had formally called for such legislation, abandoning his initial reluctance. But on Nov. 22, 1963, before Congress could take action, JFK was assassinated.

Kennedy's vice president and successor, Johnson, a Southerner who had spent decades in the House and Senate, steered the Civil Rights Act of 1964 to enactment. The law prohibited racial discrimination in schools, employment and in all facilities open to the public.

Southern Democrats in the Senate had mounted a 57-day filibuster against the bill. But a 71-29 vote forced consideration of the bill. Joining to achieve that result were 54 Democrats and 27 Republicans. [31]

When the legislation reached the House (where it had originated before being modified in the Senate), members passed it on a 289-126 vote. On the winning side were 153 Democrats and 136 Republicans. Voting "no" were 35 Republicans and 91 Democrats, all but three of them from the South. [32]

After signing the bill into law on July 2, Johnson told an aide, "I think we just delivered the South to the Republican Party for a long time to come." [33]

The following month, events forced Johnson's Democratic Party into a second repudiation of its Southern political traditions. Delegates from an insurgent, racially integrated group of activists, the Mississippi Freedom Democratic Party (MFDP), demanded to be seated at the party's presidential nominating convention in Atlantic City, N.J., charging the all-white, official delegation had denied the vote to African Americans. [34]

Despite a compromise in which two MFDP members were seated, most of the regular Mississippi delegates walked out, along with most of their Alabama counterparts. [35]

The MFDP grew out of the "Mississippi Summer Project," in which volunteers, including hundreds of white college students, helped African Americans register to vote. Two of the white volunteers were murdered in Neshoba County, along with a local black civil-rights worker.

Spurred by the killings, Congress in 1965 passed the Voting Rights Act. Within three years, a majority of African Americans in the South were registered to vote.

Republican South

The Voting Rights victory followed Johnson's 1964 election — in which he lost the Deep South states of Alabama, Georgia, Louisiana, Mississippi and South Carolina to Republican Barry M. Goldwater, R-Ariz.

The failure of a politically skilled Southern Democrat to carry his entire home region signaled that — as Johnson had predicted — Democratic control of the South was eroding.

White Southern hostility to civil rights played a key role in the Republican ascendancy. Goldwater didn't

Race-Oriented Debates Invigorate Black Web Sites

Obama draws wide support, but also disagreement.

Barack Obama has vast support among African Americans, but that doesn't mean everyone agrees with him, or cheers his tactical moves. "Obama is a political opportunist who is driven more by interests than feelings," Marc Lamont Hill, a professor of urban education and American studies at Temple University in Philadelphia, wrote in March during a long-running debate in *The Root*, a new, black-oriented Web magazine. [1]

When Obama first distanced himself from his former mentor and pastor, the Rev. Jeremiah A. Wright Jr., Hill wrote: "By standing close to Wright, Obama was able to convince local people that he was 'black enough' to represent their political interests. Now that Wright is a political liability rather than a source of street cred, Obama has decided to throw his mentor under the bus to protect his own image." [2]

Melissa Lacewell-Harris, a political science professor at Princeton University, immediately shot back, "I refuse to buy into any Barack bashing on this topic." She added, "I wish we could have a reasoned conversation about race in this country. . . . But I think it is somewhat unfair to ask Obama to perform this same function in the middle of an election with a racially tone-deaf audience." [3]

The Hill-Lacewell-Harris exchanges reflect an explosion of political debate on the black side of the Web, which has been energized by the presidential race. One site, Black Blog Watch, simply alerts surfers to new postings. [4]

Much of the commentary scalds the major media for their coverage of racial issues. "First Obama wasn't black enough," blogger and memoirist Ta-Nehisi Coates wrote,

responding to a piece in *The New York Times* (by *Times* reporter Marcus Mabry, himself African American). [5] "Then he was so black that he couldn't win the nomination. Now the question is 'How black is too black?' " [6]

Writing from a liberal perspective, Coates argued that Obama has been handling the race issue just right: "Obama emphasized race about as much as most black people on the street emphasize race . . . the same issues that keep white folks up at night — the war, the economy, health care — are the same damn issues that keep black folks up at night." [7]

Journalist Marjorie Valbrun questioned his decision to start wearing a flag lapel pin, after some criticized its absence. (*See "At Issue," p. 17.*) "People who don't support you are not going to be swayed by a pin on your lapel," she wrote. "I suspect they point to the flag pin as another reason that they don't like or trust you." [8]

Some commentators are ranging past the views of black Americans, and past Obama himself. Author John McWhorter, a senior fellow at the conservative-leaning Manhattan Institute, argued in a Web video discussion that some white voters were being tagged as racists simply for opposing Obama on the grounds that his appointees would run to the likes of Black Muslim leader Louis Farrakhan. "That's not, to me, racism," said McWhorter, who brutally critiqued hip-hop culture. "That's a kind of ignorance, [a] kind of grand view of history that doesn't take detail into account. But that person doesn't hate black people." [9]

In an exchange on *The New York Times*' *Bloggingheads* Web site, McWhorter's discussion partner, Brown

proclaim opposition to racial integration itself, but he had voted against the civil rights bill — and made sure his Southern audiences knew it. "Forced integration is just as wrong as forced segregation," he said. [36]

Just as important, Goldwater's ally in some of his Southern travels was ex-Dixiecrat Thurmond, by then a South Carolina senator and still a fierce segregationist. (After Thurmond's death, it was revealed that he had fathered a daughter with an African American woman who had been a maid in Thurmond's parents' home.) [37]

In the midst of the race, Thurmond switched his party affiliation to Republican.

Goldwater was the first Republican to receive the votes of a majority — 55 percent — of white Southerners. Since then, every Republican presidential candidate has outpolled his Democratic rival among Southern white voters.

President Richard M. Nixon, in his winning 1968 campaign, appealed to white Southerners' misgivings or outright opposition to civil rights, while avoiding depicting himself as a civil rights enemy. On the advice of

University economist Glenn Loury, agreed, taking McWhorter's point even further. "Race is a central aspect of my being," said Loury, a conservative turned liberal. "Am I willing to grant that some whites might have their 'race' — I use the word with inverted commas — also to be a constituent aspect of how they understand themselves? . . . How can you have the blackness genie out of the bottle . . . and not have the whiteness genie out of the bottle?" [10]

Others in the black commentariat were focusing on another kind of white genie.

"Jill Tubman," a pseudonymous blogger on the *Jack and Jill Politics* site, echoed another black Web commentator who ridiculed the discredited rumor that Michelle Obama had denounced "whitey." Citing a sitcom from the 1970s, Tubman noted, "The only person I ever heard saying 'honkey' or 'whitey' growing up was George Jefferson on TV. . . . This rumor was started probably by someone who wasn't black." [11]

Black Agenda Report publishes blog-style pieces and longer articles that grow out of left-wing and sometimes black nationalist perspectives. "To make himself acceptable to whites, Obama finds it necessary to shout out how unacceptable he finds the conduct of other Blacks," the site's executive editor, veteran journalist Glen Ford, wrote about Obama's denunciation of male irresponsibility — explicitly including black males. "Can one imagine Obama or any other presidential aspirant repeatedly hectoring any other ethnic group on moral issues? . . . But there are large regions of the white body politic in which it is not only acceptable, but damn near required, that politicians demonstrate their impatience with the alleged moral shortcomings of Black people." [12]

Clearly, whatever the effects of Obama's candidacy on black America, promoting lockstep conformity isn't one of them. One of his toughest, politically conservative critics sees political diversity on the upswing among African Americans. And he says it promotes — rather than weakens — black identity.

"What black America needs more than anything is individuals," says Shelby Steele, a senior fellow at the Hoover Institution at Stanford University. "In white America there is this clear right and left division, and people on both sides have legitimacy. We're just getting there in black America, but we are getting there. So I feel very much a member of the group."

[1] See Marc Lamont Hill, "Obama's Response to Jeremiah Wright," *The Root*, March 17, 2008, http://blogs.theroot.com/blogs/downfromthetower/archive/2008/03/17/obama-s-response-to-jeremiah-wright.aspx.

[2] *Ibid.*

[3] See Melissa Harris-Lacewell, "Obama's Response to Wright [Response]," *The Root*, March 18, 2008, http://blogs.theroot.com/blogs/downfromthetower/archive/2008/03/18/obama-s-response-to-wright-response.aspx.

[4] See Courtney Payne, *Black Blog Watch*, www.blackblogwatch.com/v1/index.cfm.

[5] See Marcus Mabry, "Where Whites Draw the Line," *The New York Times*, June 2008, www.nytimes.com/2008/06/08/weekinreview/08mabry.html?_r=1&ref=weekinreview&oref=slogin.

[6] See Ta-Nehisi Coates, Message to the White Man: We're not Thinking About You, blog, June 8, 2008, www.ta-nehisi.com/2008/06/message-to-the-white-man-were-not-thinking-about-you.html. Coates is author of *The Beautiful Struggle: A Father, Two Sons, and an Unlikely Road to Manhood* (2008).

[7] *Ibid.*

[8] See Marjorie Valbrun, "A Flag Pin? Come On!" *The Root*, May 16, 2008, www.theroot.com/id/46544.

[9] "Bloggingheads: Is Racism Over?" *The New York Times* video, undated, http://video.on.nytimes.com/?fr_story=4044856890331225e87fadb6969199e3e28a70c8.

[10] *Ibid.*

[11] See Jill Tubman, "Black People Just Don't Say Whitey . . . Ever," *Jack and Jill Politics*, June 19, 2008, www.jackandjillpolitics.com/2008/06/black-people-just-dont-say-whiteyever.html.

[12] See Glen Ford, "Obama Insults Half a Race," *Black Agenda Report*, June 18, 2008, www.blackagendareport.com/index.php?option=com_content&task=view&id=661&Itemid=1.

Thurmond aide Harry S. Dent, for instance, Nixon favored some "freedom of choice" in school-desegregation plans and opposed mandatory busing.

Democrats were hobbled that year by the insurgent, third-party campaign of former Gov. George C. Wallace of Alabama, who ran a Dixiecrat-style campaign that drew votes from Jim Crow Democrats like himself. Thurmond, meanwhile, was campaigning for Nixon with the message that voters who valued the fading Southern way of life would be better advised to choose

Nixon than to waste a vote on Wallace.

As the South realigned, the Democratic Party fought Republican expansion in the South by wooing African Americans' votes. In 1976, Democrat Jimmy Carter — a former governor of Georgia — won the White House thanks in part to 82 percent support from black Southerners, despite losing most white Southerners to President Gerald R. Ford.

Once Republican Reagan launched his 1980 presidential campaign, he and the party took an overwhelm-

Latinos May Play Crucial Role in Election

But their voting strength lags.

Barack Obama is poised to hand African Americans a victory in their centuries-old fight for a place in the political sun. But if he wins, it may be voters from another minority group — Latinos — who put him over the top.

Both Obama and Republican nominee John McCain are angling for Latino votes. In early July, Obama was leading McCain among Hispanic voters. McCain himself has a pro-immigration record, but that sets him apart from many in his party.

Other pro-immigration Republicans acknowledge the handicap. "If politicians want to deport your mother, people get this odd view that you don't like them," says veteran GOP strategist Grover Norquist, president of Americans for Tax Reform.

For his part, Obama consistently trailed his primary opponent, Hillary Rodham Clinton, among Latinos. But a summary of May surveys showed Obama registering 62 percent nationwide support among Hispanics nationwide, vs. 29 percent for McCain. [1]

More important, perhaps, Obama was ahead in key swing states. In New Mexico, Colorado and Nevada, as well as Arizona, he was leading McCain 57 percent to 31 percent. [2]

In these states, Hispanics make up sizable shares of the registered voter populations. Hence, Latinos are seen as critical to both parties' fortunes in the swing states (Arizona occupies a special category because it's McCain's home state, where he has enjoyed strong support in the past from Hispanic constituents). In Colorado and Nevada, Hispanics make up 12 percent of the electorate and 37 percent in New Mexico. [3]

In Florida, another possible swing state, where Hispanics account for 14 percent of the voting population, the odds appear tougher for Obama. A poll showed Obama and McCain running virtually even, at 43 percent-42 percent. Cuban Americans — 45 percent of Florida's Hispanic electorate — traditionally favor Republicans. However, the Cuban Americans' presence is lessening; they accounted for 90 percent of Florida Hispanic votes in 1988. [4]

Because large numbers of Cuban Americans vote — a 70 percent turnout is routine — and because they typically vote as a bloc, national interest in Hispanic voting has centered on South Florida. [5]

Along with Latinos' concentration in some key states, their new status as the nation's biggest minority — there are 45.5 million Latinos vs. 40.7 million African Americans — has given them increased attention this presidential season. Nonetheless, Hispanic voting strength lags behind that of the black population. [6]

The nonpartisan Pew Hispanic Center calculates there were 24 million eligible African American voters in 2007, or 66 percent of the black population. Among Hispanics, only 40 percent of the Hispanic population — 18 million people — were eligible to vote. The reasons for the low percentage of eligible voters: More than one-third of the Hispanic population is under age 18, and 26 percent aren't citizens. [7] In addition, Latinos (Cuban Americans excepted) have a weak voting record. In 2004, 47 percent of Latinos nationwide turned out, in contrast with 64 percent for the population as a whole. [8]

"We recognize we must work very hard . . . to do better with Latino voters in the general election," said Federico Peña, an Obama supporter and past secretary of Transportation and Energy in President Bill Clinton's administration. [9]

Tensions between Hispanics and African Americans could prove problematic as well for the Democrats. A survey late last year showed 44 percent of Latinos reporting they feared blacks "because they are responsible for most of the crime" (50 percent disagreed). And 51 percent of blacks said Latinos were taking jobs, housing and political power from African Americans (45 percent disagreed). [10]

ing share of the white Southern Protestant majority. Most of its members now had gone to college and lived in metropolitan areas. Reagan's praise of low taxes and free-market capitalism, coupled with his patriotic rhetoric, found a ready audience.

The civil rights protest era had ended, but memories of the time remained fresh. And Reagan, Democrats said, seemed to exploit white resentment. In fact, in August 1980 he gave his first speech as official Republican presidential nominee in Mississippi's

"There's a lot of angst among blacks about Latinos moving in," says Paula McClain, a Duke University political scientist. But she adds that African Americans tend not to support anti-immigration activists. "The notion of who's an American — black Americans have dealt with that," she says. "Historically, to be American meant to be white."

McCain hasn't associated himself with the immigration-restriction strain of the political culture, either. He even joined with Democratic icon Sen. Edward M. Kennedy, D-Mass., on a bill that would have allowed illegal immigrants to apply for legal status.

Since then, McCain has said border security must come first. But he's never endorsed the views of Reps. Tom Tancredo, R-Colo., who pushed legislation to build a wall along the Mexican border, and James Sensenbrenner, R-Wis., who tried to make entering the country illegally a felony. [11] Their "strategy has been seen by Hispanics as not just anti-undocumented immigrant but anti-Hispanic," says Simon Rosenberg, president of NDN, a think tank and advocacy organization linked to the Democratic Party.

Latinos tend to rate McCain highly as an individual, says Sergio Bendixen, a Miami-based Democratic pollster specializing in the Latino population. However, "He is definitely not hanging around with people that the Hispanic community respects," Bendixen says, citing the old saw, "Tell me who you go around with, and I'll tell you who you are."

An anti-immigration stance will turn off most Latino voters, Bendixen says, but, beyond that, immigration isn't their main concern. The substantive issues are health insurance, the economy and the Iraq war — all matters on which

Cubans in Miami celebrate on Aug. 1, 2006, after Fidel Castro temporarily handed over power to his brother Raul.

Hispanics had rated Obama's primary opponent, Hillary Clinton, more highly than Obama. But, Bendixen says, "The issues are so powerful that they are overwhelming whatever lack of comfort or lack of familiarity the Hispanic electorate might have with Sen. Obama."

[1] See Peter Wallsten, "Obama leads in battle for Latino vote," *Los Angeles Times*, June 6, 2008, www.latimes.com/news/politics/la-na-latinos6-2008jun06,0,5793717.story.

[2] See "Latino voters favor Obama over McCain, according to UW pollsters," University of Washington, June 16, 2008, http://uwnews.washington.edu/ni/article.asp?articleID=42497.

[3] See Paul Taylor and Richard Fry, "Hispanics and the 2008 Election: A Swing Vote?" Pew Hispanic Center, Dec. 6, 2007, p. ii, pewhispanic.org/files/reports/83.pdf.

[4] Ibid.; see also Tal Abbady, "Cuban American voters make South Florida a logical stop," *South Florida Sun-Sentinel*, www.sun-sentinel.com/news/local/cuba/sfl-flrndcuba20sbmay20,0,3422003.story.

[5] *Ibid.*

[6] See Howard Witt, "Latinos still the largest, fastest-growing minority," *Los Angeles Times*, May 1, 2008, p. A18.

[7] See Taylor and Fry, *op. cit.*, pp. 13-15.

[8] *Ibid.*

[9] Quoted in Alec MacGillis, "Obama Campaign Redoubles Efforts to Reach Hispanic Voters," *The Washington Post*, May 25, 2008, p. A1.

[10] See "Deep Divisions, Shared Destiny: A Poll of African Americans, Hispanics and Asian Americans on Race Relations," *New American Media*, Dec. 12, 2007, pp. 3, 9-10, http://media.newamericamedia.org/images/polls/race/exec_summary.pdf. The survey was conducted for New American Media, a San Francisco-based alliance of ethnic news organizations.

[11] See Kathy Kiely, "GOP leaders oppose immigration felony," *USA Today*, April 4, 2006, ww.usatoday.com/news/washington/2006-04-12-immigration-congress_x.htm. For background, see Alan Greenblatt, "Immigration Debate," *CQ Researcher*, Feb. 1, 2008, pp. 97-120.

Neshoba County, where the three civil rights workers had been murdered 16 years earlier. Before an almost entirely white crowd, Reagan said: "I believe in states' rights; I believe in people doing as much as they can at the private level." [38]

Democrats seized on Reagan's remark. "You've seen in this campaign the stirrings of hate and the rebirth of code words like 'states' rights' in a speech in Mississippi," said President Carter, whom Reagan was running to unseat. [39]

After Reagan's two-term administration, the GOP became the South's dominant party. But the enfranchisement of African Americans led to the elections of growing numbers of blacks, virtually all Democrats.

By 1999, 62 percent of America's 8,936 black elected officials served in the 11 states of the Old Confederacy. Mississippi, where 33 percent of the voting-age population was black, led the nation in elected African Americans, with 850 officeholders. [40] (*See graph, p. 6.*)

Racial Politics

As civil rights laws and affirmative-action programs took effect, supporting "separation of the races" became unacceptable for politicians, except on the fringes.

But racial politics didn't vanish.

When George H. W. Bush, was running for president in 1987-88, his campaign ran a TV ad accusing Massachusetts Gov. Michael Dukakis, the Democratic candidate, of coddling criminals. The controversial ad noted that under a prison furlough program — begun by Dukakis' Republican predecessor — a murderer serving a life sentence without parole raped a woman and slashed her husband after being released for a weekend furlough. [41]

The criminal, William "Willie" Horton, was black, his victim white. Official Bush campaign ads didn't feature Horton's face, though at least one commercial and some fliers produced by independent pro-Bush groups did.

"As a white Southerner, I have always known I had to go the extra mile to avoid being tagged a racist by liberal Northerners," said the late Lee Atwater, Bush's campaign manager, after Bush won. And Roger Ailes, a media consultant to the campaign (now Chairman and CEO of Fox News), said, "I did not do the Willie Horton ad. I thought it was a crude ad and probably would stir up the idea of racism with the media." [42]

Indeed, Democratic leaders accused the Bush campaign of exploiting racist emotions as soon as the explosive Horton ads began appearing. Ensuing news coverage made the campaign's avoidance of Horton's photo irrelevant, because the media frequently showed the image.

In 1992, it was Democratic presidential candidate Bill Clinton who capitalized on a racially charged issue, criticizing a comment made by the rap singer Sister Souljah about the 1992 Los Angeles riots sparked by the acquittal of white police officers who had beaten black motorist Rodney King. Referring to the beating of a white truck driver, she said, "If black people kill black people every day, why not have a week and kill white people?" [43]

She explained later she'd merely been trying to convey the mind-set of young, inner-city blacks. But Clinton equated the comment to what a white racist would say about blacks. [44]

As a leading Democrat, Clinton was praised for drawing the line at offensive speech from one of his party's key voting blocs. Since then, a "Sister Souljah moment" has come to signify precisely that action — especially when a Democrat is dissenting from liberal orthodoxy about a racial issue. [45]

Patriotism and Race

Meanwhile, Clinton kept the faith on a key issue for black Democrats — affirmative action. In February 1995, as he was preparing to fight for reelection amid the first stirrings of the sex scandals that would soon engulf his presidency, the future Republican candidate, Sen. Bob Dole of Kansas, launched an attack on affirmative action. "Why did 62 percent of white males vote Republican in 1994? I think it's because . . . sometimes the best-qualified person does not get the job because he or she may be of one color — and I'm beginning to believe that may not be the way it should be in America." [46]

Seeing a campaign issue in the making, Clinton ordered a high-level review of affirmative-action policies, which gave him the intellectual ammunition to defend them. "When affirmative action is done right, it is flexible, it is fair and it works," he said in July, promising to "mend it, not end it." [47]

Political analysts credited Clinton with lowering the temperature on the issue to the point that affirmative action nearly vanished as a campaign topic. Clinton won reelection thanks in part to 84 percent support among African Americans. [48]

In the 1999-2000 presidential campaign season, race played a role chiefly in the fight between Texas Gov. George W. Bush and Sen. McCain for the Republican nomination — a fight that spilled over into the larger arena.

Bush and McCain backed South Carolina's decision to keep flying the Confederate flag over the state capitol. The battle pitted Southerners who insisted they were expressing Carolinian pride against African Americans and white allies, who called talk of heritage a cover for racist sentiment.

Vice President Gore and his Democratic nomination rival, ex-New Jersey Sen. Bill Bradley, attacked the

Is race an important factor in the 2008 presidential election?

YES   Marjorie Valbrun
Journalist, contributing writer, TheRoot.com

Written for *CQ Researcher*, July 2008

Race is certainly an important factor in the coming election. Is there really any doubt that fascination with the presidential campaign is due largely to the fact that a black candidate has garnered support from voters of all racial stripes and is considered a viable prospect for the White House? This is not necessarily a bad thing. We Americans have been dancing around the subject of race for a long time, and Barack Obama's candidacy offers us a great opportunity to address it.

While John McCain is considered an experienced and able public servant, it is Obama who has struck an emotional chord with those who see his political ascendancy as representational of the American ideal. Many voters are excited by the possibility of electing the country's first black president and the impact it can have on American race relations and on the nation's image internationally.

To be sure, there are also many voters who are uncomfortable with Obama precisely because of his race, and they have not been shy about saying so. Democratic voters have even said in polls and interviews that they would not support Obama because he is a black man. Such views offer further proof that race is a key factor in the election.

Although Obama's candidacy has not been subject to the blatant and ugly race-based tactics that defined past elections involving candidates of different races, he has not been entirely spared of it either. (Who can forget the public furor over Jeremiah Wright?) Still, things seem different this time. Obama's avoidance of racially divisive issues signals that he is more interested in forging racial ties than in refighting the racial battles of the past. This gives voters room to write a new narrative about how race affects our politics. That Obama is a biracial, post-civil-rights-era candidate who pledges to bring Americans of all hues together has made it somewhat easier for us to talk honestly about what keeps us apart.

Pretending race is not an issue in the election won't make it so. Race has a firm hold on the American psyche, and Obama's candidacy has forced white Americans to explore their biases or fears and perhaps come to terms with the idea of a black man occupying the White House. It has also given hope — and some might argue proof — to people of color that the United States is indeed capable of living up to its most noble ideals about equality.

NO   Grover G. Norquist
President, Americans for Tax Reform

Written for *CQ Researcher*, July 2008

Barack Obama will lose to John McCain in November for many reasons. The color of his skin is not one of those reasons.

Bill and Hillary Clinton argued that many white voters would not vote for Obama because his father was black, and this was offered as a reason for the superdelegates to save the party by snatching the nomination away from Obama and giving it to Hillary.

Bill and Hillary lost that argument. They deserved to. They were wrong.

In early 2008, the Obama groundswell was driven in large part by Obama's content-free call for hope and change and his presentation of himself as a post-racial candidate. He was not Jesse Jackson or Al Sharpton. And if you supported his candidacy, you were making a public statement that you were post-racial also.

Obama faltered when the nation began to see videos of his church and minister that were decidedly not "post-racial." Obama attended a church dripping with racial grievance and bizarre hatred of America — we invented AIDS as genocide. And the replacement minister — who was white — was just as hostile to America as the Rev. Jeremiah Wright.

Then Obama announced at a billionaire's house in San Francisco that he didn't like a Middle America that was "bitter" and "clings" to their guns and religious faith. He doesn't like rural and suburban America, churchgoers and hunters.

Americans do not vote for people who express contempt for them. Hispanics do not vote for Tom Tancredo. Millions of Americans will not vote for Mr. Obama, the snob who looks down at them, their families and communities. He is a snob with a tan, but no one is voting against the tan.

In three years, the 2001 and 2003 tax cuts end. Obama says he wants to let them lapse so your capital gains tax rate will jump from 15 percent to 20 percent. The tax on dividend payments will jump from 15 percent to 35 percent. The top rate for individual taxes will jump from 35 percent to 39.5 percent, and Obama envisions a top rate of 55 percent by extending the Social Security tax to all incomes. A vote for Obama is a vote for the largest tax hike in American history. Also for liberal judges. And gun control. And vast increases in federal spending — beyond the Bush nonsense.

The Democrats often run presidential candidates like this guy: Dukakis, Carter, Mondale, Gore and Kerry. They lose. Changing the color of the liberal won't help. Or hurt.

Republicans' stand. Gore noted the flag began flying over the capitol in 1962, during the civil rights protest era, "as a symbol of resistance to justice for African Americans." [49]

The issue might have remained purely partisan — except that McCain months later reversed course, saying he'd been dishonest. Though some of his ancestors fought for the Confederacy, McCain said, "I don't believe their service, however distinguished, needs to be commemorated in a way that offends, that deeply hurts, people whose ancestors were once denied their freedom by my ancestors." [50]

In another blatantly racial incident during the South Carolina campaign, anonymous opponents of McCain used so-called push polling to suggest that McCain's Bangladeshi-born adopted daughter was his own, illegitimate black child. [51]

A more recent issue with racial dimensions surfaced during the Florida vote-counting controversy following the 2000 presidential election. On Election Day the names of some eligible voters appeared on a list of about 100,000 people said to be dead or to have felony convictions that barred them from casting ballots. Exactly how many eligible voters were kept away isn't known, but the "purge" list, assembled by a contractor for the state of Florida, was disproportionately weighted with African Americans — 66 percent in Miami-Dade County, and 54 percent in Hillsborough County (Tampa). [52]

The voter-roll purge roused attention because of the closeness of the election, in which 90 percent of black voters who did cast ballots supported Gore. "They rejected the Bush candidacy in a resounding manner," said Bositis of the Joint Center for Political and Economic Studies, "and the events in Florida . . . have convinced them that the election was won because black votes were not counted." [53]

Four years later, Obama, then a relatively unknown Senate candidate, wowed the Democratic National Convention with a speech that touched on his biracial, binational origins, the ties that bind Americans and "the hope of a skinny kid with a funny name who believes that America has a place for him, too." [54]

CURRENT SITUATION

The Women's Vote

McCain and other Republicans are effusively praising Sen. Clinton after her loss — perhaps hoping to attract the votes of her embittered backers.

Their bitterness is seen by some Obama supporters as bordering on racism. Even before she conceded Obama's victory, McCain said, "I admire her and I respect her." "She has inspired generations of American women to believe that they can reach the highest office in this nation." [55]

After the last primary, McCain went further. "The media often overlooked how compassionately she spoke to the concerns and dreams of millions of Americans, and she deserves a lot more appreciation than she sometimes received." [56] The remark resonated with many Clinton backers, who said reporters were swooning for Obama while recycling sexist insults to Clinton.

Most of the anger at the media focused on television, especially cable TV news. News executives and journalists tended to blame the outrage over coverage on the fact that Clinton lost. But "CBS Evening News" Anchor Katie Couric agreed with the critics. "I feel that Sen. Clinton received some of the most unfair, hostile coverage I've ever seen," she said. [57]

Pioneering feminist writer and activist Gloria Steinem argued in *The New York Times* in January that the obstacles confronting Clinton were just as big as those Obama was facing. "What worries me is that he is seen as unifying by his race," Steinem wrote, "while she is seen as divisive by her sex. . . . What worries me is that some women, perhaps especially younger ones, hope to deny or escape the sexual caste system." [58]

McCain is hoping, however, that not all of Clinton's backers will remain loyal to the Democratic Party. The top woman in the McCain campaign, former Hewlett-Packard CEO Carly Fiorina, made a point of appealing to female Democrats in a June TV appearance.

"No one should take a woman's vote for granted, and the Democratic Party should certainly not take it for granted," she said on "Good Morning America." "I'm a woman, and as a woman, I'm really proud Hillary Clinton ran for president. I am enormously proud of what she did, and frankly, I have enormous sympathy for what she went through." [59]

Feminist Democrats, meanwhile, have been cautioning that McCain would be a bad bet for progressive women. "He voted against legislation that established criminal and civil penalties for those who use threats and violence to keep women from gaining access to reproductive health clinics," wrote Arianna Huffington, founder of *The Huffington Post*, a liberal Web site. [60]

And activist Tim Wise, who writes frequently about racism, authored an essay in the form of a letter to white feminists threatening to vote for McCain or to abstain from voting altogether. Black voters, he said, "would have supported the white woman — hell, for many black folks, before Obama showed his mettle they were downright excited to do so — but you won't support the black man. And yet you have the audacity to insist that it is you who are the most loyal constituency of the Democratic Party, and the ones before whom party leaders should bow down, and whose feet must be kissed? Your whiteness is showing." [61]

The attention being paid to women's political power, meanwhile, may have prompted McCain's cancellation of a June fundraiser in Texas to have been hosted by former gubernatorial candidate Clayton Williams. During his campaign, he had made what he thought was a humorous comparison between weather and rape: "As long as it's inevitable, you might as well lie back and enjoy it." [62]

Targeting Michelle?

Democratic strategists say there are clear indications McCain backers will target Michelle Obama on racial issues. The candidate's outspoken wife, who rose from a working-class family on Chicago's South Side to graduate from Harvard Law School, came under fire early in his campaign for remarks during the Wisconsin primary campaign.

"What we have learned over this year is that hope is making a comeback," she said. "And let me tell you something — for the first time in my adult lifetime, I am really proud of my country. And not just because Barack has done well, but because I think people are hungry for change. And I have been desperate to see our country moving in that direction and just not feeling so alone in my frustration and disappointment. I've seen people who are hungry to be unified around some basic common issues, and it's made me proud." [63]

The next day, McCain's wife, Cindy, told a rally in Wisconsin. "I'm proud of my country. I don't know about you — if you heard those words earlier — I'm very proud of my country." [64]

Since then, Republicans have indicated they will keep reminding voters of Michelle Obama's comments. In June, former Secretary of State Lawrence Eagleburger introduced Cindy McCain at a fundraiser by calling her someone who is "proud of her country, not just once, but always." The audience caught the reference, Politico reported. [65]

Most of the commentary Michelle Obama unleashed — not all of it unfavorable — didn't touch on race. But one sympathetic journalist did sense a racial dimension to the emotions behind Mrs. Obama's remark.

"A lot of voters did and will wonder: how could someone who graduated from Princeton and Harvard Law School and won a job at a high-paying Chicago law firm — who was in some way a beneficiary of affirmative action — sound so alienated from her country?" asked *Newsweek* Editor-at-Large Evan Thomas. [66]

He cited her Princeton senior thesis, which examined relations between black Princeton graduates and the larger black community, and revealed the loneliness she had felt. "It is perhaps unsurprising that, for an unguarded moment on the campaign trail, she reflected the alienation she felt at being a working-class black woman at a rich, white man's school long ago." [67]

Obama's thesis did, however, give rise to a slanderous e-mail rumor campaign — one with no apparent links to the McCain camp. The e-mail claimed the thesis "stated that America was a nation founded on 'crime and hatred' " and that whites in America were "ineradicably racist," according to the *Politifact.com* Web site. *Politifact* examined the thesis and said it did not contain those statements. [68]

A subsequent attempt — also evidently unconnected to McCain's campaign — to attack Obama through his wife also focused on race. Conservative broadcaster Rush Limbaugh, blogger Larry Johnson, an ex-CIA agent, and Roger Stone, a former Republican operative, spread word by radio and the Web of a rumor that a tape existed of Michelle giving a talk in which she attacked "whitey." [69]

No such tape has surfaced. After investigating, the Obama campaign said the rumor of the talk was bogus. [70]

OUTLOOK

Changing Attitudes

Students of political and social trends say Obama's candidacy both reflects and stimulates deep changes in Americans' treatment of racial and ethnic differences — and that the changes appear unstoppable.

"It's not just about race," says Bositis of the Joint Center for Political and Economic Studies, citing growing acceptance of gay marriage among young people. "The younger generation is more tolerant. It has grown up with more integration. People under 35 grew up in a world where having overt, negative racial attitudes is not acceptable."

The changes in attitude reflect an underlying demographic shift. By 2050, whites will be outnumbered by blacks, Latinos, Asians and Native Americans, according to the U.S. Census Bureau. [71]

Some Republican politicians see the changes as further evidence that their party is falling behind the times. "The demographics of the country are changing," says Minnesota Gov. Pawlenty. "That doesn't mean you change your philosophy, but our party is going to have to do a better job," including diversifying Republicans' largely white-male candidate ranks.

As the only black Republican in the House during his tenure, former Oklahoma Rep. Watts agrees the GOP should make a stronger effort to reach out to minorities. But he also questions whether politics is the best vehicle for social change, because parties exist to fight for power, using the most effective weapons at hand. "When people say you ought to take the politics out of politics, it wouldn't be politics if you do that — it would be jacks," says Watts.

The Hoover Institution's Steele argues that Obama is bound to disappoint those who see him as the one-man cure for America's racial ills. "People have the illusion that he will be the endgame in terms of our racial conflict. My feeling is that he will be another chapter. He won't resolve anything. White people will realize that a black man in the White House will not save them from the suspicion of being racist."

Steele's skepticism aside, Obama's youthful cadres are changing the national political dynamic, some observers say.

"What you're getting in this election is another youth movement," says the University of Michigan's Walton. "It's not like the youth movement of the '60s; it's in the political arena. The old notion that young people don't vote is going to fall on its face. Young people are not as consumed with iPods and videos as you think. They are caught up in this presidential campaign."

The excitement has caught on abroad as well, and not only among young people. "Everyone is, in fact, impressed with the historical moment, that it is the first time an African American has won the nomination of a party," said Wamiq Zuberi, editor of *The Business Recorder*, a Pakistani newspaper. [72]

NOTES

1. For electoral vote estimates, see Greg Giroux, "At the Starting Gate, State by State," *CQ Weekly*, June 9, 2008, p. 1513. For the *Washington Post*-ABC News poll, see Dan Balz and Jon Cohen, "Poll Finds Independent Voters Split Between McCain, Obama," *The Washington Post*, June 17, 2008, p. A1.

2. Hart quoted in Jackie Calmes, "Obama Leads McCain, But Race Is Looking Tight," *The Wall Street Journal*, June 12, 2008, p. A8. Gingrich quoted in Jackie Kucinich, "Gingrich warns Republican Party of 'real disaster' this fall," *The Hill*, May 5, 2008, the-hill.com/leading-the-news/gingrich-warns-republican -party-of-real-disaster-this-fall-2008-05-06.html.

3. Adam Nagourney and Megan Thee, "Poll Finds Obama Candidacy Isn't Closing Divide on Race," *The New York Times*, July 16, 2008, p. A1. *The New York Times*/CBS News telephone poll was conducted July 7-14 among 1,796 adults, including 1,338 whites and 297 blacks.

4. Quoted in Caren Bohan, "Obama says Republicans will use race to stoke fear," Reuters, June 20, 2008, http://news.yahoo.com/s/nm/20080620/pl_nm/usa _politics_obama_race_dc&printer=1;_ylt=AsqCgl.Al. 3gFyN2gkkVh70b.3QA.

5. Quoted in Charles Babington, "Obama braces for race-based ads," The Associated Press, June 23, 2008, http://news.yahoo.com/s/ap/20080623/ap_on_el_pr/ obama_racial_ads.

6. Quoted in Kevin Merida, "Racist Incidents Give Some Obama Campaigners Pause," *The Washington Post*, May 13, 2008, p. A1; and Paul Harris, "Democrats in rural strongholds refuse to give backing to Obama," *The Observer*, June 8, 2008, www.guardian.co.uk/ world/2008/jun/08/barackobama.hillaryclinton.

7. Quoted in Juan Williams, "Obama's Color Line," *The New York Times*, Nov. 30, 2007, p. A23.

8. See Simon Rosenberg, "On Obama, race and the end of the Southern Strategy," Jan. 4, 2008, www.ndn.org/advocacy/immigration/obama-race-and-end-of.html; and Howard Witt, "Latinos still the largest, fastest-growing minority," *Los Angeles Times*, May 1, 208, p. A18.

9. For a lengthier excerpt of the sermon than the clips commonly broadcast, and a clip of Wright later explaining his language to Bill Moyers of PBS, see "Long excerpt of Wright's 'God Damn America' speech," YouTube [undated], www.youtube.com/ watch?v=bV-oI__bHA4.

10. See "Remarks of Senator Barack Obama: 'A More Perfect Union,' " March 18, 2008, www.barack-obama.com/2008/03/18/remarks_of_senator_barack _obam_53.php.

11. See "Newsweek Poll, Obama and the Race Factor," *Newsweek*, May 23, 2008, /www.newsweek.com /id/138462.

12. See "On the Second Amendment, Don't Believe Obama," National Rifle Association — Institute for Legislative Action, June 6, 2008, www.nraila.org/ Legislation/Federal/Read.aspx?id=3991.

13. For full transcript see Mayhill Fowler, "Obama: No Surprise That Hard-Pressed Pennsylvanians Turn Bitter," *Huffington Post*, April 11, 2008, www.huff-ingtonpost.com/mayhill-fowler/obama-no-surprise-that-ha_b_96188.html.

14. Quoted in Alec MacGillis, "Maybe Not 'Bitter,' But Aware of the Loss," *The Washington Post*, April 19, 2008, p. A6.

15. See Earl Black and Merle Black, *Divided America: The Ferocious Power Struggle in American Politics* (2007), pp. 84-85.

16. *Ibid.*, pp. 83-84.

17. Quoted in Kathy Kiely and Jill Lawrence, "Clinton makes case for staying in," *USA Today*, May 8, 2008, p. A1.

18. See David Paul Kuhn, "Why Clinton won Pennsylvania," *Politico*, April 23, 2008, www.politico .com/news/stories/0408/9812.html; Katharine Q. Seelye, "The Race Factor in Pa. Primary," *The New York Times*, The Caucus blog, April 23, 2008, http://thecaucus.blogs.nytimes.com/2008/04/23/the-race-factor-in-pa-primary/.

19. See "Exit Poll: Whites Back Clinton in Kentucky," MSNBC (The Associated Press), May 20, 2008, www.msnbc.msn.com/id/24736399.

20. See Eric Alterman, "The Hollywood Campaign," *The Atlantic*, September 2004, www.theatlantic.com/doc /200409/alterman; Landon Thomas Jr., "New Role For Rubin: Policy Guru," *The New York Times*, Sept. 8, 2006, p. C1; "Quadrangle, Investment Team," undated, www.quadranglegroup.com/rattner.html.

21. Quoted in Jeff Zeleny, "Obama Says He'd Roll Back Tax Cuts for the Wealthiest," *The New York Times*, May 14, 2007, www.nytimes.com/2007/05/14/us/

politics/14talk.html. See also, Jonathan Kaufman, "Fair Enough?" *The Wall Street Journal*, June 14, 2008, p. A1.

22. *Ibid.*

23. Quoted in Peter Nicholas, "Obama's ex-pastor strides back on stage," *Los Angeles Times*, April 29, 2008, p. A1.

24. See Frank Schaeffer, "If Wright is Anti-American, Why Wasn't My Dad?" *beliefnet*, March 18, 2008, http://blog.beliefnet.com/castingstones/2008/03/frank -schaffer-if-wright-is-an.html.

25. See Neela Banerjee and Michael Luo, "McCain Cuts Ties to Pastors Whose Talks Drew Fire," *The New York Times*, May 23, 2008, www.nytimes.com/2008 /05/23/us/politics/23hagee.html.

26. Quoted in William M. Welch, "Obama's ties to minister may be 'a big problem,' some say," *USA Today*, March 17, 2008, p. A4.

27. See Katharine Q. Seelye, "Jackson: Not Upset by Clinton Remarks," The Caucus blog, *The New York Times*, Jan. 28, 2008, http://thecaucus.blogs.nytimes .com/2008/01/28/jackson-not-upset-by-clinton-remarks/?hp.

28. Except where noted, this subsection is drawn from *ibid.*, and Earl Black and Merle Black, *The Vital South: How Presidents Are Elected* (1992); and Richard M. Valelly, ed., *The Voting Rights Act: Securing the Ballot* (2006).

29. See Black and Black, *Divided America, op. cit.*, p. 74.

30. See *ibid.*, p. 217.

31. See "Senate Votes Cloture on Civil Rights Bill, 71-29," CQ Electronic Library, *CQ Almanac Online Edition*, cqal64-1304621, http://library.cqpress.com/cqal-manac/cqal64-1304621.

32. *Ibid.*

33. Quoted in Black and Black, *The Vital South, op. cit.*, p. 6.

34. See *Congress and the Nation*, CQ Press, Vol. 1 (1945-1964), p. 57.

35. *Ibid.*

36. Quoted in Black and Black, *The Vital South, op. cit.*, p. 152.

37. See Jeffrey Gettleman, "Thurmond Family Struggles With Difficult Truth," *The New York Times*, Dec. 20, 2003, p. A1.

38. Quoted in Douglas E. Kneeland, "Reagan Campaigns at Mississippi Fair," *The New York Times*, Aug. 4, 1980, p. A11.

39. Quoted in Martin Schram, "Carter Said Reagan Injects Racism," *The Washington Post*, Sept. 17, 1980, p. A1.

40. See David A. Bositis, "Black Elected Officials: A Statistical Summary, 1999," Joint Center for Political and Economic Studies, 2000, pp. 10, 12, www.jointcenter.org/publications_recent_publications/black_elected_officials/black_elected_officials_a_statistical_summary_1999."

41. This subsection draws on extensive coverage of the issue by Sidney Blumenthal, "Willie Horton & the Making of an Election Issue," *The Washington Post*, Oct. 28, 1988, p. D1; John Buckley, "The Positive Purpose in Negative Campaigns," *Los Angeles Times*, Oct. 2, 1988, pp. 3, 5; Andrew Rosenthal, "Foes Accuse Bush of Inflaming Racial Tension," *The New York Times*, Oct. 24, 1988, p. A1; Tali Mendelberg, *The Race Card: Campaign Strategy, Implicit Messages, and the Norm of Equality* (2001).

42. Atwater quoted in Blumenthal, ibid. Ailes quoted in Josh Barbanel, "Roger Ailes: Master Maker of Fiery Political Darts," *The New York Times*, Oct. 17, 1989, p. B1.

43. Quoted in Jeff Chang, *Can't Stop Won't Stop: A History of the Hip-Hop Generation* (2007), p. 394.

44. For background, see Peter Katel, "Debating Hip-Hop," *CQ Researcher*, June 15, 2007, pp. 529-552.

45. See Joan Vennochi, "Sister Souljah moments," *The Boston Globe*, Sept. 16, 2007, www.boston.com/news/nation/articles/2007/09/16/sister_souljah_moments/; Mickey Kaus, *Kausfiles* (blog); Slate, Jan. 22, 2008, www.slate.com/id/2182569/#obamaescape.

46. Quoted in Steven A. Holmes, "On Civil Rights, Clinton Steers Bumpy Course Between Right and Left," *The New York Times*, Oct. 20, 1996, p. A16.

47. *Ibid.*

48. See Michael A. Fleter, "Clinton Move to Center, Cabinet Changes Leave Black Supporters Concerned," *The Washington Post*, Nov. 15, 1996, p. A10.

49. Quoted in James Gerstenzang and Matea Gold, "Gore Looks South as He Stumps in North," *Los Angeles Times*, Feb. 20, 2000, p. A39. See also "Confederate-Flag Battle to Continue in S.C.," *Los Angeles Times* (The Associated Press), June 20, 2000, p. A27.

50. Quoted in "Excerpts From McCain's Remarks on Confederate Flag," *The New York Times*, April 20, 2000, p. A22.

51. Richard H. Davis, "The Anatomy of a Smear," *The Boston Globe*, March 21, 2004. Davis was campaign manager for John McCain in 2000.

52. See Lisa Getter, "Florida Net Too Wide in Purge of Voter Rolls," *Los Angeles Times*, May 21, 2001, p. A1.

53. Quoted in "Can Bush Mend His Party's Rift With Black America?" *The New York Times*, Dec. 17, 2000, Sect. 4, p. 17.

54. See "Transcript: Illinois Senate Candidate Barack Obama," *The Washington Post*, July 27, 2004, www.washingtonpost.com/wp-dyn/articles/A19751-2004Jul27.html.

55. Quoted in "McCain praises Clinton's campaign," CNN, *politicalticker* blog, June 2, 2008, http://politicalticker.blogs.cnn.com/2008/06/02/mccain-praises-clinton%E2%80%99s-campaign.

56. *Ibid.*

57. Quoted in "Couric Gets Honored in D.C.," June 11, 2008, *fishbowlDC*, www.mediabistro.com/fishbowlDC/television/couric_gets_honored_in_dc_86823.asp.

58. See Gloria Steinem, "Women Are Never Front-Runners," *The New York Times*, Jan. 8, 2008, www.nytimes.com/2008/01/08/opinion/08steinem.html.

59. Juliet Eilperin, "McCain, Obama Reaching Out to Female Voters," *The Washington Post*, June 12, 2008, p. A1.

60. See Arianna Huffington, "Unmasking McCain: His Reactionary Record on Reproductive Rights," *Huffington Post*, May 26, 2008, www.huffingtonpost.com/arianna-huffington/unmasking-mccain-his-reac_b_103580.html.

61. See Tim Wise, "Your Whiteness is Showing," *counterpunch*, June 7-8, 2008, www.counterpunch.org/wise06072008.html.

62. See "McCain Cancels Event With Controversial Fundraiser," *ABC Political Radar* blog, June 13, 2008, http://blogs.abcnews.com/politicalradar/2008/06/mccain-cancels.html.

63. See Ariel Alexovich, "Blogtalk: Michelle Obama Under Fire," *The New York Times*, *The Caucus* blog, Feb. 19, 2008, http://thecaucus.blogs.nytimes.com /2008/02/19/blogtalk-michelle-obama-under-fire.

64. See Michael Cooper, "Cindy McCain's Pride," *The New York Times*, *The Caucus* blog, Feb. 19, 2008, http://thecaucus.blogs.nytimes.com/2008/02/19/cindy -mccains-pride.

65. See Carrie Budoff Brown, "Michelle Obama becomes GOP target," *Politico*, June 13, 2008, http://dyn.politico.com/printstory.cfm?uuid=7EC4 ACB1-3048-5C12-00B24E3D753ACFCF.

66. See Evan Thomas, "Alienated in the U.S.A.," *Newsweek*, May 13, 2008, www.newsweek.com/id/123024.

67. *Ibid.*

68. See Angie Drobnic Holan, "Digging up dirt on Michelle Obama," *Politifact*, May 30, 2008, www.poli- tifact.com/truth-o-meter/article/2008/may/30/digging -dirt-college-years/. *Politifact* is produced by *Congressional Quarterly* and *The St. Petersburg Times*.

69. See "Fight the Smears," undated, http://my.barack- obama.com/page/content/fightthesmearshome/; "CNN Reliable Sources," June 15, 2008, transcript, http://transcripts.cnn.com/TRANSCRIPTS/0806 /15/rs.01.html.

70. *Ibid.*, and Larry Johnson, "The Michelle Obama Diversion," *No Quarter* blog, June 4, 2008, http://noquarterusa.net/blog/2008/06/04/the-michelle- obama-diversion/.

71. See June Kronholz, "Racial Identity's Gray Area," *The Wall Street Journal*, June 12, 2008, p. A10.

72. Quoted in Alan Cowell, "Foreign Reaction to Obama's Claim is Favorable," *The New York Times*, June 5, 2008, www.nytimes.com/2008/06/05/world /05react.html?_r=1&oref=slogin.

BIBLIOGRAPHY

Books

Black, Earl, and Merle Black, *Divided America: The Ferocious Power Struggle in American Politics*, Simon & Schuster, 2007.
Twin-brother political scientists analyze 21st-century political polarization, including its racial dimension.

Obama, Barack, *Dreams From My Father: A Story of Race and Inheritance*, Crown, 2007 (new edition).
Originally published in 1995, the Democratic candidate tells of his search for a place in American culture.

Schaller, Thomas F., *Whistling Past Dixie: How Democrats Can Win Without the South*, Simon & Schuster, 2008.
A University of Maryland political scientist says chang- ing demographics allow the Democrats to win the West.

Steele, Shelby, *A Bound Man: Why We Are Excited About Obama and Why he Can't Win*, Free Press, 2008.
A conservative who shares Obama's mixed racial heritage says Obama is trapped by liberal political culture, which requires him to mask his beliefs to fit the definition of a black politician.

Articles

Bello, Marisol, "Blacks come to terms with Obama- Wright schism," *USA Today*, May 5, 2008, p. A6.
African American churchgoers reflect a variety of opinions concerning the Rev. Wright's effect on Obama's campaign.

Kronholz, June, "Racial Identity's Gray Area," *The Wall Street Journal*, June 12, 2008, p. A10.
Obama's mixed racial ancestry reflects the growing diversity of a country where Italians, Slavs and other non-Anglo Saxon peoples used to have to argue to be classified as "white."

McWhorter, John, "Racism in Retreat," *The New York Sun*, June 5, 2008, www.nysun.com/opinion/racism- in-retreat/79355/.
An African American author argues Obama's success so far shows that racism is eroding, even if it hasn't disappeared.

Merida, Kevin, "Incidents Give Some Obama Campaigners Pause," *The Washington Post*, May 13, 2008, p. A1.
Obama campaign workers tell of running into frank expressions of racial prejudice.

Mirengoff, Paul, "Loathing of Fear on the Campaign Trail, Part One," *Power Line* blog, May 14, 2008.
A conservative blogger rebuts Democratic conventional wisdom that the Republican Party exploits race-based fears.

Rohter, Larry, and Michael Luo, "Groups Respond to Obama's Call for National Discussion About Race," *The New York Times,* **March 20, 2008, p. A21.**
Campaign reporters find Obama's call for dialogue to be generally well-received.

Rosenbaum, Ron, "In Praise of Liberal Guilt," *Slate,* **May 22, 2008, www.slate.com/id/2191906/.**
The author of a book on Hitler and evil argues that conservatives who mock liberals' sensitivity to U.S. racial history are disregarding the moral value of acknowledging guilt.

Schone, Mark, "What role did race play with white Democrats?" *Salon,* **June 3, 2008, www.salon.com /news/feature/2008/06/03/roundtable/index.html.**
The liberal Web magazine sponsors a debate about the extent to which white voters are racist.

Thomas, Evan, "A Memo to Senator Obama," *Newsweek,* **June 2, 2008, p. 21.**
The lead story in a cover report on race in the presidential election says race still haunts American politics.

VandeHei, Jim, and John F. Harris, "Racial problems transcend Wright," *Politico,* **March 19, 2008.**
Top political reporters conclude that Obama's acclaimed Philadelphia speech didn't resolve all his racial problems.

Reports and Studies

"Deep Divisions, Shared Destiny," New American Media, Dec. 12, 2007, http://media.newamericamedia .org/images/polls/race/exec_summary.pdf.
A report on relations between African Americans, Latinos and Asian Americans shows tensions, but also a sense of solidarity.

"Obama Weathers the Wright Storm, Clinton Faces Credibility Problem," The Pew Research Center for People and the Press, March 27, 2008, http://people-press.org/reports/ pdf/407.pdf.
Obama's handling of the Rev. Wright drama won him a largely favorable response, the nonpartisan Pew report concludes.

"Race, Class & Obama," Princeton Survey Research Associates International, April 26, 2008, www.newsweek .com/id/138462.
Taken for *Newsweek* before the end of the primaries, the poll showed Obama suffering the effects of the Wright episode and facing relatively low support among white working-class voters — but not because of racial prejudice.

For More Information

Black Agenda Report, www.blackagendareport.com. A Web magazine and blog heavy on political reporting and commentary, much of it critical of Obama.

BlackPoliticsontheWeb, (813) 464-7086; http://blackpoliticsontheweb.com. The site compiles news, avoiding ideological guidelines, and runs reader comments.

ColorofChange.org, http://colorofchange.org/. A Web-based organization that organizes campaigns to e-mail lawmakers involved in social-policy and racial-justice issues.

Jack and Jill Politics, www.jackandjillpolitics.com. A blog publishing commentary on a variety of political issues, from a middle-class, or "black bourgeois," perspective.

Joint Center for Political and Economic Studies, 1090 Vermont Ave., N.W., Suite 1100, Washington, DC 20005; (202) 789-3500; www.jointcenter.org. A think tank dedicated to issues critical to the African American community.

Pew Research Center, 1615 L St., N.W., Suite 700, Washington, DC 20036; (202) 419-4300; http://pewresearch.org/. A nonpartisan organization that tracks public opinion on a wide variety of issues, including race and the presidential election.

The Root, www.theroot.com. Published by Washington post.Newsweek Interactive, a black-oriented Web magazine that presents a variety of political viewpoints.

2

Changing U.S. Electorate

Alan Greenblatt

White, working-class Americans like this Ford worker in Wayne, Mich., have helped New York Sen. Hillary Clinton beat Barack Obama in California, Pennsylvania and other large states. Since the Great Depression, working-class whites had been loyal Democrats, but many of them defected in the 1970s and '80s due to liberal Democratic policies. Sen. John McCain, the presumptive Republican presidential nominee, may appeal to working-class voters, who sometimes support GOP candidates because of their conservative social stances.

From *CQ Researcher*, May 30, 2008.

G iven the historic nature of the Democratic presidential primary contest — with the nomination coming down to a battle between a white woman and an African American man — perhaps it's not surprising that there have been splits among voters along racial, geographic, age, income and educational divides. [1]

"I don't think there's any way this election could have been anything but demographically focused, given the candidates left standing," says Scott Keeter, associate director of the Pew Research Center for People & the Press.

The Democrats' internal splits have them nervous about repairing the breaches in order to get all party supporters on board for the fall contest against Arizona Sen. John McCain, the Republican nominee. McCain might well appeal to white, working-class voters, including the so-called Reagan Democrats, who have sometimes supported GOP candidates because of their relatively conservative stances on social issues.

New York Sen. Hillary Rodham Clinton has repeatedly pointed out that, thanks to working-class support, she has beaten Illinois Sen. Barack Obama in the largest states — California, New York, Ohio, among others — which a Democrat would need to carry in order to win in November against McCain.

In an interview with *USA Today* conducted the day after the May 6 Indiana and North Carolina primaries, Clinton cited an Associated Press report "that found how Sen. Obama's support among working, hard-working Americans, white Americans, is weakening again, and how whites in both states who had not completed college were supporting me." [2]

More Americans Moving to the Suburbs

Half of all Americans lived in suburbs in 2000, a sevenfold increase from 90 years earlier. The Democratic Party has been making significant inroads into the traditional GOP turf in the suburbs. Meanwhile, the percentage of Americans in central cities has remained at around 30 percent since 1930, also favoring Democrats.

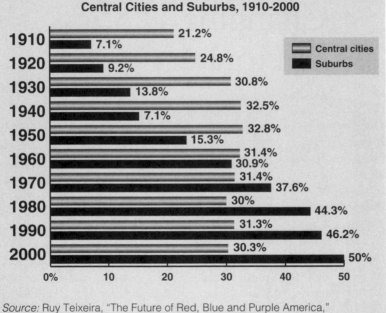

Percentage of Total Population Living in Central Cities and Suburbs, 1910-2000

Year	Central cities	Suburbs
1910	21.2%	7.1%
1920	24.8%	9.2%
1930	30.8%	13.8%
1940	32.5%	7.1%
1950	32.8%	15.3%
1960	31.4%	30.9%
1970	31.4%	37.6%
1980	30%	44.3%
1990	31.3%	46.2%
2000	30.3%	50%

Source: Ruy Teixeira, "The Future of Red, Blue and Purple America," Brookings Institution, January 2008

In exit polls conducted during the April 22 Pennsylvania Democratic primary, 16 percent of white voters said that race had influenced their decision, with almost half of these saying they would not support Obama in the fall. Only 60 percent of Catholics said they would vote for him in November.

"Mr. Obama was supposed to be a transformational figure, with an almost magical ability to transcend partisan difference," writes Paul Krugman, a *New York Times* columnist who has been supporting Clinton. "Well, now he has an overwhelming money advantage and the support of much of the Democratic establishment — yet he still can't seem to win over large blocs of Democratic voters, especially among the white working class. As a result, he keeps losing big states." [3]

Obama supporters, meanwhile, are concerned that his supporters — particularly young people and African Americans — will feel disenfranchised if Clinton wins the nomination through a coronation by party officials, because it seems certain she will trail Obama in delegates and overall popular vote support after all the primaries are concluded on June 3.

"We keep talking as if it doesn't matter, it doesn't matter that Obama gets 92 percent of the black vote, [that] because he only got 35 percent of the white vote he's in trouble," House Majority Whip James E. Clyburn, D-S.C., the highest-ranking African American in Congress, told *The Washington Post* following the Pennsylvania primary.

"Well, Hillary Clinton only got 8 percent of the black vote. . . . It's almost saying black people don't matter. The only thing that matters is how white people respond." [4]

Whatever the outcome, Obama's candidacy has already highlighted many of the ways in which the American electorate is starting to shift — as well as the ways that it hasn't changed quite yet.

"The biggest trend is that the U.S. is no longer going to be a majority-white country," says Scott Page, a University of Michigan political scientist. Given the growth of the Asian and, particularly, the Hispanic share of the population, most demographers predict that whites will no longer comprise a majority by 2050.

"Within 40 years, no single racial group will be a majority," Page says. "Second, interracial marriage is increasing, and many of these marriages are in the upper-income groups, which means that many of our future leaders will be multiracial," like Obama.

In leading the battle for Democratic delegates and total votes, Obama has forged a coalition unlike any seen before in his party. It's typical for one candidate to appeal to educated elites, as Obama does, while a rival appeals to "beer track" blue-collar voters, as Clinton does.

What Obama has done differently is wed African Americans, who typically vote along with lower-income whites in Democratic primaries, to his base among elites. "This is the first time African Americans have sided with the educated class," says David Bositis, an elections analyst at the Joint Center for Political and Economic Studies.

Referring to the leading contenders of the 1984 Democratic primary race, Bositis continues, "Obama is Gary Hart, but with the black vote. Hillary Clinton is Walter Mondale but without any black support. Obama's going to be the first nominee who represents the more educated and higher-income Democrats."

Assuming he does ultimately win the nomination, an Obama victory will be the result not only of this historic shift in black voting but also the fact that educated and upper-income voters are both growing in number and becoming more Democratic. He has also benefited from unusually high levels of support among young voters of all races.

But the white working-class vote, while shrinking as a share of the total electorate, is still a predominant factor in American politics. Many Democrats — as well as Republicans — believe that Obama's inability to appeal to this group will prove an Achilles' heel.

"Hillary supporters are going to be very unhappy," says Herbert I. London, president of the conservative Hudson Institute. London predicts that McCain will do very well in the fall among the older Democrats who have supported Clinton — and could make inroads into other Democratic constituencies as well.

"This age gap [between Clinton and Obama] is so persistent that I would be concerned about it," says Robert David Sullivan, managing editor of *CommonWealth* magazine, "especially because McCain might have a particular appeal to older independents."

"Older whites are really going to stick with McCain," echoes Dowell Myers, a University of Southern California demographer. "They're going to think that he

Whites Moving to More Republican Areas

The percentage of whites living in what are considered Republican counties has steadily increased since 1970. Thirty and 29 percent lived in what are considered "Republican landslide" and "Republican competitive" counties, respectively, in 2000, compared to 24 and 25 percent three decades earlier. By contrast, the number of whites living in what are considered "Democratic landslide" counties has decreased by 7 percentage points during the 30-year span.

Percentage of Population That Is White, 1970-2000*
(by county type)

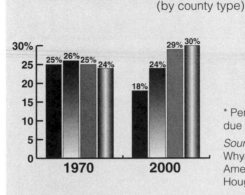

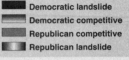

Political Leaning of County
- Democratic landslide
- Democratic competitive
- Republican competitive
- Republican landslide

* Percentages may not add to 100 due to rounding

Source: Bill Bishop, "The Big Sort: Why the Clustering of Like-Minded America Is Tearing Us Apart," Houghton Mifflin, May 2008

speaks to their interests."

William H. Frey, a demographer at the Brookings Institution, suggests that Obama's candidacy does represent a possible future for American politics. His candidacy has been "post-ethnic" in terms of his appeal to upper-income whites, as well as other white voters in states such as Wisconsin and Virginia. It's also "post-boomer," with Obama appealing to millions of "millennial" voters (referring to the generation born since 1982) and seeking, not entirely successfully, to move politics beyond the culture clashes that have marked American politics since the 1960s.

"Obama got a lot of initial support from people who liked his post-boomer sensibility — a way to get beyond moralistic politics," says Pew's Keeter. But as for a post-boomer period, he adds, "I don't think we're there yet."

Frey also cautions that Obama's candidacy may represent the shape of a political future that hasn't yet fully arrived. The trends that have benefited Obama — the rise of the youth vote, the increasing size of the upscale Democratic electorate — will continue, but may not yet be sufficiently in place to overcome the type of traditional,

AFP/Getty Images/Robyn Beck

AFP/Getty Images/Emmanuel Dunand

AFP/Getty Images/Craig Mitchelldyer

The Candidates

Sens. Hillary Rodham Clinton, D-N.Y., and Barack Obama, D-Ill., have carved out distinct groups of voters as they battle for the Democratic presidential nomination. Sen. John McCain, R-Ariz., the Republican nominee, is seeking to appeal to conservatives, blue-collar workers and religious fundamentalists.

white working-class voters who have long dominated American politics and have fueled Clinton's campaign.

"Maybe 20 years down the road there will be more of the Obama group overall, but for now everything is split," Frey says. "It's not 2030 yet."

Many demographic trends appear to be moving more generally in the Democrats' favor, including support from voters in their 20s, the increasing number of unmarried adults and secular-minded voters, the party's inroads into traditional GOP turf in the suburbs and the support of a majority of Hispanics — the nation's largest and fastest-growing minority group, who have been put off by the hard line many Republicans have taken on illegal immigration.

In seven states that held primaries in March and April alone, 1 million new voters registered as Democrats, while Republican numbers mostly "ebbed or stagnated." In Indiana and North Carolina, which held their Democratic primaries on May 6, the rate of new registrants tripled from 2004. [5]

Ruy Teixeira, another Brookings scholar and coauthor of the 2002 book *The Emerging Democratic Majority*, not surprisingly suggests that all these trends should help his party. But he concedes that Republicans still have some potent arrows in their quiver.

"The good news for the Republicans is that despite some of these various demographic factors that are moving against them, they have held the loyalties of lower-income white voters pretty well," he says.

Other structural advantages that Republicans have enjoyed in recent years — dominance of the South and the interior West, the rock-solid support of regular churchgoers, large margins of victory in the nation's fastest-growing communities — also remain in place.

And McCain's candidacy may dash Democratic hopes of running up a bigger margin among Hispanics that could help them prevail in states President Bush has carried, such as Nevada, New Mexico and Colorado. McCain has famously taken a more conciliatory stance toward immigrants than much of his party. "McCain takes Democrats out of their Western strategy entirely," says John Morgan, a Republican demographer.

With Democrats not quite settled on a candidate, it's premature to guess how the persistent demographic differences that have played out in the primaries will manifest themselves in the fall. Bositis suggests that Clinton's performance has been an indication of support for her among white women, in particular — not of white antipathy toward Obama. White working-class Democrats will mainly "come home" to support Obama in the fall, he suggests.

McCain's candidacy also has engendered some concerns on the Republican side that evangelicals — the conservative Christians who have been the party's most loyal supporters of late — will not support him with any enthusiasm. McCain consistently trailed among evangelical white Protestants during his primary race against former Govs. Mike Huckabee of Arkansas and Mitt Romney of Massachusetts.

How all these crosscurrents of support — or lack thereof — will play out in the fall remains to be seen, of course. What this year's election season has indicated more than anything, however, is that the nature and shape of the American electorate is in a state of flux just now, with the allegiances of various groups shifting between and within the two major parties — and with new constituencies making their presence very much felt.

"We're seeing more people registering now than we've ever seen before," says Kimball Brace, a Democratic consultant. "How that is going to change the demographics and nature of voting is one of the larger questions coming into play."

As the election season wears on, here are some of the other questions being asked about America's changing electorate:

Are whites losing political clout?

After the release of the 2000 census figures, some Republican strategists recognized that their party faced a

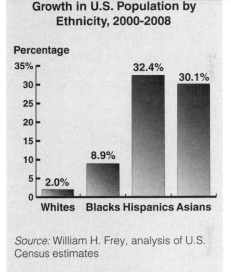

Hispanic Population Grew Rapidly

The number of Hispanics in the United States has grown by nearly a third since 2000. By contrast, blacks and whites have only grown by 9 and 2 percent, respectively. Democrats are favored by a majority of Hispanics — the nation's largest and fastest-growing minority group — who have been put off by the hard line many Republicans have taken on illegal immigration.

Growth in U.S. Population by Ethnicity, 2000-2008

Percentage

- Whites: 2.0%
- Blacks: 8.9%
- Hispanics: 32.4%
- Asians: 30.1%

Source: William H. Frey, analysis of U.S. Census estimates

serious long-term demographic challenge. Rich Bond, a former Republican National Committee chairman, told *The Washington Post*, "We've taken white guys about as far as that group can go. We are in need of diversity, women, Latino, African American, Asian . . . That is where the future of the Republican Party is." [6]

Republicans count on a disproportionate share of the white vote. Even in 2006, as Democrats regained control of Congress, white males supported GOP candidates by an eight-percentage-point margin. [7] The overall white vote that year favored Republicans by 4 percentage points — although that was down from a 15 percent margin in 2004. Whites were, in effect, outvoted by Hispanics, blacks and Asians, who gave massive margins

Hispanics' Share of U.S. Electorate Increasing

The number of Hispanics living in the United States is expected to total about 48 million in 2010, or about 16 percent of the total U.S. population. This represents a fivefold increase compared to 1970. By 2050, a quarter of the electorate is projected to be Hispanic, numbering just over 100 million people.

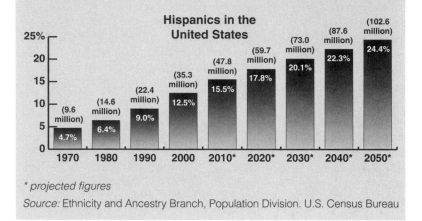

Hispanics in the United States

1970	4.7% (9.6 million)
1980	6.4% (14.6 million)
1990	9.0% (22.4 million)
2000	12.5% (35.3 million)
2010*	15.5% (47.8 million)
2020*	17.8% (59.7 million)
2030*	20.1% (73.0 million)
2040*	22.3% (87.6 million)
2050*	24.4% (102.6 million)

projected figures

Source: Ethnicity and Ancestry Branch, Population Division. U.S. Census Bureau

"You really have to have those votes in order to win," he says.

During the 1950s, whites made up more than 90 percent of the electorate (95 percent in 1952). [10] During the decades since then, blacks have secured their place in the voting booth through passage of voting-rights laws, and the Latino share of the population has skyrocketed. White males alone made up nearly half of the electorate in 1952, according to Emory University political scientist Alan Abramowitz. Their share had dropped to 33.1 percent by 2004.

"Thanks to the recent growth in the Latino population . . . the white male share is now dropping about a percentage point a year, accelerating a decline that began with the increased enfranchisement of African Americans in the civil rights era," Thomas F. Schaller wrote in *Salon* last September. "In [this] year's election, white males may account for fewer than one out of three voters. Bubba is no longer a kingmaker." [11]

But not everyone is convinced that whites are in any danger of losing their sway over elections. Karlyn Bowman, a senior fellow at the American Enterprise Institute (AEI), points out that "the black share of the electorate doesn't appear to be growing. That could change if Obama's the nominee, but at least at this point it doesn't appear to be growing. Asians are growing, but they are still a small percentage."

Despite the rapid growth and spread of Hispanics, their political power does not yet mirror their numbers, which, after all, includes millions of non-citizens. And the median age of Hispanics in the U.S. is just 27 compared to 39 for Anglos, meaning that a much higher percentage of Hispanics don't vote simply because they're too young. [12]

"White people are going to have less power," says Teixeira at the Brookings Institution, "but it's not going to be as fast as you think because of the lack of eligible voters" among Latinos.

Fernando Guerra, a political scientist at Loyola Marymount University in Los Angeles, also disputes the notion that growing minority populations will translate

to Democratic candidates (favoring Democrats by 39-, 79- and 25-point margins, respectively). [8]

Obama, the leading Democratic candidate, appears to be prevailing despite his inability to win a majority among white voters. He's doing well among young and well-educated whites and has carried 9 out of 10 black voters. But Clinton has carried the overall white vote in many states. In an analysis of the primary vote through the end of April, former *Los Angeles Times* editor Bill Boyarsky concluded that Obama's share of the white vote was "short [of] a majority, but still substantial." [9]

So if Democrats can nominate a candidate who fails to receive a majority of the white vote, and if whites' share of the total vote is shrinking, does that mean that white voters are losing influence?

Ronald Walters, a University of Maryland political scientist, believes that white influence will decline, given the growth in both immigration and naturalization. "I would think in the future you're going to have substantial demographic shifts bringing in more Hispanics and African Americans," he says. "What it will mean in terms of whites is that they will have to adjust to the loss of political power."

Walters estimates that 13 states — comprising 43 percent of the Electoral College — have combined black and Hispanic populations topping 25 percent of their total.

either into monolithic voting patterns or influence exceeding that of Anglos.

"Whites continue to be the majority or plurality everywhere, with the exception of some cities and counties," Guerra says. "There are states where African Americans and Latinos make up more than 30 percent of the population, but none are above 50 percent."

It's become conventional wisdom in the South, where the black share of the vote tops 35 percent in some states — and is a share that votes heavily Democratic — that Republicans have to take at least 60 percent of the white vote in order to prevail in statewide elections. But they've had no apparent problem doing so.

Guerra notes that whites represent a majority of the electorate even in states with exceptionally large minority populations, such as California, New Mexico and Hawaii. Myers, the USC demographer, has reached a similar conclusion about his own state.

"In California, whites are already down to 45 percent of the population, but they're about 70 percent of the voters," Myers says. "Whites will remain a majority [of the state electorate] until 2031. Despite their shrinking numbers, they're older, and older people tend to vote. Also, they're all citizens."

Nationwide, whites still make up a large and disproportionate share of the electorate. According to Brookings demographer Frey, whites' share of the population is down to 66 percent, but they still make up 74 percent of eligible voters and 78 percent of actual voters.

"The role of whites is diminishing," says Clark Bensen, a Republican demographer and consultant. "Whether it actually reaches a critical mass where it doesn't matter is another story."

Are suburbs shifting to the Democrats?

The vote in most states splits along predictable geographic lines. Big cities are primarily Democratic, while rural areas are reliably Republican. The suburbs have become the most important battlegrounds, the biggest trove of votes nationwide, with enough numbers to sway most statewide elections.

Because of their success in fast-growing counties — President Bush carried 97 of the nation's 100 fastest-growing counties in 2004 — Republicans have been hopeful that their appeal to suburban voters on issues such as tax rates and national security would be enough to assure victory in most presidential contests for the foreseeable future. [13]

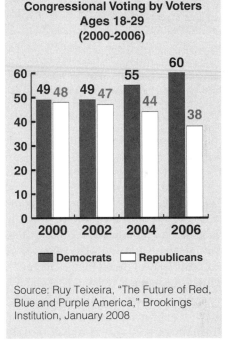

Young Voters Trending Democratic

Three out of every five voters ages 18 to 29 voted Democratic in 2006, an 11-percentage-point increase from 2000. Republican votership declined by a similar amount during the same period.

Congressional Voting by Voters Ages 18-29 (2000-2006)

■ Democrats □ Republicans

Year	Democrats	Republicans
2000	49	48
2002	49	47
2004	55	44
2006	60	38

Source: Ruy Teixeira, "The Future of Red, Blue and Purple America," Brookings Institution, January 2008

"Suburban and exurban areas . . . were central to Republican political guru Karl Rove's grand scheme for cementing GOP dominance for decades in the wake of President Bush's 2004 re-election victory," writes political journalist David Mark. [14]

Voters in exurban areas — counties on the fringe of metropolitan areas — seem naturally receptive to the GOP's overarching message about the need to limit government spending. They tend to be highly sensitive to tax increases and have sought out areas where the private sector, rather than local governments, provides services — from privately owned cars for transportation to homeowners' associations for parks and gated communities for maintenance of streetscapes.

Nascar fans stand during the prayer before a race at the California Speedway in Fontana. Nascar fans tend to be blue-collar, patriotic and Republican. In recent elections, candidates of all stripes have sought to "microtarget" voters — tailoring messages to appeal to particular demographic niches, such as "Nascar dads," "soccer moms" and "angry white males."

Joel Kotkin, an expert on development and living patterns at Chapman University in Anaheim, Calif., told Minnesota Public Radio in February that for the past 40 years cities have lost middle-class white people with children who moved to suburbs seeking better schools, more space and increased security. That left cities with what Kotkin calls an array of demographic "niches."

"And that niche tends to be either minorities, poor people, young people or people without children — all of whom tend to be much more liberal."

Democratic author and researcher Teixeira agrees "there's a density gradient for Democratic voting. The question is, where does it tip?" Teixeira argues that, despite the long-standing notion that suburban voters are more conservative than city folks, voters in older, more established "inner-ring" suburbs are increasingly favoring Democrats.

Democrats carried nearly 60 percent of the 2006 U.S. House vote in the inner-ring suburbs of the nation's 50 largest metropolitan areas — up from 53 percent in 2002 — according to an analysis by the Metropolitan Institute at Virginia Tech. They won nearly 55 percent of the next ring of "mature" suburbs, up from 50 percent four years earlier. [15]

In Virginia, Republicans pinned their hopes for retaining control of the state Senate last fall on campaigns that stressed a hard line against illegal immigration. They lost the chamber and lost state House seats by

ceding Northern Virginia suburbs that had once been firm GOP territory.

In Minnesota in 2006, Republicans lost 19 state House seats, and control of that chamber, largely in suburban districts around the Twin Cities, where voters were skeptical of the GOP's emphasis on social issues. And, in a particularly painful symbolic loss in March, Democrat Bill Foster picked up the suburban Chicago House seat formerly occupied by Republican Speaker Dennis Hastert.

"I doubt the Karl Roves of the world would disagree with the fact that the Democrats have been able to push out more into the suburbs, and Republicans have to push them back," says AEI's Bowman.

Demographer Robert Lang of Virginia Tech says that population growth rates are highest in Republican-leaning emerging suburbs — about 17 percent, he says, compared with just 4 percent growth in the inner-ring and mature suburbs. But the existing population in the latter category is so much greater that their growth in absolute numbers is about the same as the outer suburbs.

"The outer suburbs are not gaining everything," he says. "The rural and exurban growth cannot offset urbanizing suburbs much longer."

Republican demographer Morgan agrees that the older suburbs are filling up with people coming out from cities — including immigrants increasingly drawn to suburbs. But he says Republicans are moving to outer suburbs and exurban areas.

"The main county [in a metropolitan area] is no longer Republican, or it breaks about even," he says. "But what we have is hundreds of counties becoming exurban Republican. Around Atlanta, all of North Georgia is exurban and all Republican."

What's happening is that some inner-ring suburbs are coming to resemble center cities in their population density and makeup. Morgan says, "The older suburbs aren't genuinely suburbs, so many people are coming out from the cities."

Michael Barone, an AEI resident fellow and senior writer for *U.S. News & World Report*, notes that Arlington, Va., just outside Washington, was once "family territory, with young families and was Republican. In Arlington now, most people live in apartments, it's full of singles and it's become very heavily Democratic." Barone notes that similar changes have happened in other metropolitan areas as well.

The key to suburban control, as Teixeira suggests, is determining how far the line of Democratic dominance extends out from the core city. Republicans concede they are losing the inner suburbs, while Teixeira notes that "the exurbs are likely to remain solidly Republican.

"The question," he says, "is will the emerging suburbs" — the areas growing in population but closer to the city than the exurbs on the fringe — "remain competitive, as they were in 2006, or will they be solidly Republican? If the GOP can't keep the emerging suburbs solidly Republican, the math suggests they'll lose the suburbs overall."

Others are not willing to concede the suburbs to the Democrats quite yet. "This trend of the close-in suburbs becoming more Democratic seems to have started in the North, but there's still some question of whether it will happen in the South," says Robert David Sullivan, managing editor of *CommonWealth* magazine.

"If the suburbs of Atlanta act in the same way as the suburbs of Boston and Chicago, that is good news for the Democrats, but it hasn't started happening yet. That's a question for this fall."

Are young voters more liberal?

In April, the Pew Research Center for the People & the Press released survey data that suggested voters in their 20s strongly identified with the Democratic Party. More than half — 58 percent — identified with the Democrats, compared with 33 percent who affiliated with the GOP. [16] "This makes Generation Next the least Republican generation," according to the center. [17]

The findings received a good deal of attention, with some observers speculating that the unpopular presidency of George W. Bush and the war in Iraq might cost the Republicans a generation's support. The overwhelming preference for Obama among young voters in this year's Democratic primaries and caucuses also spoke to the party's hopes for winning over this fresh cohort of voters.

Voters ages 18 to 29 gave 60 percent of their support to Democrats in 2006, giving the party a 22-point margin, compared with a closer 55-to-44 percent split in 2004. [18]

"Clearly, George Bush does not appeal to them positively," says Barone, the political commentator and AEI fellow. "Unlike Presidents Reagan and Clinton, he has not attracted young voters to his party.

"Certainly, they did not go through the experiences of the 1970s — stagflation, the overregulation of the econ-omy — that left a lot of Americans skeptical about big-government policies," Barone continues. "That's been a help to Republicans in preceding years. It's not now."

Morley Winograd and Michael D. Hais, the Democratic authors of the new book *Millennial Makeover: MySpace, YouTube and the Future of American Politics*, go so far as to suggest that the party capturing the White House this year has "a historic opportunity to become the majority party for at least four more decades." [19]

But even though many conservatives such as Barone — and even some Republican political consultants — are willing to concede an advantage for Democrats among young voters today, they argue that such an advantage could prove fleeting. Today's young may be sour on the Republican "brand," but that doesn't mean they'll be life-long liberals who will remain loyal to the Democrats.

"This is a generation that's up for grabs," says Bowman, Barone's AEI colleague. She concedes that "they're leaning very heavily Democratic today" but argues that their attitudes toward both big government and big business could "tip them Republican as they start their careers."

"Democrats may have the young for a couple of elections," Republican demographer Morgan says.

Bowman also argues that, although today's young people tend to be more tolerant toward gays than their forebears, "attitudes on abortion and drugs have not become more liberal over time. They're not so much liberal or conservative," she says. "They're just different."

James Gimpel, a political scientist and expert on demographics at the University of Maryland, says that young voters are skewing more liberal on social and cultural issues, but he suggests that the Democrats' current success among them has as much to do with the party's active recruitment and appeal to these voters as ideology.

"The Democrats and progressive forces have been much more aggressive," he says. "Republicans have been very slow at recruiting younger people. The Republicans are maybe hanging back and hoping when people get into their 30s, they'll switch."

Gimpel suggests that the potential for intergenerational warfare — with younger voters resentful about having to pay high payroll taxes to support Social Security and health benefits for aging boomers — could redound to the GOP's benefit. "The opportunity is there for Republican candidates who offer lower taxes and smaller government," he says.

1950s-1960s *Democratic dominance of American politics starts to ebb.*

1952 Dwight D. Eisenhower is elected president — the only Republican president from 1933 to 1969.

1954 Supreme Court's *Brown v. Board of Education* ruling overturns "separate but equal" segregation policies in schools, leading to "white flight" from cities. . . . Democrats gain House and Senate majorities that endure for decades.

1965 President Lyndon B. Johnson signs Voting Rights Act, guaranteeing suffrage for black Americans. . . . Johnson also signs an immigration law that moves away from quotas favoring Western Europeans, signaling the beginning of enormous Latino immigration.

1966 In response to Johnson's Great Society programs, Republicans gain 47 House seats, three Senate seats and eight governorships.

1968 Assassination of Rev. Martin Luther King Jr. sparks riots in more than 100 cities. . . . Richard M. Nixon wins the presidency by pursuing a "Southern strategy" that addresses whites' concerns about law and order and changing social mores. His is the first of five Republican wins out of six elections.

1970s-1980s *Republicans dominate voting for the White House, but Democratic majorities in Congress mostly endure.*

1970 For the first time, suburban residents outnumber city dwellers.

1973 Supreme Court's *Roe v. Wade* decision legalizing abortion spurs evangelicals to greater political involvement.

1974 President Nixon resigns amidst the Watergate scandal; 75 new Democrats, "known as Watergate babies," are elected to the House, compared to just 17 Republicans.

1980 Ronald Reagan addresses 20,000 evangelicals at a gathering later called "the wedding ceremony of evangelicals and the Republican Party"; in his first election, Reagan moves millions of white working-class voters and much of the South into the GOP's column.

1990s-2000s *Political parity and increasing polarization lead to close competition between the two parties.*

1992 Democrat Bill Clinton wins the White House by appealing on economic issues to working-class voters who "play by the rules."

1994 Republicans win House for first time in 40 years, along with the Senate, through the support of "angry white males."

2000 Church attendance becomes a predictor of Republican voting; George W. Bush carries 74 percent of evangelical vote.

2004 Record 40 percent of Latinos vote for President Bush. . . . Nearly 50 percent of Americans live in "landslide counties" where one of the presidential candidates won by 20 percent or more; the figure in 1976 was 27 percent.

2005 Republican Party Chairman Ken Mehlman apologizes to African American voters for seeking "to benefit politically from racial polarization." . . . House Republicans pass an immigration bill that would reclassify illegal immigrants as felons, angering Hispanics. . . . Twenty-eight percent of adults hold college degrees, compared with 5 percent in 1940.

2006 Democrats regain control of Congress; whites give marginal support to Republicans but are outvoted by heavy Democratic voting among blacks, Hispanics and Asians.

2008 Christian leader James Dobson says he would not vote for Sen. John McCain, R-Ariz., "under any circumstances" (Jan. 13). . . . Sen. Hillary Clinton, D-N.Y., carries 67 percent of the Hispanic vote in Texas (March 4). . . . Answering criticism about the Rev. Jeremiah Wright, his former pastor, Sen. Barack Obama gives widely praised speech on race in America (March 18). . . . Obama tells San Francisco fundraiser that working-class voters are "bitter" and "cling to guns or religion" for solace (April 4). . . . Bush's disapproval rating hits 69 percent (April 22). . . . Voters in Montana, South Dakota close out Democratic primary season (June 3).

But not everyone believes that waiting for changing conditions will prove a winning strategy for the GOP. Myers, the USC demographer, says that each younger generation tends to exaggerate the political climate of the time in which they came to maturity. He argues that despite the fact people's voting habits change to some extent due to their place in the "life cycle" — people with children tend to become more conservative, for instance — "these cohorts tend to hold their orientations for the rest of their lives."

Mark Grebner, a Democratic consultant based in Michigan, agrees. He says that people who came of age under Reagan were heavily Republican and have remained so. "The people born around 1962, 1964, they're about as Republican as any age cohort that we've seen in a long time," he says.

But the people who are coming up under the Bush presidency, Grebner argues, are strongly Democratic. "People who are now 18 to 28 are much more Democratic — dramatically," he says.

A poll of 18-to-24-year-olds conducted in March and April for Harvard University's Institute of Politics found that they favor Obama over McCain, 53 percent to 32 percent, while giving Clinton a much smaller margin over McCain (44 to 39 percent). [20]

"Certainly the Bush presidency has not been a big plus for the Republican Party," Grebner says.

BACKGROUND

After the New Deal

American politics in recent decades has been a massive square dance, with regions and demographic groups switching parties. The Northeast, for example, was the most solidly Republican part of the country into the 1960s but now is the Democrats' strongest base. Conversely, the "solid South" is no longer wholly Democratic but mostly Republican.

Roman Catholics, once predominantly Democratic in their voting habits, now divide their votes evenly between the parties. African Americans in the North, for whose allegiance both parties competed effectively up until about 1960, are now the most loyal voting bloc for Democrats. The list of groups shifting loyalties between the parties goes on and on and will remain a crucial factor this year, as Democrats struggle to hold onto a sizable share of the white working-class vote, which will likely prove decisive.

White working-class voters for decades comprised the majority of the Democratic vote as the largest bloc within the New Deal coalition, which dominated U.S. politics from 1932, with the election of Franklin D. Roosevelt as president, until 1968.

Republicans had enjoyed near-permanent occupancy of the White House since the Civil War, winning 14 of the 18 presidential elections since 1860. But in 1932, in response to the federal government's weak response to the Great Depression, Roosevelt not only won big but put together an enduring political coalition that included members of labor unions, big-city political machines in the North, farm groups, intellectuals, minority groups including Jews and the South.

The New Deal coalition propelled Democrats to victory in all but two of the nine presidential elections from 1932 to 1964. "The Republicans were the party of the Northeast, of business, of the middle classes and of white Protestants, while the Democrats enjoyed a clear majority among the working classes, organized labor, Catholics and the South" at all political levels, wrote pollster Everett Carll Ladd Jr. [21]

Even during the Democrats' years in the wilderness — the two-term presidency of Dwight D. Eisenhower — New Deal-style politics and programs continued to dominate the national agenda, with the expansion of government social-welfare programs continuing unabated. Eisenhower, for instance, oversaw the creation of the Department of Health, Education and Welfare. [22] In addition, during Eisenhower's second year in office, Democrats won majorities in the House and Senate that would endure for 40 and 26 years, respectively.

The high-water mark for Democrats came with the election of 1964, when Lyndon B. Johnson won the largest share of the popular presidential vote in modern times, and the party took two-thirds of the House and Senate seats. Their landslide led to the passage of a slew of domestic legislation known as the Great Society, including the creation of Medicare, the Voting Rights Act of 1965 and a rewrite of the nation's immigration law, abolishing a system of quotas that had limited immigration mainly to newcomers from Western Europe.

The price tag and policy directions of many of these bills prompted a backlash in 1966, when Republicans gained 47 House seats, three Senate seats and eight governorships, including the election of Ronald Reagan in California. Notably, the election represented a breakthrough for the

The Gap Between Blacks and Hispanics

Will racial politics affect the Democratic nomination?

One of the most notable racial divides in voting this year has been the gap between African Americans and Hispanics during the Democratic primary campaign. Blacks have been supporting Illinois Sen. Barack Obama by margins as great as 9-to-1, while Hispanics have given New York Sen. Hillary Clinton a 2-to-1 advantage in multiple states.

Is this just a fluke, or does it speak to some underlying enmity between the nation's two largest minority groups? There does appear to be evidence of tension between blacks and Hispanics in some areas, based on economic and political competition. But many observers say that claims of a deep divide are overblown.

A widely cited comment by Sergio Bendixen, Clinton's Hispanic pollster, set the template for debate about this issue on the presidential campaign trail. "The Hispanic voter — and I want to say this very carefully — has not shown a lot of willingness or affinity to support black candidates," Bendixen told *The New Yorker* in January. [1]

There have been some schisms between the two groups. Traditionally black areas such as South Los Angeles and Compton have become majority Latino, and Hispanics have also made strong inroads in Southern states such as North Carolina and Georgia, "bringing change to communities where blacks had gained economic and political power after years of struggle against Jim Crow laws," writes Stephan Malanga, a senior fellow at the Manhattan Institute. [2]

Studies of Southern cities conducted by Duke University political scientist Paula D. McClain have found that blacks believe Latinos have robbed them of jobs, while Hispanics regard blacks as "slothful and untrustworthy." [3]

"There is considerable anger among African Americans about the immigrant labor force that has taken over whole sections of the economy and excluded African Americans from those jobs," says Ronald Walters, director of the University of Maryland's African American Leadership Center. Walters notes that Hispanics sometimes complain in turn that black mayors or members of Congress don't do much for them in areas where black and brown residents live together.

In local elections, there have been examples both of coalitions built between the two groups, and of one constituency's refusal to vote for candidates drawn from the other. In Democratic primary campaigns over the years in New York and Texas, Hispanics have tended to vote for whites over blacks, and blacks have returned the favor when it comes to contests between Anglos and Hispanics. [4] On the other hand, Hispanics have lent overwhelming support to several black big-city mayors, while at least eight African American congressmen currently represent areas that are heavily Latino. [5]

In Los Angeles, Latinos now represent 46.5 percent of the population — up from just 18.5 percent 30 years ago. The black share of the population, in the meantime, has shrunk from 17 percent to 11.2 percent, fueling some animosity from both sides as blacks continue to enjoy disproportionate sway. [6] Antonio Villaraigosa, a Latino politician, carried just 20 percent of the black vote in his first race for mayor of Los Angeles against James Hahn, who is Anglo.

GOP in the South, which had given virtually all of its support to Democrats since the Civil War. Several Southern states were among the few to support Arizona Sen. Barry M. Goldwater over Johnson in 1964. Further breaking with tradition, about a third of the South's House districts elected Republicans in 1966.

The South began to turn mainly for one reason — the passage of federal civil rights laws granting equal opportunity and voting privileges to African Americans. The share of Southern blacks registered to vote rose from 29 percent in 1960 to 62 percent in 1970, but their presence on the voter rolls was not enough to offset the conservative and increasingly Republican voting patterns of white Southerners. [23]

Other demographic patterns began to work in the GOP's favor, including the explosive growth during the post-World War II era of the suburbs, triggered by a combination of factors that included the nationwide construction of new highways and the postwar "baby boom." The suburbs also gained population due to "white flight,"

But Villaraigosa carried blacks during his successful rematch against Hahn in 2005. "When people say to me, African Americans didn't vote for you in your first race, I say, well, they didn't know me," Villaraigosa told the *Chicago Tribune*. "In my second race, they did, and they voted for me overwhelmingly." [7]

Hahn's family had enjoyed a long history of support from L.A.'s black community. Such personal ties, as opposed to racial preferences, may go a long way toward explaining Clinton's performance among Hispanics this year.

Hispanics were big supporters of Bill Clinton and have proven to be a key constituency for Hillary Clinton as well. According to exit polling, she took 64 percent of the Latino vote in the Nevada caucuses, to Obama's 26 percent. Her share of the Hispanic vote in California was 67 percent, while in Texas it was 64 percent.

"If you look at the demographics of Latinos — working class, lower educational attainment — it's very similar to the demographics of whites who are supporting Hillary," says Loyola Marymount University political scientist Fernando Guerra.

Guerra adds that, "African Americans would be supporting Hillary overwhelmingly, if everything about Obama's

Los Angeles Mayor Antonio Villaraigosa.

Getty Images/Neilson Barnard

background and platform were the same, but he was white."

David Bositis, an expert on black voting behavior at the Joint Center for Political and Economic Studies, says that Hispanics are choosing to support Clinton, as opposed to voting against Obama. Taken as a group, Hispanics did well economically during her husband's time in the White House.

Although that is also true about African Americans, the latter group has been motivated by Obama's historic candidacy but put off by the Clinton campaign's occasional injection of his race as an issue. "If Hillary hadn't blown it with them, she would have been receiving at least a third of the black vote, instead of none," Bositis says.

[1] Ryan Lizza, "Minority Reports," *The New Yorker*, Jan. 21, 2008.

[2] Stephen Malanga, "The Rainbow Coalition Evaporates," *City Journal*, winter 2008, p. 35.

[3] Arian Campo-Flores, "Everything to Everyone," *Newsweek*, Feb. 4, 2008, p. 33.

[4] James Traub, "The Emerging Minority," *The New York Times Magazine*, March 2, 2008, p. 15.

[5] Clarence Page, "Clinton's Hispanic Edge Over Obama," *Chicago Tribune*, Jan. 30, 2008, p. 21.

[6] Susan Anderson, "The Clout That Counts," *Los Angeles Times*, Nov. 11, 2007, p. M4.

[7] Clarence Page, "When the Melting Pot Boils Over," *Chicago Tribune*, Feb. 6, 2008, p. 25.

with white parents taking their children out of urban school districts that were undergoing integration by race.

During this era, the Supreme Court issued numerous rulings that did not sit well with conservatives, including requirements that white families send their children by bus to schools dominated by blacks; a ban on prayer in public schools; the lifting of restrictions on contraception; and increased protections for criminal defendants. The Republican Party platform began to complain about "moral decline and drift."

Cultural ferment extended well beyond the reach of the court, with peaceful civil rights marches giving way to riots in hundreds of cities in 1967 and 1968. Republican Richard M. Nixon played to the fears of the "silent majority," promising in 1968 to restore law and order — a message that had particularly strong partisan resonance after rioting took place at that year's Democratic National Convention in Chicago.

Nixon also devised a "Southern strategy" of appealing to the fears of whites in response to the growing political

Diversity Blamed for 'Social Isolation'

Do Obama's problems in mixed states prove the point?

One of the many striking features of this year's Democratic presidential primary contest has been the difference in the kinds of states Illinois Sen. Barack Obama has won and lost. He easily carried states with large African American populations such as Mississippi and South Carolina, as well as nearly all-white states such as Maine, Vermont and Idaho, yet he lost nearly all the states with a broader demographic mix, including Pennsylvania, California, Ohio and New York.

"As some bloggers have shrewdly pointed out, Obama does best in areas that have either a large concentration of African American voters or hardly any at all, but he struggles in places where the population is decidedly mixed," writes political reporter Matt Bai in *The New York Times Magazine*. "What this suggests, perhaps, is that living in close proximity to other races — sharing industries and schools and sports arenas — actually makes Americans less sanguine about racial harmony rather than more so." [1]

If that is indeed the case, the Obama campaign may serve as an important illustration of a point made last year by Robert D. Putnam, a Harvard University political scientist. In a study that attracted widespread attention and engendered a good deal of controversy despite its appearance in a journal called *Scandinavian Political Studies*, Putnam posited that diversity — despite its near-universal approbation as one of America's major strengths — actually causes significant social harm, at least in the near-term.

Putnam and his team conducted detailed telephone interviews with 30,000 Americans — a far larger sample than usual in such surveys — and dug more deeply into 41 communities across the country. Even controlling for factors such as income disparities and local crime rates, Putnam found that residents of diverse communities are less likely to trust their neighbors — even those of their own race — than people who live in more homogenous areas.

"Diversity seems to trigger . . . social isolation," Putnam writes in the study. "In colloquial language, people living in ethnically diverse settings appear to 'hunker down' — that is, to pull in like a turtle. . . .

"Inhabitants of diverse communities tend to withdraw from collective life, to distrust their neighbors, regardless of the color of their skin, to withdraw even from close friends, to expect the worst from their community and its leaders, to volunteer less, give less to charity and work on community projects less often, to register to vote less, to agitate for social reform more, but have less faith that they can actually make a difference and to huddle unhappily in front of the television." [2]

Other social scientists have reached similar conclusions. A pair of Harvard economists found that about half the difference in social-welfare spending between Europe and the U.S. could be attributed to greater ethnic diversity in America. Two other economists reviewed 15 recent studies and concluded that ethnic diversity was linked to lower school funding and trust, as well as declines in other measures of "social capital" (a phrase Putnam helped popularize with his 2000 best-seller *Bowling Alone*). [3]

Putnam's work on diversity was soon seized upon by conservatives who saw it as a necessary corrective to the "Politically Correct Police" who had championed diversity power and demands of African Americans. Nixon strategist Kevin Phillips popularized the phrase, explaining that Republicans would never get more than 20 percent of "the Negro vote" but nevertheless would enforce the Voting Rights Act. "The more Negroes who register as Democrats in the South, the sooner the Negrophobe whites will quit the Democrats and become Republicans," he explained to *The New York Times*. [24]

The Democratic share of the presidential vote plummeted from a record 61 percent in 1964 to just 43 percent in 1968, with third-party candidate George Wallace appealing even more directly to voter anxiety than Nixon. In his 1969 book *The Emerging Republican Majority*, Phillips wrote, "This repudiation visited upon the Democratic Party for its ambitious social programming, and inability to handle the urban and Negro revolutions, was comparable to that given conservative Republicanism in 1932 for its failures to cope with the economic crisis of the Depression." [25]

as an unquestionable virtue — and as a warning against the effects of immigration, both legal and illegal. "I'm not at all surprised by what Mr. Putnam has found in his study," says Herbert I. London, president of the Hudson Institute. "[Diversity's] going to breed resentment and, to some extent, hostility."

The Orange County Register ran an editorial called "Greater Diversity Equals More Misery," while Putnam's work was favorably cited on the Web site of former Ku Klux Klan leader David Duke. [4] This sort of response clearly left Putnam uncomfortable. "It certainly is not pleasant when David Duke's Web site hails me as the guy who found out racism is good," the liberal Putnam said. [5]

More important than his discomfort, though, was Putnam's frustration that the second half of his argument was often left out of the commentary — that both immigration and diversity, over the long term, would prove to be pluses. We forget, he suggested in an interview, that there were similar levels of discomfort among communities receiving European immigrants a century or more ago.

He maintains that the current waves of immigrants can be successfully assimilated over time if social divisions are subsumed within the sort of shared identity that has always unified Americans. The areas that are attracting immigrants today are among the nation's most economically vibrant, Putnam points out.

"Immigration policies may at first seem tangential to productivity, but they are not," says Scott Page, a University of Michigan political scientist and author of a 2007 book about diversity called *The Difference.* "Diversity is crucial to the development of a nation, especially economically. Diverse people bring diverse skills, which prove invaluable for innovation and growth."

"Chief diversity officers" have become a staple of *Fortune* 500 companies, not to please the P.C. Police but to keep abreast of demographic trends that are changing the makeup of the skilled workforce. "If you define the global talent pipeline as all those individuals around the world who have at least a college degree, only 17 percent of this pipeline comprises white males," says Sylvia Ann Hewlett, an economist at the New York-based Center for Work-Life Policy. "Increasingly, talent management is diversity management."

As Putnam himself argues, diversity may be uncomfortable, but it's beneficial — and inevitable — over the long haul. "The most certain prediction that we can make about almost any modern society is that it will be more diverse a generation from now than it is today," he writes in his study.

In the short term, however, one of the most important political questions of the year is whether Obama, assuming he's the Democratic nominee, will be able to win over the white working-class voters who have largely supported New York Sen. Hillary Clinton in the more mixed states that she has won.

"Rather than serving to heal America's racial wounds," writes conservative columnist Jonah Goldberg, "maybe Obama's campaign is more like a dye marker that helps us better diagnose the complexity of the problem." [6]

---

[1] Matt Bai, "What's the Real Racial Divide?," *The New York Times Magazine,* March 16, 2008, p. 15.

[2] Robert D. Putnam, "E Pluribus Unum: Diversity and Community in the Twenty-First Century," *Scandinavian Political Studies,* June 2007, p. 137.

[3] Michael Jonas, "The Downside of Diversity," *The Boston Globe,* Aug. 5, 2007, p. D1.

[4] Ilana Mercer, "Greater Diversity Equals More Misery," *The Orange County Register,* July 22, 2007; available at www.ocregister.com/opinion/putnam-diversity-social-1781099-racial-greater.

[5] Jonas, *op. cit.*

[6] Jonah Goldberg, "Obama: Winning White Votes in White States," *The Kansas City Star,* Feb. 14, 2008, p. B9.

Reagan Democrats

Republicans would go on to win all but one of the next six presidential elections. (The one exception came in 1976, when the party was punished for the Watergate scandal that ended the Nixon presidency.) The GOP appeared to have a lock on the Electoral College, with victory virtually assured throughout the South, the Rocky Mountain West and the Plains states. The Sun Belt, which had about as many electoral votes as Snow Belt states in the 1970s, continues to pick up votes with each census. [26]

Underlying Republican success, however, was the fracturing of the New Deal coalition and the GOP's ability to tap into white working-class votes that had long been denied its candidates. Reagan's presidential campaigns of 1980 and 1984 moved the South further into the GOP corner. Despite his antagonism toward unions, Reagan's hard line on foreign policy appealed to working-class voters, as did his economic optimism — which was borne out by a lengthy period of economic expansion on his watch.

The white working class had been loyal to Democrats in previous decades largely because of economic policies the party pursued that redistributed income toward lower-income voters. But many of them were put off by Democratic platforms during the 1970s and '80s that seemed to emphasize liberal stances on social and cultural issues. Blue-collar voters had been 12 percent more Democratic than the electorate as a whole in 1948, but by 1972 they were 4 percent less. (There was a similar drop in Democratic support among urban Catholics). [27]

In 1972, when the National Election Survey asked who composed the Democratic Party, respondents still made it sound like it was still the party of the New Deal

> **With the rapid growth of Hispanics and other minority groups, some GOP strategists were concerned that their party's dependence on white male voters, in particular, was too limiting. In 2000, Bush sought to portray himself as an inclusive candidate, featuring many black and Hispanic speakers at his nominating convention.**

— the poor, working class, blacks, Catholics and unions. By 1984, responses to the same survey painted a different picture, saying the party was made up of black militants, feminists, civil rights leaders, people on welfare, gays and unions. [28]

Even as Democrats were losing some of their traditional supporters, Republicans were benefiting from the re-emergence of an important force — white evangelical Protestants. They had largely retreated from politics following the battles during the 1920s and '30s over Prohibition and evolution. As late as 1965, the Rev. Jerry Falwell said that pastors should win souls, not concern themselves with fighting communism and political reform.

The liberal decisions of the Supreme Court, particularly in the 1973 *Roe v. Wade* case that legalized abortion, angered evangelicals, however. In May 1979, secular conservative leaders met with Falwell and urged him to form an organization that would mobilize fundamentalists. He did so a month later, founding the Moral Majority.

The following year, Reagan appealed for their support directly, addressing a gathering of 20,000 evangelicals, praising their efforts and questioning evolution. Ralph Reed, later the executive director of the Christian Coalition, which would supersede the Moral Majority as the leading force among Christian-right groups during the 1990s, called the meeting "the wedding ceremony of evangelicals and the Republican Party." [29] Evangelicals in recent election cycles have generally been estimated to represent 40 percent of the GOP primary vote.

Clinton and Bush

Bill Clinton in 1992 would become the only Democratic presidential candidate of the post-Reagan era to carry any Southern states. He won back a larger share of the white working-class vote by emphasizing economic issue (his campaign's unofficial slogan was "it's the economy, stupid") and signaled a shift away from "identity politics" by promising to "end welfare as we know it."

But Clinton's success did not translate into victories for his party. Democrats relinquished their 40-year hold on the House in 1994 and lost the Senate as well, as white male voters turned against the party, particularly in the South. By 2004, Clinton's home state of Arkansas was unique among Southern states in sending more Democrats than Republicans to Congress. There were 16 Republican senators from the region that year, compared with just four Democrats. [30]

Although he lost the popular vote in 2000, George W. Bush benefited from the demographic trends that had been moving voters into the Republican column. He carried every Southern state, as well as 74 percent of the evangelical vote. [31] The most certain predictor of support for Bush in both his elections was regular church attendance.

With the rapid growth of Hispanics and other minority groups, some GOP strategists were concerned that their party's dependence on white male voters, in particular, was too limiting. In 2000, Bush sought to portray

Do demographic trends favor Democrats?

YES Ruy Teixeira
Visiting fellow The Brookings Institution

From "The Future of Red, Blue and Purple America," The Brookings Institution, January 2008

A new wave of demographic and geographic change is currently washing over the United States and is sure to have profound effects on our future politics, just as earlier changes helped give birth to the politics we know today. Here is a quick outline of several of the political and demographic trends that are leading to a Democratic and center-left majority in the United States:

- **Immigration and minorities.** Immigration and differential fertility have driven minority voters from about 15 percent of voters in 1990 to 21 percent today, and will produce a voting electorate that is about one-quarter minority by the middle of the next decade. Presently, with some exceptions — such as President Bush's 40 percent support among Hispanics in the 2004 election — these rising constituencies tend to give the Democrats wide margins (69-30 percent among Hispanics and 62-37 percent among Asians in the 2006 congressional elections).
- **Family changes.** Changes in household structure and differences in fertility are reshaping American families. Consider these dramatic trends: Married couples with children now occupy fewer than one in four households. Single women have recently become a majority of all adult women. These trends intersect in increasingly important ways with political behavior. Married voters are far more likely to vote Republican than are unmarried voters, eclipsing the effects of the celebrated gender gap. In the 2006 congressional election, married voters slightly favored Republicans (50-48 percent), while unmarried voters favored Democrats (64-34 percent).
- **Suburbs.** Much will ride on how the changing mix of residents votes in the different parts of suburbia. In 2006, Democratic House pickups in areas like suburban Denver, suburban Philadelphia, Connecticut and southern Florida were powered by coalitions where professionals and minorities took a leading role. Jim Webb's Senate victory in Virginia was largely due to his margin in Northern Virginia's high-tech suburbs.
- **Young voters.** According to one standard definition, 80 million Americans today are Millennials (birth years 1978-1996). By 2008, the number of citizen-eligible Millennial voters will be nearing 50 million. Now they seem to be leaning Democratic. In the 2006 congressional election, the first election in which almost all 18-to-29-year-olds were Millennials, they supported Democrats by a 60-38 percent margin.

NO Michael J. New
Assistant Professor, University of Alabama

Written for *CQ Researcher*, May 2008

In recent years, many observers have argued that the rising Hispanic population in America will do serious damage to the electoral prospects of the Republican Party. However, these analysts overlook a number of other trends that bode favorably for Republicans. For instance, investors are a reliable Republican constituency. In 1980 only 20 percent of American households owned stock. Today that number is up to 50 percent, and rising. Other groups that consistently vote for Republicans, including gun owners and home-schoolers, are growing rapidly as well. Better yet, many policies that have been advanced by the Republican Party, including concealed carry laws and expanded IRAs, have successfully expanded these Republican constituencies.

Furthermore, the membership trends of various religions should give serious pause to those who think that demographic trends favor Democrats. Indeed, many religious groups whose members are likely to support Republicans, including Evangelical Protestants, Mormons and Orthodox Jews, are seeing their memberships grow. Conversely, religious groups whose memberships are mostly Democrats, including mainline Protestants and Reform Jews, are actually getting smaller. It should also be noted that other important Democratic constituencies, including labor unions, are seeing their memberships shrink in absolute terms as well.

These demographic trends will strengthen a number of political trends that already favor Republicans. For instance, in close presidential elections in 2000 and 2004, President Bush won 30 and 31 states, respectively. Since Republican Senate candidates should be at an advantage in these states, Republicans should eventually accumulate over 60 Senate seats — good for a filibuster-proof majority. The rise of the Internet and talk radio has given conservatives greater ability to promote their ideas, free of interference from the mainstream media.

Finally, there is evidence to suggest that Hispanics may not be a lost cause for the Republican Party. First, Hispanics who are evangelical Protestants and those from Cuba are already likely to support Republican candidates. Furthermore, Republicans have been successful in capturing a large percentage of the Hispanic vote in states like Florida and Texas, which have pro-immigrant governors and less generous welfare benefits.

The best strategy might be to follow the lead of these governors and implement policies that will create and expand Republican constituencies among Hispanic voters. One way this can be done is to continue to pursue policies that will make Hispanics more sensitive toward taxes and less supportive of government programs.

A poll worker in New Orleans signs up a voter last February. Barack Obama has added African Americans, who typically vote along with lower-income whites in Democratic primaries, to his base among elites. If Obama wins the nomination, it will reflect this historic shift in black voting and also the fact that educated and upper-income voters are growing in number and becoming more Democratic.

himself as an inclusive candidate, featuring many black and Hispanic speakers at his nominating convention. He was also careful not to take as hard a line against immigrants as some members of his party.

But many suburban and highly educated voters began to turn against the GOP, concerned about the party's stances on social issues, such as opposition to stem-cell research, skepticism about evolution and political interference with the decision about keeping alive Terri Schiavo, a brain-dead Florida woman.

Bush's attempts to reach beyond his political base proved futile during his second term, as when the Republican-controlled House in 2006 refused to vote on a moderate Senate-passed immigration bill that had been negotiated with his administration. But what drove down Bush's approval ratings and cost his party control of Congress in 2006 was, primarily, the war in Iraq.

Bush's widely criticized handling of the devastation in New Orleans wrought by Hurricane Katrina erased any small gains his party had made among African Americans, while a tougher immigration bill passed by the House drove down GOP support among Hispanics from 40 percent in 2004 to 30 percent or less in 2006. [32]

Brother political scientists Earl Black and Merle Black wrote last year, "In modern American politics, a Republican Party dominated by white Protestants faces a Democratic Party in which minorities plus non-Christian whites far outnumber white Protestants." [33]

CURRENT SITUATION

'The Big Sort'

Despite the close balance between the parties in recent years — neither party has enjoyed a large majority in either congressional chamber for years, and no presidential candidate received a majority of the popular vote from 1992 until 2004 — comparatively few geographical areas remain in close contention.

Nationwide, the parties might be nearly tied, but candidates on either side can count on blowouts one way or the other within most counties. Compare the results of the presidential elections of 1976 and 2004, both of which were extremely close. In 1976, fewer than 25 percent of Americans lived in "landslide counties" that one candidate or the other carried by a margin of 20 points or greater. By 2004, nearly half the country — 48.3 percent — lived in a landslide county. [34]

Today, suggests journalist Bill Bishop in his new book *The Big Sort*, "Zip codes have political meaning. . . . As Americans have moved over the past three decades, they have clustered in communities of sameness, among people with similar ways of life, beliefs and, in the end, politics." [35]

It's not that liberals or conservatives ask their real-estate agents for printouts of precinct voting data when they're shopping for houses, but they do make lifestyle choices that place them among people who tend to live — and vote — much the way they do.

"There are lifestyle differences between liberals and conservatives that there weren't 30 years ago," says Notre Dame political scientist David Campbell. "The parties are well sorted ideologically, and we live in an era when it's easy to signal where you stand on these things by the type of car you drive and whether you shop at the farmer's market or Sam's Club. It's a way of constructing an identity, and those identities are playing out in politics."

Political analyst Charles Cook sometimes jokes that Democratic candidates have trouble carrying any district that doesn't include a Starbucks. [36] Rural areas are strongly Republican, cities are Democratic and the two parties fight their major turf wars in the suburbs, with fast-growing outer suburbs favoring the GOP and inner-ring suburbs becoming denser and more Democratic.

Such generalizations have long carried an element of truth, but some experts think the truth grows more compelling with each passing election year. "Even if you drop below the broad regional level, you find that neighborhoods and communities are looking more homogeneous than they ever have before," says Gimpel at the University of Maryland. "You have Republicans settling in around Republicans and Democrats settling around Democrats."

Lack of Competition

Although it's something of a myth that there are Republican "red" or Democratic "blue" states — plenty of states vote one way for president and the opposite for senator or governor — increasingly there are red and blue counties. That's why there are so few competitive House or state legislative seats.

Redistricting has been widely blamed for the fact that few legislative seats — perhaps less than 10 percent — are competitive at either the congressional or state level. It's become normal for a major state such as California to pass through an entire election cycle with none of its legislative seats — U.S. House, state Assembly or state Senate — changing partisan hands.

It's true that partisan redistricting, in which lines are generally drawn by state legislators for both Congress and their own seats, lumps together as many Republicans or Democrats together into districts that heavily favor one party or another. But most political scientists seem to believe that such partisan mapmaking simply exaggerates the natural ideological or partisan sorting that people are already doing by settling within like-minded communities.

In 2004, a third of U.S. voters lived in counties that had voted for the same party in each presidential election dating back all the way to 1968; just under half hadn't switched allegiances since 1980; and 73 percent lived in counties that had voted the same way in every election since 1992 — four in a row. [37]

Along with the geographical sorting, there is also an ideological sorting in terms of media choices, with citizens turning to media that gibe with their established worldview. Conservatives watch Fox News Channel and read blogs such as Instapundit, while liberals tune into National Public Radio and leave comments at DailyKos.com.

Journalist Bishop argues in his book that all this self-sorting amplifies people's natural preferences — that progressives grow more liberal in the exclusive company of left-leaning neighbors and media outlets, with the same "echo chamber" effect pushing conservatives further to the right. He contends it's one of the major rea-

sons for today's heated partisan bickering and lack of interparty cooperation.

"Like-minded, homogeneous groups squelch dissent, grow more extreme in their thinking and ignore evidence that their positions are wrong," Bishop writes. "As a result, we now live in a giant feedback loop." [38]

Picking Out Raisins

Candidates and consultants are well aware of the way counties or districts are likely to favor one party or another. In recent election years, they have sought to "microtarget" voters — tailoring messages to appeal to particular groups of voters within a community, rather than the community as a whole.

Every recent election cycle seems to bring about talk of new niche demographic groups who are being courted by candidates and consultants, such as "angry white males," "soccer moms" and "Nascar dads." Microtargeting represents an effort to appeal to dozens of different demographic groups, generally defined by their lifestyle and consumer choices.

Only a few years ago, party databases still targeted voters solely by precinct. Now they crack open each subdivision and make a good guess about which residents are socially liberal and which ones are anti-tax conservatives. Sophisticated campaigns are trying to become more precise with their messages, as well. Rather than sending out six or seven pieces of mail districtwide, they may send 20 different mailings to five different groups, such as veterans, seniors or gun owners.

How do they know which voter should get which piece of mail — and, more important, which swing voters should have the candidate show up personally on their doorsteps? Consultants such as Mark Grebner, an Ingham County commissioner in Michigan, look at every piece of information they can find about each voter — their ethnicity; whether they live in a precinct that turns out for hot Democratic primaries but not Republican ones; which magazines they subscribe to; and whether they ever have signed a petition to put an initiative or a candidate on a ballot. (To learn more about voters for his clients in Wisconsin, where he has less data, Grebner pays a fellow in Bangladesh to read every letter to the editor in state papers via the Web and code them according to likely party preference.)

Grebner takes all this information, runs a bunch of statistical analyses and assigns a percentage to each voter's likelihood of voting Democratic. Further narrowing the universe of potentially receptive voters is what winning close campaigns is all about. "If you don't want raisins in your cereal," Grebner says, "buy cereal that doesn't have raisins — don't pick them out one at a time."

OUTLOOK

Creating a New Map

In Bishop's analysis, it's Republicans who "were the winners in the big sort." From 1980 to 2006, Republican counties outgrew Democratic ones, on average, by more than 1 million people a year. Nearly all of that was due to people moving in, not natural population growth. "From 1990 to 2006 alone, 13 million people moved from Democratic to Republican counties." [39]

Republicans have taken advantage of the fact that much recent domestic migration has been toward the South and West, lending them added advantages in the Electoral College. Brookings demographer Frey predicts that the states that voted for Bush in 2004 will gain an additional 17 electoral votes (and House seats) by 2030. [40]

"In 2012, we gain a 15-electoral-vote advantage over the Democrats, on top of the earlier advantage," says GOP consultant Morgan. "That leaves the Dems really scrambling, like 270 [electoral votes] would be out of reach for them."

That is based on two assumptions. The first is that recent state population trends will continue through the rest of the decade, which is not necessarily the case. "The increase we've had in population growth in a lot of areas has just evaporated, except for Arizona and Texas," says Clark Bensen, another Republican consultant.

The other assumption is that states will continue to vote the way they have in the past. That has seemed like a good bet through the early part of this decade, with only three small states — New Hampshire, Iowa and New Mexico — switching their votes between 2000 and 2004. But nothing in politics is static.

Although Brookings scholar and author Teixeira is optimistic that demographic trends favor Democrats, including increasing support from Hispanics and "millennials" now in their 20s, the fact that parts of the electorate are changing can cause an opposite reaction in other parts. Republicans benefited from the rise of the Christian Right and their gains in the South, but these gains cost them support among moderate voters in the Northeast and suburbs in general.

"The very fact that the Democrats are benefiting from demographic trends, such as the rise of single women, could drive other voters into the arms of Republicans," he says. "They might not like Democrats as the party of single people."

Teixeira and other Democrats believe that this year's election represents a chance for their party not only to consolidate the demographic trends that have been breaking their way but also to capitalize on the unpopularity of President Bush, the war in Iraq and uncertainty about the economy.

"Even though McCain was probably the best person Republicans could nominate, I think the Democrats win no matter who ends up being the nominee, Clinton or Obama," says Guerra, the Loyola Marymount political scientist. "It's not only the changing demographics that is going to reward Democrats. We get tired of a certain party, and we're going to punish Republicans for their policies, even if McCain was not always on their side."

But as they wrap up the primary season, even Democrats are debating whether they might blow an election in which they appear to have many advantages. A lot of that debate comes down to the question of demographics. If Clinton is the nominee, African-Americans and the young will not be as motivated as they would be by an Obama candidacy. But Obama has yet to prove he can carry white working-class voters in the preponderance of swing states.

Head-to-head polls have shown as many as 14 states breaking different ways, depending on the Democratic nominee. Political analyst Rhodes Cook suggests that Clinton would likely carry 18 to 22 states — roughly the same group that Al Gore carried in 2000 and John Kerry won in 2004. Cook predicts that Obama, however, might win as many as 30 states — or as few as 10.

Although Obama lost the Pennsylvania primary, he carried the state's 300,000 newly registered Democrats by about 20 points. Republican registrations in the state were down by 70,000. Obama has launched a voter-registration effort that seeks to replicate such new-minted support in all 50 states.

"Hillary goes deeper and stronger in the Democratic base than Obama, but her challenge is that she doesn't go as wide," said Peter Hart, a Democratic pollster. "Obama goes much further reaching into the independent and Republican vote, and has a greater chance of creating a new electoral map for the Democrats." [41]

NOTES

1. Alan Greenblatt, "The Partisan Divide," *CQ Researcher*, April 30, 2004, pp. 373-396.

2. Kathy Kiely and Jill Lawrence, "Clinton Makes Case for Staying In," *USA Today*, May 8, 2008, p. 1A.

3. Paul Krugman, "Self-Inflicted Confusion," *The New York Times*, April 25, 2008, p. A27.

4. Jonathan Weisman and Matthew Mosk, "Party Fears Racial Divide," *The Washington Post*, April 26, 2008, p. A1.

5. Eli Saslow, "Democrats Registering in Record Numbers," *The Washington Post*, April 28, 2008, p. A1.

6. Thomas B. Edsall, "Census a Clarion Call for Democrats, GOP," *The Washington Post*, July 8, 2001, p. A5.

7. Susan Page, "GOP Coalition Fractured by Opposition to War," *USA Today*, Nov. 8, 2006, p. 1A.

8. Larry J. Sabato, *The Sixth-Year Itch* (2008), p. 22. For background, see the following *CQ Researcher* reports: David Masci, "Latinos' Future," Oct. 17, 2003, pp. 869-892; Alan Greenblatt, "Race in America," July 11, 2003, pp. 593-624, and Nadine Cohodas, "Electing Minorities," Aug. 12, 1994, pp. 697-720.

9. Bill Boyarsky, "Courting the White Vote," *Truthdig*, April 24, 2008, www.truthdig.com/report/item/20080425_courting_the_white_vote/.

10. Earl Black and Merle Black, *Divided America* (2007), p. 10.

11. Thomas F. Shaller, "So Long, White Boy," *Salon*, Sept. 17, 2007, www.salon.com/opinion/feature/2007/09/17/white_man/.

12. Alan Greenblatt, "Slow March to the Polls," *Governing*, June 2006, p. 17.

13. Ronald Brownstein and Richard Rainey, "GOP Plants Flag on New Voting Frontier," *Los Angeles Times*, Nov. 22, 2004, p. A1.

14. David Mark, "The Battle Over Suburban, Exurban Vote," Politico, Dec. 4, 2007. Mary H. Cooper, "Smart Growth," *CQ Researcher*, May 28, 2004, pp. 469-492.

15. Jill Lawrence, "Democratic Gains in Suburbs Spell Trouble for GOP," *USA Today*, Nov. 26, 2006, p. 6A.

16. Scott Keeter, *et al.*, "Gen Dems: The Party's Advantage Among Young Voters Widens," Pew Research Center for the People & the Press, April 28, 2008.

17. "A Portrait of 'Generation Next': How Young People View Their Lives, Futures and Politics," Pew Research Center for the People & the Press, Jan. 9, 2007; available at http://people-press.org/reports/pdf/300.pdf.

18. Sabato, *op. cit.*, p. 22.

19. Michiko Kakutani, "Why Are These Democrats Smiling? It's Cyclical," *The New York Times*, April 22, 2008, p. E7.

20. "Obama Dominating Highly-Charged Youth Vote in Presidential Race, Harvard Poll Finds," Harvard Institute of Politics, news release April 24, 2008.

21. Everett Carll Ladd Jr., "The Shifting Party Coalitions, 1932 to 1976," in Seymour Martin Lipset, ed., *Emerging Coalitions in American Politics* (1978), p. 83.

22. Kenneth S. Baer, *Reinventing Democrats* (2000), p. 14.

23. Barbara Sinclair, *Party Wars* (2006), p. 17.

24. James Boyd, "Nixon's Southern Strategy," *The New York Times*, May 17, 1970, p. 215.

25. Kevin Phillips, *The Emerging Republican Majority* (1969), p. 25.

26. Kenneth Jost and Greg Giroux, "Electoral College," *CQ Researcher*, Dec. 8, 2000, pp. 977-1008.

27. Ladd, *op. cit.*, p. 94.

28. Baer, *op. cit.*, p. 35.

29. Sinclair, *op. cit.*, p. 49.

30. *Ibid.*, p. 14.

31. *Ibid.*, p. 51.

32. "Latinos and the 2006 Midterm Election," Pew Hispanic Center, Nov. 27, 2006.

33. Black and Black, *op. cit.*, p. 29.

34. Bill Bishop, *The Big Sort* (2008), p. 6.

35. *Ibid.*, p. 5.

36. Alan Greenblatt, "Whatever Happened to Competitive Elections?", *Governing*, October 2004, p. 22.

37. Bishop, *op. cit.*, p. 45.

38. *Ibid.*, p. 39.

39. *Ibid.*, p. 56.

40. William H. Frey, "The Electoral College Moves to the Sun Belt," The Brookings Institution, May 2005, p. 4.

41. Patrick Healy, "For Democrats, Questions Over Race and Electability," *The New York Times*, April 24, 2008, p. A1.

BIBLIOGRAPHY

Books

Bishop, Bill, with Robert G. Cushing, *The Big Sort: Why the Clustering of Like-Minded America is Tearing Us Apart*, Houghton Mifflin, 2008.
A journalist shows how many more Republicans and Democrats are moving into communities that are partisan enclaves, contributing to the polarization of U.S. politics.

Bowman, Karlyn, and Ruy Teixeira, eds., *Red Blue and Purple America; The Future of Election Demographics*, Brooking Institution Press (forthcoming).
In a book coming this fall, a group of political scientists and demographers examine how trends in religion, geography, immigration and income and class are affecting voting habits.

Fisher, Claude S., and Michael Hout, *Century of Difference: How America Changed in the Last Hundred Years*, Russell Sage Foundation, 2006.
University of California, Berkeley sociologists draw on census data and polling surveys to present a comprehensive description of demographic, economic and cultural changes since 1900.

Singer, Audrey, Susan W. Hardwick and Caroline B. Brettell, eds., *Twenty-First Century Gateways: Immigrant Immigration in Suburban America*, Brookings Institution Press, 2008.
Academic authors examine the impact of immigrants no longer settling in urban cores so much as the suburbs.

Articles

Brownstein, Ron, "The Warrior and the Priest," *Los Angeles Times*, March 25, 2007, p. M1.
An influential column argues Barack Obama would appeal to upscale voters while Hillary Clinton would assume the role of "warrior" defending the interests of blue-collar voters.

Curry, Tom, "How Reagan Hobbled the Democrats," MSNBC.com, June 7, 2004, www.msnbc.msn.com/id /5151912/.
Curry examines how the Republican president captured lower- and middle-income whites and the South through clear economic and foreign policies.

Frum, David, "Why the GOP Lost the Youth Vote," *USA Today*, April 9, 2008, p. 12A.
A former speechwriter for President George W. Bush says Republicans must pay more attention to payroll taxes and environmental and social issues to woo young voters.

Healy, Patrick, "For Democrats, Questions Over Race and Electability," *The New York Times*, April 24, 2008, p. A1.
The split among Democratic primary voters has party leaders debating who has the best chance to prevail in the fall.

Malanga, Steven, "The Rainbow Coalition Evaporates," *City Journal*, Winter 2008.
A conservative author examines tensions between African Americans and immigrants in urban neighborhoods.

Mark, David, "The Battle Over Suburban, Exurban Vote," *Politico*, Dec. 4, 2007.
A political journalist looks at how emerging suburbs have become a contested battleground.

Schaller, Thomas F., "So Long, White Boy," *Salon*, Sept. 17, 2007.
White males have abandoned the Democrats, so party candidates should learn to win without their support.

Reports and Studies

Frey, William H., "The Electoral College Moves to the Sun Belt," The Brookings Institution Research Brief, May 2005.
Sun Belt states, which had a nearly equal amount of electoral votes as the Northeast and Midwest in 1972, will have 146 more by 2030.

Keeter, Scott, Juliana Horowitz and Alex Tyson, "Gen Dems: The Party's Advantage Among Young Voters Widens," Pew Research Center for the People & the Press, April 28, 2008, http://pewresearch.org/pubs/813/gen-dems.
Fifty-eight percent of voters under 30 are leaning toward the Democrats, fueling party growth much as young voters drove GOP growth during the 1990s.

Marcelo, Karlo Barrios, *et al.*, "Young Voter Registration and Turnout Trends," Rock the Vote and the Center for Information & Research on Civic Learning and Engagement, February 2008.
The turnout of young voters — typically low since 18-year-olds got the vote in 1972 — rose in both the 2004 and 2006 elections and is likely to increase again this year.

McKee, Seth C. and Daron S. Shaw, "Suburban Voting in Presidential Elections," *Presidential Studies Quarterly*, March 2003.
The decisive suburban vote edged away from Republican candidates during the 1990s in the North, but not in the South.

Putnam, Robert D., "E Pluribus Unum: Diversity and Community in the Twenty-First Century," *Scandinavian Political Studies*, June 2007, p. 137.
Based on a nationwide survey, the Harvard political scientist finds decreased levels of trust and social participation in communities that are more diverse.

For More Information

American Enterprise Institute, 1150 17th St., N.W., Washington, DC 20036; (202) 862-5800; www.aei.org. A conservative public policy think tank that conducts research and education on politics, economics and social welfare.

Atlas of U.S. Elections; uselectionatlas.org. A Web site providing comprehensive mapping of election results by state, city and county.

Brookings Institution, 1775 Massachusetts Ave., N.W., Washington, DC 20036; (202) 797-6000; www.brookings.edu. A centrist think tank that issues regular reports on politics, immigration and demographics through its Metropolitan Policy and Governance Studies programs.

Joint Center for Political and Economics Studies, 1090 Vermont Ave., N.W., Suite 1100, Washington, DC 20005; (202) 789-3500; (202) 789-3500; www.jointcenter.org. Studies issues of importance to African Americans.

Patchwork Nation Project, *The Christian Science Monitor*, 210 Massachusetts Ave., Boston, MA 02115; (617) 450-2000; www.csmonitor.com/patchworknation. Tracks political demographic information and hosts blogs by residents of 11 representative types of communities.

Pew Research Center for The People & The Press, 1615 L St., N.W., Suite 700, Washington, DC 20036; (202) 419-4300; people-press.org. Conducts public opinion polls and research on media and political issues.

UCLA Higher Education Research Institute, 2005 Moore Hall/Box 951521, Los Angeles, CA 90095; www.gseis.ucla.edu/heri/. Has conducted nationwide surveys of college freshmen for more than 40 years.

U.S. Census Bureau, 4600 Silver Hill Rd., Suitland, MD 20746; (202) 501-5400; www.census.gov. The primary source for information about the U.S. population.

William C. Velásquez Institute, 206 Lombard St., San Antonio, TX 78226; (210) 992-3118; www.wcvi.org. Conducts research as part of its mission of improving the level of political participation among Latinos.

3

Affirmative Action

Peter Katel

JESSICA PECK CORRY
Colorado Civil Rights Initiative

MELISSA HART
Coloradans for Equal Opportunity

TV screenshot courtesy "DemocracyNow"

Law student Jessica Peck Corry, executive director of the Colorado Civil Rights Initiative, supports Constitutional Amendment 46, which would prohibit all government entities in Colorado from discriminating for or against anyone because of race, ethnicity or gender. Attorney Melissa Hart counters that the amendment would end programs designed to reach minority groups.

From *CQ Researcher*, October 17, 2008.

N o white politician could have gotten the question George Stephanopoulos of ABC News asked Sen. Barack Obama. "You said . . . that affluent African Americans, like your daughters, should probably be treated as pretty advantaged when they apply to college," he began. "How specifically would you recommend changing affirmative action policies so that affluent African Americans are not given advantages and poor, less affluent whites are?" [1]

The Democratic presidential nominee, speaking during a primary election debate in April, said his daughters' advantages should weigh more than their skin color. "You know, Malia and Sasha, they've had a pretty good deal." [2]

But a white applicant who has overcome big odds to pursue an education should have those circumstances taken into account, Obama said. "I still believe in affirmative action as a means of overcoming both historic and potentially current discrimination," Obama said, "but I think that it can't be a quota system and it can't be something that is simply applied without looking at the whole person, whether that person is black, or white or Hispanic, male or female." [3]

Supporting affirmative action on the one hand, objecting to quotas on the other — Obama seemed to know he was threading his way through a minefield. Decades after it began, affirmative action is seen by many whites as nothing but a fancy term for racial quotas designed to give minorities an unfair break. Majority black opinion remains strongly pro-affirmative action, on the grounds that the legacy of racial discrimination lives on. Whites and blacks are 30 percentage points apart on the issue, according to a 2007 national survey by the nonpartisan Pew Research Center. [4]

Americans Support Boost for Disadvantaged

A majority of Americans believe that individuals born into poverty can overcome their disadvantages and that society should be giving them special help (top poll). Fewer, however, endorse race-based affirmative action as the way to help (bottom).

	Agree	Disagree
We should help people who are working hard to overcome disadvantages and succeed in life.	93%	6
People who start out with little and work their way up are the real success stories.	91	7
Some people are born poor, and there's nothing we can do about that.	26	72
We shouldn't give special help at all, even to those who started out with more disadvantages than most.	16	81

If there is only one seat available, which student would you admit to college, the high-income student or the low-income student?

	Percentage selecting:	
	Low-income student	High-income student
If both students get the same admissions test score?	63%	3%
If low-income student gets a slightly lower test score?	33	54
If the low-income student is also black, and the high-income student is white?	36	39
If the low-income student is also Hispanic, and the high-income student is not Hispanic?	33	45

Source: Anthony P. Carnevale and Stephen J. Rose, "Socioeconomic Status, Race/Ethnicity, and Selective College Admissions," The Century Foundation, March 2003

Now, with the candidacy of Columbia University and Harvard Law School graduate Obama turning up the volume on the debate, voters in two states will be deciding in November whether preferences should remain in effect in state government hiring and state college admissions.

Originally, conflict over affirmative action focused on hiring. But during the past two decades, the debate has shifted to whether preference should be given in admissions to top-tier state schools, such as the University of California at Los Angeles (UCLA) based on race, gender or ethnic background. Graduating from such schools is seen as an affordable ticket to the good life, but there aren't enough places at these schools for all applicants, so many qualified applicants are rejected.

Resentment over the notion that some applicants got an advantage because of their ancestry led California voters in 1996 to ban affirmative action in college admissions. Four years later, the Florida legislature, at the urging of then-Gov. Jeb Bush, effectively eliminated using race as an admission standard for colleges and universities. And initiatives similar to the California referendum were later passed in Washington state and then in Michigan, in 2006.

Race is central to the affirmative action debate because the doctrine grew out of the civil rights movement and the Civil Rights Act of 1964, which outlawed discrimination based on race, ethnicity or gender. The loosely defined term generally is used as a synonym for advantages — "preferences" — that employers and schools extend to members of a particular race, national origin or gender.

"The time has come to pull the plug on race-based decision-making," says Ward Connerly, a Sacramento, Calif.-based businessman who is the lead organizer of the Colorado and Nebraska ballot initiative campaigns, as well as earlier ones elsewhere. "The Civil Rights Act of 1964 talks about treating people equally without regard to race, color or national origin. When you talk about civil rights, they don't just belong to black people."

Connerly, who is black, supports extending preferences of some kind to low-income applicants for jobs — as long as the beneficiaries aren't classified by race or gender.

But affirmative action supporters say that approach ignores reality. "If there are any preferences in operation in our society, they're preferences given to people with white skin and who are men and who have financial and other advantages that come with that," says Nicole Kief, New York-based state strategist for the American Civil Liberties Union's racial justice program, which is opposing the Connerly-organized ballot initiative campaigns.

Yet, of the 38 million Americans classified as poor, whites make up the biggest share: 17 million people. Blacks account for slightly more than 9 million and Hispanics slightly less. Some 576,000 Native Americans are considered poor. Looking beyond the simple numbers, however, reveals that far greater percentages of African Americans and Hispanics are likely to be poor: 25 percent of African Americans and 20 percent of Hispanics live below the poverty line, but only 10 percent of whites are poor. [5]

In 2000, according to statistics compiled by *Chronicle of Higher Education* Deputy Editor Peter Schmidt, the average white elementary school student attended a school that was 78 percent white, 9 percent black, 8 percent Hispanic, 3 percent Asian and 30 percent poor. Black or Hispanic children attended a school in which 57 percent of the student body shared their race or ethnicity and about two-thirds of the students were poor. [6]

These conditions directly affect college admissions, according to The Century Foundation. The liberal think tank reported in 2003 that white students account for 77 percent of the students at high schools in which the greatest majority of students go on to college. Black students account for only 11 percent of the population at these schools, and Hispanics 7 percent. [7]

A comprehensive 2004 study by the Urban Institute, a nonpartisan think tank, found that only about half of black and Hispanic high school students graduate,

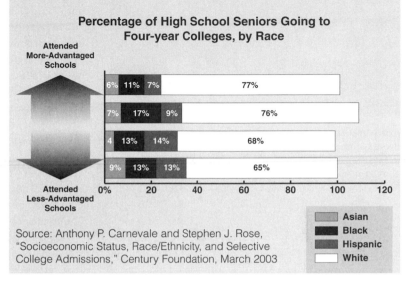

Elite Schools Graduate Fewest Minorities

Among college-bound blacks and Hispanics, larger percentages graduated from "less advantaged" high schools than from the "most advantaged" schools.

Percentage of High School Seniors Going to Four-year Colleges, by Race

Attended More-Advantaged Schools

| 6% | 11% | 7% | 77% |

| 7% | 17% | 9% | 76% |

| 4 | 13% | 14% | 68% |

| 9% | 13% | 13% | 65% |

Attended Less-Advantaged Schools

0%   20   40   60   80   100   120

Asian ▨
Black ▨
Hispanic ▨
White ▢

Source: Anthony P. Carnevale and Stephen J. Rose, "Socioeconomic Status, Race/Ethnicity, and Selective College Admissions," Century Foundation, March 2003

compared to 75 and 77 percent, respectively, of whites and Asians. [8]

Politically conservative affirmative action critics cite these statistics to argue that focusing on college admissions and hiring practices rather than school reform was a big mistake. The critics get some support from liberals who want to keep affirmative action — as long as it's based on socioeconomic status instead of race. "Affirmative action based on race was always kind of a cheap and quick fix that bypassed the hard work of trying to develop the talents of low-income minority students generally," says Richard D. Kahlenberg, a senior fellow at The Century Foundation.

Basing affirmative action on class instead of race wouldn't exclude racial and ethnic minorities, Kahlenberg argues, because race and class are so closely intertwined.

President Lyndon B. Johnson noted that connection in a major speech that laid the philosophical foundations for affirmative action programs. These weren't set up for another five years, a reflection of how big a change they represented in traditional hiring and promotion practices, where affirmative action began. "You do not take a person who, for years, has been hobbled by chains and liberate him, bring him up to the starting line of a race and then say, 'You are free to compete with all the others,' and still

Liasion/Lara Joe Regan

Asian-American enrollment at the University of California at Berkeley rose dramatically after California voters in 1996 approved Proposition 209, a ballot initiative that banned affirmative action at all state institutions. Enrollment of African-American, Hispanic and Native American students, however, plunged.

justly believe that you have been completely fair," Johnson said in "To Fulfill These Rights," his 1965 commencement speech at Howard University in Washington, D.C., one of the country's top historically black institutions. [9]

By the late 1970s, a long string of U.S. Supreme Court decisions began setting boundaries on affirmative action, partly in response to white job and school applicants who sued over "reverse discrimination." The court's bottom line: Schools and employers could take race into account, but not as a sole criterion. Setting quotas based on race, ethnicity or gender was prohibited. (The prohibition of gender discrimination effectively ended the chances for passage of the proposed Equal Rights Amendment [ERA], which feminist organizations had been promoting since 1923. The Civil Rights Act, along with other legislation and court decisions, made many supporters of women's rights "lukewarm" about the proposed amendment, Roberta W. Francis, then chair of the National Council of Women's Organizations' ERA task force, wrote in 2001). [10]

The high court's support for affirmative action has been weakening through the years. Since 1991 the court has included Justice Clarence Thomas, the lone black member and a bitter foe of affirmative action. In his 2007 autobiography, Thomas wrote that his Yale Law School degree set him up for rejection by major law firm interviewers. "Many asked pointed questions unsubtly suggesting that they doubted I was as smart as my grades indicated," he wrote. "Now I knew what a law degree

from Yale was worth when it bore the taint of racial preference." [11]

Some of Thomas' black classmates dispute his view of a Yale diploma's worth. "Had he not gone to a school like Yale, he would not be sitting on the Supreme Court," said William Coleman III, a Philadelphia attorney who was general counsel to the U.S. Army in the Clinton administration. [12]

But that argument does not seem to impress Thomas, who was in a 5-4 minority in the high court's most recent affirmative action ruling, in which the justices upheld the use of race in law-school admissions at the University of Michigan. But even Justice Sandra Day O'Connor, who wrote the majority opinion, signaled unease with her position. In 25 years, she wrote, affirmative action would "no longer be necessary." [13]

Paradoxically, an Obama victory on Nov. 4 might be the most effective anti-affirmative action event of all.

"The primary rationale for affirmative action is that America is institutionally racist and institutionally sexist," Connerly, an Obama foe, told The Associated Press. "That rationale is undercut in a major way when you look at the success of Sen. [Hillary Rodham] Clinton and Sen. Obama."

Asked to respond to Connerly's remarks, Obama appeared to draw some limits of his own on affirmative action. "Affirmative action is not going to be the long-term solution to the problems of race in America," he told a July convention of minority journalists, "because, frankly, if you've got 50 percent of African American or Latino kids dropping out of high school, it doesn't really matter what you do in terms of affirmative action; those kids are not getting into college." [14]

As critics and supporters discuss the future of affirmative action, here are some of the questions being debated:

Has affirmative action outlived its usefulness?

In the United States of the late 1960s and '70s, even some outright opponents of race-based affirmative action conceded that it represented an attempt to deal with the consequences of longstanding, systematic racial discrimination, which had legally ended only shortly before.

But ever since opposition to affirmative action began growing in the 1980s, its opponents themselves have invoked the very principles that the civil rights movement had embraced in its fight to end discrimination. Taking a job or school applicant's race or ethnicity into account is immoral, opponents argue, even for supposedly benign purposes. And a policy of racial/ethnic preferences, by definition, cannot lead to equality.

In today's United States, critics say, minority applicants don't face any danger that their skin color or ethnic heritage will hold them back. Instead, affirmative-action beneficiaries face continuing skepticism from others — and even from themselves, that they somehow were given an advantage that their academic work didn't entitle them to receive.

Meanwhile, opponents and supporters readily acknowledge that a disproportionate share of black and Latino students receive substandard educations, starting in and lasting through high school. Affirmative action hasn't eliminated the link between race/ethnicity and poverty and academic deprivation, they agree.

Critics of race preferences, however, say they haven't narrowed the divide that helped to trigger affirmative action in the first place. Affirmative action advocates favor significantly reforming K-12 education while simultaneously giving a leg up to minorities who managed to overcome their odds at inadequate public schools.

And some supporters say affirmative action is important for other reasons, which transcend America's racial history. Affirmative action helps to ensure continuation of a democratic political culture, says James E. Coleman Jr., a professor at Duke University Law School.

"It's not just about discrimination or past discrimination," says Coleman, who attended all-black schools when growing up and then graduated from Harvard College and Columbia Law School in the early 1970s, during the early days of affirmative action. "It's in our self-interest. We want leaders of all different backgrounds, all different races; we ought to educate them together."

But Connerly, the California businessman behind anti-affirmative action ballot initiatives, says that race and gender preferences are the wrong tool with which to promote diversity, because they effectively erode academic standards. "Excellence can be achieved by any group

Few Poor Students Attend Top Schools

Nearly three-quarters of students entering tier 1 colleges and universities come from the wealthiest families, but only 3 percent of students from the bottom quartile enter top schools. Far more students from poorer backgrounds enroll in less prestigious schools, and even more in community colleges.

Socioeconomic Status of Entering College Classes

School prestige level	First quartile (lowest)	Second quartile	Third quartile	Fourth quartile (highest)
Tier 1	3%	6%	17%	74%
Tier 2	7	18	29	46
Tier 3	10	19	36	35
Tier 4	16	21	28	35
Community Colleges	21	30	27	22

Source: Anthony P. Carnevale and Stephen J. Rose, "Socioeconomic Status, Race/Ethnicity, and Selective College Admissions," The Century Foundation, March 2003

of people," says Connerly, a former member of the University of California Board of Regents. "So we will keep the standards where they ought to be, and we will expect people to meet those standards."

But legislators interested in a "quick fix" have found it simpler to mandate diversity than to devise ways to improve schools. "There are times when someone has to say, 'This isn't right. We're going to do something about it,'" Connerly says. "But in the legislative process, I can find no evidence of leadership anywhere."

Like others, Connerly also cites the extraordinary academic achievements of Asian American students — who haven't benefited from affirmative action. Affirmative action supporters don't try to dispute that point. "At the University of California at Berkeley, 40 percent of the students are Asian," says Terry H. Anderson, a history professor at Texas A&M University in College Station. "What does that say about family structure? It makes a big statement. Family structure is so important, and it's something that affirmative action can't help at all."

But if encouraging minority-group enrollment at universities doesn't serve as a social and educational cure-all, says Anderson, who has written a history of affirmative

Few Poor Students Score High on SAT

Two-thirds of students who scored at least 1300 on the SAT came from families ranking in the highest quartile of socioeconomic status, compared with only 3 percent of students from the lowest-income group. Moreover, more than one-fifth of those scoring under 1000 — and 37 percent of non-test-takers — come from the poorest families.

SAT Scores by Family Socioeconomic Status*

Score	First Quartile (lowest)	Second Quartile	Third Quartile	Fourth Quartile (highest)
>1300	3%	10%	22%	66%
1200-1300	4	14	23	58
1100-1200	6	17	29	47
1000-1100	8	24	32	36
<1000	21	25	30	24
Non-taker	37	30	22	10

* The maximum score is 1600

Note: Percentages do not add to 100 due to rounding.

Source: Anthony P. Carnevale and Stephen J. Rose, "Socioeconomic Status, Race/Ethnicity, and Selective College Admissions," The Century Foundation, March 2003

how talented they are, but what sorts of opportunities they've had."

Does race-based affirmative action still face powerful public opposition?

At the state and federal level, affirmative action has generated enormous conflict over the decades, played out in a long chain of lawsuits and Supreme Court decisions, as well as the hard-fought ballot initiatives this year in Arizona, Missouri and Oklahoma — all three of which ended in defeat for race, ethnic and gender preferences.

But today's political agenda — dominated by the global financial crisis, the continuing downward slide of real estate prices, the continuing conflict in Iraq and escalated combat in Afghanistan — would seem to leave little space for a reignited affirmative action conflict.

Nevertheless, supporters and opponents of affirmative action fought hard in five states over proposed ballot initiatives, two of which will go before voters in November.

Nationally, the nonpartisan Pew Research Center reported last year that black and white Americans are divided by a considerable margin on whether minority group members should get preferential treatment. Among blacks, 57 answered yes, but only 27 percent of whites agreed. That gap was somewhat bigger in 1991, when 68 percent of blacks and only 17 percent of whites favored preferences. [15]

Obama's statement to ABC News' Stephanopoulos that his daughters shouldn't benefit from affirmative action reflected awareness of majority sentiment against race preference. [16]

Still, the exchange led to some predictions that it would resurface. "The issue of affirmative action is likely to dog Sen. Obama on the campaign trail as he seeks to win over white, blue-collar voters in battleground states like Michigan," *The Wall Street Journal* predicted in June. [17]

action, the policy still serves a valuable purpose. "It's become part of our culture. On this campus, it's been 'out' to be racist for years and years. I'm looking at kids born in 1990; they just don't feel self-conscious about race or gender, they just expect to be treated equally."

Standing between the supporters and the enemies of affirmative action's racial/ethnic preferences are the affirmative action reformers. "I don't think it's time to completely abolish all forms of affirmative action," says the Century Foundation's Kahlenberg. "But it's clear there are strong legal, moral and political problems with relying solely on race."

And at the practical level, race isn't the only gauge of hardship that some students must overcome, even to be capable of competing for admission to a top-tier school. "There are students from low-income backgrounds," Kahlenberg says, "who aren't given the same opportunities as wealthier students are given, and they deserve a leg up in admissions. Someone's test scores and grades are a reflection not only of how hard they work and

Just two and a half weeks before the election, that forecast hadn't come to pass. However, earlier in the year interest remained strong enough that campaigners for state ballot initiatives were able to gather 136,589 signatures in Nebraska and about 130,000 in Colorado to require that the issue be put before voters in those states.

Meanwhile, the initiative efforts in Arizona, Missouri and Oklahoma were doomed after the validity of petition signatures was challenged in those states. Connerly, the chief organizer of the initiatives, blames opponents' tactics and, in Oklahoma, an unusually short, 90-day window during which signatures must be collected. But once initiatives get on ballots, he says, voters approve them. "There is something about the principle of fairness that most people understand."

Without congressional legislation prohibiting preferences, Connerly says, the initiatives are designed to force state governments "to abide by the moral principle that racial discrimination — whether against a white or black or Latino or Native American — is just wrong."

But reality can present immoral circumstances as well, affirmative action defenders argue. "Racial discrimination and gender discrimination continue to present obstacles to people of color and women," says the American Civil Liberties Union's (ACLU) Kief. "Affirmative action is a way to chip away at some of these obstacles."

Kief says the fact that Connerly has played a central role in all of the initiatives indicates that true grassroots opposition to affirmative action is weak in states where initiatives have passed or are about to be voted on.

However, The Century Foundation's Kahlenberg points out that pro-affirmative action forces work hard to block ballot initiatives, because when such initiatives have gone before voters they have been approved. And the most recent successful ballot initiative, in Michigan in 2006, passed by a slightly bigger margin — 57 percent to 43 percent — than its California counterpart in 1996, which was approved by 54-46. [18]

Further evidence that anti-affirmative action initiatives are hard to fight surfaced this year in Colorado, where the group Coloradans for Equal Opportunity failed to round up enough signatures to put a pro-affirmative action initiative on the ballot.

Kahlenberg acknowledges that affirmative action politics can be tricky. Despite abiding public opposition to preferences, support among blacks is so strong that Republican presidential campaigns tend to downplay

Democratic presidential candidate Sen. Barack Obama, speaking in Philadelphia on Oct. 11, 2008, represents the new face of affirmative action in the demographically changing United States: His father was Kenyan and a half-sister is half-Indonesian.

affirmative action, for fear of triggering a huge turnout among black voters, who vote overwhelmingly Democratic. In 1999, then-Florida Gov. Jeb Bush kept a Connerly-sponsored initiative out of that state largely in order to lessen the chances of a major black Democratic mobilization in the 2000 presidential election, in which his brother would be running. [19]

"When you have an initiative on the ballot," Kahlenberg says, "some Republicans think that it increases minority turnout, so they're not sure whether these initiatives play to their party or not." Republican opposition to affirmative action goes back to the Reagan administration. Reagan, however, passed up a chance to ban affirmative action programs throughout the federal government, displaying a degree of GOP ambivalence. However, Connerly is an outspoken Republican. [20]

Nevertheless, an all-out Republican push against affirmative action during the past decade failed to catch on at the national level. In 1996, former Republican Senate Majority Leader Bob Dole of Kansas was running for president, and the affirmative action initiative was on the same ballot in California. "The initiative passed, but there was no trickle-down help for Bob Dole," says Daniel A. Smith, a political scientist at the University of Florida who has written on affirmative action politics.

This year, to be sure, anxieties growing out of the financial crisis and economic slowdown could rekindle passions over preferences. But Smith argues the economic environment makes finger-pointing at minorities less likely. "Whites are not losing jobs to African Americans," he says. "Whites and African Americans are losing jobs to the Asian subcontinent — they're going to Bangalore. The global economy makes it more difficult to have a convenient domestic scapegoat for lost jobs."

Has affirmative action diverted attention from the poor quality of K–12 education in low-income communities?

If there's one point on which everyone involved in the affirmative action debate agrees, it's that public schools attended by most low-income students are worsening.

"The educational achievement gap between racial groups began growing again in the 1990s," Gary Orfield, a professor of education and social policy at Harvard University, wrote. "Our public schools are becoming increasingly segregated by race and income, and the segregated schools are, on average, strikingly inferior in many important ways, including the quality and experience of teachers and the level of competition from other students. . . . It is clear that students of different races do not receive an equal chance for college." [21]

The decline in education quality has occurred at the same time various race-preference policies have governed admission to the nation's best colleges and universities. The policies were designed to provide an incentive for schools and students alike to do their best, by ensuring that a college education remains a possibility for all students who perform well academically.

But the results have not been encouraging. In California alone, only 36 percent of all high school students in 2001 had taken all the courses required for admission to the state university system, according to a study by the Civil Rights Project at Harvard University. Among black students, only 26 percent had taken the prerequisites, and only 24 percent of Hispanics. Meanwhile, 41 percent of white students and 54 percent of Asians had taken the necessary courses. [22]

In large part as a result of deficient K–12 education, decades of race-preference affirmative action at top-tier colleges and universities have yielded only small percentages of black and Hispanic students. In 1995, according to an exhaustive 2003 study by The Century Foundation, these students accounted for 6 percent of admissions to the 146 top-tier institutions. [23]

Socioeconomically, the picture is even less diverse. Seventy-four percent of students came from families in the wealthiest quarter of the socioeconomic scale; 3 percent came from families in the bottom quarter. [24]

For race-preference opponents, the picture demonstrates that efforts at ensuring racial and ethnic diversity in higher education would have been better aimed at improving K–12 schools across the country.

"If you've tried to use race for 40-some years, and you still have this profound gap," Connerly says, "yet cling to the notion that you have given some affirmative action to black and Latino and American Indian students — though Asians, without it, are outstripping everybody — maybe the way we've been doing it wasn't the right way to do it."

Meanwhile, he says, making a point that echoes through black, conservative circles, "Historically black colleges and universities (HBCUs) — if you look at doctors and pharmacists across our nation, you'll find them coming from schools that are 90 percent black. These schools are not very diverse, but they put a premium on quality."

But not all HBCUs are in that class, affirmative action supporters point out. "A lot of people who come out with a degree in computer science from minority-serving institutions know absolutely no mathematics," says Richard Tapia, a mathematics professor at Rice University and director of the university's Center for Equity and Excellence in Education. "I once went to a historically black university and had lunch with a top student who was going to do graduate work at Purdue, but when I talked to her I realized that her knowledge of math was on a par with that of a Rice freshman. The gap is huge."

Tapia, who advocates better mentoring for promising minority students at top-flight institutions, argues that the effect of relegating minority students to a certain defined group of colleges and universities, including historically black institutions, limits their chances of advancement in society at large. "From the elite schools you're going to get leadership."

Still, a question remains as to whether focusing on preferential admissions has helped perpetuate the very conditions that give rise to preferences in the first place.

"At the K–12 level you could argue that affirmative action has led to stagnation," says Richard Sander, a professor of law at UCLA Law School. "There's very little forward movement, very little closing of the black-white gap of the past 20 to 30 years."

Coleman of Duke University agrees that public education for most low-income students needs help. But that issue has nothing to do with admissions to top-drawer universities and professional schools, he says. "Look at minority students who get into places like that," he says. "For the most part, they haven't gone to the weakest high schools; they've often gone to the best."

Yet the affirmative action conflict focuses on black students, who are assumed to be academically under-qualified, Coleman says, while white students' place at the best schools isn't questioned. The classroom reality differs, he says. "We have a whole range of students with different abilities. All of the weak students are not minority students; all of the strong students are not white students."

BACKGROUND

Righting Wrongs

The civil rights revolution of the 1950s and '60s forced a new look at the policies that had locked one set of Americans out of most higher-education institutions and higher-paying jobs.

As early as 1962, the Congress of Racial Equality (CORE), one of the most active civil-rights organizations, advocated hiring practices that would make up for discrimination against black applicants. "We are approaching employers with the proposition that they have effectively excluded Negroes from their work force a long time, and they now have a responsibility and obligation to make up for their past sins," the organization said in a statement from its New York headquarters. [25]

Facing CORE-organized boycotts, a handful of companies in New York, Denver, Detroit, Seattle and Baltimore changed their hiring procedures to favor black applicants.

In July 1964, President Lyndon B. Johnson pushed Congress to pass the landmark Civil Rights Act, which had been championed by President John F. Kennedy since his 1960 presidential election campaign.

The law's Title VII, which prohibits racial, religious or sexual discrimination in hiring, said judges enforcing the law could order "such affirmative action as may be appropriate" to correct violations. [26]

Title VII didn't specify what kind of affirmative action could be decreed. But racial preferences were openly discussed in the political arena as a tool to equalize opportunities. Official working definitions of affirmative action didn't emerge until the end of the 1960s, under President Richard M. Nixon.

In 1969, the administration approved the "Philadelphia Plan," which set numerical goals for black and other minority employment on federally financed construction jobs. One year later, the plan was expanded to cover all businesses with 50 or more employees and federal contracts of at least $50,000. The contracts were to set hiring goals and timetables designed to match up a firm's minority representation with the workforce demographics in its area. The specified minorities were: "Negro, Oriental, American Indian and Spanish Surnamed Americans." [27]

The sudden change in the workplace environment prompted a wave of lawsuits. In the lead, a legal challenge by 13 black electric utility workers in North Carolina led to one of the most influential U.S. Supreme Court decisions on affirmative action, the 1971 *Griggs v. Duke Power Co.* case. [28]

In a unanimous decision, the high court concluded that an aptitude test that was a condition of promotion for the workers violated the Civil Rights Act. Duke Power may not have intended the test to weed out black applicants, Chief Justice Warren E. Burger wrote in the decision. But, he added, "Congress directed the thrust of the Act to the consequences of employment practices, not simply the motivation." [29]

If the point of the Civil Rights Act was to ensure that the consequences of institutions' decisions yielded balanced workforces, then goals and timetables to lead to that outcome were consistent with the law as well. In other words, eliminating racial discrimination could mean paying attention to race in hiring and promotions.

That effort would produce a term that captured the frustration and anger among white males who were competing with minority-group members for jobs, promotions or school admissions: "reverse discrimination."

The issue went national with a challenge by Allan Bakke, a white, medical school applicant, to the University of California. He'd been rejected two years in a row while minority-group members — for whom 16 slots in the 100-member class had been set aside — were admitted with lower qualifying scores.

After the case reached the Supreme Court, the justices in a 5-4 decision in 1978 ordered Bakke admitted and prohibited the use of racial quotas. But they allowed race to be considered along with other criteria. Representing the University of California was former Solicitor General Archibald Cox, the Watergate special prosecutor who was fired on orders of President Nixon in 1973. Cox's grand-

1960s *Enactment of civil rights law opens national debate on discrimination.*

1964 Civil Rights Act of 1964 bars discrimination in employment and at federally funded colleges.

1965 President Lyndon B. Johnson calls for a massive national effort to create social and economic equality.

1969 Nixon administration approves "Philadelphia Plan" setting numerical goals for minority employment on all federally financed building projects.

1970s-1980s *Affirmative action expands throughout the country, prompting legal challenges and growing voter discontent, leading to new federal policy.*

1971 The U.S. Supreme Court's landmark *Griggs v. Duke Power Co.* decision, growing out of a challenge by 13 black electric utility workers in North Carolina, is seen as authorizing companies and institutions to set out goals and timetables for minority hiring.

1978 Supreme Court's decision in *University of California Regents v. Bakke*, arising from a medical-school admission case, rules out racial quotas but allows race to be considered with other factors.

1980 Ronald W. Reagan is elected president with strong support from white males who see affirmative action as a threat.

1981-1983 Reagan administration reduces affirmative action enforcement.

1985 Attorney General Edwin Meese III drafts executive order outlawing affirmative action in federal government; Reagan never signs it.

1987 Supreme Court upholds job promotion of a woman whose advancement was challenged by a male colleague claiming higher qualifications.

1990s *Ballot initiatives banning race and gender preferences prompt President Bill Clinton to acknowledge faults in affirmative action.*

1994 White voter discontent energizes the "Republican revolution" that topples Democrats from control of Congress.

1995 Supreme Court rules in *Adarand Constructors v. Peña* that affirmative action programs must be "narrowly tailored" for cases of extreme discrimination. . . . Clinton concedes that affirmative action foes have some valid points but concludes, "Mend it, but don't end it." . . . Senate votes down anti-affirmative action bill.

1996 California voters pass nation's first ballot initiative outlawing racial, ethnic and gender preferences. . . . 5th U.S. Circuit Court of Appeals rules that universities can't take race into account in evaluating applicants.

1998 Washington state voters pass ballot initiative identical to California's.

2000s *Affirmative action in university admissions stays on national agenda, leading to major Supreme Court ruling; Sen. Barack Obama's presidential candidacy focuses more attention on the issue.*

2003 Supreme Court's *Gratz v. Bollinger* ruling rejects University of Michigan undergraduate admission system for awarding extra points to minority applicants, but simultaneous *Grutter v. Bollinger* decision upholds UM law school admissions policy, which includes race as one factor among many. . . . Justice Sandra Day O'Connor writes in 5-4 majority opinion in Grutter that affirmative action won't be necessary in 25 years. . . . Century Foundation study finds strong linkage between socioeconomic status, race and chances of going to college.

2006 Michigan passes nation's third ballot initiative outlawing racial, ethnic and gender preferences.

2008 Opponents of affirmative action in Arizona, Missouri and Oklahoma fail to place anti-affirmative action initiatives on ballot, but similar campaigns succeed in Colorado and Nebraska. . . . U.S. Civil Rights Commission opens study of minority students majoring in science and math. . . . Saying his daughters are affluent and shouldn't benefit from race preferences, Obama endorses affirmative action for struggling, white college applicants.

daughter, Melissa Hart, helps lead the opposition to an anti-affirmative action ballot initiative in Colorado (*see p. 63*). [30]

In 1979 and 1980, the court upheld worker training and public contracting policies that included so-called set-asides for minority-group employees or minority-owned companies. But in the latter case, the deciding opinion specified that only companies that actually had suffered discrimination would be eligible for those contracts. [31]

Divisions within the Supreme Court reflected growing tensions in the country as a whole. A number of white people saw affirmative action as injuring the educational and career advancement of people who hadn't themselves caused the historical crimes that gave rise to affirmative action.

Reversing Course

President Ronald W. Reagan took office in 1981 with strong support from so-called "Reagan Democrats" — white, blue-collar workers who had turned against their former party on issues including affirmative action. [32]

Initially, Reagan seemed poised to fulfill the hopes of those who wanted him to ban all preferences based on race, ethnicity and gender. The latter category followed an upsurge of women fighting to abolish limits on their education and career possibilities.

Yet Reagan's appointees were divided on the issue, and the president himself never formalized his rejection of quotas and related measures. Because no law required the setting of goals and timetables, Reagan could have banned them by executive order. During Reagan's second term, Attorney General Edwin Meese III drafted such an order. But Reagan never signed it.

Nevertheless, the Reagan administration did systematically weaken enforcement of affirmative action. In Reagan's first term he cut the budgets of the Equal Employment Opportunity Commission and the Office of Federal Contract Compliance — the two front-line agencies on the issue — by 12 and 34 percent, respectively, between 1981 and 1983. As a result, the compliance office blocked only two contractors during Reagan's two terms, compared with 13 that were barred during President Jimmy Carter's term.

The Justice Department also began opposing some affirmative action plans. In 1983, Justice won a partial court reversal of an affirmative action plan for the New Orleans Police Department. In a police force nearly devoid of black supervisors, the plan was designed to expand the number — a move considered vital in a city whose population was nearly one-half black.

Affirmative action cases kept moving through the Supreme Court. In 1984-1986, the court overturned plans that would have required companies doing layoffs to disregard the customary "first hired, last fired" rule, because that custom endangered most black employees, given their typically short times on the job.

And in 1987, a 5-4 Supreme Court decision upheld an Alabama state police plan requiring that 50 percent of promotions go to black officers. The same year, the court upheld 6-3 the promotion of a woman employee of Santa Clara County, Calif., who got promoted over a male candidate who had scored slightly higher on an assessment. The decision marked the first court endorsement of affirmative action for women.

In the executive branch, divided views persisted in the administration of Reagan's Republican successor, George H. W. Bush. In 1990 Bush vetoed a pro-affirmative action bill designed to reverse recent Supreme Court rulings, one of which effectively eased the way for white men to sue for reverse discrimination.

The legislation would have required "quotas," Bush said, explaining his veto. But the following year, he signed a compromise, the Civil Rights Act of 1991. [33] Supported by the civil rights lobby, the bill wrote into law the *Griggs v. Duke Power* requirement that an employer prove that a job practice — a test, say — is required for the work in question. A practice that failed that test could be shown to result in discrimination, even if that hadn't been the intention.

Bush also reversed a directive by his White House counsel that would have outlawed all quotas, set-asides and related measures. The administration's ambivalence reflected divided views in American society. Local government and corporate officials had grown appreciative of affirmative action for calming racial tensions. In 1985, the white Republican mayor of Indianapolis refused a Justice Department request to end affirmative action in the police department. Mayor William Hudnut said that the "white majority has accepted the fact that we're making a special effort for minorities and women." [34]

Yet among white males, affirmative action remained a very hot-button issue. "When we hold focus groups," a Democratic pollster said in 1990, "if the issue of affirmative action comes up, you can forget the rest of the session. That's all . . . that's talked about." [35]

'Percent Plans' Offer Alternative to Race-Based Preferences

But critics say approach fails to level playing field.

In recent years, voters and judges have blocked race and ethnicity preferences in university admissions in three big states with booming minority populations — California, Florida and Texas. Nonetheless, lawmakers devised a way to ensure that public universities remain open to black and Latino students.

The so-called "percent plans" promise guaranteed admission based on a student's high school class standing, not on skin tone. That, at least is the principle.

But the man who helped end racial affirmative action preferences in two of the states involved argues affirmative action is alive and well, simply under another name. Moreover, says Ward Connerly, a black businessman in Sacramento, Calif., who has been a leader in organizing anti-affirmative action referendums, the real issue — the decline in urban K-12 schools — is being ignored.

"Legislatures and college administrators lack the spine to say, 'Let's find the problem at its core,' " says Connerly, a former member of the University of California Board of Regents. "Instead, they go for a quick fix they believe will yield the same number of blacks and Latinos as before."

Even Connerly's opponents agree "percent plans" alone don't put high schools in inner cities and prosperous suburbs on an equal footing. "In some school districts in Texas, 50 percent of the graduates could make it here easily," says Terry H. Anderson, a history professor at Texas A&M University in College Station. "Some school districts are so awful that not one kid could graduate here, I don't care what race you're talking about."

All the plans — except at selective schools — ignore SAT or ACT scores (though students do have to present their scores). The policy troubles Richard D. Kahlenberg, a senior fellow at The Century Foundation, who champions "class-based" affirmation action. "The grade of A in one high school is very different from the grade of A in another," he says.

Texas lawmakers originated the percent plan concept after a 5th U.S. Circuit Court of Appeals decision in 1996 (*Hopwood v. Texas*) prohibited consideration of race in college admissions. Legislators proposed guaranteeing state university admissions to the top 10 percent of graduates of the state's public and private high schools. Then-Gov. George W. Bush signed the bill, which includes automatic admission to the flagship campuses, the University of Texas at Austin and Texas A&M. [1]

In California, the impetus was the 1996 voter approval of Proposition 209, which prohibited racial and ethnic preferences by all state entities. Borrowing the Texas idea, California lawmakers devised a system in which California high school students in the top 4 percent of their classes are eligible for the California system, but not necessarily to attend the two star institutions, UC Berkeley and UCLA. (Students in the top 4 percent-12.5 percent range are admitted to community colleges and can transfer to four-year institutions if they maintain 2.4 grade-point averages.) [2]

Connerly was active in the Proposition 209 campaign and was the key player — but involuntarily — in Florida's adoption of a percent plan. In 1999, Connerly was preparing to mount an anti-affirmative action initiative in Florida. Then-Gov. Jeb Bush worried it could hurt his party's standing with black voters — with possible repercussions on his brother George's presidential campaign. Instead Gov. Bush launched "One Florida," a percent plan approved by the legislature.

In Florida, the top 20 percent of high school graduates are guaranteed admission to the state system. To attend the flagship University of Florida at Gainesville they must meet tougher standards. All three states also require students to

Mending It

From the early 1990s to 2003 race-based affirmative action suffered damage in the political arena and the courts.

In 1994, white male outrage at preferences for minority groups and women was a key factor in congressional elections that toppled Democrats from control of both houses. As soon as the Congress changed hands, its new leaders targeted affirmative action. "Sometimes the best-qualified person does not get the job because he or she may be one color," Majority Leader Dole said in a television interview. "That may not be the way it should be in America." [36]

have completed a set of required courses.

Percent plan states also have helped shape admissions policies by experimenting with ways to simultaneously keep academic standards high, while ensuring at least the possibility that promising students of all socioeconomic circumstances have a shot at college.

In Florida, the consequences of maintaining high admissions standards at UF were softened by another program, "Bright Futures," which offers tuition reductions of 75 percent — or completely free tuition — depending on completion of AP courses and on SAT or ACT scores.

The effect, says University of Florida political scientist Daniel A. Smith, is to ensure a plentiful supply of top students of all races and ethnicities. "We have really talented minorities — blacks, Latinos, Asian-Americans — because 'One Florida' in combination with 'Bright Futures' has kept a lot of our talented students in the state. We have students who turned down [partial] scholarships to Duke and Harvard because here they're going for free."

At UCLA, which also has maintained rigorous admission criteria, recruiters spread out to high schools in low-income areas in an effort to ensure that the school doesn't become an oasis of privilege. The realities of race and class mean that some of that recruiting work takes place in mostly black or Latino high schools.

"It's the fallacy of [Proposition] 209 that you can imme-

Getty Images/Neilson Barnard

"The time has come to pull the plug on race-based decision-making," says Ward Connerly, a Sacramento, Calif., businessman who spearheaded anti-affirmative action ballot initiatives in Colorado, Nebraska and other states.

diately move to a system that doesn't take account of race and that treats everybody fairly," said Tom Lifka, a UCLA assistant vice chancellor in charge of admissions. He said the new system meets legal standards. [3]

Consciously or not, Lifka was echoing the conclusion of the most thorough analysis of the plans' operations in the three states. The 2003 study, sponsored by Harvard University's Civil Rights Project, concluded that the states had largely succeeded in maintaining racial and ethnic diversity on their campuses.

But the report added that aggressive recruitment, academic aid to high schools in low-income areas and similar measures played a major role.

"Without such support," wrote Catherine L. Horn, an education professor at the University of Houston, and Stella M. Flores, professor of public policy and higher education at Vanderbilt, "the plans are more like empty shells, appearing to promise eligibility, admission and enrollment for previously excluded groups but actually doing very little." [4]

[1] Catherine L. Horn and Stella M. Flores, "Percent Plans in College Admissions: A Comparative Analysis of Three States' Experiences," Civil Rights Project, Harvard University, 2003, pp. 20-23, www.civilrightsproject.ucla.edu/research/affirmativeaction/tristate.pdf.

[2] *Ibid.*

[3] Quoted in David Leonhardt, "The New Affirmative Action," *The New York Times Magazine*, Sept. 30, 2007, p. 76.

[4] Horn and Flores, *op. cit.*, pp. 59-60.

The following year, the U.S. Supreme Court imposed limits on the use of preferences, ruling on a white, male contractor's challenge to a federal program that encouraged general contractors to favor minority subcontractors. Justice O'Connor wrote in the 5-4 majority opinion in *Adarand Constructors v. Peña* that any racial or ethnic pref-

erences had to be "narrowly tailored" to apply only to "pervasive, systematic and obstinate discriminatory conduct." [37]

Some justices had wanted all preferences overturned. Though that position failed to win a majority, the clear unease that O'Connor expressed added to the pressure on politicians who supported affirmative action.

Supporters of affirmative action in Lansing, Mich., rally against a proposed statewide anti-affirmative action ballot initiative in September 2006; voters approved the proposal that November. The initiative followed a 2003 U.S. Supreme Court ruling upholding the use of race in law-school admissions at the University of Michigan. Justice Sandra Day O'Connor, who wrote the majority 5-4 opinion, predicted, however, that in 25 years affirmative action would "no longer be necessary."

In that climate, President Bill Clinton gave a 1995 speech at the National Archives in Washington in which he acknowledged that critics had a point. He said he didn't favor "the unjustified preference of the unqualified over the qualified of any race or gender." But affirmative action was still needed because discrimination persisted, Clinton added. His bottom line: "Mend it, but don't end it." [38]

The slogan seemed to match national politicians' mood. One day after Clinton's speech, the Senate voted down a bill to abolish all preferences, with 19 Republicans siding with Democrats in a 61-36 vote.

But in California, one of the country's major affirmative action laboratories, the "end it" argument proved more popular. Racial/ethnic preferences had become a major issue in a state whose minority population was booming. California's higher-education system also included two of the nation's top public institutions: the University of California at Berkeley (UCB) and UCLA.

Among many white, Anglo Californians, affirmative action had come to be seen as a system under which black and Latino applicants were getting into those two schools at the expense of whites or Asians with higher grades and SAT scores.

By 1996, the statewide university system's majority-Republican Board of Regents voted to end all race, ethnic and gender preferences in admissions. The board did allow universities to take applicants' socioeconomic circumstances into account.

And in the same year, California voters approved Proposition 209, which outlawed all race, ethnicity and gender preferences by all state entities. Connerly helped organize that referendum and followed up with successful campaigns in Washington state in 1998 and in Michigan in 2003.

Meanwhile, the "reverse discrimination" issue that had been decided in the *Bakke* case flared up in Texas, where Cheryl Hopwood and two other white applicants to the University of Texas law school challenged their rejections, pointing to the admissions of minority students with lower grades and test scores. In 1996, the 5th U.S. Circuit Court of Appeals decided for the plaintiffs, ruling that universities couldn't take race into account when assessing applicants.

The appeals judges had overruled the *Bakke* decision, at least in their jurisdiction of Texas, Mississippi and Louisiana, yet the Supreme Court refused to consider the case.

But in 2003, the justices ruled on two separate cases, both centering on admissions to another top-ranked public higher education system: the University of Michigan. One case arose from admissions procedures for the undergraduate college, the other from the system for evaluating applicants to the university's law school. [39]

The Supreme Court decided against the undergraduate admissions policy because it automatically awarded 20 extra points on the university's 150-point evaluation scale to blacks, Latinos and American Indians. By contrast, the law school took race into account in what Justice O'Connor, in the majority opinion in the 5-4 decision, called a "highly individualized, holistic review" of each candidate aimed at producing a diverse student population. [40]

CURRENT SITUATION

'Formal Equality'

In the midst of war and the Wall Street meltdown, affirmative action may not generate as many headlines as it used to. But the issue still packs enough punch to have put anti-affirmative action legislation up for popular vote in Colorado and Nebraska this year.

"This is a progressive approach," said Jessica Peck Corry, executive director of the Colorado Civil Rights Initiative, which is campaigning for proposed Constitutional Amendment 46. The amendement would prohibit all state government entities from discriminating for or against anyone because of race, ethnicity or gender. "America is too diverse to put into stagnant race boxes," she says.

Melissa Hart, a co-chair of "No On 46," counters that the amendment would require "formal equality" that shouldn't be confused with the real thing. She likens the proposal to "a law that says both the beggar and the king may sleep under a bridge." In the real world, she says, only one of them will spend his nights in a bedroom.

Unlike California, Michigan and Washington — the states where voters have approved initiatives of this type over the past 12 years — the Colorado campaign doesn't follow a major controversy over competition for university admissions.

To be sure, Corry — a libertarian Republican law student, blogger and past failed candidate for state Senate — has publicly opposed affirmative action for several years. [41] But Corry, who is also a policy analyst at the Denver-based Independence Institute, a libertarian think tank, acknowledges that the referendum campaign in Colorado owes its start to Connerly. He began taking the ballot initiative route in the 1990s, after concluding that neither state legislatures nor Congress would ever touch the subject.

"They just seem to lack the stomach to do what I and the majority of Americans believe should be done," Connerly says. "Clearly, there's a disconnect between elected officials and the people themselves."

Connerly's confidence grows out of his success with the three previous initiatives. But this year, his attempts to get his proposal before voters in Arizona, Missouri and Oklahoma all failed because his campaign workers didn't gather enough valid signatures to get the initiatives on the ballot.

Connerly blames what he calls an overly restrictive initiative process in Oklahoma, as well as organized opposition by what he calls "blockers," who shadowed signature-gatherers and disputed their explanations of the amendments.

Opponents had a different name for themselves. "Our voter educators were simply that — voter educa-tors," said Brandon Davis, political director of the Service Employees International Union in Missouri. "Ward Connerly should accept what Missourians said, and he should stop with the sore-loser talk." [42]

The opposition began deploying street activists to counter what they call the deliberately misleading wording of the proposed initiatives. In Colorado, Proposition 46 is officially described as a "prohibition against discrimination by the state" and goes on to ban "preferential treatment to any individual or group on the basis of race, sex, color, ethnicity or national origin." [43]

"We want an acknowledgement that disadvantage cannot be specifically determined based on looking at some race data or gender data," Corry says. But tutoring, counseling and other activities should be extended to all who need help because of their socioeconomic circumstances, she contends.

Likewise, a project to interest girls in science and math, for instance, would have to admit boys. "In a time when America is losing its scientific advantage by the second, why are you excluding potential Nobel prize winners because they're born with the wrong biology?" she asks rhetorically.

Hart says that many tutoring and similar programs tailored to low-income students in Colorado already welcome all comers, regardless of race or ethnicity. But she questions why a math and science program tailored for girls should have to change its orientation. Likewise, Denver's specialized public schools for American Indian students would have to change their orientation entirely. "Class-based equal opportunity programs are not substitutes for outreach, training and mentoring on the basis of race and gender," she says.

The issue of class comes up in personal terms as well. Corry portrays herself as the product of a troubled home who had to work her way through college and graduate school. Though her father was a lawyer, her mother abandoned the family and wound up living on the streets. And Corry depicts Hart as a member of the privileged class, a granddaughter of former Solicitor General Cox and a graduate of Harvard University and Harvard Law School. "People like Melissa, I believe, are well-intentioned but misguided," Corry says. "The worst thing you can do to someone without connections is to suggest that they can't make it without preferences."

Hart, rapping Corry for bringing up personal history rather than debating ideas, adds that her father and his part of the family are potato farmers from Idaho.

The Preference Program Nobody Talks About

How "legacies" get breaks at top colleges.

Many critics say race-based affirmative action gives minority college applicants an unfair advantage. But reporter Peter Schmidt found an even more favored population — rich, white kids who apply to top-tier schools.

"These institutions feel very dependent on these preferences," Schmidt writes in his 2007 book, *Color and Money: How Rich White Kids Are Winning the War Over College Affirmative Action.* "They throw up their hands and say, 'There's no other way we can raise the money we need.' "

Colleges admit these students — "legacies," in college-admission lingo — because their parents are donation-making graduates. Offspring of professors, administrators or (in the case of top state universities) politically influential figures get open-door treatment as well.

"Several public college lobbyists, working in both state capitals and with the federal government in and around Washington, have told me that they spend a significant portion of their time lobbying their own colleges' admissions offices to accept certain applicants at the behest of public officials," Schmidt writes. [1]

Especially in regard to legacies and the families' donations, Schmidt says, "There is a utilitarian argument that the money enables colleges to serve students in need. But there isn't a correlation between how much money they're bringing in and helping low-income students."

As deputy editor of the *Chronicle of Higher Education*, Schmidt has been covering affirmative action conflicts since his days as an Associated Press reporter writing about protests over racial tensions at the University of Michigan in the mid-1990s.

His book doesn't deal exclusively with applicants from privileged families — who, by the nature of American society, are almost all white and academically well-prepared. But Schmidt's examination of privileged applicants frames his reporting on the more familiar issues of preferences based on race, ethnicity and gender.

According to Schmidt, Harvard as of 2004 accepted about 40 percent of the legacies who applied, compared to about 11 percent of applicants overall. In the Ivy League in general, children of graduates made up 10-15 percent of the undergraduates.

Though the issue is sensitive for college administrators, Schmidt found some members of the higher-education establishment happy to see it aired.

"Admissions officers are the ones who are finding the promising kids — diamonds in the rough — and getting emotionally invested in getting them admitted, then sitting down with the development officer or the coach and finding that these kids are knocked out of the running," he says.

Some education experts dispute that conclusion. Abigail Thernstrom, a senior fellow at the conservative Manhattan Institute and vice-chair of the U.S. Commission on Civil Rights, opposes "class-based" affirmative action (as well as racial/ethnic preferences), calling it unnecessary. She says that when top-tier schools look at an applicant from a disadvantaged background "who is getting a poor education — a diamond in the rough but showing real academic progress — and compare that student to someone from Exeter born with a silver spoon in his mouth, there's no question that these schools are going to take that diamond in the rough, if they think he or she will be able to keep up."

But some of Schmidt's findings echo what affirmative action supporters have observed. James E. Coleman Jr., a law professor at Duke University, argues against the tendency to focus all affirmative action attention on blacks and Latinos. "The idea is that any white student who gets here deserves to be here. They're not questioned. This has always been true."

At the same time, Coleman, who is black, agrees with Schmidt that those who start out near the top of the socioeconomic ladder have access to first-class educations before they even get to college. Coleman himself, who graduated from Harvard and from Columbia Law School, says he never had a single white classmate in his Charlotte, N.C., schools until he got accepted to a post-high school preparatory program at Exeter, one of the nation's most prestigious prep schools. "I could tell that my educational background and preparation were woefully inadequate compared to students who had been there since ninth grade," he recalls. "I had to run faster."

Schmidt says the politics of affirmative action can give rise to tactical agreements between groups whose interests might seem to conflict. In one dispute, he says, "Civil rights groups and higher-education groups had a kind of uneasy alliance: The civil rights groups would not challenge the admissions process and go after legacies as long as affirmative action remained intact."

But, he adds, "There are people not at the table when a deal like that is struck. If you're not a beneficiary of one or the other side of preferences, you don't gain from that agreement."

---

[1] Peter Schmidt, *Color and Money: How Rich White Kids Are Winning the War Over College Affirmative Action* (2007), p. 32.

Would many black and Latino science and math majors be better off at lesser-ranked universities?

YES
Rogers Elliott
Professor emeritus, Department of Psychology and Brain Sciences, Dartmouth College

From testimony before U.S. Civil Rights Commission, Sept. 12, 2008

Race preferences in admissions in the service of affirmative action are harming the aspirations, particularly, of blacks seeking to be scientists.

The most elite universities have very high levels in their admission standards, levels which minorities — especially blacks — don't come close to meeting.

[Thus], affirmative action in elite schools, which they pursue vigorously and successfully, leaves a huge gap, probably bigger than it would be for affirmative action at an average school. That is what constitutes the problem.

At elite schools, 90 percent of science majors [got] 650 or above on the SAT math score. About 80 percent of the white/Asian group are 650 or above, but only 25 percent of the black group have that score or better. The gaps that are illustrated in these data have not gotten any better. They have, in fact, gotten a little bit worse: The gap in the SAT scores between blacks and whites, which got to its smallest extent in about 1991 — 194 points — is back to 209.

The higher the standard at the institution, the more science they tend to do. But the [lower-ranking schools] still do science, and your chances of becoming a scientist are better. Now, obviously, there are differences. The higher institutions have eliteness going for them. They have prestige going for them, and maybe getting a degree from Dartmouth when you want to be a doctor will leave you better off in this world even though you're not doing the thing you started with as your aspiration.

Seventeen of the top 20 PhD-granting institutions for blacks in this country, are HBCUs [historically black colleges and universities].

Elite institutions are very performance-oriented. They deliberately take people at a very high level to begin with — with a few exceptions — and then they make them perform, and they do a pretty good job of it. If you're not ready for the first science course, you might as well forget it. Some of these minority students had mostly A's . . . enough to get to Dartmouth or Brown or Cornell or Yale. They take their first course, let's say, in chemistry; at least 90 percent of the students in that course are bright, motivated, often pre-med, highly competitive whites and Asians. And these [minority] kids aren't as well-prepared. They may get their first C- or D in a course like that because the grading standards are rigorous, and you have to start getting it from day one.

NO
Prof. Richard A. Tapia
Director, Center on Excellence and Equity, Rice University

From testimony before U.S. Civil Rights Commission, Sept. 12, 2008

The nation selects leaders from graduates and faculty of U.S. universities with world-class science, technology, engineering and math (STEM) research programs. If we, the underrepresented minorities, are to be an effective component in STEM leadership, then we must have an equitable presence as students and faculty at the very top-level research universities.

Pedigree, unfortunately, is an incredible issue. Top research universities choose faculty from PhDs produced at top research universities. PhDs produced at minority-serving schools or less-prestigious schools will not become faculty at top research universities. Indeed, it's unlikely they'll become faculty at minority-serving institutions. A student from a research school with a lesser transcript is stronger than a student from a minority-serving institution with all A's.

So are the students who come from these minority-serving institutions incompetent? No. There's a level of them that are incredibly good and will succeed wherever they go. And usually Stanford and Berkeley and Cornell will get those. Then there's a level below that you can work with. I produced many PhDs who came from minority-serving institutions. Is there a gap in training? Absolutely.

We do not know how to measure what we really value: Creativity. Underrepresented minorities can be quite creative. For example, the Carl Hayden High School Robotic Team — five Mexican American students from West Phoenix — beat MIT in the final in underwater robotics. They were not star students, but they were incredibly creative.

Treating everyone the same is not good enough. Sink or swim has not worked and will not work. It pays heed to privilege, not to talent. Isolation, not academics, is often the problem. We must promote success and retention with support programs. We must combat isolation through community-building and mentoring.

Ten percent of the students in public education in Texas are accepted into the University of Texas, automatically — the top 10 percent. They could have said look, these students are not prepared well. They're dumped at our doorstep, let's leave them. They didn't. The Math Department at the University of Texas at Austin built support programs where minorities are retained and succeed. It took a realization that here they are, let's do something with them.

Race and ethnicity should not dictate educational destiny. Our current path will lead to a permanent underclass that follows racial and ethnic lines.

AP Photo/Nati Harnik

TV cameramen in Lincoln, Neb., shoot boxes of signed voter petitions that qualified a proposed initiative to be put on the ballot in Nebraska this coming November calling for a ban on most types of affirmative action.

"I am proudly the granddaughter of Archibald Cox, proud of the fact that he argued the *Bakke* case for the University of California, and proud to be continuing a tradition of standing up for opportunity in this country," she says.

The Nebraska campaign, taking place in a smaller state with little history of racial or ethnic tension and a university where competition for admission isn't an issue, has generated somewhat less heat. But as in Colorado, college-preparation and other programs of various kinds that target young women and American Indians would be threatened by the amendment, says Laurel Marsh, executive director of the Nebraska ACLU.

Over Their Heads?

The U.S. Civil Rights Commission is examining one of the most explosive issues in the affirmative action debate: whether students admitted to top universities due to racial preferences are up to the academic demands they face at those institutions.

Math and the hard sciences present the most obvious case, affirmative action critics — and some supporters — say. Those fields are at the center of the commission's inquiry because students from high schools in low-income areas — typically minority students — tend to do poorly in science and math, in part because they require considerable math preparation in elementary and high school.

Sander of UCLA, who has been studying the topic, testified to the commission that for students of all races who had scored under 660 on the math SAT, only 5 percent of blacks and 3.5 percent of whites obtained science degrees. But of students who scored 820 or above on the SAT, 44 percent of blacks graduated with science or engineering degrees. Among whites, 35 percent graduated with those degrees — illustrating Sander's point that that issue is one of academic preparation, not race.

Abigail Thernstrom, the commission's vice-chair, says that most graduates of run-of-the-mill urban schools labor under a major handicap in pursuing math or science degrees. "By the time they get to college they're in bad shape in a discipline like math, where all knowledge is cumulative," she says. "The colleges are inheriting a problem that, in effect, we sweep under the rug."

Thernstrom, a longtime affirmative action critic, bases her views both on her 11 years of service on the Massachusetts state Board of Education and on data assembled by academics, including Sander. "Test scores do predict a lot, high school grades predict a lot," Sander says in an interview, disputing critics of his work who say students from deficient high schools can make up in college what they missed earlier.

Testifying to the commission on Sept. 12, Sander presented data showing that black and Hispanic high school graduates tend to be more interested than their white counterparts in pursuing science and math careers, but less successful in holding on to majors in those fields in college. Lower high school grades and test scores seem to account for as much as 75 percent of the tendency to drop out of those fields, he says.

Sander added that a student's possibilities can't be predicted from skin color and that the key factor associated with inadequate academic preparation is socioeconomic status. "We ought to view that as good news, because that means there's no intrinsic or genetic gap," he testified.

Rogers Elliott, an emeritus psychology and brain sciences professor at Dartmouth College, told the commission that the best option for many black and Hispanic students who want to pursue science or math careers is to attend lower-rated universities. Among institutions that grant the most PhDs to blacks, 17 of the top 20 are HBCUs, Elliott said, "and none of them is a prestige university."

Richard Tapia, a Rice University mathematician, countered that consigning minority-group students who aren't stars to lower-ranking universities would be disastrous. Only top-tier universities, he argued, provide their graduates with the credibility that allows them to assert leadership. "Research universities must be responsible for providing programs that promote success," he said, "rather than be let off the hook by saying that minority students should go to minority-serving institutions or less prestigious schools."

Tapia directs such a program — one of a handful around the country — that he says has helped Rice students overcome their inadequate earlier schooling. But he accepts Sander's and Elliott's data and says students with combined SAT scores below 800 would not be capable of pursuing math or science majors at Rice.

Tapia, the son of Mexican immigrants who didn't attend college, worked at a muffler factory after graduating from a low-achieving Los Angeles high school. Pushed by a co-worker to continue his education, he enrolled in community college and went on to UCLA, where he earned a doctorate. He attributes his success to a big dose of self-confidence — something that many people from his background might not have but that mentors can nurture.

A commission member sounded another practical note. Ashley L. Taylor Jr., a Republican lawyer from Richmond, Va., who is black, argued that colleges have a moral obligation to tell applicants if their SAT scores fall within the range of students who have a shot of completing their studies. "If I'm outside that range, no additional support is going to help me," he said.

Sander agrees. "African American students and any other minority ought to know going into college the ultimate outcomes for students at that college who have their profile."

Tapia agreed as well. "I had a student that I was recruiting in San Antonio who had a 940 SAT and was going to Princeton. I said, 'Do you know what the average at Princeton is?' He said, "Well, my teachers told me it was about 950.' I said, 'Well, I think you'd better check it out.' "

In fact, the average combined math and verbal SAT score of students admitted to Princeton is 1442. [44]

OUTLOOK

End of the Line?

Social programs don't come with an immortality guarantee. Some supporters as well as critics of affirmative action sense that affirmative action, as the term is generally understood, may be nearing the end of the line.

"I expect affirmative action to die," says Tapia. "People are tired of it. And if we had to depend on affirmative action forever, then there was something wrong. If you need a jump-start on your battery, and you get it jumped, fine. If you start needing it everywhere you go, you'd better get another battery."

Tapia's tone is not triumphant. He says the decline in public school quality is evidence that "it didn't work, and we didn't do a good job." But he adds that the disparities between the schooling for low-income and well-off students is what makes affirmative action necessary. "Sure, in an ideal world, you wouldn't have to do these things, but that's not the world we live in."

UCLA's Sander, who favors reorienting affirmative action — in part by determining an academic threshold below which students admitted by preference likely will fail — sees major change on the horizon. For one thing, he says, quantities of data are now accessible concerning admission standards, grades and other quantifiable effects of affirmative action programs.

In addition, he says, today's reconfigured Supreme Court likely would rule differently than it did on the 2003 University of Michigan cases that represent its most recent affirmative action rulings.

Justice O'Connor, who wrote the majority decision in the 5-4 ruling that upheld the use of race in law-school admissions, has retired, replaced by conservative Justice Samuel A. Alito. "The Supreme Court as it stands now has a majority that's probably ready to overrule" that decision, Sander says. A decision that turned on the newly available data "could lead to a major Supreme Court decision that could send shockwaves through the system."

For now, says Kahlenberg of The Century Foundation, affirmative action has already changed form in states that have restricted use of racial and ethnic preferences. "It's not as if universities and colleges have simply thrown up their hands," he says. "They now look more aggressively at economic disadvantages that students face. The bigger picture is that the American public likes the idea of diversity but doesn't want to use racial preferences to get there."

Anderson of Texas A&M agrees that a vocabulary development marks the shift. "We've been changing affirmative action and quotas to diversity," he says. "Diversity is seen as good, and has become part of our mainstream culture."

In effect, diversity has come to mean hiring and admissions policies that focus on bringing people of different races and cultures on board — people like Obama, for example. "Obama's talking about merit, and keeping the doors open for all Americans, and strengthening the middle class," Anderson says.

Obama, whose father was Kenyan and whose half-sister is half-Indonesian, also represents another facet of the changing face of affirmative action. "Our society is becoming a lot more demographically complicated," says Schmidt, of *The Chronicle of Higher Education* and author of a recent book on affirmative action in college admissions. "All of these racial groups that benefit from affirmative action as a result of immigration — they're not groups that have experienced oppression and discrimination in the United States. And people are marrying people of other races and ethnicities. How do you sort that out? Which parent counts the most?"

All in all, Schmidt says, the prospects for affirmative action look dim. "In the long term, the political trends are against it," he says. "I don't see a force out there that's going to force the pendulum to swing the other way."

At the same time, many intended beneficiaries — African Americans whose history set affirmative action in motion — remain untouched by it because of the deficient schools they attend.

The catastrophic state of public schools in low-income America remains — and seems likely to remain — a point on which all sides agree. Whether anything will be done about it is another story.

Top schools will continue to seek diverse student bodies, says Coleman of Duke law school. But the public schools continue to deteriorate. "I haven't seen any effort by people who oppose affirmative action, or people who support it, to do anything to improve the public school system. We ought to improve the quality of education because it's in the national interest to do that."

NOTES

1. See "Transcript: Obama and Clinton Debate," ABC News, April 16, 2008, http://abcnews.go.com/Politics /DemocraticDebate/story?id=4670271&page=1.

2. *Ibid.*

3. *Ibid.*

4. See "Trends in Political Values and Core Attitudes: 1987-2007," Pew Research Center for People and the Press, March 22, 2007, pp. 40-41, http://people-press.org/reports/pdf/312.pdf.

5. See Alemayehu Bishaw and Jessica Semega, "Income, Earnings, and Poverty Data from the 2007 American Community Survey," U.S. Census Bureau, August 2008, p. 20, www.census.gov/prod/2008pubs/acs-09.pdf.

6. See Peter Schmidt, *Color and Money: How Rich White Kids Are Winning the War Over College Affirmative Action* (2007), p. 47.

7. See Anthony P. Carnevale and Stephen J. Rose, "Socioeconomic Status, Race/Ethnicity, and Selective College Admissions," The Century Foundation, March 2003, pp. 26, 79, www.tcf.org /Publications/Education/carnevale_rose.pdf.

8. See Christopher B. Swanson, "Who Graduates? Who Doesn't? A Statistical Portrait of High School Graduation, Class of 2001," The Urban Institute, 2004, pp. v-vi, www.urban.org/UploadedPDF/410 934_WhoGraduates.pdf.

9. Quoted in Ira Katznelson, *When Affirmative Action Was White: An Untold History of Racial Inequality in Twentieth-Century America* (2005), p. 175.

10. See Roberta W. Francis, "Reconstituting the Equal Rights Amendment: Policy Implications for Sex Discrimination," 2001, www.equalrightsamendment.org/APSA2001.pdf.

11. See Clarence Thomas, *My Grandfather's Son: A Memoir* (2007), p. 126.

12. Quoted in "Justice Thomas Mocks Value of Yale Law Degree," The Associated Press, Oct. 22, 2007, www.foxnews.com/story/0,2933, 303825,00.html. See also, Coleman profile in Berger&Montague, P.C., law firm Web site, www.bergermontague.com/attor neys.cfm?type=1.

13. See Linda Greenhouse, "Justices Back Affirmative Action by 5 to 4, But Wider Vote Bans a Racial Point System," *The New York Times*, June 24, 2003, p. A1.

14. "Barack Obama, July 27, 2008, Unity 08, High Def, Part II," www.youtube.com/watch?v=XIoRzNVTy H4&eurl=http://video.google.com/videosearch?q= obama%20UNITY&ie=UTF-8&oe=utf-8&rls=org .mozilla:en-US:official&c. UNITY is a coalition of the Asian American Journalists Association, the National Association of Black Journalists, the National Association of Hispanic Journalists and the

Native American Journalists Association, www.unityjournalists.org.

15. See "Trends in Political Values . . .," *op. cit.*, pp. 40-41.

16. See http://abcnews.go.com/Politics/Democratic Debate/story?id=4670271.

17. See Jonathan Kaufman, "Fair Enough?" *The Wall Street Journal*, June 14, 2008.

18. See Christine MacDonald, "Ban lost in college counties," *Detroit News*, Nov. 9, 2006, p. A16; and "1996 General Election Returns for Proposition 209," California Secretary of State, Dec. 18, 1996, http://vote96.sos.ca.gov/Vote96/html/vote/prop/prop-209.961218083528.html.

19. See Sue Anne Pressley, "Florida Plan Aims to End Race-Based Preferences," *The Washington Post*, Nov. 11, 1999, p. A15.

20. See Walter Alarkon, "Affirmative action emerges as wedge issue in election," *The Hill*, March 11, 2008, http://thehill.com/campaign-2008/affirmative-action-emerges-as-wedge-issue-in-election-2008-03-11.html.

21. *Ibid.*, p. viii.

22. Catherine L. Horn and Stella M. Flores, "Percent Plans in College Admissions: A Comparative Analysis of Three States' Experiences," The Civil Rights Project, Harvard University, February 2003, pp. 30-31, http://eric.ed.gov/ERICDocs/data/ericdocs2sql/content_storage_01/0000019b/80/1a/b7/9f.pdf.

23. See Carnevale and Rose, *op. cit.*, pp. 10-11.

24. *Ibid.*

25. Quoted in Terry H. Anderson, *The Pursuit of Fairness: A History of Affirmative Action* (2004), p. 76. Unless otherwise indicated, material in this subsection is drawn from this book.

26. For background, see the following *Editorial Research Reports*: Richard L. Worsnop, "Racism in America," May 13, 1964; Sandra Stencel, "Reverse Discrimination," Aug. 6, 1976; K. P. Maize and Sandra Stencel, "Affirmative Action Under Attack," March 30, 1979; and Marc Leepson, "Affirmative Action Reconsidered," July 31, 1981, all available in *CQ Researcher Plus Archive*.

27. Quoted in Anderson, *op. cit.*, p. 125. For more background, see Richard L. Worsnop, "Racial Discrimination in Craft Unions," *Editorial Research Reports*, Nov. 26, 1969, available in *CQ Researcher Plus Archive*.

28. *Griggs v. Duke Power*, 401 U.S. 424 (1971), http://caselaw.lp.findlaw.com/scripts/getcase.pl?court=US&vol=401&invol=424. For background, see Mary H. Cooper, "Racial Quotas," *CQ Researcher*, May 17, 1991, pp. 277-200; and Kenneth Jost, "Rethinking Affirmative Action," *CQ Researcher*, April 28, 1995, pp. 269-392.

29. *Ibid.*

30. See *University of California Regents v. Bakke*, 438 U.S. 265 (1978), http://caselaw.lp.findlaw.com/scripts/getcase.pl?court=US&vol=438&invol=265.

31. See *United Steelworkers of America, AFL-CIO-CLC v. Weber, et al.*, 443 U.S. 193 (1979), http://caselaw.lp.findlaw.com/scripts/getcase.pl?court=US&vol=443&invol=193; and *Fullilove v. Klutznick*, 448 U.S. 448 (1980), www.law.cornell.edu/supct/html/historics/USSC_CR_0448_0448_ZS.html.

32. Unless otherwise indicated, this subsection is drawn from Anderson, *op. cit.*; and Jost, *op. cit.*

33. For background, see Cooper, *op. cit.*

34. Anderson, *op. cit.*, p. 186.

35. *Ibid.*, p. 206.

36. Quoted in *ibid.*, p. 233. Unless otherwise indicated this subsection is drawn from Anderson, *op. cit.*

37. *Ibid.*, p. 242.

38. *Ibid.*, p. 244.

39. For background, see Kenneth Jost, "Race in America," *CQ Researcher*, July 11, 2003, pp. 593-624.

40. Quoted in Greenhouse, *op. cit.*

41. "Controversial Bake Sale to Go On at CU, College Republicans Protesting Affirmative Action," 7 News, Feb. 10, 2004, www.thedenverchannel.com/news/2837956/detail.html.

42. Quoted in Kavita Kumar, "Affirmative action critic vows he'll try again," *St. Louis Post-Dispatch*, May 6, 2008, p. D1.

43. "Amendment 46: Formerly Proposed Initiative 2007-2008 #31," Colorado Secretary of State, undated, www.elections.colorado.gov/DDefault.aspx?tid=1036.

44. College data, undated, www.collegedata. com/cs/data/college/college_pg01_tmpl.jhtml?schoolId=111.

BIBLIOGRAPHY

Books

Anderson, Terry H., *The Pursuit of Fairness: A History of Affirmative Action*, Oxford University Press, 2004.
A Texas A&M historian tells the complicated story of affirmative action and the struggles surrounding it.

Kahlenberg, Richard D., ed., *America's Untapped Resource: Low-Income Students in Higher Education*, The Century Foundation Press, 2004.
A liberal scholar compiles detailed studies that add up to a case for replacing race- and ethnic-based affirmative action with a system based on students' socioeconomic status.

Katznelson, Ira, *When Affirmative Action Was White: An Untold History of Racial Inequality in Twentieth-Century America*, Norton, 2005.
A Columbia University historian and political scientist argues that affirmative action — favoring whites — evolved as a way of excluding Southern blacks from federal social benefits.

Schmidt, Peter, *Color and Money: How Rich White Kids are Winning the War Over College Affirmative Action*, Palgrave Macmillan, 2007.
An editor at *The Chronicle of Higher Education* explores the realities of race, class and college admissions.

Sowell, Thomas, *Affirmative Action Around the World: An Empirical Study*, Yale University Press, 2004.
A prominent black conservative and critic of affirmative action dissects the doctrine and practice and its similarities to initiatives in the developing world, of which few Americans are aware.

Articles

Babington, Charles, "Might Obama's success undercut affirmative action," The Associated Press, June 28, 2008, www.usatoday.com/news/politics/2008-06-28-3426171631_x.htm.
In a piece that prompted a debate question to presidential candidate Barack Obama, a reporter examines a possibly paradoxical consequence of the 2008 presidential campaign.

Jacobs, Tom, "Affirmative Action: Shifting Attitudes, Surprising Results," *Miller-McCune*, June 20, 2008, www.miller-mccune.com/article/447.
A new magazine specializing in social issues surveys the long-running debate over university admissions. (*Miller-McCune* is published by SAGE Publications, parent company of CQ Press.)

Leonhardt, David, "The New Affirmative Action," *New York Times Magazine*, Sept. 30, 2007, p. 76.
A journalist specializing in economic and social policy explores UCLA's efforts to retool its admissions procedures.

Liptak, Adam, "Lawyers Debate Why Blacks Lag At Major Firms," *The New York Times*, Nov. 29, 2006, p. A1.
A law correspondent airs a tough debate over affirmative action's success, or lack of it, at big law firms.

Matthews, Adam, "The Fixer," *Good Magazine*, Aug. 14, 2008, www.goodmagazine.com/section/Features/the_fixer.
A new Web-based publication for the hip and socially conscious examines the career of black businessman and affirmative-action critic Ward Connerly.

Mehta, Seema, "UCLA accused of illegal admissions practices," *Los Angeles Times*, Aug. 30, 2008, www.latimes.com/news/local/la-me-ucla30-2008aug30,0,6489043.story.
Mehta examines the latest conflict surrounding the top-tier university's retailored admissions procedures.

Reports and Studies

Coleman, James E. Jr. and Mitu Gulati, "A Response to Professor Sander: Is It Really All About the Grades?" *North Carolina Law Review*, 2006, pp. 1823-1829.
Two lawyers, one of them a black who was a partner at a major firm, criticize Sander's conclusions, arguing he overemphasizes academic deficiencies.

Horn, Catherine L. and Stella M. Flores, "Percent Plans in College Admissions: A Comparative Analysis of Three States' Experiences," The Civil Rights Project, Harvard University, February 2003.
Educational policy experts with a pro-affirmative action perspective dig into the details of three states' alternatives to traditional affirmative action.

Prager, Devah, "The Mark of a Criminal Record," *American Journal of Sociology*, March 2003, pp. 937-975. White people with criminal records have a better chance at entry-level jobs than black applicants with clean records, an academic's field research finds.

Sander, Richard H., "The Racial Paradox of the Corporate Law Firm," *North Carolina Law Review*, 2006, pp. 1755-1822. A much-discussed article shows that a disproportionate number of black lawyers from top schools leave major law firms before becoming partners.

Swanson, Christopher B., "Who Graduates? Who Doesn't? A Statistical Portrait of Public High School Graduation, Class of 2001," The Urban Institute, 2004, www.urban.org/publications/410934.html. A centrist think tank reveals in devastating detail the disparity in high schools between races and classes.

For More Information

American Association for Affirmative Action, 888 16th St., N.W., Suite 800, Washington, DC 20006; (202) 349-9855; www.affirmativeaction.org. Represents human resources professionals in the field.

American Civil Liberties Union, 125 Broad St., 18th Floor, New York, NY 10004; www.aclu.org/racialjustice/aa/index.html. The organization's Racial Justice Program organizes legal and voter support for affirmative action programs.

American Civil Rights Institute, P.O. Box 188350, Sacramento, CA 95818; (916) 444-2278; www.acri.org/index.html. Organizes ballot initiatives to prohibit affirmative action programs based on race and ethnicity preferences.

Diversity Web, Association of American Colleges and Universities, 1818 R St., N.W., Washington, DC 20009; www.diversityweb.org. Publishes news and studies concerning affirmative action and related issues.

www.jessicacorry.com. A Web site featuring writings by Jessica Peck Corry, director of the Colorado campaign for a racial preferences ban.

Project SEAPHE (Scale and Effects of Admissions Preferences in Higher Education), UCLA School of Law, Box 951476, Los Angeles, CA 90095; (310) 267-4576; www.seaphe.org. Analyzes data on the effects of racial and other preferences.

U.S. Commission on Civil Rights, 624 Ninth St., N.W., Washington, DC 20425; (202) 376-7700; www.usccr.gov. Studies and reports on civil rights issues and implements civil rights laws.

AP Photo/W. A. Harewood

Atlanta's Morris Brown College is among several of
the nation's 103 historically black colleges and
universities (HBCUs) facing academic or financial
troubles. While well-known schools like Spelman
and Morehouse are thriving, all the nation's HBCUs
struggle to survive with far fewer resources than
predominantly white schools. Critics say HBCUs are
anachronisms in the age of integration, but fervent
supporters say they provide higher education and
support to a neglected group of Americans.

From *CQ Researcher,*
December 12, 2003. (Updated September 30, 2008)

4

Black Colleges

Kenneth Jost and Alan Greenblatt

I n 2003, the recorded message on the Morris Brown College
switchboard assured callers that the 118-year-old institution is
"still open — renewing and rebuilding." But visitors to the
Atlanta campus found a school with massive debts, no president,
fewer than 75 students and a perilously uncertain future.

Sadly, the picture five years later was not much different. The
college in 2008 was still saddled with $27 million in debt, lacked
access to federal student aid funds and graduated a total of 31 students — all but three of them "nontraditional" adult education
students. "In the spring of 2008, there were only 56 students on
campus," reported the *Atlanta Journal-Constitution.* There were
10 faculty members at Morris Brown and class size maxed out at
six students. [1]

Morris Brown has been on the ropes since late 2002 when the
Commission on Colleges of the Southern Association of Colleges
and Schools (SACS) revoked the school's accreditation because of
financial mismanagement. Student enrollment — 2,700 —
dropped by more than half within a month and plummeted further
after a SACS appeals panel in 2003 rejected Morris Brown's effort
to overturn the revocation. Since then, the school's athletic program
has been eliminated, all classrooms and offices consolidated into a
single building and the few remaining students told to settle
accounts for the current semester before enrolling in the next.
Among the school's financial mistakes: handing out scholarships
without the funds to pay them, giving laptop computers to all students and applying for membership in the NCAA's elite Division I-A
for intercollegiate athletics — an expensive proposition even for big
state schools. "They didn't think thoroughly and clearly in terms of

the financial impact," says Adam Gibbs, a former Bank of America executive who served on a three-member transition team with a mission of helping to keep Morris Brown alive.

The loss of accreditation was the final blow. The decision meant that Morris Brown students were no longer eligible for federal student loans, which account for a major part of the private school's revenues. "Once we lost accreditation, our survival was put in doubt," says Gibbs.

Morris Brown is among several of the nation's 103 historically black colleges and universities — widely referred to as HBCUs — undergoing high levels of financial, managerial or academic stress. Mary Holmes College — a private, two-year institution in West Point, Miss. — closed its doors in 2003 after losing accreditation a year earlier, and more than 20 other black colleges have closed over the years. [2]

Morris Brown's problems are mirrored at other black colleges. Empty, dilapidated buildings have also become the order of the day at Alabama A&M University, where enrollment has dwindled to fewer than 100 students. Knoxville College at the start of 2008 opened its doors for the spring semester with enrollment down to 66 students, debt standing at $7 million and its budget cut by half over the previous four years. [3]

More broadly, all of the nation's HBCUs — founded primarily during the late 19th and early 20th centuries — continue their ongoing struggle to survive with far less in financial and other resources than predominantly white colleges and universities, private or public. All told, the 103 HBCUs have endowments that lag well behind other private colleges. Howard University has the largest, at $523.7 million as of June 2007. That represented a big jump from the previous year, but left Howard at 138th in the nation. The second most generously endowed HBCU — Spelman — had just $340.3 million — less than one percent of the value of the endowment held by Harvard University, the nation's wealthiest institution of higher learning. [4] And in the Southern and Border states, which traditionally maintained dual systems of higher education, states continue to fund public black colleges at significantly lower rates than predominantly white schools — with white schools sometimes receiving more than twice as much per student as the black schools.

Despite such challenges, fervent supporters of black colleges and universities tout historical legacies and current accomplishments to justify the schools' continued existence in the post-segregation era. By offering higher education to a "neglected, oppressed and segregated group of American citizens," HBCUs have been a "major force by which some of the disparity which exists among the races has been solved," says Frederick Humphries, former president of the National Association for Equal Opportunity in Higher Education (NAFEO), which comprises virtually all of the historically black institutions.

William Gray — former president of the United Negro College Fund (UNCF), which raises funds for 39 private member HBCUs — notes that HBCUs represent only 3 percent of the nation's 3,000-plus colleges and universities but account for nearly a third of the country's black college graduates each year. "If an educational institution is producing outstanding graduates and leaders who are helping make America strong, then it's worth having," says Gray. According to a National Science Foundation study, Fisk University, a school in Nashville with fewer than 1,000 students, produces more black graduates who go on to complete doctorates in natural sciences than any other school in the nation. [5] "HBCUs today represent only 4 percent of all higher education institutions, but they graduate approximately 30 percent of all African American students, 40 percent of African American students receiving a four-year degree in STEM (science, technology, engineering and math) and 50 percent of African American teachers," Dorothy Cowser Yancy, president of Johnson C. Smith University, told the House Education and Labor Committee in March 2008.

The roster of HBCU alumni indeed includes some impressive names: from prominent government officials and well-known entertainers to high-profile journalists and top-ranked professional athletes. Overall statistics, however, are less impressive. Some of the schools graduate fewer than one-third of the students in their entering classes. And graduation rates at even the most prestigious black institutions fall short of comparable figures for black students attending the most elite predominantly white schools. Some critics say the figures show that African American students who attend HBCUs lose more than they gain from the choice. "There is a certain amount of comfort at some of these institutions," says Gerald Foster, a former professor of social work at historically black Virginia Union University in Richmond. "But what you give up is a certain amount of academic quality."

College graduation rates for blacks continue to lag well behind those of other racial groups. However, the U.S. Department of Education reports that in 2006, 142,240 blacks earned four-year degrees from American colleges and universities. That number had increased 4 percent from the previous year and was more than double the number of bachelor's degrees earned by African Americans in 1990. [6] Foster, author of a confrontational critique, *Is There a Conspiracy to Keep Black Colleges Open?,* believes racially identifiable schools have outlived their usefulness. "The whole purpose of civil rights was to get beyond the issue of segregation," says Foster, who is African American and earned degrees from Virginia Union and Howard University in Washington, D.C.

Some leading opponents of racial preferences — both black and white — also question the HBCUs' reasons for being. "These colleges were formed out of necessity," says Ward Connerly, president of the Sacramento-based American Civil Rights Institute, which opposes racial and gender preferences. "From the standpoint of public policy, I have to think that they are an idea whose time has come and probably gone," at least with regard to public funding. Connerly, who is African American, authored Proposition 209, the 1996 California initiative that barred racial preferences in admissions in the state's university system. (Connerly has since sponsored similar initiatives in other states, including Colorado and Nebraska in 2008.)

Roger Clegg, president and general counsel for the Center for Equal Opportunity, agrees. "Everyone would welcome the day when the rationale for historically black colleges would no longer apply," Clegg says, "when a special nurturing environment is no longer necessary, the problems of the inner city are not racially defined and where there are lots of institutions [focusing] on the contributions of a wide variety of different racial and ethnic groups." Clegg, who is white, has filed friend-of-the-court briefs opposing racial preferences on behalf of the center in several major cases. A widely-cited 2007 study by a pair of economists found that the historic advantage HBCUs offered to blacks in terms of graduation rates

and increased income had declined by the 1990s, leading to a "wage penalty" that led to a decline in relative wages for HBCU graduates between the 1970s and 1990s. [7] President George W. Bush and other administration officials, however, strongly supported the HBCUs. Bush called for increased federal funding for HBCUs during his 2000 campaign. His first Education Secretary Roderick Paige, who is African American and a graduate of historically black Jackson State University in Mississippi, credits the HBCUs with helping narrow the continuing gap between college attendance and graduation rates for white and black students. "The situation would be much worse without our historically black colleges and universities," Paige told the Mississippi Association of Colleges in 2003. [8]

During his presidential campaign in 2008, Barack Obama did not make HBCUs a central focus. But as a senator in 2007 he cosponsored an amendment to the Higher Education Act that offered $15 million in annual grants to Predominantly Black Institutions that did not qualify for official HBCU status, but are primarily urban and rural two-year colleges that serve at least 50 percent low-income or first-generation college students. Obama's new designation was projected to apply to 75 institutions in 17 states, benefiting approximately 265,000 students.

Abigail Thernstrom and Stephen Thernstrom, two white academics, note that HBCUs are more segregated than many "urban public schools that liberal critics routinely denounce as disastrously 'segregated.' " Still, they conclude that the HBCUs serve a useful purpose. They wrote in a 2007 *Wall Street Journal* opinion column, "Perhaps they continue to thrive because they do an excellent job of making sure their students actually get a diploma. Getting into college is not the great problem for blacks in higher education today; staying and graduating is. The dropout rate at the HBCUs is high, but considerably lower than at the typical majority-white school. Although only a 10th of all African Americans attend HBCUs, they award over a fifth of all bachelor's degrees earned by blacks. And yet they do not attract students from unusually affluent and educated homes." [9]

In 2003, nationally syndicated radio host Tom Joyner, a graduate of Alabama's Tuskegee University, donated $1 million in scholarship funds for students at embattled Morris Brown. He later offered to buy the campus, if that would save the school. As the fundraising continues, and as black colleges and universities grapple with the challenges of an increasingly competitive academic environment, here are some of the major questions being debated:

Do historically black colleges and universities still serve a useful purpose?

When William Allen was about to become executive director of Virginia's higher-education policymaking panel in June 1998, the conservative African American suggested in a newspaper interview that it was time to reconsider the role of historically black colleges and institutions. "It's always important for people to go back and review their inheritance to see if it's what they want to embrace," Allen, an opponent of racial preferences in college admissions, told *The Washington Post.*

His comment immediately drew sharp criticism from, among others, former Virginia Gov. L. Douglas Wilder, himself an alumnus of Virginia Union University. In a quick retreat, Allen told the *Post* the next day that he had a record of supporting historically black colleges and had no plans to review the status of the two black universities in the state system. [10]

The episode indicates both the strong support for historically black colleges among their alumni and the combative reaction from alumni and other supporters to any suggestion that the institutions are no longer needed. UNCF President Gray counters the idea by emphasizing that religiously founded schools survive today even though overt discrimination against Jews, Catholics and Mormons has largely disappeared. "I'll close Morehouse and say it's no longer needed when you close Notre Dame," Gray says. "I'll close Spelman and say that it's no longer needed when you close Brigham Young." Gray and other HBCU supporters insist the schools still serve a vital purpose by providing educational opportunities for all types of students — but, in particular, for African American students from economically or educationally disadvantaged backgrounds. "Some of the youngsters who are educated out of the urban inner cities or from rural, poor Southern roots would not have access to a college education but for the existence of an Alcorn or Tuskegee," says Walter Allen, a professor of sociology at UCLA. As a result, supporters say, black colleges provide greater socioeconomic diversity than many or most predominantly white schools, mixing students whose parents are professionals with sons and daughters of tenant farmers. "This is very important learning in an increasingly globalized society," says Charles Willie, professor emeritus at Harvard's Graduate School of Education.

But Connerly, who served on the University of California Board of Regents, opposes any public funding for racially identified schools. "We as taxpayers ought to be providing the funding for our kids to get an education that is free from any consideration of race," Connerly says. "If they want to make [black colleges] a privately financed enterprise, God speed. [But] I don't personally ascribe to the rationale."

Supporters of HBCUs, however, deny that black colleges are themselves promoting racial separation. They note that HBCUs have never excluded whites, and in fact today have a higher percentage of white students (nearly 10 percent) and white faculty (more than a third) than comparable statistics for black students and faculty at predominantly white institutions. HBCUs "are diverse and integrated — more racially diverse than predominantly white institutions," Gray says. In 2008, Joshua Packwood graduated from Morehouse as the school's first white valedictorian.

For his part, Virginia Union's Foster forcefully makes a separate accusation of academic inferiority against what he depicts as the middle and bottom tiers of HBCUs. "There is an ethos of academic and administrative mediocrity," he writes, "that maintains and sustains an inefficient status quo of fifty years ago and drives away bright, young, energetic faculty who are ostracized rather than embraced." Foster says the "top-tier" black schools "can compete on par with any other school of similar mission." But some of the lower-ranked schools, he says, may have outlived their usefulness. "The only thing that they're hanging their hat on is that they're black," Foster says. "That's ludicrous."

Supporters of HBCUs sharply dispute the critique. Black colleges "have been superlative with regard to the quality of teaching," says NAFEO President Humphries. "They had to be good teachers with what they had to work with. They might not have had as many resources as the rest of higher education, but nothing has been

A Who's Who of HBCU Graduates

Some of the leading figures in the African American civil rights movement graduated from historically black colleges and universities, including Booker T. Washington (Tuskegee), W.E.B. DuBois (Fisk), Thurgood Marshall (Lincoln University of Pennsylvania, Howard Law School) and the Rev. Martin Luther King Jr. (Morehouse). Today, prominent HBCU alumni can be found in many walks of public life:

Politics and Government

Mfume

Paige

Kweisi Mfume, former president, NAACP (Morgan State)

L. Douglas Wilder, former Va. governor (Virginia Union)

The Rev. Jesse L. Jackson Sr., president, Rainbow Coalition (North Carolina A&T)

Rod Paige, former U.S. secretary of Education (Jackson State)

Vernon Jordan, attorney/lobbyist (Howard)

Henry Frye, former N.C. chief justice (North Carolina A&T)

Andrew Young, human-rights activist (Howard)

Marian Wright Edelman, president, Children's Defense Fund (Spelman)

Hazel O'Leary, former U.S. secretary of Energy (Fisk)

Steve Bullock, former acting president, American Red Cross (Virginia Union)

Arts and Entertainment

Lee

Winfrey

Spike Lee, film director (Morehouse)

Oprah Winfrey, media entrepreneur (Tennessee State)

Leontyne Price, opera singer (Central State)

Lionel Richie, singer/musician (Tuskegee)

Erykah Badu, singer (Grambling State)

Keenen Ivory Wayans, actor/director (Tuskegee)

Keshia Knight Pulliam, actress (Spelman)

Samuel L. Jackson, actor (Morehouse)

Sean "Diddy" Combs, rap artist/producer (Howard)

Science and Medicine

Satcher

David Satcher, former U.S. surgeon general (Morehouse)

Jocelyn Elders, former U.S. surgeon general (Philander Smith)

Alvin H. Crawford, co-director, Spine Center University of Cincinnati Medical Center (Tennessee State)

Louis Sullivan, former U.S. secretary of Health and Human Services; founder and former president, Morehouse School of Medicine (Morehouse)

Levi Watkins Jr., cardiac surgeon, John Hopkins University (Tennessee State)

Journalism, Literature and Publishing

Morrison

Earl Graves, magazine publisher (Morgan State)

Tony Brown, journalist (West Virginia State)

Toni Morrison, novelist (Howard)

Alice Walker, novelist (Morgan State)

Athletics

Rice

Bob Hayes, Olympian & pro football player (Florida A&M)

Edwin Moses, Olympian and physicist (Morehouse)

Jerry Rice, former pro football player (Mississippi Valley State)

Lou Brock, former pro baseball player (Southern University A&M)

Source: HBCUNetwork.Com

slack about the teaching." Asked if black colleges measure up to white schools, Professor Allen replies, "Absolutely." HBCUs are "underresourced" and might not compare favorably in terms of lab facilities or the like, he says. But, he adds, "Many of those colleges produce a better product in terms of black students because they have a core of dedicated teachers who believe in the capabilities and potential of those students and who motivate those students to succeed."

In any event, says Christopher Brown, dean of the college of education at the University of Nevada-Las Vegas, HBCUs have become an essential component of U.S. higher education. "Those institutions play a tremendous role in the production of students, irrespective of race, and they play a tremendous role in the production in terms of race," Brown says. "If we remove these institutions, it would not be possible for the remaining institutions to absorb those students."

Do African American students benefit from attending a predominantly black college?

When white Americans think about historically black colleges, they naturally focus on the schools' distinctive racial identity. But for many African Americans attending HBCUs, race becomes a non-issue — perhaps for the first and maybe the only time in their lives. "Because the vast majority of students are African American, it becomes less and less of an issue in daily interaction," says Christopher Elders, a Morehouse graduate who studied at Oxford University in England in 2003 as a Rhodes scholar. "You forget that everybody around you is African American."

HBCU supporters say that experience gives African American students both comfort and self-confidence. "The schools have always had to do a job of weeding out from the minds of black students that they were second-class citizens," Humphries says. "All they need is opportunity and a fair set of conditions, and they'll do as well as anybody else. But they need to be in an environment where people believe in them."

Critics, however, question both rationales. "In this nation, we're not supposed to get our comfort from being around people with the same melanin content as ourselves," Connerly says. Foster says HBCUs "are harming more than they are benefiting students because [the schools] are not preparing them for what they will

confront when they graduate." Supporters of black colleges contrast the environment on HBCU campuses with the African American students' experiences at predominantly white schools. Black students "get to an integrated school and find they're segregated by race anyway," says Reginald Stuart, a graduate of Tennessee State University in Nashville and a longtime reporter, now a corporate recruiter with McClatchy Newspapers.

Work by two researchers published in the early 1990s does suggest that African American students fare better in many respects at HBCUs than at predominantly white schools, according to Laura Perna, an assistant professor of education policy at the University of Maryland in College Park. Perna, who is white and formerly worked at UNCF's Patterson Research Institute, says the researchers concluded that African American students who attend predominantly black schools experience "less social isolation, less alienation, less personal dissatisfaction and less personal racism than African Americans who attend predominantly white institutions." [11] But Foster disputes the idea that black students generally have problems at predominantly white campuses. "If you find yourself in a campus environment that is so stressful or distressful," he says, "one would raise questions why you would stay there. Sometimes it's easier to stay, to assume victim status. That provides an excuse for you not to excel."

HBCU supporters also say the schools do a better job than predominantly white institutions of tailoring instruction and curricula to the needs of black students, many of whom come to college with weak educational backgrounds. Black colleges "continue to offer customized teaching for the African American student," says Komanduri Murty, a professor of sociology at Clark Atlanta and co-author of a 1993 study of HBCUs. "They get a lot of special attention that they would not get in other schools." [12] Foster views this so-called "remediation" rationale less favorably. He says many of the lower-tier HBCUs admit far too many students who do not belong in college at all and are accepted only because they bring federal aid to the schools. "In this millennium," he writes, "there is neither need nor reason for substandard, mediocre colleges — black or white." [13]

Some HBCU supporters concede that black students do make some tradeoffs by attending a black college. "You will get football, but you won't get the Rose Bowl," says Brown of UNLV. But, he adds, "In terms of the academics, more often than not, you're going to gain."

UCLA Professor Allen, who is black but attended predominantly white schools, acknowledges that black students may fare better in wealth and prestige by choosing an elite white school over one of the best black colleges. On those factors, Allen says, "Harvard trumps everywhere in the country." But, he adds, "If your emphasis is on social and other cultural indicators, Harvard loses out." Rhodes scholar Elders, however, says he had no doubts about picking Morehouse over a predominantly white college. "The ultimate outcome of a successful education at a black school is that there's a real sense of security in your identity," he says. "There was no illusion that the rest of the world was like Morehouse. Everyone is aware that this is one aspect of their lives but not a microcosm for the rest of the world."

After studying the history of the Cold War at Oxford, Elders returned to the United States to attend Harvard Law School, where he is a research fellow. He says he has no concerns that his Morehouse degree leaves him at a disadvantage. "I couldn't imagine being in a better position than I am right now," he says.

Should the federal government increase support for historically black colleges?

Students leaving for college today pack many of the same things that their parents took with them a generation earlier; but at least half arrive on campus with something new: desktop or notebook computers. [14] Computers are less widespread, however, at the nation's historically black colleges and universities. A Commerce Department survey in 2000 found that only a quarter of the students at the nation's HBCUs owned personal computers. The study was based on survey replies from three-fourths of America's HBCUs. [15]

To remedy what the study called "a digital-divide issue," HBCU supporters on Capitol Hill are pushing a bill to authorize $250 million per year for five years in targeted aid to historically black and other minority-serving colleges and universities. The bill passed the Senate unanimously in 2003, but has yet to see significant further action. The bill "uses racial classifications to address a problem that is not limited to institutions or individuals of a particular racial identity," Clegg and Connerly wrote in a July 29, 2003 letter to then-Sen.

Spelman College in Atlanta is among only three HBCUs with an endowment valued in excess of $100 million, as of 2001. Black colleges have far smaller endowments than predominantly white private schools.

Courtesy Spelman College

George Allen, R-Va., chief sponsor of the Senate bill. They proposed a rewritten version with neutral criteria that they said would nevertheless probably funnel most of the proposed funds to HBCUs. [16]

For HBCU supporters, however, the episode demonstrates the continuing need to remedy more than a century of underfunding of higher education for black Americans. "It's hard to overcome the historical advantage that white schools had," says NAFEO's Humphries. "There is a historical inadequacy that is going to take a long time to make up."

The financial gap results not only from historical inequities but also from present-day disadvantages, according to Gray of the UNCF and other HBCU supporters. HBCUs have to keep tuitions relatively low to be affordable to middle- and lower-income black families. One reason the loss of accreditation at some colleges has been so devastating is that such a status keeps students from receiving federal financial aid, which is a must for most HBCU students.

In addition, although firm figures are hard to come by, most studies show that lower percentages of African American graduates donate to their alma maters than alumni from predominantly white institutions. And, with a few notable exceptions — such as media entrepreneur Oprah Winfrey or magazine publisher Earl

Graves Jr. — HBCU alumni lack the wealth to support their alma maters with the kind of six- or seven-figure contributions that predominantly white colleges sometimes receive from well-heeled alumni.

That seems to be changing, to some degree. Howard University in Washington has become something of a fundraising juggernaut. And, as president of lesser-known Bennett College, Johnetta Cole met a $50 million fundraising goal by reaching out to well-known figures such as poet Maya Angelou, comedian Bill Cosby and former Sen. Bob Dole, R-Kan. By the time Cole retired in 2006, Bennett had removed four older buildings and stuffed its endowment with at least $7 million. [17]

Initially, HBCUs sent a disproportionate number of graduates into lower-paying professions like teaching and academics — a legacy of their early mission of promoting basic education for African American students. Today more HBCU graduates are going into more lucrative professions such as business, law and medicine, but until recently their incomes were still limited because they primarily served black clienteles.

With limited alumni giving, HBCUs have been unable to amass endowments anywhere near those of predominantly white colleges and universities. Only four HBCUs had endowments valued in excess of $100 million as of 2001: Spelman, Morehouse, Hampton and Howard. As Gray notes, a $1 billion endowment, even if conservatively invested, can spin off $50 million in income without any fundraising effort by the school's president or office of development.

"A black college president is trying to do a lot with practically nothing," Gray concludes. "They have to depend on fees, tuitions [federal aid] to make ends meet — unless they're public, and even then they don't get a fair share from the state legislatures." In fact, a recent compilation shows that the predominantly white flagship state universities in nine states studied received as much as three times more per student than the historically black state schools. [18] In 2008, James T. Minor, an assistant professor of higher education at Michigan State University, surveyed four Southern states — Alabama, Louisiana, Mississippi and North Carolina — and found that only the latter showed evidence of trying to expand access and degree attainment for African Americans. And even there, HBCUs were far underfunded compared with North Carolina's flagship public

universities. The University of North Carolina at Chapel Hill and North Carolina State University each received approximately $15,700 in state funding per student, while North Carolina A&T and Fayetteville State University received about $7,800. [19]

HBCU supporters are working to increase private and public support. Gray, who resigned the UNCF post at the end of 2003, has energized the center's fundraising over the past 10 years with glitzy events featuring black celebrities such as the late singer Lou Rawls. But he and other HBCU supporters say the federal government needs to do more. Specifically, they call for making Pell Grants available to all low-income students, increasing targeted funding for HBCUs under the so-called Title III program created in 1986, and helping HBCUs gain a greater share of federal research grants. The 2007 College Cost Reduction and Access Act provided $170 million in new funding for HBCUs over two years to help expand college access and strengthen services for low-income students, as well as campus renovation. "By providing HBCUs with these much-needed federal resources, we are saying that the needs of these vital institutions and their students can no longer go ignored," said George Miller, D-Calif., the bill's sponsor and chair of the House Education and Labor Committee.

BACKGROUND

Separate and Unequal

Blacks had few opportunities for education at any level in the United States before the Civil War and only limited opportunities during the century of racial segregation that prevailed after the abolition of slavery in 1863. The segregated school systems, however, included fledgling black colleges — first private and later public institutions — that evolved by the mid-20th century into an important avenue of educational advancement for African Americans. [20]

Before the Civil War, African Americans, whether slave or free, were restricted from higher education by law in the South and — with limited exceptions — by social custom elsewhere. Blacks were admitted at only a few white colleges — notably, Berea in Kentucky and Oberlin in Ohio. Five of today's historically black colleges can trace their roots to the antebellum period, but only one

— Wilberforce University in Ohio, founded in 1843 by the African Methodist Episcopal Church — actually awarded baccalaureate degrees before the Civil War. *

All told, only 28 blacks received college degrees in the United States before 1861.

After the Civil War, missionary and church groups rushed to the South to lay the foundations for an educational system for the largely illiterate population of freed black slaves. By the end of the 19th century, more than 60 educational institutions for blacks had been founded, thanks to the efforts of Northern missionary societies, philanthropists and federal and state governments.

Although some schools, such as Fisk, had college departments from early on, most remained little more than elementary and secondary schools until the 1900s. For instance, Hampton, founded in 1868, did not award its first college degree until 1922. The differences between the early black and white colleges resulted from the black schools' limited financial resources, black students' limited educational preparation and deliberate decisions by Southern states to provide vocational instead of liberal arts curricula for black students.

Many of today's leading black private schools were established during this period and began as church-supported schools that emphasized training of ministers and teachers. Among those early church-funded schools were Atlanta University (1865), Fisk (1866), Talladega (1867) and Tougaloo (1868), all founded by the American Missionary Association; Hampton and Morehouse (1867) were supported by the American Baptist Home Mission. The church groups had the support of the Freedmen's Bureau, the federal agency established to help the former slave population. The bureau itself started Howard University, chartered by Congress in 1867 and named after the bureau's commissioner, General O. O. Howard. But the bureau drew the wrath of Southern politicians and was abolished in 1872. After the bureau's demise, some Southern and border states

began to establish separate public schools for blacks. Paradoxically, the movement was spurred in part by the Second Morrill Act of 1890, which prohibited federal aid to state systems that discriminated against blacks in tax-supported education. Within a decade, 17 of 19 Southern and Border states had responded to the law by establishing parallel higher-education systems for whites and blacks. Although the two systems were separate, they were demonstrably unequal. Virtually all of the public black colleges began as "normal" or "industrial" schools, and none initially offered baccalaureate degrees. They also received less state aid per student than their predominantly white counterparts — a tradition that continues to this day.

The Supreme Court gave its legal blessing to mandatory racial segregation with its infamous 1896 decision, *Plessy v. Ferguson*, upholding a Louisiana law requiring separation of black and white passengers on railways. A decade later, the high court also sanctioned racial segregation in higher education. The lesser-known ruling in *Berea College v. Kentucky* (1908) upheld a state law that made it a crime to teach black and white students in the same school. [21]

By the turn of the century, private black colleges had awarded more than 1,100 baccalaureate degrees. In the early 1900s they began attracting significant financial support from white philanthropic organizations — notably, the Carnegie and Rockefeller foundations, the Peabody Education Fund, the Slater Fund and the Julius Rosenwald Fund. Despite the Morrill Act's anti-discrimination provision, however, black public colleges were significantly underfunded compared to white schools. A decade after enactment, white schools were reportedly receiving appropriations 26 times greater than black schools. [22]

Opening Doors

The legal battle against racial segregation began with court cases that successfully challenged discriminatory treatment of black students in higher education. The focus turned to elementary and secondary education, however, after the Supreme Court's historic 1954 decision outlawing segregation in public schools. Only in the 1970s did civil rights groups mount comparably broad challenges to the dual systems of higher education. Those cases left the separate black and white public colleges

---

* The four other schools included the abolitionist-founded Institute for Colored Youth (1837, now Cheyney University) and the Ashmun Institute (1854, now Lincoln University), both now parts of the Pennsylvania state higher education system; the District of Columbia Teachers College (1851, merged in 1975 into the University of the District of Columbia); and St. Louis Normal College for Women (1856, now Harris-Stowe State College).

CHRONOLOGY

1901-1950 *Segregated black colleges and universities advance but still lag far behind white schools; first efforts to challenge racial segregation in courts.*

1928 Southern Association of Colleges and Schools (SACS) agrees to consider accrediting black institutions.

1944 United Negro College Fund (UNCF) formed, with 29 members.

1950 Supreme Court rules black students' rights violated by unequal treatment at state post-graduate schools in Oklahoma, Texas.

1951-1980 *Desegregation era; efforts begin to dismantle dual systems of public colleges and universities.*

1954 Supreme Court rules racial segregation in elementary and secondary schools unconstitutional; applies ruling to higher education two years later.

1964 Civil Rights Act of 1964 bars discrimination in federally funded programs by state and local governments (Title VI); Department of Health, Education and Welfare (HEW) orders 10 states in 1968 and 1969 to submit plans to dismantle dual systems of higher education.

1970 Civil rights groups sue HEW to make states dismantle dual systems of higher education (*Adams v. Richardson*); three years later judge orders states to "eliminate vestiges of racial dualism."

1977 Federal court orders white University of Tennessee at Nashville to merge with historically black Tennessee State University.

1978 HEW calls for desegregation of faculty, elimination of duplicative programs in state higher education systems.

1980s *Higher-education desegregation suits falter; Federal aid voted for historically black colleges and universities (HBCUs); Enrollment at HBCUs declines.*

1986 Congress authorizes direct aid for HBCUs in Title III of Higher Education Amendments; funding initially set at $100 million, $5 million for black graduate institutions.

1987 Federal judge dismisses higher-education desegregation suit, saying plaintiffs lacked legal standing.

1990s *HBCU enrollment levels off.*

1992 Supreme Court says states must take affirmative steps to dismantle dual systems of public higher education.

1996 Congress authorizes $29 million over five years for historic preservation at HBCUs.

2000-present *Many black colleges in trouble over finances.*

2000 GOP presidential candidate George W. Bush promises 77 percent increase in funding over five years for HBCUs; budget proposals as president fall short of promise.

2002-2003 Morris Brown and Mary Holmes colleges lose accreditation due to inadequate financing. . . . Mary Holmes College closes; Morris Brown opens with fewer than 75 students; Bennett, Grambling State and Talladega win lifting of probation placed in 2001.

2006 Former Morris Brown college president and CFO plead guilty to financial student aid fraud, having used $8 million to pay faculty salaries and other bills. . . . The UNCF launches a 10-year building program for HBCUs, quickly raising $19 million from philanthropic organizations. . . . Alabama settles a 26-year-old lawsuit, *Knight v. Alabama*, which claimed that the state's property tax system and college admissions policies were racially discriminatory. The settlement led to $56.7 million in higher education appropriations to "redress historical discrimination against African Americans" in 2007.

2007 The SACS puts Florida A&M University on probation for financial and management problems. . . . Fisk University is criticized for its plans to sell two paintings for $16 million. The paintings were donated as part of a complete collection. . . . An amendment to the Higher Education Act cosponsored by Sen. Barack Obama, D-Ill., authorizes $15 million in annual federal grants to Predominantly Black Institutions, an estimated 75 rural and urban two-year colleges with enrollment made up of more than 50 percent African Americans. The College Reduction and Access Act also provides $170 million in new funding for HBCUs for the following two years.

2008 Howard University completes a five-year, $275 million fundraising campaign. . . . More than two dozen members of Congress band together to form the House HBCU with the goal of expanding federal support for the institutions.

standing, but reduced some of the funding disparities that had disadvantaged the historically black schools.

The NAACP first focused on higher education in the 1930s as a glaring example of racial inequality and as a politically less explosive area than elementary and secondary education. The strategy yielded an initial victory in 1938 when the high court, by a 6-2 vote, ruled that the state of Missouri had violated black student Lloyd Gaines's equal-protection rights by offering to pay his tuition at an out-of-state law school rather than admit him to the state's all-white law school. The court went further in a pair of rulings in 1950, which ruled separate but evidently unequal treatment of black students unconstitutional. In one case, Texas sought to avoid admitting a black student to the University of Texas Law School by creating a new all-black school; in the other, the University of Oklahoma admitted a black graduate student but assigned him to a special seat in the classroom and special tables in the library and cafeteria. [23]

The high court unanimously jettisoned the "separate but equal" doctrine for elementary and secondary education in its 1954 decision, *Brown v. Board of Education.* A year later, the court said in the so-called *Brown II* decision that public school systems did not need to desegregate immediately. But in a higher-education case in 1956, the court said that no delay was allowed in admitting qualified black applicants to graduate professional schools on the same basis as white applicants. [24]

None of the higher-education decisions, however, addressed the status of the historically black public colleges and universities. That issue lay largely dormant until 1964 when Congress — in Title VI of the Civil Rights Act — prohibited racial discrimination by any state or local governmental program that received federal funding. [25] The Office of Civil Rights of the Department of Health, Education and Welfare (HEW) did not draw up regulations to enforce the law, but in 1968 and 1969 it ordered 10 states with dual higher-education systems to draft plans to dismantle the separate systems and create unitary systems in their place. Five states submitted plans deemed unacceptable; five others ignored the order. But the department failed to initiate enforcement proceedings against any of them.

Civil rights groups responded with a broad suit in 1970 aimed at requiring HEW to enforce Title VI. [26]

The suit — filed in the name of Kenneth Adams, a black Mississippi student, against HEW Secretary Elliott Richardson — lasted for nearly 20 years but ultimately produced only limited effects. In an initial ruling, a federal judge in Washington in 1973 not only ordered HEW to enforce the law but also directed the 10 states "to eliminate the vestiges of racial dualism" in higher education. NAFEO replied with a friend-of-the-court brief that argued for correcting disparities but preserving the public black colleges as separate institutions.

In response to a second ruling, HEW in 1978 developed criteria that called on the states to desegregate faculty at both white and black schools and to reduce or eliminate programs at white schools that duplicated similar programs at nearby black schools. By the 1980s, however, enforcement slowed to a near halt. And in 1987 the court dismissed the case on the ground that the plaintiffs lacked legal standing to bring the suit.

Four higher-education desegregation suits in individual states also lasted for decades, with somewhat limited results. [27] In Tennessee, a federal court in 1977 ordered the merger of historically black Tennessee State University (TSU) in Nashville with the University of Tennessee at Nashville, a smaller school with a largely white and predominantly part-time student body. The ruling marks the only instance when a white school has been merged into an HBCU. Suits in Alabama, Louisiana and Mississippi took countless twists and turns from the late 1960s through the '90s. Federal courts handling the suits generally tried to establish unitary standards for admissions, promote racial diversity in faculty hiring and reduce financial disparities. Broader changes were beaten back in at least two instances: the proposed elimination of the governing board for historically black Southern University in Louisiana and the proposed closing of HBCU Mississippi Valley State University. Settlements in some of the suits stipulate that the black public colleges try to increase the percentage of whites in the student body, but the schools have fallen short of the goals — even while giving white applicants preferential admissions or scholarships. Tennessee State, for example, was to increase white enrollment to 50 percent, but whites comprised only 15 percent of the student body in 2001. Mississippi's three black public universities were to become eligible for additional funding if they reached 10 percent white enrollment, but as of 2001 none had. [28]

Historic Buildings Get Little Help

In the years immediately after its founding in 1866, Fisk University was barely able to stay afloat. To raise funds, the Nashville school hit on the idea of sending the grandly named, 11-member Jubilee Singers on a European tour.

The tours — lasting from 1871 to 1878 — helped popularize the African American spiritual and ensure the survival of one of the oldest of the nation's historically black colleges and universities (HBCUs). Some of the money raised was used to build Jubilee Hall, the first permanent structure built expressly for black education in the South and still the centerpiece of the campus.

Despite its historic importance, Jubilee Hall deteriorated over the years — the victim of deferred maintenance by a university perennially low on cash. In spring 2003, however, the building re-emerged with its past glory after a multimillion-dollar renovation financed by a $4 million grant from the federal government and a matching anonymous gift. [1]

Fisk is one of the fortunate few among black universities that have been able to take on major renovations of historic buildings in advanced states of decay or disrepair. In a federal government survey in 1998, HBCUs identified 712 historically significant properties in need of restoration, at a total estimated cost of $755 million. [2] About half were listed in the National Register of Historic Places. [3]

Two years earlier, Congress had signaled an interest in the issue by authorizing $29 million over five years to finance restoration at HBCUs as part of an omnibus National Parks bill. The legislation required colleges to match the federal funds on a 50-50 basis.

Officials at black colleges welcomed the funding but also called it inadequate. "We were quite enthusiastic about the [original] program, but it was never funded at a high enough level," David Swinton, president of Benedict College in South Carolina, remarked in late 2002. [4] Many schools also said the 50-50 match was difficult to meet.

Congress reauthorized the program in 2003 at $10 million per year for seven years. But the Interior Department appropriations bill signed into law that year provided only $3 million. However, the bill does lower the amount colleges must raise on their own to 30 percent.

Bea Smith, former vice president for government affairs at the National Association for Equal Opportunity in Higher Education (NAFEO), says the money will help but still falls short of the need. NAFEO had recommended an initial appropriation of $60 million.

"The needs were so great that we would like a large amount of money," Smith says. "Even at that, it was not going to address all the needs. We're concerned about the deferred maintenance. Many schools have buildings that are very much at risk."

"America's historically black colleges and universities have provided a strong foundation upon which generations of young African Americans have built their lives," says Richard Moe, president of the National Trust for Historic Preservation. "But now, those foundations are deteriorating. We need to take immediate action to preserve not just the historic structures that grace these campuses but also the important legacy of the schools themselves — the dreams they fulfill through the education they provide."

---

[1] For coverage, see Gail Kerr, "Jubilee Hall Renovation Breathes Life Into Fisk," *The* [Nashville] *Tennessean*, Nov. 18, 2002, p. 1B; The Associated Press, "Fisk Receives $4 Million Anonymous Donation to Renovate Historic Buildings," May 4, 2002.

[2] U.S. General Accounting Office, "Historic Preservation: Cost to Restore Historic Properties at Historically Black Colleges and Universities," February 1998 (GAO/RCED-98-51). For background, see Jacqueline Conciatore, "Fighting to Preserve Black History," *Black Issues in Higher Education*, July 20, 2000, p. 18.

[3] Conciatore, *ibid.*

[4] Quoted in Charles Dervarics, "HBCU Preservation Bill Dies in Congress," *Black Issues in Higher Education*, Dec. 19, 2002, p. 6.

The Supreme Court addressed the higher-education desegregation issues only once, in a 1992 decision in the Mississippi desegregation case. In its 8-1 ruling in *United States v. Fordice*, the court held that the adoption of race-neutral policies was not sufficient to dismantle the state's dual system of higher education — five historically white schools and three HBCUs. The justices sent the case back to lower federal courts to consider, among other steps, eliminating duplicative programs or possibly closing one or more of the schools. In a significant concurring opinion, Justice Clarence Thomas, the court's only African American member, stressed that the ruling did not require the closure of historically black schools. "It would be ironic, to say the least, if the institutions that sustained blacks during segregation were themselves destroyed in an effort to combat its vestiges," he wrote. [29]

Debating Quality

The court battles over desegregation played out against a background debate in educational circles over the HBCUs' role and academic quality. The debate was touched off by an article written in 1967 by two Harvard University sociologists sharply criticizing historically black colleges as academically inferior. HBCU supporters said the critique was unfounded — based on anecdotes more than research — and ignored the schools' contributions under adverse circumstances.

The debate has roots in a pedagogical dispute that raged in the late 19th and early 20th centuries between the first two great proponents of black education: Booker T. Washington and W.E.B. DuBois. Washington (1856-1915), who founded Tuskegee Institute in 1880, advocated industrial-arts education for blacks. Vocational training, he argued, was the best way for blacks to improve their lives without unnecessarily confronting the white power establishment. DuBois (1868-1963), a professor at Atlanta University and one of the founders of the NAACP, favored instead a liberal arts education for what he called "the talented tenth" of the black population. He viewed this intellectual elite as the key to blacks' advancement and regarded Washington's philosophy as amounting to acceptance of second-class status. [30]

The disagreement is today widely viewed as more theoretical than concrete and probably mattered less at the time than practical issues of funding, staffing and leadership. As a Department of Education overview relates, much of the instruction being offered at black colleges in the early 20th century was at the elementary or secondary level. [31] The schools were predominantly controlled by white administrators and teaching staffs, many of whom tended to be overly authoritarian toward students and accommodationist toward their local white communities. And — despite support from northern philanthropists — they were woefully underfunded.

Some gains began by the 1920s. Howard got its first black president in 1926. The Southern Association of Colleges and Schools agreed in 1928 to consider accredi-

Morehouse College in Atlanta boasts three Rhodes scholars in recent years, including political science majors Christopher Elders (left), who plans a career in public policy after law school, and Oluwabusayo Folarin, who hopes to work for the United Nations.

tation for black institutions. Despite the Great Depression, enrollment at HBCUs increased by 66 percent during the 1930s — outpacing the 36 percent rise for all colleges — while expenditures more than doubled after adjustment for inflation. And in an important financial development Tuskegee President Frederick D. Patterson called in 1943 for other black college presidents to join in cooperative fundraising. Patterson's initiative resulted in the formation the next year of the United Negro College Fund, with 27 member colleges at the time.

By mid-century, black colleges and universities were still largely invisible to the white educational community, even though they enrolled about 90 percent of all African American higher-education students. The schools drew attention in the 1950s and '60s as some of their students took part in the growing civil rights movement. North Carolina A&T students, for example, mounted the seminal Greensboro sit-in campaign in 1960. But the visibility came at the price of political disfavor and in some instances retaliation. The Louisiana legislature demanded that Southern University expel all students and fire all teachers taking part in the demonstrations. [32]

Unfavorable attention of a different sort came in 1967 when a leading education journal published an article, "The American Negro College," written by two well-regarded Harvard University sociologists: Christopher Jencks and David Riesman. [33] Jencks and Riesman were critical of segregation and insightful and sympathetic toward the black colleges' financial and political difficulties. Still, their central conclusion was that the majority of black colleges were — and were likely to remain — "academically inferior institutions . . . in terms of student aptitudes, faculty creativity and intellectual and moral ferment." They added that they had "the impression" that black colleges "do even less than comparable white colleges to remedy their students' academic inadequacies."

African Americans were "outraged" by the article, according to Marybeth Gasman, an associate professor at the University of Pennsylvania's Graduate School of Education in Philadelphia. They said the article used little research and relied on anecdotes and hearsay, she recalls. Riesman, in fact, told an education conference in 1976 that his views had changed. In a book-length response two years after that, Harvard's Professor Willie insisted Jencks and Riesman had made an unfair comparison to white schools. The real question, Willie wrote, was, "How have black colleges and universities done so much, so well, with so little?" Phasing out black schools, Willie added, "would be an academic disaster." [34]

The controversy spurred efforts to raise the HBCUs' profile and strengthen their finances. The UNCF in 1972 launched a public-awareness campaign with its now-famous slogan, "A mind is a terrible thing to waste." Two years later, the fund staged its first telethon, which evolved in 1979 into Lou Rawls' "Parade of Stars" — now called "An Evening of Stars" and set to mark its 30th anniversary in January 2009. The ongoing desegregation suits sought in part to increase states' financial support for the public black colleges and universities. And in 1986 Congress approved the first general federal-aid program for HBCUs. Title IIIB of the Higher Education Amendments of 1986 authorized $100 million for HBCUs and $5 million for historically black graduate and professional schools.

Researchers in the early 1990s painted a more favorable picture of HBCUs than Jencks and Riesman had done a quarter-century earlier. In a broad study of colleges, researchers Ernest Pascarella and Patrick Terenzini found that black students performed better academically at HBCUs than at white undergraduate schools. Similarly, they found that attendance at HBCUs had a more positive effect on later educational attainment than attendance at a white school. [35] Two professors at histor-

ically black Clark Atlanta University — Julian Roebuck and Komanduri Murty — reported similar findings following a survey of HBCUs. The result, they wrote, was "a growing conviction that HBCUs can best prepare black students for service and leadership roles in the black community." [36]

CURRENT SITUATION

Aiming High

Florida A&M officials were flying high when *Time* magazine designated it as "College of the Year" for the 1997-98 academic year. Five years after capturing the title on the strength of its academics, the nation's largest single-campus black university took aim this summer at another prestigious distinction. It began the expensive process of applying for membership in the NCAA's elite Division I-A of intercollegiate sports.

Suddenly, however, school spirit on the Tallahassee campus has turned from upbeat to downcast amid financial turmoil and high-level administrative buck-passing. The university's financial books are off by $1.8 million. The school needs $1.5 million to pay overdue bills. Students are getting financial aid months late. And the state's financial chief temporarily cut off checks for the university's president and 18 top administrators until they turned over financial records that were six weeks late. "All of this has been a tremendous blow to the university," Jim Corbin, chairman of the school's board of trustees, told the *St. Petersburg Times* in late November. "I don't think there's any excuse for it." [37] Four years later, the school was put on academic probation due to financial mismanagement and other administrative problems.

Florida A&M's fall from academic celebrity to notoriety provides only one example — if one of the most dramatic — of an array of financial and managerial problems besetting several of the nation's historically black colleges and universities in recent years. [38] Three schools — Grambling State University in Louisiana, Talladega University in Alabama and Bennett College, a private women's school in Greensboro, N.C. — learned late in 2003 that the Southern Association of Colleges and Schools had rewarded their efforts to work out years of financial mismanagement by lifting academic probation imposed by the accrediting body in December 2001.

Other schools, however, are facing bearish financial conditions, managerial disorder or both.

To stave off what its trustees called a potential "disaster," Clark Atlanta University decided in 2003 to close five academic programs: the School of Library and Information Studies, the Systems Sciences doctorate program and the departments of Engineering, International Affairs and Development and Allied Health Professions. The effort was aimed at turning the college's $7.5 million deficit into a surplus by summer 2004. However, the school — formed by the 1989 merger of undergraduate Clark College and Atlanta University, then exclusively a graduate institution — was by the summer of 2008 still $25 million in debt and had only a $40 million endowment.

Meanwhile, public HBCUs throughout the South are facing the same budget squeezes plaguing most other state colleges and universities. [39] In Louisiana, Dillard University and Southern University at New Orleans faced the additional challenge of trying to stay in business after Hurricane Katrina left their respective campuses uninhabitable in 2005. "We are the only New Orleans college with no hope of coming back to our campus in the fall," said Victor Ukpolo, Southern's chancellor, in May 2006. But even without a campus, the university continued its work. Some 2,100 of the university's 3,600 students enrolled in the spring 2006 semester at a temporary campus of 400 trailers located just north of the closes campus. [40]

The turmoil at Florida A&M included unsavory finger-pointing between the school's current leaders — Corbin and university president Fred Gainous — and the previous president, Humphries. In his 16 years as president, Humphries gained a reputation for raising funds from big corporations, winning government grants, promoting academic excellence and personally recruiting and befriending students. He prided himself on regularly vying with Harvard for the best record in enrolling African American students designated as National Achievement Scholars. Gainous succeeded to the post after Humphries resigned in 2001 to become president of NAFEO, the association that represents black colleges and universities. Gainous took steps to deal with financial problems by firing some administrators and instituting greater accountability. Today, Corbin says Humphries "left the place in a financial mess," while Humphries

denies any responsibility. "I left no problems for FAMU," he told the *St. Petersburg Times.*

"There still is a lot to be done to move the university forward," Gainous said in late November 2003. "We must get our financial house in order." But Gainous was fired a year later, with auditors finding problems such as no-bid contracts, late payments to vendors and sloppy accounting practices.

Saving Morris Brown

Friends of Morris Brown College are trying to raise millions of dollars to dig the 123-year-old school out of a financial hole, which many blame on unsustainable ambition and inattentive oversight. Today the school is a shell of its previous self, and leading experts on black colleges doubt its ability to survive. "It's going to be a very uphill fight," says Gray, president of the UNCF. "The fiscal mismanagement that apparently occurred there was so deep, so large that I don't know how they're going to overcome it very quickly."

Morris Brown's problems stem primarily from what transition team member Gibbs acknowledges were "errors in judgment" by past administrations. But they also are rooted, to some extent, in the school's governance structure and in its historical mission of serving economically and educationally disadvantaged African American youths.

The college was founded in 1885 by leaders of the African Methodist Episcopal (AME) Church and remains today one of the few black institutions to have been established and operated under African American patronage. The school began by serving a constituency that was "unskilled, untrained, and economically unstable," the college says in an historical overview posted on its Web site. When the civil rights revolution came along in the 1960s, Morris Brown was ahead of other schools — both black and white — in serving disadvantaged youth. [41]

The school's Web site boasts a handful of prominent alumni, including the Rev. Hosea Williams, the late civil rights leader; and James McPherson, the Pulitzer Prize-winning historian of the Civil War. But the college's supporters emphasize above all Morris Brown's continuing commitment to serving students who — as transition team member Watson puts it — "don't test so well" or "sometimes aren't as prepared as they could be or should

Philip Neely/Fisk University

The 2003 academic year for freshmen at Fisk University begins with the fall convocation. Graduation rates are significantly lower for students at HBCUs than for blacks at predominantly white schools.

be." That philosophy translated into an admissions policy that looked beyond an applicant's grades, test scores or ability to pay. [42] Grateful alumni sang the college's praises, but the school lacked the reputation of the other HBCUs that comprise the six-member Atlanta University Center. Morris Brown was the only one of the undergraduate institutions in the consortium that did not make *Black Enterprise* magazine's most recent list of top 50 colleges for African Americans. [43]

The college was also financially challenged. The school faced a possible shutdown in 1993 over a $10 million shortfall, averted only by $7 million in emergency fund-raising and $2 million in budget cuts. The financial squeeze was exacerbated by a series of ambitious moves by Dolores Cross, who served as the college's president from 1998 to 2002. Under Cross, the college increased enrollment, decided to buy laptops for all students, and sought to move into the NCAA's top-ranked Division I-A.

Over the years, the Negro College Fund provided $24 million in aid to the college even though Gray says he warned against some of the policies. "All we can do is give money," Gray told one newspaper as the school faced loss of accreditation in 2002. "I cannot control how it is spent." [44] The fund also approved a special

$1 million donation to Morris Brown in March 2003, as the college was appealing its loss of accreditation.

The Southern Association of Colleges and Schools cited an array of financial issues in placing the school on probation in December 2000. "Concerns were expressed about their financial status, the way they were handling student aid, planning, oversight," explains James Rogers, the association's executive director. "Those are all very serious areas."

Cross resigned in 2003 after an additional disclosure that the college had withdrawn $8 million from a federal student-aid account to pay overdue bills. Cross and CFO Parvesh Singh pled guilty in 2006 to financial aid fraud. After his arrival, Morris Brown's next president, Charles Taylor, estimated the school's debt at $23 million — and then upped it to $27 million. The U.S. Department of Education meanwhile was demanding repayment of $5.4 million in allegedly mishandled student-aid funds.

The school plans to apply for reaccreditation in 2009. Rogers says it is "rare" for a college to regain accreditation. "It is a steep mountain, but there are other institutions that have been able to climb those steep mountains," he says.

OUTLOOK

Changing Times

When Oluwbusayo Folarin graduated from high school in Grand Prairie, Texas, in 2000, he expected to take a year off to travel before enrolling in college. But he changed his plans after Morehouse College flew him all-expenses paid to the historically black Atlanta college for a summer conference with other top-ranking African American students — and then offered him what amounted to a full scholarship.

Four years later, Folarin graduated with a degree in political science and a ticket to Oxford University on a prestigious Rhodes scholarship. Having left Morehouse twice to study at predominantly white campuses — Bates College in Maine and the University of Cape Town in South Africa — Folarin also has no doubts about the quality of his education or the benefits of a predominantly black institution. "Morehouse provides a bubble of empowerment," says Folarin, who grew up with his Nigerian father and American stepmother. "It

Are racially identifiable colleges and universities good for the country?

YES

William H. Gray, III
Former President and CEO, United Negro College Fund

Written for *CQ Researcher*, November 2003

Historically black colleges and universities (HBCUs) play a critical role in American higher education. They produce a disproportionate number of African American baccalaureate recipients and the undergraduate degree-of-origin for a disproportionate share of Ph.D.s to blacks. These institutions perform miracles in elevating disadvantaged youth to productive citizenship. If they did not exist, we would have to invent them.

The landscape of American higher education is composed of a diverse array of institutions, each preserving and strengthening the cultural communities from which they emerged. The role of HBCUs in this commonwealth of cultures is similar to that of Notre Dame for Catholics, Brandeis for Jews, Smith for women and Haskell Indian Nations University for American Indians. These institutions enrich diversity in America by providing access and choice to college-goers.

HBCUs are diverse institutions. Over 13 percent of students at HBCUs are white while fewer than 6 percent of students at white colleges are black. More than 25 percent of faculty at HBCUs are white compared to less than 4 percent of black faculty at white colleges. More than 10 percent of deans and administrators at HBCUs are white compared to 2 percent at white institutions who are black. Many HBCUs recruit white students. In fact, several now have majority-white enrollments, including Bluefield State University (92 percent) and West Virginia State College (86 percent).

The nation's 105 HBCUs are public, private, two-year, four-year and graduate. While HBCUs comprise only 3 percent of the nation's 3,688 institutions of higher learning, they produce 24 percent of all bachelors' degrees. These institutions also account for nine of the top 10 colleges that graduate the most black students who go on to earn Ph.D.s, and four of the top five colleges that produce black medical-school acceptances. Students select HBCUs for their educational excellence, low costs and nurturing environments.

HBCUs have evolved into diverse institutions worthy of public support, just as Catholic, Jewish, Mormon and Methodist colleges have. Yet no one suggests that those religious institutions hurt diversity in public colleges and should be closed.

HBCUs are national treasures. For decades, they have enabled underprivileged students to transition from dependence to independence and have contributed immensely to building a more competitive and skilled America.

NO

Ward Connerly
Chairman, American Civil Rights Institute

Written for *CQ Researcher*, November 2003

The American people have a decision to make. Two different ideals, both popular but mutually exclusive of each other, are at war in our colleges and universities. The first is that racial diversity is an intrinsic good that should be promoted at every opportunity on every campus. This is the position of the federal government, after the Supreme Court ruled last summer that states have a "compelling interest" in fostering diversity. It is also the position of the overwhelming majority of college and university administrations, many of which submitted briefs to the court supporting this ideal. And polls show that a sizable number of Americans agree with them.

But directly opposed to the diversity ideal are historically black colleges and universities (HBCUs). An HBCU's entire reason for being is to not be diverse. Yet Americans support HBCUs as well, understandably so given their historic origins. We show our support by channeling federal funds to HBCUs every year. Here lies the dilemma.

Very few would call for a halt in federal funds to HBCUs, just as very few would like to see publicly funded universities cease to exist. But it is hypocritical to support the public funding of HBCUs and then turn around and criticize a "lack of diversity" at other public colleges and universities, since HBCUs, by their very nature, draw away many black students who would otherwise attend racially mixed schools and affect their "diversity."

Take the University of California, for instance. Although HBCUs tend to be located in the South — not California — many black California students seek out these institutions. These students definitely do not want diversity, and presumably don't think it will add much to their education. They're specifically seeking racial homogeneity.

It seems unfair, then, to immediately blame the UC system or the command in the California Constitution that prohibits racial discrimination or preferences to any UC applicant for any perceived "lack of diversity" in the UC student body. Surely the drain of talented black California students to HBCUs must lessen the numbers of talented black students in the UC system. And those HBCUs are funded, in part, by public dollars.

So before critics condemn the public UC system for a dearth of minorities and charge it with insensitivity, or even worse, racism, those critics should look at other actions our government undertakes that undermine the ideal they hold above all others.

gives people a chance to discover themselves. You have so many schools in the Northeast that are predominantly white and have so few African Americans." Morehouse's mission, he continues, "is not to segregate. Its mission is to empower people who have been historically oppressed. There is still definitely a need for this kind of environment."

Folarin's story illustrates both the continuing appeal of historically black colleges for many African Americans and the intense recruiting efforts by many HBCUs to attract students in a competitive academic marketplace. Enrollment statistics yield a mixed picture of their success. Total enrollment at HBCUs increased about 10 percent during the 1990s, but the 218,000 black students enrolled in 2001 represented only 14 percent of all African Americans in college. And the HBCUs have had only limited success attracting white students: The number of whites attending black colleges declined by about 15 percent over the past decade — from 29,000 in 1991 to 24,000 in 2001. White enrollment continues to slip, but black enrollment at HBCUs has begun to tick back up, reaching 235,000 in 2006.

But recruiting is only one of the many ongoing challenges faced by historically black colleges today. Money is another — and the most pressing in many ways. Tight budgets and limited endowments cramp all of a school's programs and ambitions — even recruiting. Twenty HBCUs signed up to exhibit at the Heartland Black College Expo in Mt. Vernon, Ill., in October 2003, but only four showed up. The rest canceled because of budget constraints. [45]

Money is tight for all higher education institutions, HBCU supporters acknowledge — from public and private sources alike. But black colleges face special problems because of their history. Because most HBCUs have not had a lot of wealthy alumni or friendly corporate executives to give and help raise money, their endowments are sometimes perilously small. "Without some resources deliberately infused into black colleges," Harvard's Willie says, "we're going to lose a few."

Leaders of the two major HBCU organizations, however, are cautiously optimistic. And some of the HBCUs have seen enrollments tick up in recent years and improved their fundraising. In 2008, Howard University announced that it had completed a five-year, $275 million fundraising drive. "It sets the bar, that this kind of success is possible and HBCUs can compete with mainstream institutions," said William F.L. Moses, a senior program director at the Kresge Foundation. "HBCUs can compete with the best." [46]

"Hopefully, as opportunity gets equalized in American society, and we overcome the effects of our past history, then I think you're going to see these schools get stronger," said Gray, the former United Negro College Fund president. Gray acknowledges that some schools "probably will go by the wayside," but quickly adds, "Not because of their blackness but because of market forces."

In 2006, the United Negro College Fund launched the Institute for Capacity Building, a 10-year project designed to aid member HBCUs in areas such as fundraising, enrollment, curriculum and executive leaders. UNCF quickly raised $19 million toward the effort, largely from grants from Kresge and other foundations. [47]

Foster at Virginia Union also predicts that there may be fewer black colleges over time, but, unlike Gray, he welcomes the potential demise of schools among what he calls the bottom tiers of HBCUs. "If these schools are not selective in admissions criteria, are not graduating 75 percent of the students admitted, [and] are almost totally dependent on the federal trough for survival, then there is no need for them," he writes. [48]

For his part, Penn State's Brown sees a need for fundamental changes of a more positive nature — changes that will make the schools attractive to black and white students alike in a post-segregation world.

"We're going to have to reclaim our uniqueness of mission while identifying new niches of opportunity," Brown says. "We have to maintain and reassert this rich intellectual history that was burst out at a time of segregation and that did the yeoman's work of generating a national work force, and now — in the same space but at a different hour of the day — reaffirm that history, but be mindful and responsive to the fact that the segregation hour certainly by law has passed."

NOTES

1. Ernie Suggs, " 'Sense of Being' Paved Path Toward Graduation," *Atlanta Journal-Constitution*, May 10, 2008, p. 1A.

2. For background, see Susan Phillips, "Troubled Times for Black Colleges," *CQ Researcher*, Jan. 7, 1994, p. 15. Historically black colleges and universities are defined in federal law as accredited institutions established before 1964 "whose principal mission was, and is, the education of black Americans." They include colleges in Southern and Border states stretching from Pennsylvania and Ohio to Texas, the District of Columbia and the Virgin Islands. The White House Initiative on Historically Black Colleges and Universities counts the number of HBCUs as 105, the National Association for Equal Opportunity in Higher Education puts the number at 103. The total NAFEO membership of 115 includes some "predominantly black institutions" established after 1964.

3. Darren Dunlap, "Build It Back Up," *Knoxville News-Sentinel*, Feb. 17, 2008, p. 1.

4. "Black Colleges and Universities Show Impressive Endowment Growth," *The Journal of Blacks in Higher Education*, Spring 2008, p. 23.

5. "Educators Tell Congress Historically Black Colleges Are Struggling," *The Jacksonville Free Press*, March 20-March 26, 2008, p. 3.

6. "African Americans Continue to Make Solid Gains in Bachelor and Master Degree Awards," *The Journal of Blacks in Higher Education*, July 1, 2008; available at www.jbhe.com/features/60_degreeawards.html.

7. Roland G. Fryer Jr., and Michael Greenstone, "The Causes and Consequences of Attending Historically Black Colleges and Universities," MIT Department of Economics Working Paper No. 07-12, April 9, 2007.

8. Quoted in "Black, White Performance Gap Widens, Study Finds," *Black Issues in Higher Education*, Nov. 6, 2003, pp. 6-7.

9. Abigail Thernstrom and Stephen Thernstrom, "Separation Anxiety," *The Wall Street Journal*, Nov. 30, 2007.

10. See Spencer S. Hsu, "Va. Support for Black Universities Challenged," *The Washington Post*, June 12, 1998, p. C1; "Va. Appointee Retreats From Comments on Black Schools," *The Washington Post*, June 13, 1998. p. C1. Allen served in the position until July 1999.

11. See Ernest P. Pascarella and Patrick Terenzini, *How College Affects Students: Findings and Insights From Twenty Years of Research* (1992).

12. Julian B. Roebuck and Komanduri S. Murty, *Historically Black Colleges and Universities: Their Place in American Higher Education* (1993).

13. Foster, *op. cit.*, p. 94.

14. See Kenneth C. Green, *Campus Computing Study* (1999). The study, completed in 1999, estimated that 49 percent of students in colleges nationwide personally owned their own computers.

15. U.S. Department of Commerce, National Telecommunications and Information Administration, "Historically Black Colleges and Universities: An Assessment of Networking and Connectivity," October 2000 (http://search.ntia.doc.gov/nafeo.pdf). The earlier study is Kenneth C. Green, Campus Computing Study (1999).

16. For coverage, see Andrea L. Foster, "Playing Catch-Up: A Bill in Congress Could Give Minority Institutions New Money for Computer Technology," *The Chronicle of Higher Education*, June 27, 2003, p. 27. The Senate approved the bill 97-0 on April 30, 2003.

17. Diane Dole, "The Crossroads of History: America's Best Black Colleges," *U.S. News & World Report*, Sept. 28, 2007.

18. Figures from the Center for Higher Education and Educational Finance at Illinois State University cited in "Jim Crow Entrenched: Unequal Funding of State-Operated Colleges in the South," *The Journal of Blacks in Higher Education*, Spring 2002, p. 9.

19. James T. Minor, "Contemporary HBCUs: Considering Institutional Capacity and State Priorities: A Research Report," Michigan State University, 2008.

20. Background drawn from M. Christopher Brown II, *The Quest to Define Collegiate Desegregation: Black Colleges, Title VI Compliance, and Post-ADAMS Litigation* (1999); Julian B. Roebuck and Komanduri S. Murty, *Historically Black Colleges and Universities: Their Place in American Higher Education* (1993). See also Norman Anthony Meyer, "Historically Black Colleges and Universities: A

Legacy of African American Educational Achievement," master's thesis, School for Summer and Continuing Education, Georgetown University, 1991 (thesis 6120, Georgetown University Libraries).

21. The citation is 211 U.S. 405 (1908).

22. John Sekora, "Murder Relentless and Impassive: The American Academic Community and the Negro College," *Soundings*, Vol. 51 (spring 1968), p. 259, cited in Meyer, *op. cit.*, p. 22.

23. See Joan Biskupic and Elder Witt, *Congressional Quarterly's Guide to the U.S. Supreme Court* (3d ed.), 1997, p. 631. The cases are *Missouri ex rel Gaines v. Canada*, 305 U.S. 337 (1938); *Sweatt v. Painter*, 339 U.S. 629 (1950) (Texas); and *McLaurin v. Oklahoma State Regents for Higher Education*, 339 U.S. 637 (1950).

24. The case is *Florida ex rel. Hawkins v. Board of Control of Florida*, 350 U.S. 413 (1956).

25. See *Brown, op. cit.*, pp. 22-23.

26. *Ibid.*, pp. 23-28; see also Roebuck & Murty, *op. cit.*, pp. 45-47. The two principal court rulings are *Adams v. Richardson*, 356 F.Supp. 92 (D.C. Circ. 1973), and *Adams v. Bennett*, 676 F.Supp. 668 (D.C. Cir. 1987).

27. See *Brown, op. cit.*, pp. 29-53.

28. See Janita Poe, "Traditional Black Colleges Struggle to Create Diversity While Preserving Proud Histories," *Atlanta Journal-Constitution*, Nov. 4, 2001, p. 1A; Jeffrey Gettleman, "New Era for Mississippi's Black Colleges," *Los Angeles Times*, May 1, 2001, p. 1A.

29. See *United States v. Fordice*, 505 U.S. 717 (1992). Justice Byron R. White wrote the court's opinion; Justice Antonin Scalia dissented.

30. See Roebuck & Murty, *op. cit.*, pp. 30-31.

31. National Center for Education Statistics, "Historically Black Colleges and Universities, 1976-90," July 1992 (NCES 92-640).

32. See Sekora, *op. cit.*

33. Christopher Jencks and David Riesman, "The American Negro College," *Harvard Educational Review*, Vol. 37, No. 1 (1967), pp. 3-60. The article

was published as a chapter in their book *The Academic Revolution* (1968).

34. Charles V. Willie and Ronald R. Edmonds (eds.), *Black Colleges in America: Challenge, Development, Survival* (1978), p. xi.

35. Pascarella and Terenzini, *op. cit.*

36. Roebuck & Murty, *op. cit.*, p. 202.

37. Anita Kumar, "Financial Turmoil Racks FAMU," *St. Petersburg Times*, Nov. 30, 2003. Other background and quotes also drawn from article. For "College of the Year" designation, see *Time/The Princeton Review*, "The Best College for You and How to Get In," 1998 edition, p. 76.

38. For compilation of news coverage of historically black colleges and universities, see The HBCU Network (www.hbcunetwork.com: click on "About Our Schools."

39. For background, see William Triplett, "State Budget Crisis," *CQ Researcher*, Oct. 3, 2003, pp. 821-844.

40. Katherine Mangan, "Still Without a Campus, Southern U. at New Orleans Struggles to Stay in Business," *The Chronicle of Higher Education*, May 26, 2006, p. 31.

41. "College Information — History," www.morris-brown.edu (visited December 2003).

42. Some background drawn from Audrey Williams June, "Endangered Institutions," *The Chronicle of Higher Education*, Jan. 17, 2003.

43. Sonya A. Donalds, "50 Best Colleges and Universities for African Americans," *Black Enterprise*, January 2003, p. 76. Morris Brown did rank 32nd in the magazine's 1999 list.

44. Gray's statement to the *New York Daily News* is quoted in June, *op. cit.*

45. Gregory R. Norfleet, "Students at Black College Expo Experience Budget Cuts Firsthand," *The Register-News*, Oct. 20, 2003.

46. Kathryn Masterson, "Howard U. Assembles Fundraising Juggernaut," *The Chronicle of Higher Education*, June 27, 2008, p. 1.

47. Reginald Stuart, "A Decade of Turbulence," *The Crisis*, Sept. 1007-Oct. 2007, p. 15.

48. Foster, *op. cit.*, p. 24.

BIBLIOGRAPHY

Books

Brown, M. Christopher II, *The Quest to Define Collegiate Desegregation: Black Colleges, Title VI Compliance, and Post- ADAMS Litigation,* **Bergin & Garvey, 1999.**
Chronicles history of litigation to desegregate public higher education, concluding by arguing against efforts to eliminate "racially identifiable" institutions. Includes four-page list of cases, 17-page bibliography. Brown is a professor of education at Pennsylvania State University on leave in fall 2003 at the Frederick D. Patterson Research Institute, the research arm of the United Negro College Fund. For a more recent title, see M. Christopher Brown II and Kassie Freeman, *Black Colleges: New Perspectives on Policy and Practice* (Praeger, 2003).

Bullock, Henry Allen, *A History of Negro Education in the South: From 1619 to the Present,* **Harvard University Press, 1967.**
Comprehensive history of the education of African Americans in the South from Colonial era through the abolition of slavery and the early years of the civil rights revolution; originally published in 1934 and reissued in 1967. Bullock taught at several HBCUs before becoming the first black professor at the University of Texas in Austin in 1969; he died in 1973.

Foster, Gerald A., *Is There a Conspiracy to Keep Black Colleges Open?* **Kendall/Hunt, 2001.**
Strongly argues that many historically black colleges and universities (HBCUs) are academically mediocre and no longer needed. Foster, an African American, is a professor of social work at his alma mater, historically black Virginia Union University.

Garibaldi, Antoine M. (ed.), *Black Colleges and Universities: Challenges for the Future,* **Praeger, 1984.**
Sixteen contributors examine issues such as challenges faced by underfinanced private schools and by public schools on account of desegregation. Garibaldi held chief academic positions at two HBCUs — Xavier and Howard — before his current position as president of Gannon University.

Roebuck, Julian B., and Komanduri S. Murty, *Historically Black Colleges and Universities: Their Place in American Higher Education,* **Praeger, 1993.**
Survey reports positive features of HBCUs for black students along with some criticisms of "authoritarian" administrators and unfavorable climate for white students and faculty; also includes good historical overview, individual profiles of schools and 10-page list of references. Roebuck is professor emeritus and Murty professor at Clark Atlanta University.

Articles

"African American College Graduation Rates: Intolerably Low, and Not Catching Up to Whites," *The Journal of Blacks in Higher Education,* **autumn 2002, pp. 89-102.**
Special report calls black students' graduation rates "dismally low" and shows figures for many HBCUs, both public and private, well below 50 percent.

"Jim Crow Entrenched: Unequal Funding of State-Operated Colleges in the South," *The Journal of Blacks in Higher Education,* **Spring 2002, pp. 8-10.**
Shows that public HBCUs in nine Southern and Border states receive substantially less in state funds than white institutions.

Donalds, Sonya, "50 Best Colleges and Universities for African Americans," *Black Enterprise,* **January 2003, p. 76.**
Annual survey lists many HBCUs as among the best colleges or universities for African Americans.

Maxwell, Bill, " 'We're In This Struggle Together,' " *St. Petersburg Times,* **Sept. 21, 2003, p. 1D.**
Excellent overview of current conditions and problems of historically black colleges and universities.

Poe, Janita, "Traditional Black Colleges Struggle to Create Diversity While Preserving Proud Histories," *The Atlanta Journal and Constitution,* **Nov. 4, 2001, p. 1A.**
Relates efforts by black public colleges to attract white students.

Schmidt, Peter, "Colleges Seek Key to Success of Black Men in Classroom," *Chronicle of Higher Education*, Oct. 10, 2008, p. 1.

The article surveys efforts at various institutions, including the University System of Georgia and the City University of New York, to help black men succeed in college.

Stuart, Reginald, "A Decade of Turbulence," The Crisis, Sept. 2007-Oct. 2007, p. 15.

The article outlines the many financial and academic hardships afflicting HBCUs, while noting their attempts to build capacity and continue their historic mission of educating underserved populations.

Thernstrom, Abigail, and Stephen Thernstrom, "Separation Anxiety," *The Wall Street Journal*, Nov. 30, 2007.

The husband-and-wife authors of America in Black and White note that options for African American students certainly are no longer limited to HBCUs, but argue that such colleges still serve a useful purpose by producing disproportionate numbers of black graduates.

Reports and Studies

Fryer, Roland G. Jr., and Michael Greenstone, "The Causes and Consequences of Attending Historically Black Colleges and Universities," MIT Department of Economics Working Paper No. 07-12, April 9, 2007.

The Harvard and MIT economists conclude that by the 1990s the traditional advantages HBCUs offered blacks in terms of graduation rates and income after college had declined.

Minor, James T., "Contemporary HBCUs: Considering Institutional Capacity and State Priorities: A Research Report," Michigan State University, 2008.

The education professor finds that four southern states underfund their HBCUs, compared with predominantly white public institutions.

U.S. Department of Commerce, National Telecommunications and Information Administration, "Historically Black Colleges and Universities: An Assessment of Networking and Connectivity," October 2000.

Most HBCUs responding to a government survey estimate that fewer than one-fourth of their students own personal computers.

U.S. General Accounting Office, "Historic Preservation: Cost to Restore Historic Properties at Historically Black Colleges and Universities," February 1998 (GAO/RCED-98-51).

Survey of HBCUs identifies 712 historically significant properties needing restoration estimated to cost $755 million.

Web Sites

Both major organizations representing HBCUs maintain Web sites with useful information and links. For the National Association for Equal Opportunity in Higher Education, see www.nafeo.org. For the United Negro College Fund, see www.uncf.org. In addition, the HBCU Network serves as a general resource for HBCUs. See www.HBCUNetwork.com.

For More Information

American Civil Rights Institute, P.O. Box 188350, Sacramento, CA 95818; (916) 444-2278; www.acri.org. A national organization opposed to racial and gender preferences.

Center for Equal Opportunity, 7700 Leesburg Pike, Suite 231, Falls Church, VA 22043; (703) 442-0066; www.ceousa.org. A think tank opposed to racially conscious public policies in education and immigration.

National Association for Equal Opportunity in Higher Education, 209 Third Street, SE, Washington, DC 20003; (202) 552-3300; www.nafeo.org. Represents historically black colleges and universities, both public and private.

United Negro College Fund, 8260 Willow Oaks Corporate Dr., Fairfax, VA 22031; (703) 205-3400; www.uncf.org. Raises funds for 39 private black colleges and universities.

White House Initiative on Historically Black Colleges and Universities, 1900 K St., N.W., 8th floor, Washington, DC 20006; (202) 502-7900; www.ed.gov/about/inits/list/whh-bcu/edlite-index.html. Launched by President Ronald Reagan in 1981 to strengthen HBCUs.

5

Racial Diversity in Public Schools

Kenneth Jost

White enrollment at Seattle's Ballard High School is above previous guidelines five years after a racial-diversity plan was suspended because of a legal challenge. The Supreme Court's June 28 decision invalidating racial-balance plans in Seattle and Louisville, Ky., bars school districts from using race for student-placement decisions but may permit some race-conscious policies to promote diversity.

From *CQ Researcher*, September 14, 2007.

Hannah MacNeal's parents were glad to learn of an opening at the popular magnet elementary school near their upscale neighborhood in eastern Louisville, Ky. When they applied in mid-August for Hannah to enroll as a fourth-grader at Greathouse/Shryock Elementary, however, school system officials said she could not be admitted.

The reason: Hannah is white.

Only six weeks earlier, the U.S. Supreme Court had ruled that Jefferson County Public Schools (JCPS) — which includes Louisville — was violating the Constitution by assigning students to schools on the basis of their race.

Hannah's stepmother, Dana MacNeal, was surprised and upset when she learned Hannah would have been admitted to the school if she had been black. And she was all the more upset when JCPS Student Placement Director Pat Todd insisted on Aug. 14 that the Supreme Court ruling allowed the school system to continue maintaining separate attendance zones for black and white students for Greathouse/Shryock and two of the system's other three magnet elementary schools.

The school system's lawyers were surprised as well to learn of the policy. After the MacNeals decided to fight the decision keeping Hannah in her regular elementary school, officials agreed to enroll her at Greathouse/Shryock and scrap the racially separate boundary zones beginning in 2008. [1]

"Of course, they backed off from the position, knowing they were wrong," says Louisville attorney Ted Gordon, who represented the MacNeals in the latest round in his long-running battle to overturn Jefferson County's school racial-diversity policies. "They have to follow the law."

School Racial-Balance Plans in Louisville and Seattle

The Supreme Court's June 28, 2007, ruling on the school racial-diversity plans in Seattle and Jefferson County (Louisville) bars the use of racial classifications in individual pupil assignments but appears to permit some "race-neutral" policies aimed at racial diversity.

Jefferson County (Louisville) (98,000 students; 35 percent African American)

History: County was racially segregated before *Brown v. Board of Education* ruling; court-ordered desegregation plan in 1975 called for crosstown busing between predominantly African American West End and mainly white neighborhoods in eastern suburbs; court order dissolved in 2000; school board adopts pupil-assignment plan with use of racial classifications to promote diversity; assignment plan still in effect after Supreme Court decision, pending new plan expected for 2009-2010 academic year.

Details: Plan classifies students as "black" or "white" (including Asians, Hispanics and others); guidelines call for each elementary, middle or high school to have between 15 percent and 50 percent African American enrollment; residence-based system assigns students to school within residential "cluster"; most West End neighborhoods assigned to schools outside area; student applications for transfer from assigned school evaluated on basis of several factors, including effect on racial makeup; under Supreme Court decision, individual transfer requests will no longer be denied on basis of race.

Seattle (45,000 students: 58 percent "non-white")

History: No history of mandatory segregation, but racially identifiable neighborhoods: predominantly black south of downtown, predominantly white to the north; racial-balance plan with crosstown busing voluntarily adopted in 1978; school choice introduced in 1990s, with race as one "tiebreaker" to distribute students among oversubscribed schools; school board suspended the plan in 2002 because of legal challenge; Supreme Court ruling held plan invalid.

Details: Ninth-graders permitted to apply to up to three of district's 10 high schools; tiebreakers used for applications to oversubscribed schools; sibling preference was most important factor, race second; race used if school's enrollment deviated by specified percentage from overall racial demographics: 40 percent white, 60 percent non-white.

The Supreme Court's fractured ruling struck down pupil-assignment policies adopted in 2000 limiting African American enrollment at any individual school in Jefferson County to between 15 percent and 50 percent of the student body. The ruling also rejected the Seattle school system's use of race as a "tiebreaker" for assigning students to high schools; the plan had been suspended in 2002 because of the litigation. [2] (*See box, p. 98.*)

In response to the MacNeals' case, Todd's office drew up new boundary zones for the four magnet elementary schools that were approved by the school board on Sept. 10. For the longer term, officials are trying to find ways to maintain a measure of racial balance in the 98,000-student school system under the Supreme Court decision, which bars the use of racial classifications in individual pupil assignments but appears to permit some "race-neutral" policies aimed at racial diversity. (*See box, p. 99.*)

"We are going to do our best to achieve it," says JCPS Superintendent Sheldon Berman. "We are deeply committed to retaining the qualities of an integrated environment."

The court's June 28 decision dealt a blow to hundreds of school systems around the country that have adopted voluntary race-mixing plans after court-ordered desegregation plans lapsed in recent years.

Five of the justices — led by Chief Justice John G. Roberts Jr. — said using racial classifications in pupil assignments violated the Equal Protection Clause of the 14th Amendment. That is the same provision the court cited a half-century earlier in the famous *Brown v. Board of Education* (1954) ruling that found racial segregation in public schools unconstitutional. [3]

In a strong dissent, the court's four liberal justices — led by Stephen G. Breyer — said the ruling contradicted previous decisions upholding race-based pupil assignments and would hamper local school boards' efforts to prevent "resegregation" in individual schools. But one of the justices in the majority — Anthony M. Kennedy — joined the liberal minority in endorsing racial diversity as a legitimate goal. Kennedy listed several "race-neutral" policies, such as drawing attendance zones or building new schools to include students from different racial neighborhoods, that schools could adopt to pursue the goal.

The ruling drew sharp criticism from traditional civil rights advocates. "It's preposterous to think the 14th Amendment was designed to permit individual white parents to strike down a plan to help minority students have better access to schools and to prevent school districts from having integrated schools that are supported by a majority of the community," says Gary Orfield, a long-time civil rights advocate and director of the Civil Rights Project at UCLA's Graduate School of Education and Information Sciences.

Ted Shaw, president of the NAACP Legal Defense Fund, said the ruling blocks school boards from using "one of the few tools that are available" to create racially diverse schools. "The court has taken a significant step away from the promise of *Brown*," says Shaw. "And this comes on top of the reality that many school districts are highly segregated by race already."

Conservative critics of race-based school policies, however, applauded the ruling. "I don't think school districts should be drawing attendance zones or building schools for the purpose of achieving a politically correct racial mix," says Roger Clegg, president of the Center for Equal Opportunity, which joined in a

Racial Classifications Barred But Diversity Backed

The Supreme Court's June 28 decision in *Parents Involved in Community Schools v. Seattle School District No. 1* invalidating pupil-assignment plans in Seattle and Louisville bars school systems from assigning individual students to schools based on their race. In a partial concurrence, however, Justice Anthony M. Kennedy joined with the four dissenters in finding racial diversity to be a legitimate government interest and in permitting some race-conscious policies to achieve that goal.

Roberts (plurality opinion)

Scalia   Thomas   Alito

"Racial balancing is not transformed from 'patently unconstitutional' to a compelling state interest simply by relabeling it 'racial diversity.' "

Kennedy (concurring in part)

". . . [A] district may consider it a compelling interest to achieve a diverse student body. Race may be one component of that diversity. . . . What the government is not permitted to do . . . is to classify every student on the basis of race and to assign each of them to schools based on that classification."

Breyer (dissenting)

Stevens   Souter   Ginsburg

"The plurality . . . undermines [*Brown v. Board of Education*'s] promise of integrated primary and secondary education that local communities have sought to make a reality. This cannot be justified in the name of the Equal Protection Clause."

Credits: AFP/Getty Images/Paul J. Richards (Alito, Kennedy, Roberts, Souter, Scalia, Thomas); Getty Images/Mark Wilson (Ginsburg, Stevens); AFP/Getty Images/ Brendan Smialowski (Breyer)

friend-of-the-court brief supporting the white families that challenged the Seattle and Louisville school policies.

"A lot of parents out there don't like it when their students are treated differently because of race or ethnicity," Clegg adds. "After these decisions, the odds favor those

Southern Schools Least Segregated, But Slipping

Schools in the South were the least segregated in the nation in the 1970s and '80s, a distinction they maintained in the 2005 school year. But Southern schools have been resegregating steadily since 1988.

Change in Black Segregation in Southern Schools, 1954-2005

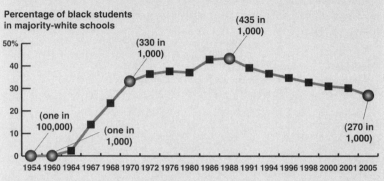

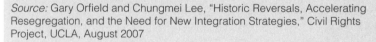

Source: Gary Orfield and Chungmei Lee, "Historic Reversals, Accelerating Resegregation, and the Need for New Integration Strategies," Civil Rights Project, UCLA, August 2007

parents and those organizations that oppose school boards that practice racial or ethnic discrimination."

School officials in Louisville and Seattle and around the country are generally promising to continue race-mixing policies within the limits of the court's decision. "School boards are going to have to do the hard work to find more tailored ways of approaching diversity in their schools," says Francisco Negrón, general counsel of the National School Boards Association.

The evidence in Louisville and nationally suggests, however, that the goal will be hard to achieve. In Louisville, nine schools are now outside the district's 15/50 guidelines, with several having more than 55 percent African American enrollment, according to Todd. "If the board wants to continue to maintain diversity, we've already had some significant slippage at some selected schools," he says. [4]

Nationally, a new report by the UCLA Civil Rights Project concludes that African American and Latino students are increasingly isolated from white students in public schools. Overall, nearly three-fourths of African American students and slightly over three-fourths of Latino students attend predominantly minority schools. Both figures have been increasing since 1980, the report says. [5] (*See graphs, p. 101.*)

Critics of race-based pupil assignments are unfazed by the trends. "We're past guidelines, we're past quotas and we need to move on," says Gordon of the Louisville statistics. He calls instead for an array of reforms focused on schools with high concentrations of low-income students.

"All other things being equal, I like racially diverse schools," says Abigail Thernstrom, a senior fellow at the conservative Manhattan Institute and a former member of the Massachusetts Board of Education. "But I do not think it works from any angle to have government entities — whether they are federal courts or local school boards — try to engineer diversity."

Supporters of racial-balance plans argue that diversity in the classroom helps boost academic achievement for minority students without adversely affecting achievement for white students. Opponents dispute those claims. (*See sidebar, p. 111.*)

The debate over diversity also highlights a secondary dispute over the widespread practice of "tracking" — the offering of separate courses for students based on ability or previous achievement. Supporters say the practice matches curriculum to students' needs and abilities, but critics say it results in consigning already disadvantaged students — including a disproportionate number of African Americans — to poor-quality education. (*See sidebar, p. 108.*)

Meanwhile, some experts and advocates are calling for shifting the focus away from race and instead trying to promote socioeconomic integration — mixing low-income and middle- and upper-class students. Richard Kahlenberg, a senior fellow with the left-of-center Century Foundation who is most closely associated with the movement, says policies aimed at preventing high concentrations of low-income students will produce academic gains along with likely gains in racial and ethnic diversity.

"Providing all students with the chance to attend mixed-income schools can raise overall levels of achievement," Kahlenberg writes in a report released on the day of the Supreme Court decision. [6]

White Students Are Racially Isolated

Segregation remained high in 2005-06 for all racial groups except Asians. White students remained the most racially isolated, although they attended schools with slightly more minority students than in the past. The average white student attended schools in which 77 percent of their peers were white. Meanwhile, more than half of black and Latino students' peers were black or Latino, and fewer than one-third of their classmates were white.

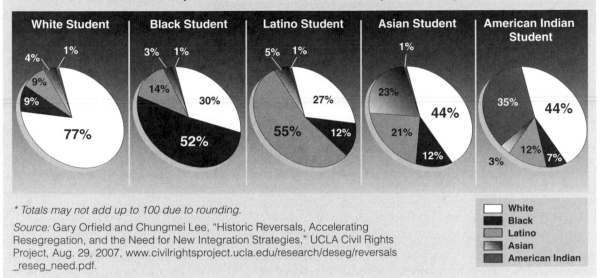

Racial Composition of Schools Attended by the Average . . .

White Student — 77%, 9%, 9%, 4%, 1%
Black Student — 52%, 30%, 14%, 3%, 1%
Latino Student — 55%, 27%, 12%, 5%, 1%
Asian Student — 44%, 23%, 21%, 12%, 1%
American Indian Student — 44%, 35%, 12%, 7%, 3%

Legend: White, Black, Latino, Asian, American Indian

* Totals may not add up to 100 due to rounding.

Source: Gary Orfield and Chungmei Lee, "Historic Reversals, Accelerating Resegregation, and the Need for New Integration Strategies," UCLA Civil Rights Project, Aug. 29, 2007, www.civilrightsproject.ucla.edu/research/deseg/reversals _reseg_need.pdf.

As the debate over diversity in public-school classrooms continues, here are the major questions being considered:

Should school systems promote racial diversity in individual schools?

School officials in Lynn, Mass., a former mill town 10 miles northeast of Boston, take pride in a pupil-assignment system that has helped maintain racial balance in most schools even as the town's Hispanic population has steadily increased over the past decade. "We work very hard to promote integration and cultural diversity so that our children are able to get along with each other," says Jan Birchenough, the administrator in charge of compliance with the state's racial-balance law.

But attorney Chester Darling says Lynn's policy of denying any transfer requests that would increase racial imbalance at an individual school "falls squarely within" the kinds of plans prohibited by the Supreme Court decision in the Louisville and Seattle cases. "It

can't be race-neutral if you use the word race," says Darling, who is asking a federal judge in Boston to reopen a previously unsuccessful suit filed by parents challenging the policy. [7]

Critics of race-based assignment plans hope the Supreme Court decision will persuade or force school districts like Lynn's to drop any use of racial classifications in pupil placement. "Most school districts will look at the decision's bottom line, will consider that the Louisville and Seattle plans were not sloppily done, and yet at the end of the day were declared unconstitutional," says Clegg of the Center for Equal Opportunity. "This cost the school boards a lot of time and money, and they're going to have to pay the other side's lawyer."

But school board officials say the court's fractured ruling leaves room for local systems to consider race in trying to create racial and ethnic mixing in individual schools. "Race is still not out of the question," says Negrón of the school boards' association. "A plurality of

Non-Racial Approaches to Integration

Some 40 school districts around the country are seeking to diversify enrollment in individual schools through socioeconomic integration — typically, by setting guidelines for the percentage of students eligible for free or reduced-price lunch. Here are some of the districts taking such approaches, as drawn from a report by the Century Foundation's Richard Kahlenberg, a strong advocate of the policies.

School District *Enrollment: Percentage of whites (W), African-Americans (B), Hispanics (H), Asian-Americans (A)*

Berkeley, Calif. (*9,000: 31% W, 29% B, 17% H, 8% A*)
Socioeconomic and racial diversity guidelines were adopted in 2004 to replace a voluntary racial-integration plan; plan being phased-in one grade at a time; in 2005-06, eight of 11 elementary schools were within 15% of the districtwide average of 40% of students receiving subsidized lunches; most parents (71%) still receive first choice of schools.

Brandywine, Del. (*11,000: 54% W, 39% B, 3% H, 4% A*)
The district — comprising parts of Wilmington and surrounding suburbs — was granted an exception in 2001 by state Board of Education to law mandating neighborhood schools; plan limits subsidized-lunch enrollment to between 16% and 73%; plan credited with maintaining racial diversity; some evidence of academic gains in higher grades.

Cambridge, Mass. (*6,000: 37% B, 35% W, 15% H, 11% A*)
Plan adopted in 2001 to replace race-conscious "controlled choice" system says individual schools should be within 15 percentage points of districtwide percentage of free/reduced lunch students; race remains a potential factor in assignments; racial diversity maintained, socioeconomic diversity increased; limited evidence finds academic gains for low-income students, no negative effect on middle-income students.

Charlotte-Mecklenburg, N.C. (*129,000: 42% B, 36% W, 14% H, 4% A*)
School board dropped racial-desegregation effort, adopted public school choice plan after school system was declared "unitary" in 2001, or no longer a dual system based on race; plan gives some priority to low-income students in schools with concentrated poverty, but transfers to higher-performing schools are permitted only if seats are available; plan seen as unsuccessful in creating racial or socioeconomic integration.

La Crosse, Wis. (*7,000: 20% minority*)
Was first district to adopt socioeconomic integration policy in 1991-92 in response to influx of Hmong refugees; plan used redrawn attendance zones and busing to spread low-income students among elementary schools and two high schools; plan largely survived political battle in 1992-93 that included recall of several school board members; plan touted as success, but enrollments at most elementary schools have been and still are outside guidelines.

Apart from the legal issue, supporters and opponents of racial-diversity plans also disagree on their educational and other effects. "There's a consensus in the academic world that there are clear educational benefits, and the benefits aren't just for minority students," says UCLA Professor Orfield.

Conversely, "racial isolation leads to reduced achievement," says Negrón.

Critics of racial-diversity policies, however, say those benefits are unproven and the logic of the claimed cause-effect relationship unconvincing. "There is very little empirical evidence," says Thernstrom, the Manhattan Institute fellow.

"I don't think how well you learn or what you learn depends on the color of the skin of the person sitting next to you," says Clegg. "Students in overwhelmingly white schoolrooms in Idaho and in overwhelmingly African American classrooms in Washington, D.C., can each learn."

Critics cite as one concrete disadvantage the time spent on buses when students are transported out of their neighborhoods for the sake of racial balance. "There's no educational benefit there, and it's a waste of their very precious time," says Thernstrom. The travel burdens also hamper student participation in extracurricular activities and parental involvement, the critics say.

In traditional desegregation plans, those burdens typically fell for the most part on African American students, who were transported out of their neighborhoods to schools in predominantly white areas. Busing was "usually a one-way street" for African Americans, says James Anderson, head of the department of educational-policy studies at the University of Illinois, Champaign-Urbana.

the court said certain things that are not the law of the land. What the majority has done is invalidate these particular programs, but certainly left the door wide open to the use of race — which continues to be a compelling government interest."

In recent years, however, school-choice policies in some communities have meant increased busing for whites as well as minority students. Negrón cites the example of Pinellas County (Clearwater), Fla., which has a universal-choice program allowing students to enroll in any school in the county and providing transportation if requested. "It is a cost," Negrón says. "But school districts are finding that it depends on the facts and circumstances."

Civil rights advocates counter that racial isolation imposes much more serious costs for minority students. "The consequences of segregation of African American students in public schools — and it is increasingly true for Latino students — have been concentration of poverty, deprivation of resources and a host of other problems that do impact on the quality of education," says the Legal Defense Fund's Shaw.

Like many of the critics, Thernstrom stops short of absolute opposition to any race-conscious school policies. "I don't mind" redrawing attendance zones for racial mixing, she says, "but I don't think we should be starry-eyed about what it's going to achieve."

Michael Rosman, president of the Center for Individual Rights, says schools should try to prevent "racial isolation" in individual schools "if it is shown to have deleterious educational effects."

But Illinois Professor Anderson says school boards should take affirmative steps to "take advantage" of diversity. "We could build wonderful, intellectually rich environments where kids really do have an exchange of ideas and an exchange of cultures and come out of that with a cos-

mopolitan sense of culture that is unique," he says. "How can you be global," he adds, "yet at the same time so parochial?"

School District *Enrollment: Percentage of whites (W), African-Americans (B), Hispanics (H), Asian-Americans (A)*

Manatee County, Fla. (*42,000: 60% W, 20% H, 15% B, 4% other*)
District south of Tampa Bay has had limited success with a plan adopted in 2002 admitting students to schools based on maintaining socioeconomic balance: Only 10 elementary schools were within guidelines in 2005-06; among 14 schools with above-average low-income enrollment, only four showed adequate academic gains.

McKinney, Tex. (*20,000: 64% W, 21% H, 11% B, 3% other*)
Dallas suburb adopted socioeconomic-balance policy in 1995 by redrawing attendance zones; low-income students perform better on statewide tests than low-income students statewide; some opposition to longer bus rides, but plan said to have broad support.

Minneapolis, Minn. (*36,000: 41% B, 28% W, 16% H, 10% A*)
Desegregation suit settled in state court in 2000 with agreement to adopt four-year experiment to encourage socioeconomic integration; plan provides transportation for low-income students to suburban schools; also requires wealthier magnet schools in Minneapolis to set aside seats for low-income students; 2,000 low-income students attended suburban schools over four-year period; legislature voted to extend program after end of experiment.

Omaha, Neb. (*47,000: 44% W, 32% B, 21% H*)
School board adopted plan aimed at socioeconomic integration after system was declared unitary in 1999; low-income students given preference in weighted lottery for admission to magnet schools; 2006 proposal to expand plan to recently annexed neighborhoods prompted backlash in state legislature, but education groups won passage of 2007 bill to establish goal of socioeconomic diversity throughout metropolitan area.

Rochester, N.Y. (*33,000: 64% B, 22% H, 13% W*)
Managed-choice plan adopted in city in 2002 includes socioeconomic-fairness guidelines; vast majority of elementary school students (83%) are economically disadvantaged; plan seen as likely to have limited effect unless interdistrict choice program is established between city and suburbs.

San Francisco (*55,000: 32% Asian, 22% H, 13% B, 9% W*)
Student-assignment plan adopted in 2001 replaced racial-desegregation scheme with plan aimed at socioeconomic diversity; seven-part definition includes SES (socioeconomic status), academic achievement, language, other factors; plan seen as fairly successful in balancing schools by SES, less so in producing racial diversity; district is consistently top-performing urban district in state.

Wake County (Raleigh), N.C. (*136,000: 54% W, 27% B, 10% H, 5% A*)
Guidelines adopted in 2000 replacing racial guidelines limit schools to 40% free/reduced lunch, 25% reading below grade level; policies credited with maintaining racial diversity; role in academic gains questioned; school-zone changes due to growth draw criticism from some families.

Sources: Richard D. Kahlenberg, Century Foundation, "Rescuing *Brown v. Board of Education*: Profiles of Twelve School Districts Pursuing Socioeconomic School Integration," Century Foundation, June 28, 2007, www.tcf.org; news accounts.

Should school systems seek to promote socioeconomic integration in individual schools?

The consolidated school system in Wake County, N.C. — encompassing the rapidly growing Research Triangle Park area (near Raleigh and Durham) — made nationwide news in 2000 by dropping the use of racial guidelines in favor of socioeconomic-integration policies. The "Healthy School" assignment guidelines call for limiting individual schools to no more than 40 percent enrollment of students receiving free or reduced-price lunches or 25 percent enrollment of students performing below grade level.

Seven years later, the policies are a bragging point for the school system and exhibit No. 1 for advocates of socioeconomic integration. "Classrooms that are balanced from a diversity point of view are important to maintaining academic performance," says Michael Evans, the school system's communications director, citing the district's declining achievement gap for African American, Hispanic and low-income students.

Some Wake County parents are not sold, however. Dave Duncan, the one-time president of the now largely inactive advocacy group Assignment by Choice, discounts the claimed academic gains by pointing to the relatively small percentage of students assigned under the guidelines and the comparable academic gains statewide. The school system "used the diversity issue as a smoke screen when there is criticism or opposition to the way they do the student-assignment process," Duncan says.

As the most prominent advocate of socioeconomic integration, the Century Foundation's Kahlenberg acknowledges varied results in districts with such policies. But he strongly argues that the policy of mixing students by socioeconomic background offers educational benefits in its own right and practical advantages for districts trying to promote racial diversity without running afoul of the Supreme Court's new limits on race-based assignments.

"There's a wide body of research that the single, best thing you can do for low-income kids is to give them the opportunity to attend a middle-class school," says Kahlenberg. Despite some well-publicized exceptions, schools with "concentrated levels of poverty" tend to have more student-discipline problems, lower caliber teachers and principals and less parental involvement than predominantly middle- or upper-class schools, he explains. Socioeconomic integration, he says, results in higher academic achievement for low-income students

and no adverse effect on others as long as there is "a strong core of students with middle-class background."

Kahlenberg says socioeconomic integration is also likely to produce some racial and ethnic mixing since the poverty rate among African Americans and Latinos is higher than among whites. In educational terms, however, he says socioeconomic diversity is more valuable than racial diversity because the academic gains of mixing by class and income appear to be well established, while the claimed gains of race mixing are in dispute.

Traditional civil rights advocates like the Legal Defense Fund's Shaw do not quarrel with socioeconomic integration but insist that it is "not an adequate substitute for racial integration."

Orfield agrees that socioeconomic integration is "a good idea" but quickly adds, "You can't achieve racial integration very well by using social and economic integration."

"If you talk to districts that have relied solely on that, it doesn't reach all of the students that they need to reach," says Negrón at the school boards association.

For their part, conservatives raise fewer objections to mixing students by socioeconomic background than by race, but they worry the practice may merely be a pretext for racial classifications. "It has fewer constitutional problems," says Thernstrom. "It is less politically controversial."

"It's better than race-based student assignments," says Clegg at the Center for Equal Opportunity. "But if you're using socioeconomic status simply as a proxy for race, many of the same policy and legal problems remain."

Thernstrom is unconvinced, however, of the claimed academic benefits. "There are no proven results from it," she says. She scoffs at what she calls "the notion that if you sit next to somebody, differences [in values] are going to somehow melt away."

In any event, Clegg says he opposes either racial or socioeconomic mixing if it requires assigning students to schools distant from their homes. "Neighborhood schools are the preferable means of assignment," he says, "because you're not having to pay for busing and you're not having to put children on long bus rides, which keep them from engaging in extracurricular activities."

Kahlenberg disagrees. "I haven't heard anyone make a convincing case that from an educational perspective the best way to assign students is the place where their parents can afford to live," he says. "That's the way we do it, but there's no argument that's the best way to educate kids in our society."

From opposite perspectives, however, both Orfield and Thernstrom agree that socioeconomic integration engenders some of the same kinds of opposition that racial integration does. "You do have a lot of middle-class flight as a result," Thernstrom says. "It's not really more popular than racial integration," Orfield says.

Despite the resistance, Kahlenberg believes the policy would fulfill a fundamental goal of public education in the United States. "Most people believe at least in theory that education is the way for kids of any background to do well," he says. "As long as we have economically segregated schools, that promise is broken."

Is the focus on diversity interfering with efforts to improve education in all schools?

As he wrapped up his legal challenge to the Louisville pupil-assignment plan before the Supreme Court, attorney Gordon depicted the case as a choice between "diversity" and "educational outcome."

"For me," Gordon told the justices during the Dec. 4 arguments, "I would use all these millions of dollars. I would reduce teacher-student ratio. I would give incentive pay to the better teachers. I would [build] more magnet schools, more traditional schools."

"We presuppose that we're going to have bad schools and good schools in this country," he continued. "I don't think we can no [sic] longer accept that."

Gordon describes himself as a civil rights liberal, but his argument parallels the views of conservatives like Clegg. "School districts should be worrying less about the racial and ethnic mix than about improving the education that's offered at all schools," Clegg says.

"If you're just focusing on racial diversity, as it's called, for its own sake without trying to assess whether you're improving the educational outcomes," says Rosman, "then you're detracting from the overall goal of achieving educational excellence. In some instances, that's happened."

"The solution is to reduce the gap, the racial gap, the ethnic gap, the socioeconomic gap," says Thernstrom. "Then kids will be looked at as just kids without any kind of assumptions made about, you know, are they like me?"

Traditional civil rights groups and advocates insist that diversity and educational reform complement rather than conflict with each other. In any event, they say, the push for diversity is neither so strong nor so extensive as the critics contend.

"We haven't had any federal policy of promoting diversity since 1981," says Orfield, referring to the first year of Ronald Reagan's presidency. "We haven't had any new lawsuits to integrate schools for a long time. Ever since 1980, most desegregation plans have had voluntary choice and magnet schools, and almost all of them are part and parcel of educational reform plans."

John Trasviña, president and general counsel of the Mexican American Legal Defense and Educational Fund (MALDEF), calls the claimed conflict between diversity and educational quality "a diversion." Referring to educational reform, he says, "We aren't doing that either. It's always easy to say let's address some other issue. When it comes to do that, it's not done."

Diversity advocates dispute critics' suggestion that racial or economic integration has been pursued solely for its own sake with no attention to improving educational quality. "I don't think anybody ever thought that school integration by itself was a sufficient policy," Orfield says.

"The whole reason for economic integration is to promote academic achievement and raise the quality of schooling," says Kahlenberg. "No one has figured out how to make separate schools for rich and poor work well, certainly not for poor kids."

Orfield and Kahlenberg also dismiss concerns that the transportation costs entailed in some diversity plans take scarce dollars from other, more promising school-improvement initiatives. "We've spent billions and billions of dollars on low-income schools, which hasn't produced a lot of results," Kahlenberg says.

Orfield is even blunter about recent efforts to reduce the racial gap. "It's been a failure," he says. Desegregation and anti-poverty programs of the 1960s and '70s did narrow the racial-achievement gap, Orfield writes in the recent UCLA Civil Rights Project report. But he says "most studies" find that President Bush's No Child Left Behind law — which specifically calls for narrowing the achievement gap between white and minority pupils — has had "no impact" on the disparities so far. [8]

From opposite perspectives, Thernstrom and Trasviña lay out demanding agendas for schools to try to close the racial gap. "I want more learning going on," says Thernstrom. "You need really good schools. The day should be longer, the teachers should be better, the principals should have more authority.

"Our kids aren't learning enough in school," she continues. "That will level the playing field."

CHRONOLOGY

Before 1950 *Free, universal public education is enshrined as American ideal and advances in practice, but African Americans, Hispanics and Asian Americans are consigned to separate and unequal schools in much of the country.*

1950s-1960s *Racial segregation in public schools is ruled unconstitutional, but desegregation is slow.*

1954, 1955 Supreme Court's unanimous decision in *Brown v. Board of Education* (1954) outlaws mandatory racial segregation in public schools; a year later court says school districts must dismantle dual systems "with all deliberate speed" (*Brown II*). "Massive resistance" in South stalls integration.

1964, 1965 Civil Rights Act of 1964 authorizes Justice Department to file school-desegregation suits; Title I of Elementary and Secondary Education Act provides targeted aid to school districts for low-income students.

1968 Supreme Court tells school districts to develop plans to dismantle dual systems "now."

1970s-1980s *Busing upheld as desegregation tool but draws strong protests in North and West as well as South; Supreme Court, Justice Department withdraw from desegregation cases.*

1971 Supreme Court unanimously upholds federal courts' power to order crosstown busing to desegregate schools.

1973 Supreme Court rejects federal constitutional right to equal school funding; one month later, New Jersey supreme court is first to sustain funding-equity suit under state constitution.

1974 U.S. Supreme Court, 5-4, bars court-ordered desegregation between inner cities and suburbs; decision is first in series of closely divided rulings that limit desegregation remedies.

1983 U.S. Department of Education report "A Nation at Risk" paints critical picture of rising mediocrity in U.S. schools, shifts agenda away from equity issues.

1990s *Racial isolation increases for African Americans, Latinos; "reverse discrimination" suits by white students backed in some federal courts, fail in others.*

1991 LaCrosse, Wis., becomes first school district to aim to balance enrollment by students' income status: "socioeconomic integration."

1995 Supreme Court signals federal courts to wrap up desegregation cases; lower courts respond by generally granting "unitary" status to school systems seeking to be freed from desegregation orders.

1998, 1999 Federal appeals courts in Boston, Richmond, Va., bar racial preferences in public school admission.

2000-Present *Socioeconomic integration advances; Latinos become largest ethnic minority; Supreme Court ruling bars racial classifications in pupil assignments.*

2000 Wake County (Raleigh), N.C., becomes largest school district to try socioeconomic integration.

2001 President George W. Bush wins congressional approval of No Child Left Behind Act, requiring school districts to meet achievement benchmarks, including closing racial gap.

2001-2005 White families challenge racial-diversity plans in Seattle and Louisville, Ky; federal courts back school districts, ruling plans are "narrowly tailored" to achieve "compelling" interest in diversity.

2005, 2006 Bush nominates John G. Roberts Jr. and Samuel A. Alito Jr. to Supreme Court; both win Senate confirmation, strengthening conservative majority on court.

2007 Supreme Court ruling in Louisville and Seattle cases limits use of race in pupil assignments, but five justices say race-neutral measures can be used to promote compelling interest in diversity; school boards vow to try to maintain racial diversity; advocates push socioeconomic integration on legal, political grounds.

"We clearly need to improve the quality of our schools," says Trasviña. He calls for steps to reduce the dropout rate and to channel more students into so-called STEM courses (science, technology, engineering and math). But diversity helps, not hurts reform efforts, he says.

"While it is true that simply putting children of different backgrounds in seats in the same classroom does not necessarily improve the classroom experience by itself, [diversity] adds to it," Trasviña says. "And it adds to the political will to make sure that people understand that these are our schools."

BACKGROUND

The 'Common School'

The idea of free, universal public education has been espoused in the United States since the Revolutionary Era and still holds a central place in American thought as a tool for personal development and social cohesion. But the ideal of equal educational opportunity for all has never obtained in practice. Even as education became more nearly universal in the 20th century, African Americans and other racial and ethnic minorities faced blatant discrimination that was only partly alleviated by landmark court rulings outlawing legally mandated segregation. [9]

George Washington and Thomas Jefferson were among the nation's early leaders to call in general terms for mass public education, but the educational "system" of the early 19th century consisted of private academies, rural district schools and a handful of "charity" schools in cities. Horace Mann, the so-called father of American public education, used his appointment as Massachusetts' first commissioner of education in 1837 to advocate the "common school" — publicly supported and open to all. As University of Wisconsin educational historian William Reese explains, Mann saw education as a way to restore social harmony at a time of social tensions between rich and poor and between native-born and immigrants. Others saw the same connection. His fellow New Englander Alpheus Packard wrote in the 1840s of the "sons of wealth and poverty" gaining mutual respect by sitting side by side in a public school. [10]

Abolitionist Mann's vision had no practical meaning, however, for African American slaves before the Civil War and only limited significance for their descendants for decades after slavery was abolished. Both before and after the Civil War, the vast majority of African

Americans "lived in states that were openly and explicitly opposed to their education," according to the University of Illinois' Anderson.

After emancipation slaves who had learned to read and write became teachers in rudimentary schools, aided by Northern missionaries and philanthropists and some sympathetic white Southerners. With the end of Reconstruction, however, Southern leaders "pushed back the gains that had been made," Anderson says. In a racially segregated system in the early 20th century, per capita spending for black pupils in the South amounted to one-fourth to one-half of the amount spent on whites. [11]

Education was becoming nearly universal for white Americans, even as racial segregation became entrenched for African Americans and, in many places, for Mexican- and Asian Americans. [12] Elementary school attendance was nearly universal by the 1920s. High schools — once viewed as fairly selective institutions — began doubling in enrollment each decade after 1890 thanks to a declining market for child labor and the growing enforcement of new compulsory education laws. Secondary school enrollment increased from 50 percent of 14–17-year-olds in 1920 to nearly 95 percent of that age group by the mid-1970s. Meanwhile, the average school year was also increasing — from 144 days in 1900 to 178 days in 1950. And per capita investment in education rose during the same period from 1.2 percent of national income to 2 percent.

The Supreme Court's 1954 decision in *Brown* outlawing racial segregation in public schools capped a half-century-long campaign by the NAACP to gain a measure of equal educational opportunity for African Americans. [13] The legal campaign — directed by the future Supreme Court justice, Thurgood Marshall — was waged at a deliberate pace even as many black students and families were agitating for better schools at the local level. The eventual decision seemed far from inevitable beforehand. Only after 1950 did the NAACP decide to ask the court to abolish segregation rather than try to equalize the separate school systems. And the justices were closely divided after the first round of arguments in 1952; they joined in the unanimous ruling in 1954 only after a second round of arguments and shrewd management of the case by the new chief justice, Earl Warren. *

---

* California, home to the nation's largest concentration of Asian-Americans and the second-largest concentration of Mexican-Americans after Texas, had abolished racial segregation in schools by law in 1947.

'Tracking' Leads to Racial Separation in Classes

But grouping students by ability has wide support.

Ballard High School sits on a spacious campus in an overwhelmingly white suburban neighborhood in the eastern end of Jefferson County, Ky. As part of Jefferson County Public Schools' racial balance policies, however, Ballard's attendance zone includes neighborhoods on the opposite side of the county in Louisville's predominantly African American West End section.

By drawing students from the West End, the school achieved around 25 percent black enrollment in the 2006-07 academic year. But despite the measure of racial balance in overall enrollment, Ballard students say blacks and whites are less than fully integrated inside. "Kids naturally separate," remarks Ben Gravel, a white 12th-grader, as he arrives at school on Aug. 13 for the opening of a new school year.

At Ballard — and in schools around the country — the racial separation is especially pronounced in the classroom itself. African American students are disproportionately enrolled in less challenging, "low-track" classes and underrepresented in higher-track classes, such as advanced placement (AP) courses and international baccalaureate (IB) programs. In 2006, for example, African Americans comprised about 13 percent of graduating high school seniors but only 6 percent of the total number of students who took advanced placement exams administered by the College Board. [1]

The widespread practice of tracking — or "ability grouping" as supporters prefer to call it — has been a con-tentious issue within education circles for more than two decades. "Detracking" advocates have had occasional success in pushing reforms, but the practice has persisted — in part because of strong resistance from parents of students enrolled in higher-track courses. [2]

Supporters say the practice matches curricular offerings to students' abilities and achievement level. "It doesn't make sense to the average person that you would put a non-reader in the same English classroom as some kid who's reading Proust," says Tom Loveless, director of the Brown Center on Educational Policy at the Brookings Institution in Washington.

Critics say the practice simply keeps already-disadvantaged students on a path to lower academic achievement. "If you have classes that are structured to give kids less of a challenge, those kids tend to fall farther behind," says Kevin Welner, an associate professor at the University of Colorado's School of Education in Boulder.

Civil rights advocates say the enrollment patterns reflect what they call "segregation by tracking." In her critique of the practice, Jeannie Oakes, director of urban schooling at UCLA's Graduate School of Education and Information Studies, cited research evidence indicating that African American and Latino students were more likely to be assigned to low-track courses than white students even when they had comparable abilities or test scores. [3]

The high court's "remedial" decision one year later in *Brown II* directed school districts to desegregate "with all deliberate speed." Many Southern politicians lent support to a campaign of "massive resistance" to the ruling by diehard segregationists. A decade after *Brown*, fewer than 5 percent of black students in the South were attending majority-white schools; more than three-fourths were attending schools with 90 percent minority enrollment. [14] In 1968, an evidently impatient Supreme Court declared that school districts had to develop plans to dismantle dual systems that promised "realistically" to work — and to work "now." Three years later, a new chief justice, Warren E. Burger, led a unanimous court in upholding the authority of local federal courts to order school districts to use cross-neighborhood busing as part of a desegregation plan. [15]

'Elusive' Equality

The campaign to desegregate schools stimulated broader efforts in the late 20th century to equalize educational opportunity at national, state and local levels. Initially, desegregation advanced in the South and to a lesser extent in other regions. But integration eventually stalled in the face of white opposition to busing, ambivalence among blacks and Supreme Court decisions easing pressure on local school districts to take affirmative steps to

"I wouldn't use the phrase 'segregation by tracking.' A lot of it is self-tracking," counters Abigail Thernstrom, a senior fellow at the conservative Manhattan Institute and co-author of a book on the educational gap between white and minority students. "Is it terrible that we have so few Latino and black students who are prepared to take the most educationally rigorous courses?" she adds. "Of course, it's terrible."

Sixth-graders study science as part of the international baccalaureate curriculum at Harbour Pointe Middle School in Mukilteo, Wash.

opt for a lesser education?"

Loveless says under a random-assignment system, high-achieving students "would lose quite a bit," middle-range students "would lose a bit" and lowest-achieving students "would probably benefit a little bit" — mainly by reducing the concentration of students with behavioral issues in low-track classes.

Welner disagrees that high-achieving students are necessarily harmed by reforms. "Good detracking doesn't take anything away from these kids," he says. "The high achievers are not only holding their own but are doing better after the reform."

Welner acknowledges minority students often choose low-track courses, but faults school systems instead of the students. Minority parents and students often lack the information needed to understand the different course offerings, he says. And students "sometimes don't want to be the only minority in the high-track class," he says.

Loveless acknowledges the critics' complaints about low-track classes, but says the solution is to reform not to abolish them. "Let's fix the low-track classes," he says. Despite the critics' doubts, he says many private, charter and parochial schools have developed low-track curricula that more effectively challenge students than those often found in public schools.

"If we know how to create a high-track class, why would we then create a separate set of classes that don't have those opportunities?" Welner asks. "Why would we let students

Despite the recurrent clashes at the local level, Loveless predicts that tracking will continue to be a widespread practice. "Polls are very clear," he says. "Parents, teachers and students favor ability grouping. Those are three important constituency groups."

[1] College Board, "Advanced Placement: Report to the Nation 2006," p. 11 (www.collegeboard.com). For background, see Marcia Clemmitt, "AP and IB Programs," *CQ Researcher*, March 3, 2006, pp. 193-216.

[2] For opposing views, see Tom Loveless, *The Tracking Wars: State Reform Meets School Policy* (1999); Jeannie Oakes, *Keeping Track: How Schools Structure Inequality* (2d ed.), 2005.

[3] *Ibid.*, pp. 230-231.

mix white and black students. School funding reform efforts produced some results, but as the 21st century began educational equality remained — in Professor Reese's word — "elusive." [16]

The Supreme Court's unanimity in school race cases broke down in the 1970s, and a continuing succession of closely divided decisions reduced districts' obligations to develop effective integration plans. In one of the most important rulings, the justices in 1974 divided 5–4 in a case from Detroit to bar court-ordered desegregation between predominantly black inner cities and predominantly white suburban districts. Three years later, the court essentially freed school districts from any obliga-

tion to prevent resegregation after adopting a racially neutral assignment plan. The decisions coincided with widespread opposition to busing for racial balance among white families in many communities, most dramatically in Boston in the 1970s, where police escorts were needed for buses taking pupils from predominantly black Roxbury to predominantly white South Boston.

African American students and families, meanwhile, had mixed reactions to desegregation generally and busing in particular, according to Professor Anderson. In many districts, desegregation meant the closing or transformation of historically black schools that had provided a good education for many students. In the South,

More Blacks and Latinos Attend Poorest Schools

The vast majority (79 percent) of white students attend schools where less than half the student body is poor, compared with 37 percent of black students and 36 percent of Hispanics. For schools where at least 91 percent of the students are poor, whites made up just 1 percent of the student body compared with 13 and 15 percent, respectively, for blacks and Hispanics.

Distribution of Students in Public Schools by Percentage Who Are Poor, 2005-2006

Percent Poor	Percentage of each race				
	White	Black	Latino	Asian	American Indian
0-10%	20	5	7	23	17
11-20%	17	5	5	14	6
21-30%	16	7	7	12	8
31-40%	14	9	8	11	9
41-50%	12	11	9	9	11
51-60%	9	11	10	8	11
61-70%	6	12	11	6	11
71-80%	3	13	12	6	10
81-90%	2	14	14	6	8
91-100%	1	13	15	4	9

* Totals may not add up to 100 due to rounding.

Source: Gary Orfield and Chungmei Lee, "Historic Reversals, Accelerating Resegregation, and the Need for New Integration Strategies," Civil Rights Project, UCLA, August 2007

Total number of students (in millions)	
White	28
Black	8
Latino	10
Asian	2
American Indian	1

national agenda in 1965 by passing a law as part of President Lyndon B. Johnson's "war on poverty" to provide federal aid targeted to poor children. [17] By the end of the century, however, Title I of the Elementary and Secondary Education Act was seen as having produced mixed results at best — in part because allocation formulas shaped by the realities of congressional politics directed much of the money to relatively well-to-do suburban districts.

Meanwhile, advocates of educational equity had turned to the courts to try to reduce funding disparities between school districts — with mixed results. [18] The Supreme Court ruled in 1973 that funding disparities between districts did not violate the federal Constitution. One month later, however, the New Jersey Supreme Court became the first state tribunal to find differential school funding to run afoul of a state constitutional provision. Over the next three decades, school funding suits resulted in court rulings in at least 19 states finding constitutional violations and ordering reforms. But funding disparities persisted. In a wide-ranging survey in 1998, *Education Week* gave 16 states a grade of C- or below on educational equity between school districts. [19]

desegregation also often meant the loss of black principals and teachers. And busing was a "one-way street" for African Americans: most plans entailed the transportation of black students away from their neighborhoods to a mixed reception at best in predominantly white communities.

From the start, the NAACP and other civil rights groups had viewed desegregation not only as a goal in its own right but also — and perhaps more importantly — as an instrument to equalize educational opportunities for black and white pupils. In the heady days of the civil rights era, Congress had put educational equality on the

At the same time, school policymakers were focusing on clamorous calls to improve educational quality stimulated by the publication in 1983 of a report by the Reagan administration's Department of Education sharply criticizing what was depicted as rising mediocrity in U.S. schools. The debate generated by "A Nation at Risk" brought forth all manner of proposals for imposing educational standards, revising curricula or introducing competition within public school systems or between public and private schools. The debate diverted policymakers' attention to some extent from diversity issues and led many white

Do Racial Policies Affect Academic Achievement?

Most studies find beneficial effects from integration.

When the Supreme Court outlawed racial segregation in schools in 1954, it relied heavily on research by the African-American psychologist Kenneth Clark purporting to show that attending all-black schools hurt black students' self-esteem. Over time, the court's reliance on Clark's study drew many critics, who questioned both the research and its prominent use in a legal ruling.

A half-century later, as they considered challenges to racial-diversity plans in Seattle and Louisville, Ky., the justices were deluged with sometimes conflicting research studies on the effects of racial policies on educational achievement. Among 64 friend-of-the-court briefs, nearly half — 27 — cited social science research. Most found beneficial effects from racial integration, but a minority questioned those claims.

The National Academy of Education, a select group of education scholars, created a seven-member committee to evaluate the various studies cited in the various briefs. Here are the committee's major conclusions from the research, released on June 29 — one day after the court found the school districts' plans unconstitutional:

Academic achievement. White students are not hurt by desegregation efforts or adjustments in racial composition of schools. African-American student achievement is enhanced by less segregated schooling, although the magnitude of the influence is quite variable. The positive effects for African-American students tend to be larger in the earlier grades.

Near-term intergroup relations. Racially diverse schools and classrooms will not guarantee improved intergroup relations, but are likely to be constructive. The research identifies conditions that need to be present in order for diversity to have a positive effect and suggests steps schools can take to realize the potential for improvement.

Long-term effects of school desegregation. Experience in desegregated schools increases the likelihood over time of greater tolerance and better intergroup relations among adults of different racial groups.

The critical-mass question. Racial diversity can avoid or mitigate harms caused by racial isolation, such as tokenism and stereotyping, particularly when accompanied by an otherwise beneficial school environment. Some briefs suggest a minimum African-American enrollment of 15 percent to 30 percent to avoid these harms, but the research does not support specifying any particular percentage.

Race-neutral alternatives. No race-neutral policy is as effective as race-conscious policies for achieving racial diversity. Socioeconomic integration is likely to marginally reduce racial isolation and may have other benefits. School choice generally and magnet schools in particular have some potential to reduce racial isolation, but could also increase segregation.

Source: Robert L. Linn and Kevin G. Welner (eds.), "Race-Conscious Policies for Assigning Students to Schools: Social Science Research and the Supreme Court Cases," National Academy of Education, June 29, 2007 (www.naeducation.org/Meredith_Report.pdf).

---

parents to worry more about their own children's education than about educational equity or diversity. [20]

By the end of the 1990s, federal courts were all but out of the desegregation business, and racial isolation — "resegregation" to civil rights advocates — was on the rise. In a trio of cases in 1991, 1993 and 1995, the Supreme Court gave federal courts unmistakable signals to withdraw from superintending desegregation plans. School districts that sought to be declared "unitary" — or no longer dual in nature — and freed from desegregation decrees, like Jefferson County, invariably succeeded. By 2001, at least two-thirds of black students and at least half of Latino students nationwide were enrolled in predominantly minority schools. And after narrowing in the 1980s, the educational-testing gaps between white and black students began to widen again in the 1990s. In 2000, the typical black student scored below about 75 percent of white students on most standardized tests. [21]

'Diversity' Challenged

Even as courts reduced the pressure on school districts to desegregate, hundreds of school systems adopted voluntary

Minnijean Brown, 15, one of the Little Rock Nine, arrives at Central High School on Sept. 25, 1957, guarded by soldiers sent by President Dwight. D. Eisenhower. Brown and eight other African American students desegregated the Arkansas school three years after the Supreme Court's landmark *Brown v. Board of Education* ruling.

measures aimed at mixing students of different racial and ethnic backgrounds. Some plans that made explicit use of race in pupil assignments drew legal challenges from white families as "reverse discrimination." Meanwhile, several dozen school systems were adopting — and achieving some success with — diversity plans tied to socioeconomic status instead of race. Support for socioeconomic integration appeared to increase after the Supreme Court's June 28 decision in the Seattle and Louisville cases restricting the use of race in pupil assignments but permitting race-neutral policies to achieve diversity in the classroom.

School boards that voluntarily sought to achieve racial and ethnic mixing claimed that the policies generally improved education for all students while benefiting disadvantaged minorities and promoting broad political support for the schools. Many plans — like those in Seattle and Louisville — explicitly considered race in some pupil assignments, and several drew legal challenges. In November 1998 the federal appeals court in Boston struck down the use of racial preferences for blacks and Hispanics for admission to the prestigious Boston Latin School. Then in fall 1999, the federal appeals court in Richmond, Va., ruled in favor of white families challenging race-based policies in two districts in the Washington, D.C., suburbs. The rulings struck down a weighted lottery that advantaged blacks and Hispanics in Arlington County, Va., and a transfer policy in Montgomery

County, Md., that limited students from changing schools in order to maintain racial balance. [22]

The idea of socioeconomic integration first gained national attention when the midsized town of La Crosse, Wis., redrew attendance zones in the early 1990s to shift students from an overcrowded, predominantly affluent high school to the town's second high school in the blue-collar section with a growing Hmong population. In Kahlenberg's account, the plan survived concerted political opposition, produced measurable educational progress and now enjoys widespread support. Cambridge, Mass., substituted socioeconomic integration policies for racial busing in 1999 after the federal appeals court ruling in the Boston Latin case. Wake County, N.C., similarly dropped its racial balancing plan in 2000 in favor of an assignment plan tied to free or reduced-lunch status to comply with the rulings by the Richmond-based appeals court in the Arlington and Montgomery County cases. By 2003, Kahlenberg claimed some 500,000 students nationwide were enrolled in school systems that used economic status as a factor in pupil assignments. [23]

In the main, however, school districts that had adopted racial balancing plans stuck with them despite legal challenges. Seattle adopted its "open choice" plan in 1998 — some two decades after it had become the largest school district in the nation to voluntarily adopt a racial busing plan. The ad hoc group Parents Involved in Community Schools filed its suit challenging the use of race as a "tiebreaker" in pupil assignments in July 2000. That same year, Jefferson County Public Schools adopted its controlled choice plan after a federal judge freed the system from a desegregation decree dating to 1975. Parent Crystal Meredith challenged the race-based assignments in April 2003. Federal district judges upheld the plans — in April 2001 in the Seattle case and in June 2004 in the Jefferson County case. The 4th U.S. Circuit Court of Appeals in Cincinnati then upheld the Jefferson County plan in July 2005. The Seattle case followed a more complicated appellate route. The school district suspended the plan after an initial setback in 2002, but eventually the 9th U.S. Circuit Court of Appeals in San Francisco upheld the plan in October 2005.

The Supreme Court's decision to hear the two cases immediately raised fears among civil rights advocates that the conservative majority fortified by President George W. Bush's appointments of Chief Justice Roberts and

Is racial diversity in the classroom essential to a good education?

YES

Janet W. Schofield
Professor of Psychology, University of Pittsburgh

Written for *CQ Researcher*, September 2007

Education in a democratic society serves three basic purposes. It provides students with workforce skills, prepares them to function as thoughtful and informed citizens in a cohesive country and enriches their lives by awakening them to new knowledge, perspectives and possibilities. Racial diversity in schools and classrooms enhances the attainment of each of these goals.

The ability to work effectively with individuals from diverse backgrounds is a fundamental workplace skill, as the well-known report "What Work Requires of Schools," issued by President George H.W. Bush's administration, points out. Yet, many students never develop this skill because our country's neighborhoods, social institutions and religious organizations are often highly segregated. Racially diverse schools provide a milieu essential to the development of this crucial skill.

Racially diverse schools also have a vital role to play in developing fair-minded citizens and in promoting social cohesion. Research demonstrates that in-school contact with individuals from different backgrounds typically reduces prejudice, a fundamentally important outcome in our increasingly diverse society. In addition, students who attend diverse schools are more likely than others to choose diverse work and residential settings as adults, thus promoting social cohesion.

Racially diverse schools also enrich students' understanding and expand their perspectives by placing them in contact with others whose views and life experiences may be very different. Just as visiting a foreign country is a much richer and more powerful experience than reading about it, interacting with students from different backgrounds brings their perspectives and experiences alive in a way not otherwise possible.

Even individuals who discount the arguments above must acknowledge that heavily segregated minority schools disadvantage the very students most in need of an excellent educational environment. Such schools typically have relatively impoverished curricular offerings, great difficulty recruiting experienced teachers and high teacher-turnover rates, all of which may help to explain why research suggests that attending such schools typically undermines students' achievement relative to similar peers in more diverse schools.

Racial diversity in and of itself does not guarantee a good education, but as a recent report by the National Academy of Education suggests, it creates preconditions conducive to it. In our increasingly diverse democracy, the educational cost of segregated schools is too high for majority and minority students alike.

NO

Abigail Thernstrom
Senior Fellow, Manhattan Institute
Co-author, No Excuses: Closing the Racial Gap in Learning

Written for *CQ Researcher*, September 2007

Racially diverse classrooms are desirable — of course. But are they essential to a good education? Absolutely not. If they were, big-city school districts would be stuck providing lousy educations for America's most disadvantaged children into the indefinite future. A large majority of students in 26 out of the 27 central-city districts with a public school population of at least 60,000 are non-white. The white proportion in these districts averages 16 percent. Thus, big-city schools will not be racially "diverse" unless we start flying white kids from Utah into, say, Detroit.

Or rather, they will not be racially "diverse" according to the Seattle school board's definition in the racial balancing plan the Supreme Court condemned last term. Seattle had divided students into only two racial groups: white and non-white. If schools were half-Asian, half-white, that was fine; if they were 30 percent white with the rest Asian, they weren't sufficiently "diverse," and educational quality would be somehow lacking.

What racial stereotyping! Do all non-white students express the same non-white views — with all white students having a "white" outlook? In fact, why is racial diversity the only kind that counts for those concerned about the group clustering in certain schools? What about a social class or religious mix?

And on the subject of racial stereotyping, do we really want to embrace the ugly assumption that black kids are incapable of learning unless they're hanging around some white magic? Good inner-city schools across the country are teaching the children who walk through the door. In excellent schools, if every one of the students is black — reflecting the demography of the neighborhood — the expectations for educational excellence do not change. And happily, there are no compelling studies showing enormous positive gains for black students when they attend schools with large numbers of whites.

Good education is not confined to academic learning. But there is no evidence that schools engaging in coercive racial mixing build a lifelong desire to "socialize with people of different races," as Seattle assumed. Visit a school lunchroom! Racial and ethnic clustering will be very much in evidence.

Those who insist school districts should turn themselves inside out to engineer racial diversity haven't a clue as to the limits of social policy. And they demean the capacity of non-Asian minority kids to learn, whatever the color of the kid in the seat next to them.

Justice Samuel A. Alito Jr. would strike down the plans. Questions by Roberts and Alito during arguments on Dec. 4, 2006, left little doubt about their positions. The high-drama announcement of the decision on June 28 lasted nearly 45 minutes with Roberts, Kennedy and Breyer each delivering lengthy summaries of his opinion from the bench.

"The way to stop discrimination on the basis of race," Roberts declared as he neared his conclusion, "is to stop discriminating on the basis of race."

Breyer was equally forceful in his dissent. "This is a decision that the court and this nation will come to regret," he said.

Almost immediately, however, Kennedy's pivotal concurrence began to draw the closest scrutiny as advocates and observers tried to discern what alternatives remained for school boards to use in engineering racial diversity. The National School Boards Association urged local boards to continue seeking diversity through "careful race-conscious policies." Administrators in Seattle and Louisville said they planned to do just that.

But Clegg of the Center for Equal Opportunity said school systems would be better off to drop racial classifications. "At the end of the day, these two plans didn't pass muster," he said. "And the impact will be to persuade other school districts that this is not a good idea." [24]

CURRENT SITUATION

'Resegregation' Seen

The Louisville and Seattle school systems are in the opening weeks of a new academic year, with few immediate effects from the Supreme Court decision invalidating their previous pupil-assignment plans. Officials in both districts are working on new pupil-assignment plans to put into effect starting in fall 2009, with racial diversity still a goal but race- or ethnic-based placements no longer permitted.

Both school systems, however, are reporting what civil rights advocates call "resegregation" — higher percentages of African American students in predominantly minority schools. Critics of racial-diversity policies object to the term, arguing that segregation refers only to legally enforced separation of the races. Whatever term is used, a new report documents a national trend of "steadily increasing separation" in public schools between whites

and the country's two largest minority groups: Latinos and African Americans.

The report by the UCLA Civil Rights Project shows, for example, that the percentage of black students in majority-white schools rose from virtually zero in 1954 to a peak of 43.5 percent in 1988 before beginning a steady decline. In 2005 — the most recent year available — 27 percent of black students attended majority-white schools.

Meanwhile, the proportion of African Americans attending majority-minority schools has been slowly increasing over the past two decades — reversing gains in integration in the 1960s and '70s — while the percentage of Latino students in majority-minority schools has grown steadily since the 1960s. In 2005, 73 percent of black students were in majority-minority schools, and more than one-third — 38 percent — were in "intensely segregated" schools with 90 to 100 percent minority enrollment. For Latinos, 78 percent of students were in majority-minority schools.

By contrast, Asian Americans are described in the report as "the most integrated" ethnic group in public schools. In 2005, the average Asian student attended a school with 44 percent white enrollment — compared to 30 percent white enrollment for the average black student and 27 percent white enrollment for the average Latino. The report attributed the higher integration for Asians to greater residential integration and relatively small numbers outside the West.

Seattle was already experiencing increasing racial isolation after suspending its previous placement plan, which included race as one "tiebreaker" in pupil assignments. "There has been a decline in racial diversity since suspension of the plan," says Seattle Public Schools spokeswoman Patti Spencer.

In Louisville, nine schools now have African American enrollment above the previous guideline limit of 50 percent — most of them in predominantly black neighborhoods in Louisville's West End or the heavily black areas in southwestern Jefferson County. Black enrollment in some schools in the predominantly white East End has declined, though not below the minimum figure of 15 percent in the previous guidelines.

The 15/50 guidelines remain "a goal," according to Student Placement Director Todd. "We're trying to prevent as much slippage as possible."

In Seattle, outgoing Superintendent Raj Manhas told reporters after the Supreme Court ruling that the school district would look at "all options available to us" to try to preserve racial diversity in the schools. [25] The new superintendent, Maria Goodloe-Johnson, is an African American who was sharply critical of racial policies in her previous position as superintendent in Charleston, S.C. Since taking office in Seattle in July, however, Goodloe-Johnson has not addressed racial balance, according to Spencer. [26]

Opponents of the race-based policies say school districts should refocus their efforts. "Where school districts should focus is on education standards, not creating a specific racial mix of students," says Sharon Browne, a staff attorney with the Pacific Legal Foundation, the conservative public interest law firm that supported the legal challenges in Louisville and Seattle.

"The guidelines are gone," says attorney Gordon in Louisville. "They're past tense."

In Seattle, Kathleen Brose, the longtime school activist who founded Parents Involved in Community Schools to challenge the use of race for high school placements, says diversity is "important," but parental choice is more important. "The school district has been so focused on race," she adds, "that, frankly, I think they forgot about academics."

Legal Options Eyed

School boards around the country are re-examining their legal options for promoting diversity. At the same time, they are bracing for new legal challenges to their diversity plans that, so far, have not materialized.

The National School Boards Association plans to provide local boards with advisories on what policies can be used under the Supreme Court's decision to promote racial balance. But General Counsel Negrón expects few changes as a result of the ruling.

"School districts are not going to be changing their policies drastically to the extent that they will be abandoning their choices of diversity or integration as their goal, if that's what they've chosen to do," Negrón says. "School districts are going to comply with the law as they understand it. And there's a lot of room in Justice Kennedy's concurrence for school districts to be creative and innovative."

Barring any consideration of race, Negrón adds, "was just not what the decision stood for."

Pacific Legal Foundation attorney Browne, however, worries that school districts are not complying with the ruling. "We are very disappointed that there are school districts who are ignoring the decision by the U.S. Supreme Court and continuing to use race [in pupil assignments]," she says.

Browne says school districts should have begun developing contingency plans for assigning students on a non-racial basis after the oral arguments in the Seattle and Louisville cases in December indicated the court would find both plans unconstitutional.

The Louisville and Seattle cases themselves are still pending in lower federal courts, with winning lawyers in both cases asking the courts to order the school boards to pay attorneys' fees.

In Seattle, the firm of Davis Wright Tremaine is seeking $1.8 million in attorneys' fees despite having previously said that it was handling the parents' case pro bono — for free. "Congress specifically and explicitly wrote into the law that if the government is found to have violated citizens' civil rights, then the prevailing party should seek fee recovery," explained Mark Usellis, a spokesman for the firm. The school system reported spending $434,000 in legal fees on the case. [27]

Louisville solo practitioner Gordon is asking to be paid $200 per hour for the "hundreds of hours" he devoted to the case plus a bonus for the national impact of the case. Without specifying a figure, he also wants to be reimbursed for spending his own money on expenses and court costs. Meanwhile, plaintiff Crystal Meredith is asking for $125,000 in damages, which she attributes to lost wages, invasion of privacy and emotional distress. [28]

Gordon says he received several complaints from parents whose applications for transfers for their children had been denied on the basis of limited capacity at the school they had chosen. Gordon says he suspected school officials were actually denying the transfers on racial grounds, but the MacNeals' case was the only "smoking gun" he found.

The Pacific Legal Foundation is following up on "many inquiries" received from parents since the Supreme Court ruling, according to Browne, but no new cases have been filed. She declined to say where the complaints originated. The foundation has suits pending in California courts against the Los Angeles and Berkeley school districts over race-based policies.

If any new legal challenges are filed, Negrón expects federal courts will defer to local school boards' decisions, for the most part. The [Supreme Court] didn't tell us exactly what to do," he explains. "School districts will be trying their best to come up with something that meets the requirements of the law and at the same time meets their educational interest in regard to diversity."

OUTLOOK

'Minimal Impact'?

In striking down the Seattle and Jefferson County racial-balance plans, Chief Justice Roberts cited figures from the two school districts showing that the policies actually affected relatively few students — only 52 pupils in Seattle and no more than 3 percent of the pupil assignments in Jefferson County. The "minimal impact," he wrote, "casts doubt on the necessity of using racial classifications."

Writing for the dissenters, however, Justice Breyer cast the stakes in broader terms by citing the growing percentage of black students in majority non-white schools nationwide. The Louisville and Seattle school boards, Breyer said, were asking to be able to continue using tools "to rid their schools of racial segregation." The plurality opinion, he concluded, was "wrong" to deny the school boards' "modest request."

Two months after the ruling, civil rights advocates are continuing to voice grave concerns that the decision will hasten what they call the resegregation of public schools nationwide. "We're going to have a further increase in segregation of American schools," says UCLA's Orfield. "School districts are going to have to jump through a whole series of hoops if they want to have some modest degree of integration."

Legal Defense Fund President Shaw fears new challenges not only to pupil-assignment plans but also to mentoring and scholarship programs specifically targeting racial minorities. "Our adversaries are not going to go away," says Shaw. "They're going to continue to attack race-conscious efforts to address racial inequality."

Opponents of racial-balance plans either discount the fears of increased racial isolation or minimize the harms of the trend if it materializes.

"I don't think there will be dramatic consequences from these decisions," says Rosman of the Center for Individual Rights. School systems with an interest in racial diversity "will find a way to do that legally," he says. "For schools that use race explicitly, it will still be a contentious matter."

"There's going to be less and less focus on achieving politically correct racial and ethnic balance and more focus on improving education," says the Center for Equal Opportunity's Clegg. "That's where the law's headed, and that's where policy's headed. We ought to be worrying less about integration anyhow."

For his part, the Century Foundation's Kahlenberg stresses that the number of school districts with race-conscious policies — guesstimated at around 1,000 — is a small fraction of the nationwide total of 15,000 school systems. Many of the districts that have been seeking racial balance will likely shift to socioeconomic integration, he says, "because that's a clearly legal way to raise academic achievement for kids and create some racial integration indirectly."

In Louisville, the county school board did vote on Sept. 10 to broaden its diversity criteria to include socioeconomic status. "Race will still be a factor," Superintendent Berman said, "but it will not be the only factor." [29] Meanwhile, Student Placement Director Todd says Jefferson County's use of non-contiguous school-attendance zones to mix students from different racially identifiable neighborhoods is likely to be continued.

In his concurring opinion, Justice Kennedy suggested "strategic site selection" as another permissible policy to promote racial diversity — placing new schools so they draw students from different racial neighborhoods. The suggestion may prove impractical in many school districts. Jefferson County opened one new school this fall — in the rapidly growing and predominantly white eastern end, far removed from the African American neighborhoods in the West End. As Breyer noted in his opinion, many urban school systems are unlikely to be building new schools because they are losing not gaining enrollment.

Changing demographics and changing social attitudes are inevitably bringing about changes in the schools. Within a decade or so, demographers expect white students will no longer comprise a majority of public school enrollment. And, as Abigail Thernstrom notes, young people have different attitudes toward race than their parents or grandparents.

"In terms of racial attitudes, we're on a fast track," Thernstrom says. "Young kids are dating across racial and ethnic lines. America is changing in very terrific ways and has been for some time. I expect that change to continue."

But University of Wisconsin educational historian Reese cautions against expecting racial issues to disappear. "It's like a never-never land to imagine that racial issues can somehow disappear," he says. "It's a nice thing to say that we should live in a kind of perfect world, but we don't. I can't imagine that it will disappear. It couldn't have disappeared in the past, and it won't disappear in the future."

NOTES

1. For coverage, see Chris Kenning, "Separate attendance zones voided," *The* [Louisville] *Courier-Journal*, Aug. 29, 2007, p. 1A.

2. The decision is *Parents Involved in Community Schools v. Seattle School District No. 1*, 552 U.S. _ _ _ (2007); the companion case was *Meredith v. Jefferson County Public Schools*. For a detailed chronicle of the cases, see Kenneth Jost, "Court Limits Use of Race in Pupil Assignments," in *The Supreme Court Yearbook 2006-2007*, http://library.cqpress.com/scyb/.

3. For background, see Kenneth Jost, "School Desegregation," *CQ Researcher*, April 23, 2004, pp. 345-372.

4. See Chris Kenning, "JCPS sees change in racial makeup," *The* [Louisville] *Courier-Journal*, Sept. 2, 2007, p. 1A.

5. Gary Orfield and Chungmei Lee, "Historic Reversals, Accelerating Resegregation, and the Need for New Integration Strategies," UCLA Civil Rights Project (formerly based at Harvard University), August 2007, pp. 29, 35.

6. Richard D. Kahlenberg, "Rescuing *Brown v. Board of Education*: Profiles of Twelve School Districts Pursuing Socioeconomic School Integration," June 28, 2007, p. 3.

7. For coverage, see Peter Schworm, "AG Urges Court to Uphold Lynn Plan," *The Boston Globe*, July 18, 2005, p. B4.

8. Orfield and Lee, op. cit., pp. 7-8. For background, see Barbara Mantel, "No Child Left Behind," *CQ Researcher*, May 27, 2005, pp. 469-492.

9. Background drawn in part from William J. Reese, America's Public Schools: From the Common School to "No Child Left Behind" (2005); R. Freeman Butts, *Public Education in the United States: From Revolution to Reform* (1978).

10. Reese, *op. cit.*, pp. 10-11, 25-26.

11. For background, see James Anderson, *The Education of Blacks in the South, 1860-1935* (1988). See also Heather Andrea Williams, *Self-Taught: African American Education in Slavery and Freedom* (2003).

12. For background, see "School Desegregation," *op. cit.*, p. 350 (Latinos), pp. 356-357 (Asian Americans), and sources cited therein.

13. Some background drawn from James T. Patterson, Brown v. Board of Education: *A Civil Rights Milestone and Its Troubled Legacy* (2001).

14. For data, see *ibid.*, pp. 228-230.

15. The decisions are *Green v. County School Board of New Kent County*, 391 U.S. 430 (1968), and *Swann v. Charlotte-Mecklenburg County Board of Education*, 402 U.S. 1 (1971).

16. Reese, *op. cit.*, p. 246. For background on later school desegregation cases, see Patterson, *op. cit.*

17. For background, see H. B. Shaffer, "Status of the War on Poverty," in *Editorial Research Reports*, Jan. 25, 1967, available at *CQ Researcher Plus Archive*, http://library.cqpress.com.

18. Background drawn from Kathy Koch, "Reforming School Funding," *CQ Researcher*, Dec. 10, 1999, pp. 1041-1064.

19. The decisions are *San Antonio Independent School District v. Rodriguez*, 411 U.S. 1 (1973), and *Robinson v. Cahill*, 62 A.2d 273 (N.J. 1973).

20. For background, see Charles S. Clark, "Attack on Public Schools," *CQ Researcher*, July 26, 1996, pp. 649-672.

21. See Patterson, *op. cit.*, p. 214 n.19, p. 234.

22. The decisions are *Wessmann v. Gittens*, 160 F.3d 790 (1st Cir. 1998); *Tuttle v. Arlington County School Board*, 195 F.3d 698 (4th Cir. 1999), *Eisenberg v. Montgomery County Public Schools*, 197 F.3d 123 (4th Cir. 1999). For coverage, see Beth Daley, "Court Strikes Down Latin School Race Admission Policy," *The Boston Globe*, Nov. 20, 1998, p. A1; Jay Mathews, "School Lottery Loses on Appeal," *The Washington Post*, Sept. 26, 1999, p. C1 (Arlington County); Brigid Schulte, "School Diversity Policy Is Overruled," *ibid.*, Oct. 7, 1999, p. A1 (Montgomery County).

23. See Richard D. Kahlenberg, *All Together Now* (2003 ed.)., p. xiii.

24. Quoted in Andrew Wolfson, "Desegregation Decision: Some Find 'Sunshine' Amid Rain," *The* [Louisville] *Courier-Journal*, June 29, 2007, p. 6K.

25. Quoted in Jessica Blanchard and Christine Frey, "District Vows to Seek Out Diversity Answers," *Seattle Post-Intelligencer*, June 29, 2007, p. A1.

26. See Emily Heffter, "First Day of School for Chief," *Seattle Times*, July 10, 2007, p. B1.

27. See Emily Heffter, "Law firm wants school district to pay $1.8M," *Seattle Times*, Sept. 6, 2007, p. B5.

28. Chris Kenning and Andrew Wolfson, "Lawyer in schools case seeks fees, bonus," *The* [Louisville] *Courier-Journal*, July 29, 2007, p. 1A.

29. Quoted in Antoinette Konz, "Schools adopt guidelines for assignment plan," *The* [Louisville] *Courier-Journal*, Sept. 11, 2007.

BIBLIOGRAPHY

Books

Frankenberg, Erika, and Gary Orfield (eds.), *Lessons in Integration: Realizing the Promise of Racial Diversity in American Schools*, University of Virginia Press, 2007.
Twelve essays by 19 contributors examine the educational and social effects of desegregation and the disadvantages to students in segregated schools. Orfield is co-director of the Civil Rights Project, UCLA Graduate School of Education and Information Studies (formerly, the Harvard Civil Rights Project); Frankenberg is a study director for the project. Includes notes, 46-page bibliography.

Loveless, Tom, *The Tracking Wars: State Reform Meets School Policy*, Brookings Institution Press, 1999.
The director of the Brown Center on Educational Policy at Brookings depicts tracking as a traditional educational practice and detracking as "a gamble" that may hurt rather than help students in low-achievement schools. Includes detailed notes.

Oakes, Jeannie, *Keeping Track: How Schools Structure Inequality* (2d ed.), Yale University Press, 2005.
The director of urban schooling at UCLA's Graduate School of Education and Information Studies updates the landmark critique of tracking that launched a detracking reform movement after its publication in 1985. Includes detailed notes.

Patterson, James T., *Brown v. Board of Education: A Civil Rights Milestone and Its Troubled Legacy*, Oxford University Press, 2001.
An emeritus professor of history at Brown University gives a compact account of the landmark school desegregation case and a legacy described as "conspicuous achievement" along with "marked failures."

Reese, William J., *America's Public Schools: From the Common School to "No Child Left Behind,"* Johns Hopkins University Press, 2005.
A professor of educational-policy studies at the University of Wisconsin-Madison provides an accessible overview of the history of U.S. public education from Horace Mann's advocacy of the "common school" through 20th-century developments.

Thernstrom, Abigail, and Stephan Thernstrom, *No Excuses: Closing the Racial Gap in Learning*, Simon & Schuster, 2003.
The authors decry the persistent achievement gap between white and black students but discount the importance of racial isolation in schools as a cause. Includes extensive statistical information, notes. Both authors are senior fellows with the Manhattan Institute; Abigail Thernstrom is vice chair of the U.S. Civil Rights Commission, Stephan Thernstrom a professor of history at Harvard.

Articles

Simmons, Dan, "A Class Action: Leaders Tried to Rein In Effects of Poverty in Public Schools; Voters Were in No Mood for Busing," *La Crosse* (Wis.) *Tribune*, Jan. 21, 2007, p. 1.
The story and an accompanying sidebar ("Balance by Choice") examine the history and current status of the La Crosse school district's 15-year experiment with socioeconomic integration.

Reports and Studies

Kahlenberg, Richard D., "Rescuing *Brown v. Board of Education*: Profiles of Twelve School Districts Pursuing Socioeconomic School Integration," Century Foundation, June 28, 2007, www.tcf.org.
The 42-page report describes the mixed results of socioeconomic integration in 12 school systems, with lengthy treatment of three: La Crosse, Wis.; Cambridge, Mass.;

and Wake County (Raleigh), N.C. For a book-length treatment, see Kahlenberg, *All Together Now: Creating Middle-Class Schools through Public School Choice* (Brookings Institution Press, 2001).

Linn, Robert L., and Kevin G. Welner (eds.), "Race-Conscious Policies for Assigning Students to Schools: Social Science Research and the Supreme Court Cases," National Academy of Education, June 29, 2007, www.naeducation.org/Meredith_Report.pdf.
The 58-page report details social-science research on the effects of racial diversity in schools and finds "general support" for the conclusion that the overall academic and social effects of increased racial diversity are "likely to be positive."

Orfield, Gary, and Chungmei Lee, "Historic Reversals, Accelerating Resegregation, and the Need for New Integration Strategies," UCLA Civil Rights Project, Aug. 29, 2007, www.civilrightsproject.ucla.edu.
The 50-page report finds "accelerating isolation" of African American and Latino students in public schools and recommends a variety of measures to counter the trend, including an attack on housing segregation, socioeconomic integration of schools and congressional initiatives "to require and/or to support racial progress."

On the Web

The Courier-Journal has an extensive compilation of articles, photographs and information on the course of school desegregation in Louisville and Jefferson County (www.courier-journal.com/desegregation). Current coverage can be found on the Web sites of Seattle's two newspapers, the *Seattle Times* (http://seattletimes.nw source.com/html/education/) and the *Seattle Post-Intelligencer* (http://seattlepi.nwsource.com/).

For More Information

American Educational Research Association, 1430 K St., N.W., Suite 1200, Washington, DC 20005; (202) 238-3200; www.aera.net. National research society encouraging scholarly research in efforts to improve education.

Center for Equal Opportunity, 7700 Leesburg Pike, Suite 231, Falls Church, VA 22043; (703) 442-0066; www.ceo usa.org. Think tank devoted to equal opportunity and racial harmony.

Center for Individual Rights, 1233 20th St., N.W., Suite 300, Washington, DC 20036; (202) 833-8400; www.cir-usa.org. Nonprofit public-interest law firm opposed to racial preferences.

Century Foundation, 41 E. 70th St., New York, NY 10021; (212) 535-4441; www.tcf.org. Public-policy institution promoting methods for socioeconomic integration in education.

Mexican American Legal Defense and Educational Fund, 634 S. Spring St., 11th floor, Los Angeles, CA 90014; (213) 629-2512; www.maldef.org. Protects and promotes the civil rights of Latinos living in the United States.

NAACP Legal Defense and Educational Fund, 99 Hudson St., Suite 1600, New York, NY 10013; (212) 965-2200; www.naacpldf.org. Serves as legal counsel on issues of race, with emphasis on education, voter protection, economic justice and criminal justice.

National School Boards Association, 1680 Duke St., Alexandria, VA 22314; (703) 838-6722; www.nsba.org. Seeks to foster excellence and equity in public education by working with school board leadership.

Here is contact information for the school districts involved in the Supreme Court decision, Parents Involved in Community Schools v. Seattle School District No. 1:

Jefferson County Public Schools, VanHoose Education Center, 3332 Newburg Rd., P.O. Box 34020, Louisville, KY 40232-4020; (502) 485-3949; www.jefferson.k12.ky.us.

Seattle School District No. 1, 2445 Third Ave. South, Seattle, WA 98134; (206) 252-0000; www.seattleschools.org.

6

Hate Speech

Marcia Clemmitt

The Rutgers University women's basketball team answers media questions about the derogatory remark made by popular shock jock Don Imus. The team later met with Imus and accepted his apology, but he was fired after public outrage led advertisers to abandon his program.

From *CQ Researcher*,
June 1, 2007.

When radio host Don Imus offhandedly referred to the Rutgers University women's basketball team as "nappy-headed hos" on April 4, it was far from the first time that radio's original shock jock had used racist and sexist jokes on his program. Insults were long a stock in trade of "Imus in the Morning," the 10th-highest-rated radio talk show in the nation last April and also a staple on MSNBC's cable TV lineup, where ratings were rising.

To name just a few examples, in the early 1990s, Imus referred to then-*New York Times* White House correspondent Gwen Ifill, an African American, as "the cleaning lady." [1] In December 2006, he used an anti-Semitic stereotype, calling the "Jewish management" of his employer, CBS Radio, "money-grubbing bastards." [2]

In 2001, *Chicago Tribune* columnist Clarence Page, then a regular guest on the program, asked Imus to promise to stop using phrases like "knuckle-dragging apes" to refer to black athletes and words like "thugs, pimps and muggers" to refer to non-criminal African Americans. Imus agreed but quickly broke his pledge. [3]

The incident with the Rutgers team had a different outcome, however.

A liberal media-criticism group, Media Matters for America, noted the April 4 remark on its Web site. By April 6 the National Association of Black Journalists called for the 66-year-old Imus to be fired, and the Rev. Al Sharpton and other individuals and groups soon followed suit.

"Imus has a pathetic yet well-documented history of resorting to racist, sexist and homophobic commentary" and should resign or be fired, said National Association of Hispanic Journalists President Rafael Olmeda in a statement. [4]

Conservatives Are Top Talk Hosts

With at least 13.5 million weekly listeners, political commentator Rush Limbaugh drew the largest talk radio audience in fall 2006, followed by fellow conservatives Sean Hannity and Michael Savage. Don Imus, whose show was later canceled, was tied for 10th place.

Top Talk Radio Hosts, fall 2006

Host	Minimum Weekly Listeners	Host	Minimum Weekly Listeners
1. Rush Limbaugh	13.5 million	10. Dr. Joy Browne	2.25 million
2. Sean Hannity	12.5 million	Don Imus	
3. Michael Savage	8.25 million	Kim Komando	
4. Dr. Laura Schlessinger	8 million	Jim Rome	
5. Laura Ingraham	5 million	11. Bob Brinker	1.75 million
6. Glenn Beck	3.75 million	Tom Leykis	
Neal Boortz		12. Rusty Humphries	1.5 million
Mike Gallagher		Lars Larson	
7. Jim Bohannon	3.25 million	G. Gordon Liddy	
Clark Howard		Mancow	
Mark Levin		13. Alan Colmes	1.25 million
Bill O'Reilly		Al Franken	
8. Bill Bennett	3 million	Bill Handel	
Jerry Doyle		Hugh Hewitt	
Dave Ramsey		Lionel	
Ed Schultz		Stephanie Miller	
Doug Stephan		Randi Rhodes	
9. Michael Medved	2.75 million	14. Dr. Dean Edell	1 million
George Noory		Opie & Anthony	
		Michael Reagan	

Source: Talkers magazine, 2007

Imus' show has long been a popular stop for politicians such as Sens. John McCain, R-Ariz., and John Kerry, D-Mass., as well as powerful Washington journalists like "Meet the Press" host Tim Russert. Though some long-time guests like former *Boston Globe* columnist Tom Oliphant defended their friend and depicted his remark as a joke that misfired, advertisers including General Motors and American Express became concerned about the burgeoning public scrutiny and intensifying coverage of the flap in the press and pulled ads from the show. On April 11, MSNBC canceled "Imus in the Morning"; CBS followed suit the next day. [5]

Beyond derailing Imus' nearly four-decade run as a radio host, the incident triggered a widespread debate about the public use of racist and sexist language, especially by shock jocks and some commentators, and in the lyrics of gangsta-rap music, which often refer to women as "bitches" and "hos," as Imus did.

Racist and sexist insults are common currency among radio shock talkers, who delight in "bringing private behavior out into public," giving the audience "the thrill of crossing that line," according to John Baugh, a professor of linguistics at Washington University in St. Louis. But when private language goes public, "a tremendous amount of bigotry can be exposed that's beneath the veneer" of polite society, Baugh says.

In the weeks since the Imus incident, radio networks have responded more firmly than usual to shock-jock forays into racist and sexist clowning, firing or suspending several hosts for comments not strikingly different from their usual fare.

Imus' former employer CBS Radio indefinitely suspended two New York shock jocks, JV and Elvis, for airing prank calls to Chinese restaurants that included terms like "shrimp flied lice." On May 15 XM Satellite Radio, a subscriber-only service not even carried over public airwaves, suspended shock jocks Gregg "Opie" Hughes and Anthony Cumia for 30 days for on-air comments surrounding a segment about a homeless man who declared he wanted to rape Secretary of State Condeleeza Rice and other women.

Some media analysts, noting that edgy content sells, predict the shock-jock crackdown is probably temporary.

Unlike some activists, the advertisers who abandoned "Imus in the Morning" "never intended to kill the show" and generally don't rule out sponsoring Imus again in the future, wrote Steve McClellan of *AdWeek* magazine.

The program "helped sell marketers' products to more than 2 million mostly affluent viewers and listeners each week," garnering $33 million in ads annually for MSNBC and another $11 million for WFAN, the New York radio station where it originated. [6]

But some conservative commentators warn that those liberal activist groups that pushed for Imus' firing are carrying on with their agendas in the hope of ending the dominance of conservative talk on radio and television. One possible way of doing this would be advocating for the restoration of the Federal Communications Commission's Fairness Doctrine, a rule requiring broadcasters who air programs on controversial subjects to give significant time to all sides of an issue. The agency repealed it in 1987.

"It wasn't exactly clear to me how [liberals] intended to bring back the Fairness Doctrine," Cliff Kincaid, chief writer and editor at the conservative media-criticism group Accuracy in Media, said at an April 13 forum at the conservative Washington-based think tank Free Congress Foundation. "But I think now with the Imus affair, we know." It's a "short leap from firing Imus to going after [conservative commentator] Rush Limbaugh." [7]

Some of the loudest criticisms that followed the Imus affair were aimed not at racist and sexist language used by whites like Imus and Limbaugh but by black musicians — mainly in gangsta-rap lyrics.

"Now that we've gotten Imus taken care of, can we finally address what's going on with the misogyny among rappers?" asked columnist Sue Hutchison in the April 13 *San Jose Mercury News.* [8]

"Hypocrisy abounds" around the Imus firing because the same terms Imus used "go on in rap music on hundreds of radio stations around the country" without any protest from the same African Americans who protested Imus' language, said Dick Kernan, vice president of the Specs Howard School of Broadcasting in Southfield, Mich. [9]

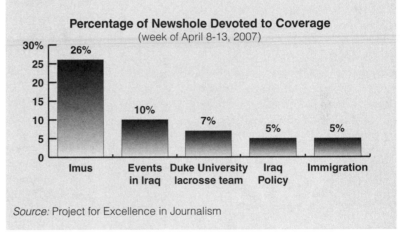

Imus Controversy Ignited Media Flood

In early April 2007, newspapers devoted more than a quarter of their "newshole" — the space devoted to news — to the controversy over Don Imus' racist remark about the Rutgers University women's basketball team. The next biggest topic was the Iraq War, which garnered just 10 percent of the newshole. Of all news stories so far in 2007 (not shown on graphic), only coverage of President Bush's troop "surge" in Iraq, in early January received more coverage (34 percent of the newshole). Total coverage of the Imus controversy received 26 percent of the coverage. Much of the Imus coverage revolved around the Rev. Al Sharpton, who skewered Imus on his talk show on April 9 and helped lead the campaign for Imus' firing.

Percentage of Newshole Devoted to Coverage
(week of April 8-13, 2007)

Category	Percentage
Imus	26%
Events in Iraq	10%
Duke University lacrosse team	7%
Iraq Policy	5%
Immigration	5%

Source: Project for Excellence in Journalism

Others argue that gangsta-rap lyrics and a radio broadcast aren't necessarily comparable forms of media. Hip-hop "was a quick and easy scapegoat," says Tony N. Brown, a sociologist at Vanderbilt University. But the offensive lyrics generally aren't on display to the general public, he says. "To get these particular lyrics that people are talking about, you have to buy them," and radio bleeps or deletes them, he says.

Anger about sexist lyrics and use of other derogatory language like "nigger" in some rap music has been protested in African American communities for years, although that fact hasn't been much noticed by the mainstream media, wrote journalist Richard Prince of the Maynard Institute for Journalism Education in Oakland, Calif. At soul singer James Brown's funeral last December, the Rev. Sharpton recalled that Brown had asked him, "What happened that we went from saying, 'I'm black and I'm proud' to calling us niggers and hos and bitches?"

Civil rights activist and radio host the Rev. Al Sharpton became one of the first voices to call for the firing of Don Imus after he made a racial and gender slur against the Rutgers University women's basketball team. Some conservative commentators complained Sharpton hasn't made such high-profile protests against sexist lyrics by black rappers.

"Sharpton has been out there talking about these lyrics for a long time," says Lee Thornton, a journalism professor at the University of Maryland, College Park, and a former broadcaster.

To some analysts, aggressive language throughout the media is disturbing evidence that popular culture in the United States lacks civility.

"Mainstream media is becoming more like Imus" all the time, says Sheri Parks, associate professor of American studies at the university. "Ridicule and insults are the way we laugh now. We're moving closer and closer to that culture of meanness being completely mainstream."

As broadcasters, lawmakers and social critics debate the values and dangers of shock media to American culture, here are some of the questions being asked:

Have ethnic jokes and insults become too pervasive in society?

Ethnic putdowns and comedy making light of someone's gender have long been part of American culture. But social critics and other commentators argue that shock jocks, gangsta rappers and other personalities have taken things to the extreme by using slurs to target political opponents or other public figures, increasingly poisoning public discourse. The question is whether practitioners have gone over the line — and where exactly the line is?

Talk radio, at least, "is not getting dirtier, not getting cleaner" although the medium continues to expand, says Michael Harrison, founder and editor of *Talkers* magazine and a longtime observer of the phenomenon. "There's no trend toward nastiness."

In fact, ethnic humor and insults are ancient traditions and have long been a feature of American culture, says Leon Rappoport, professor emeritus of psychology at Kansas State University and author of a recent book on ethnic humor. "Dialect humor" stereotyping groups ranging from "operatic Italians to money-grubbing Jews" was a staple of the music halls and vaudeville stages of the early 20th century, for example, says Rappoport.

Later, when stage performers migrated to radio, joking based on ethnic stereotypes continued, says Rappoport. For example, radio comedian Fred Allen based much of his humor on a cast of invented characters representing stereotyped Irish, Jewish and Southern characters, among others.

Early radio and television talk-show host Joe Pyne regularly ridiculed his guests, sometimes with ethnic insults, through the 1960s, says Douglas Gomery, professor emeritus of journalism at the University of Maryland and resident scholar at the university's Library of American Broadcasting.

In 1968, when blacks rioted in several American inner cities, Pyne was suspended for a week after he pulled a gun out of his drawer while talking with an African American guest. [10]

But some analysts argue that ethnic and gender slurs, along with other name-calling, have become disturbingly prevalent in media over the past few decades and foster hatred and intolerance.

Imus is "emblematic of our uncivil times," said Charles Haynes, a senior scholar at the First Amendment Center, an education organization in Arlington, Va. "In the Internet age, the impulse to offend apparently knows no bounds. People feel increasingly emboldened to say or write anything — however ugly, vulgar or downright hateful. . . . The anything-goes Web world has raised the bar for what counts as 'offensive speech' in America's public square," and "offensive speech sells," said Haynes. [11]

The open use of ethnic and gender slurs "has gotten worse" in recent years, says E. Faye Williams, a lawyer and businesswoman who chairs the National Congress of Black Women, a group that has long protested the stereotyping of African American women, including in gangsta rap. Today's American media is rife with comedy, movies and music that negatively stereotype black women, in particular, she says.

Williams says the trend is especially troubling because programming with offensive material is sold to other countries. "It breaks my heart when I go to other countries and see that those negative stereotypes have been exported," Williams says.

Negative stereotypes of African Americans are evident among Asian and Latin American immigrants to the United States. Many arrive "with anti-black stereotypes in their heads" that they picked up from American media viewed abroad, says Joe R. Feagin, a professor of sociology at Texas A&M University and author of numerous books documenting race-related experiences and attitudes.

In a recent study, for example, rural Taiwanese people who had never seen a black person "had anti-black attitudes" based on viewing American media, he says.

To some, the ethnic and racial putdowns are symptoms of a broader coarsening of American society. Name-calling and stereotyping go "way back in Western culture," says Deborah Tannen, professor of linguistics at Georgetown University and author of the 1999 book *The Argument Culture: Stopping America's War of Words.* But, she adds, "I've found lots and lots of evidence that it got worse in the 1990s," as name-calling and shouting replaced more civil debate in realms ranging from television shows to the courts. For example, several former U.S. senators have declared that they voluntarily left Congress in the 1990s because discourse there became vicious and harshly adversarial. Numerous lawyers say they left their

Former conservative journalist David Brock founded the liberal media-watchdog group Media Matters for America, credited with bringing shock jock radio host Don Imus' racially offensive remark to public attention by posting it on the group's Web site the same day he made the comment. The growing prominence of such Internet activism means fewer media gaffes now escape public scrutiny, analysts say.

profession for the same reason, Tannen says.

There's no doubt "we have become a coarse society" over the past few decades, says Maryland's Thornton, whose network television jobs included a seven-year stint booking guests for the Rev. Jesse Jackson's "Both Sides" talk show on CNN.

"I cannot imagine dropping a person from the 1940s into our climate," says Thornton. "Decades ago, although there was racism underneath, people clothed themselves in a mannerly way. There were lines of public behavior. I don't think we know anymore in our culture what the lines are. That's why Imus was as surprised as anyone to find that he had crossed one," she says.

The insult culture "has gone to the point of no return, and we don't know how to rein it in," says Thornton. "The whole shock jock thing has contributed to the coarsening of dialogue," she says. Nevertheless, "The public appetite for this is overrated" by media outlets.

A Who's Who of Shock Jocks

In the beginning was Imus.

Don Imus

Howard Stern

Don Imus began his career as the first true "shock jock" in 1970 at a Cleveland radio station as a DJ. He quickly developed a popular repertoire of comic and raunchy bits such as asking female callers, "Are you naked?"

In the 1990s, the "Imus in the Morning" show gravitated toward news and political talk, with a growing list of influential guests including members of Congress and journalists from major news organizations such as NBC and *Newsweek*. The show mixed political talk with shock-jock banter. For example, Imus referred to *Washington Post* media reporter Howard Kurtz, a frequent guest, as a "boner-nosed . . . beanie-wearing Jewboy" and described New York Knicks basketball player Patrick Ewing as a "knuckle-dragging moron."

Imus was fired in April by both CBS Radio and MSNBC television, which had simulcast his radio program to rising ratings, after calling the Rutgers University women's basketball team "nappy-headed hos." Fired in the first months of a five-year, $40 million contract, Imus is suing CBS.

Radio's second iconic shock jock is **Howard Stern**, who got his first radio job in 1976 and transitioned into shock-jock stunts gradually a few years later. Stern's specialty is sex talk, though he's also done parodies like "Hill Street Jews." In 1985 NBC Radio briefly canceled Stern's show over a new segment called "Bestiality Dial-a-Date."

His employer in the early 1990s, Infinity Broadcasting, racked up $1.7 million in Federal Communications Commission (FCC) indecency fines over Stern's show between 1990 and 1993. In 1992, for example, stations carrying Stern earned a $600,000 fine after Stern combined indecency with racial stereotypes when he said "the closest I came to making love to a black woman was I masturbated to a picture of Aunt Jemima on a pancake box."

Despite frequent suspensions, cancellations and station changes, Stern has been employed on radio consistently for more than three decades. Currently he hosts "The Howard Stern Show" on Sirius Satellite Radio.

To some observers, using ethnic stereotypes as veiled or overt insults is an especially egregious form of argument and has gone too far in the media.

The liberal media-monitoring group Media Matters for America was chagrined when conservative radio talk-show host Limbaugh aimed racial stereotypes at both civil rights activist Sharpton and Democratic presidential candidate Sen. Barack Obama by playing a satirical song titled "Barack the Magic Negro," in which a singer impersonating Sharpton urges listeners not to vote for Obama because he's not a "real" black man like rapper Snoop Dogg.

However, others argue that racial stereotyping is no more harmful than strong, argumentative language.

Accuracy in Media's Kincaid says there's no essential difference between denigrating people through racial

stereotypes or denigrating them for their individual actions, as liberal MSNBC host Keith Olbermann does in his nightly feature dubbing several individuals "the worst people in the world" for that day. In either case, it's a matter of "holding people up for public ridicule," says Kincaid.

Should the government do more to restrain hate speech?

The Federal Communications Commission (FCC) has the authority to limit sexually explicit speech and other public discourse it deems "indecent." Some observers believe the agency should adopt a similar approach toward "hate speech" involving demeaning racial or ethnic stereotypes. But such an expansion of regulatory power could collide with First Amendment concerns,

Shock talker **Doug "Greaseman" Tracht** has been an on-air personality since the early 1970s at several East Coast stations. He's most infamous for racist comments he made while working at Washington, D.C.-area stations, where he's spent most of his career.

Douglas Tracht

In 1985, he was widely criticized for saying of the Martin Luther King Day holiday that "they should shoot four more of them and give us a whole week off." Between 1999 and 2002, Tracht was off the air entirely after he was fired over another racist comment. Tracht's broadcast features often-raunchy on-air skits and stories employing a large cast of fictional characters he developed over the years.

Bubba

After two decades on broadcast radio, **Bubba the Love Sponge** was fired by Clear Channel Communications in 2004 after the FCC fined the company $755,000 based on complaints about Bubba's show, which has featured stunts like butchering a hog on air, shocking guests with electric collars and giving his co-workers a massive dose of laxatives to see who would be the last to move their bowels. Currently the program is carried on Sirius.

Anthony Cumia and Gregg Hughes

Jocks Gregg "Opie" Hughes and Anthony Cumia — **Opie and Anthony** — have migrated from broadcast radio to satellite and back again. Among other incidents, they were fired from a Boston station in 1998 for an April Fool's hoax claiming that then-Boston Mayor Thomas Merino had been killed in a car crash.

In May 2007, in an unusual twist, the two were fired by the unregulated subscription-radio service XM Satellite Radio but not by the CBS broadcast network, which also airs their show, after they joked about a homeless man raping Secretary of State Condoleezza Rice.

JV and Elvis — Jeff Vandergrift and Dan Lay — inhabited shock radio's "The Dog House with JV and Elvis" until their show was canceled by CBS in May 2007, in the wake of Imus' firing. Vandergrift and Lay aired a prank phone call in fake accents to a Chinese restaurant, requesting "shrimp flied lice," among other Asian-stereotyping jokes. The call — typical fare for the show — was made before Imus made his "nappy-headed hos" comment, but CBS didn't fire the two until after it fired Imus.

particularly the libertarian belief that individuals, not the government, should be responsible for reining in inappropriate speech.

"The FCC needs to take a close look at its policies when it comes to the kind of language people use," says Ohio State University sociologist K. Sue Jewell, author of the book *From Mammy to Miss America and Beyond: Cultural Images and the Shaping of U.S. Social Policy.* Jewell believes name-calling and stereotyping insults by high-profile media figures can strongly influence public opinion, particularly among young people, and "easily escalate to violence."

Williams of the National Congress of Black Women believes the FCC should remove shock jocks for offensive remarks on public airwaves, since they can find new homes on subscription satellite radio stations. She and other experts contend the FCC and Congress could easily justify expanding the agency's mandate, citing historical precedent.

"There are certain words that have historical baggage, and they probably shouldn't be used on the airwaves, which are owned by all of us. Given our national history of racial discrimination, I don't see why the FCC can't make that argument," says Leonard Baynes, a professor at New York's St. John's University School of Law. Baynes says the FCC should even consider levying similar restrictions on cable television content, noting cable operators currently are required to scramble indecent programming and take other steps to police content in order to get franchise licenses.

AP Photo/Richard Drew

Angela Burt-Murray, editor-in-chief of *Essence* magazine, is one of several prominent black journalists — including Gwen Ifill of PBS and Al Roker of NBC — who called for CBS Radio to take a harder stance on Don Imus' April 4 remark about the Rutgers women's basketball team after he was suspended for two weeks. He was eventually fired by CBS on April 12.

But some experts prefer the status quo be maintained, saying they fear government agencies will find it difficult to walk the center line and fight off the temptation to regulate speech that conflicts with an administration's political agenda.

"I support the FCC's ability to regulate obscenity — but I don't want to see their powers expanded" to sanction language that's racist or homophobic, for example, says Accuracy in Media's Kincaid. The answer to speech that offends people is more speech from the side that was offended, he says. "I want to see more speech, not less."

The best response "would be for people [like Imus] to bring onto their shows the people that disagree with them," says Kincaid, who co-hosted CNN's "Crossfire" talk program in the 1980s. Harking back to his on-air experience, Kincaid says, "I liked that show because of the two views" that were part of every program. But ensuring that opposing views are part of every discussion should be left to television and radio networks and hosts, not the government, he adds.

Even the FCC's current powers to regulate for "decency" can be misused to push a political agenda instead, said liberal writer and commentator Ted Rall, who contends the decision to pull shock jock Howard Stern's show from Clear Channel Communications' radio stations in 2004 had less to do with inappropriate remarks than with statements critical of the Bush administration. [12]

"If you don't think me going after Bush got me thrown off those stations, you got another think coming," said Stern. His days on broadcast radio were "numbered because I dared to speak out against the Bush administration and . . . the religious agenda of George W. Bush concerning stem cell research and gay marriage," he said. "What he is doing with the FCC is pushing this religious agenda." [13]

Some legal experts worry that legitimate free speech can be caught up in a dragnet of enforcement actions if the government more stringently polices the airwaves.

"Racist speech is — or should be — always over the line, and Imus' coarse and racist reference to the Rutgers team was all the worse because it seemed so casually uttered," said New York City-based First Amendment lawyer Floyd Abrams. Nevertheless, he said, "I am concerned about policing even errant speech to the point that we risk losing the enlivening and sometimes even acute commentary that accompanies it and of which even offensive speech is sometimes a part." [14]

Radio is by its nature a spontaneous medium, and that means inadvisable words will be uttered from time to time, says *Talkers* magazine's Harrison. "The spontaneity is what keeps people interested," he says. 'The more they regulate radio the more they'll kill it."

Harrison notes that radio has become such a niche medium that there's little reason to apply a new regulatory regime. Broadcast radio today is "just one little street down a much wider avenue" of largely unregulated media, making additional content regulation both unfair and pointless, he says.

Harrison says talk about new regulations smacks of hypocrisy when all types of objectionable discourse and pornography are conveyed on the Internet, which is unregulated.

L. Brent Bozell, founder of the conservative Media Research Center, adamantly opposes increased government regulation of argumentative speech. He argues, however, that a different kind of federal rule would help media consumers squelch such speech on their own, if they chose, at least on cable television. Under a "cable choice" set-up, cable subscribers could order and cancel channels individually, rather than being restricted to a cable company's prepackaged channel tiers.

A rule permitting such "cable choice" would "be a real market solution" to problems like Imus' racist speech, which was carried over MSNBC, says Bozell. "If the customer had the right" to stop paying for individual channels, "NBC and BET [Black Entertainment Television] would be very very careful about who they offended," and "if 2 percent of the people watched a certain network, the other 98 percent wouldn't have to pay for it," as happens today, he says.

Should Don Imus have been fired?

Few people defend the language Imus used to describe the Rutgers players. But while many commentators say his firing was justified, others find it hypocritical, in light of language found elsewhere in the media. And they wonder whether keeping him on the air might have helped spark a more enduring dialogue about racism and misogyny.

Firing Imus "was an appropriate response, and it should have happened sooner," says Ohio State's Jewell, adding that the public airwaves "should not be used to demean a culture."

"Blacks were more likely to want him to be fired," which illustrates the stark "racial divide" in America, says Baynes of St. John's Law School. In the dominant white culture, "there really isn't an appreciation and understanding of this minority point of view," which is the product of a longstanding historical linkage between use of racially demeaning language and racist actions, Baynes says.

"When someone uses that kind of language, it makes the hair on the back of your neck stand up because you don't know what that person would do in terms of firing you without cause or refusing to rent an apartment to you," Baynes says.

In contrast, he continues, "white people know the person who used the language as a friend, an aunt, an uncle, a grandpa, someone who may have loved them and been generous to them." In such a scenario, they are reluctant to speak out against racist language while acknowledging that someone who can be loving to friends and family also is capable of being hurtful.

Imus was fired largely because civil rights activists wielded economic power over advertisers to get him off the air — a positive but not extremely significant outcome, says Marc Lamont Hill, assistant professor of American studies at Temple University. The firing doesn't address any of the real racial problems afflicting African Americans, such as poor schools or hiring and housing discrimination, says Hill. "I'd take a hundred Imuses if it meant that black people could have access to good health care," he says.

More important than Imus being fired was "the conversation on language that impugns people that's begun" in the wake of the incident, says Karl Frisch, media relations director at the liberal media-criticism organization Media Matters for America, one of the groups that first brought public attention to Imus' slur.

Some who are skeptical about the firing say that a better conversation on race might have ensued had Imus stayed on the job, however.

The firing was understandable but unfortunate, says Tom Taylor, editor of *Inside Radio* magazine. Earlier in Imus' career, after he beat personal problems with drugs and alcohol, "he did a great job of getting other guys alerted to that problem" through public-service work and his radio program. "To me, we've lost the opportunity" to see if "he could have done the same thing with racist language," Taylor says.

Radio is a niche medium where loyal but small audiences are in large part created and sustained by the particular talents of individual on-air personalities. Imus' niche was an unusual one, and his departure will be felt, Taylor says.

The Imus audience "was never large" — 2 and a half to 3 million listeners, says Taylor. "But it was a very interesting audience," made up of "the type of American who watches the Sunday TV talk shows and would like to meet authors." The program "was sort of like an 18th-century Paris salon where you get this volatile mixture of guys" discussing a wide range of topics, he says. In particular, "publishers have been in tears" since the firing because Imus' show "was an almost irreplaceable stop on the book circuit."

CHRONOLOGY

1960s-1970s *Supreme Court debates whether government bans on radio shock talk violate the Constitution. In sitcoms and standup comedy, insult humor replaces physical comedy, which is deemed too violent.*

1969 Supreme Court declares that the Federal Communications Commission's (FCC) Fairness Doctrine — requiring on-air controversial discussions to present all sides of the issue — is consistent with the First Amendment guarantee of free speech.

1968 Don Imus takes his first radio job in Cleveland.

1978 In a case involving comedian George Carlin's use of "seven dirty words," Supreme Court upholds FCC's right to bar broadcast of "indecent" material.

1980s *Raucous, risqué "morning zoo" programs become drive-time radio favorites.*

1984 Denver shock host Alan Berg is murdered by right-wing fanatics angered by his outspoken left-wing political and sex talk.

1987 FCC rescinds the Fairness Doctrine.

1990s *Talk radio burgeons after the Fairness Doctrine is scrapped. Political talk hosts pick up shock talk, especially ethnic and gender insults. A new form of hip-hop, gangsta rap, features sexist, violent lyrics.*

1993 St. Louis shock jocks Steve Shannon and D.C. Chymes are fired after telling a caller she is "acting like a nigger." They are soon hired by another local station.

1996 New York radio personality Bob Grant, who has a history of anti-black statements, is fired after a joke about Commerce Secretary Ron Brown, an African-American, who had just died in a plane crash.

1997 Imus is named one of *Time* magazine's 25 most influential Americans.

1999 Washington, D.C., shock jock Doug "Greaseman" Tracht is fired after saying, "Now you understand why they drag them behind trucks," referring to the Texas murder in which James Byrd, an African-American, was dragged behind a truck.

2000s *Shock talkers fired from broadcast radio find new homes on unregulated Internet and satellite radio.*

2003 Conservative radio host Rush Limbaugh is hired then quickly fired by ESPN after he says a biased liberal media pushed black Philadelphia Eagles quarterback Donovan McNabb to star status despite mediocre skills. . . . Rochester, N.Y., shock talker Bob Lonsberry is fired after comparing the city's African-American mayor to a monkey but is soon rehired by the same station.

2004 Rapper Nelly cancels a charity appearance at Spelman College, a historically black school for women in Atlanta, after students protest his sexist videos.

2005 Sportscaster Sid Rosenberg is banned from "Imus in the Morning" after saying singer Kylie Minogue, who has breast cancer, "won't look so good when she's got a bald head with one titty." He later returns to the show as a frequent guest. . . . New York radio host Miss Jones is briefly suspended for a song mocking tsunami victims as "Africans drowning, little Chinamen swept away. You could hear God laughing, 'Swim, you bitches, swim.' "

2006 Shock jock Howard Stern leaves the public airwaves for Sirius Satellite Radio.

2007 On April 4, Imus refers to Rutgers University female basketball players as "nappy-headed hos" and is fired a week later after advertisers pull their spots. Fired three months into a five-year $40 million contract with CBS Radio, Imus is suing the network. . . . CBS Radio fires New York shock jocks Jeff Vandergrift and Dan Lay — J.V. and Elvis — for a prank phone call to workers at a Chinese restaurant. . . . Some in the newly Democrat-controlled Congress mull regulating media violence and reviving the Fairness Doctrine.

Some critics believe firing Imus was hypocritical when one considers the offensive or questionable material that can be found on a daily basis in the media. Kincaid of Accuracy in Media cites MSNBC's decision to air the profanity-laced video made by Seung-Hui Cho, the student who carried out the April 16 Virginia Tech University massacre.

The double standard isn't a particular surprise, however, since both MSNBC and CBS employed Imus because he was an edgy shock jock, then fired him for saying something shocking, says Kincaid. MSNBC, in particular, "helped to make him a star by putting their people on his show" as journalist-guests, he says.

"The policy ought to be that the media is in favor of free speech," says Kincaid. "So if you hire a commentator who's known for saying shocking things, then you accept that he will say shocking things. . . . People can apologize on the air and move on. That's freedom with responsibility."

"I thought CBS overreacted because I think that his intentions weren't derogatory," says Dennis Rome, a professor of criminal justice at the University of Wisconsin, Parkside.

Rome says while the language Imus used was objectionable, it continues to be widely used. He notes that gangsta rappers use words like "hos," saying it's a different thing for African Americans to demean each other. "I don't agree," he says. "The real problem is that the language is being kept alive, no matter who's using it, and what we need to do is move on from it."

Rome adds, "Rush Limbaugh and others have said a lot worse" than the statement that lost Imus his job, and the damage potentially done by media personalities who use racial and gender stereotyping as part of political discourse "is far stronger, because they intend to be derogatory," Rome says. He predicts nothing will come of the Imus incident because he was quickly fired and the incident was swept under the rug.

"A better approach would have been, 'What do we do to balance this? What else can we put on the air to show more points of view?' " he says.

BACKGROUND

Historical Stereotypes

Imus sought to excuse his use of the phrase "nappy-headed hos" by saying he and his producers had picked up the words from hip-hop music, as well as from the Spike Lee film "School Daze." But historians and linguists say the words have a history stretching back to the days of slavery. [15]

Blacks' "nappy hair" was one of the physical characteristics seized upon by white slave owners to prove that "neither human physiology nor human nature was uniform" as a way of justifying their ownership of other humans, said Zine Magubane, assistant professor of sociology at Boston College. [16]

Slavery in America flourished at the same time many Europeans and American settlers were embracing the ideals of the Enlightenment, including human equality, as the inspiration for the French and American revolutions, Magubane said. To reconcile that apparent contradiction, some focused on physical differences between blacks and whites they said were signs blacks didn't have to be included on equal terms in a social contract.

For example, in his "Notes on the State of Virginia," Thomas Jefferson concluded that blacks couldn't be politically enfranchised members of the new American union because of their "physical and moral" differences from whites, such as not having long, flowing hair, Magubane wrote. [17]

Descriptions like "nappy headed" and "ho" to refer to African American women are part of "a white, racial frame that we whites invented in the 1600s to explain how we as good Christians could enslave thousands of human beings," says Feagin of Texas A&M. The stereotypes persist, including in some black music like gangsta rap, because "350 of our 400 years of history were years of extreme racial oppression. So in order to see ourselves as good people, we had to come up with" reasons for considering African Americans lesser people and "hammer it into everybody's head, including black people," Feagin says.

While "ho" itself is a newer coinage, originating in the black community, words stereotyping African American women as oversexed and as prostitutes — such as "wench" — were common from slavery days, largely to provide a rationale for the growth of a large mulatto class of mixed-race children, says Ohio State sociologist Jewell. "Where were all those mulatto children coming from?" — from "Jezebel — the bad black girl," she says. Words like "wench," "ho" and "Jezebel" convey the message that "these women of African descent are very hyper-sexed, worldly seductresses, and if you aren't careful, they will seduce you," she says.

Societal Conversation on Race Seems Unlikely

Racism experts say they are not surprised.

Soon after radio host Don Imus referred to the Rutgers University women's basketball team as "nappy-headed hos," groups like the National Association of Black Journalists and some media commentators began calling for a national "conversation on race." Such a dialogue was needed, some said, to confront the simmering differences that saw many African-Americans calling for the shock jock's firing while many whites saw the comments as no big deal.

But while some dialogue did soon begin about the sexism inherent in the gangsta-rap lyrics from which Imus said he picked up the term "ho," conversation about the radio host's casual use of a racist, sexist insult never really happened. Many racism experts say they're not surprised.

Racism "isn't on the docket as an issue," despite occasional flurries of attention when a celebrity like Imus crosses the line in public comments, says Marc Lamont Hill, an assistant professor of American studies at Temple University.

When whites who use words like "nappy-headed" say, " 'I said that, but I'm not a racist,' I do think that they're being serious," says Hill, who is black. "I believe that Imus could honestly say, 'I don't think I'm better than a black person.' " But "the broader context that makes the whole notion of 'nappy-headed' and 'ho' so painful is that he has the power to put a name on someone," Hill says.

"Being called a nigger isn't just an epithet. It's putting you in a certain position" because a white man has the power to do so, while African-Americans don't, says Hill. "I can call you a cracker, but I can't treat you like a cracker."

In the 1960s, during the civil rights era, "we had a way to talk about race" because discussion centered on laws that could quell overt oppression and segregation, says Shawn J. Parry-Giles, associate professor of communication at the University of Maryland, College Park. Today, with those laws on the books, "There is a sense among the majority group that we've done everything that we need to do." So when a potentially racist incident occurs, "we just individualize it," hoping that firing Imus, for example, ends the problem, Parry-Giles says.

The shock-radio era has "paralleled a societal era of ignoring race, on the grounds that our society should be colorblind," says Lee Anne Bell, director of the education program at Barnard College. "But if you can't talk about it, you can't confront it, and that makes colorblindness very insidious."

Overt racism among whites has drastically receded, but young, white men, especially, "still love to go for a beer with [white] friends and tell racist jokes," says Joe R. Feagin, a professor of sociology at Texas A&M University and co-author of a recent book on racist language and opinions among today's white college students.

And while Imus and the students Feagin surveyed generally excuse their private language, saying it doesn't make them racists, "it does mean something," Feagin says. When comedian and former "Seinfeld" actor Michael Richards railed at some African-American hecklers at a stand-up gig last year, he made "seven uses of the N-word," says Feagin. "That comes from something pretty deep."

If America ever does get serious about having a race conversation, scholars and educators on race and prejudice have some suggestions:

- Everyone must acknowledge, up front, that we routinely act to protect our own individual interests, and that those interests have race, gender and class implications, says Tony N. Brown, assistant professor of sociology at Vanderbilt University. "People say, 'I'm

Today, the stereotypes persist, although Americans generally think that the days of racism are over, says Feagin. "We passed civil rights laws in the 1960s, and now we think all the racial problems are over," he says. But if that had happened, it would mean "hundreds of years of history had been canceled, and that doesn't happen quickly."

In fact, the same racist language, including heavy use of "nigger," continues to be common among white people speaking in all-white groups, says Leslie Houts Picca, a sociologist at the University of Dayton. "We were really quite shocked at just how prevalent casual use of the N-word is," says Picca, who with coauthor Feagin recently published a book detailing race-related incidents that white college students revealed in diaries.

When asked about their objectionable speech, many white students said the words "had lost their racial connotations," says Picca. But in fact they "are centuries-old

not racist or sexist in my language,' "Brown says. "Nevertheless, "in my day-to-day actions, I do reinforce my own racial and gender and class interests, sometimes to the detriment of others' interests. I don't think positive things about the homeless," for example.

Comedian and former "Seinfeld" actor Michael Richards appears on the Rev. Jesse Jackson's radio show on Nov. 26, 2006, to make amends for a Nov. 17 racist outburst at a West Hollywood comedy club. When loud talk from a group of African-American audience members interrupted his act, Richards unleashed a racial tirade, calling the men "niggers" and alluding to lynching.

- Whites, the majority culture, "must be willing to admit there are things we don't know about racism, because people of color have to know when racism is operating just to get along in the world, but white people have our racism detectors set at a very low level," says Tim Wise, a lecturer on race and gender bias and founder of the Nashville-based Association for White Anti-Racist Education. Whites should "start with the assumption that when people of color say, 'Racism is operating,' they probably know what they're talking about, because they've spent a lifetime learning to distinguish between what's racism and what's just everyday insensitivity," Wise says.

- Everyone should hear as many first-person — preferably in-person — stories of Americans of all ethnicities as possible, says Feagin. "The more voices people read or encounter, the more they understand" others' points of view, he says.

- Conversation should "start with objective facts — that women earn 76 cents on the dollar compared to men, for comparable work; that black men are incarcerated at a very high rate," says Brown. "Then we can ask people to give their individual explanations for those facts," he says. "In those explanations, attitudes and beliefs would be revealed" and could then be examined and discussed, he says.

- Everyone should be willing to take responsibility for what they can control, not shift the discussion to what others are doing, says Wise. The nearly immediate shift of the Imus-spurred race discussion from his language to racism and misogyny expressed by hip-hop lyrics shows "how white Americans are so used to shifting the conversation away from things that are our responsibility," he says.

"Why can't we just stop and talk about ourselves for a minute, about our personal responsibility to challenge white people" over racist comments? asks Wise. "Our personal responsibility is to say, 'Cool. The next time something like Imus happens, we whites will deal with our people, just as we expect people of color to hold their group responsible for things like violent rap lyrics,' " he says. Black or white, "own the piece of the problem that's yours, and maybe we can jumpstart the conversation."

Few believe that a true cross-racial conversation on racial matters will begin in America any time soon, Imus or no Imus, however. Says Georgetown University professor of linguistics Deborah Tannen: "Things happen all the time that could spark that conversation, but they don't."

stereotypes, like lazy and criminal. They are not inventing them" but "bringing them down from history."

When used in public, as in Imus' comment, the words call up memories of a painful past for African Americans, but not for whites, and this deepens the racial divide, says Feagin.

"Mulattos did not come from interracial marriage, and for every time a black man raped a white woman, there were a 1,000 cases the other way" in the days of slavery and legal segregation, a fact that haunts elderly African American women, in particular, to this day, he says. "One of my grad students has been interviewing elderly African Americans who lived under legal segregation," Feagin says. In one commonly remembered story, a white man enters a black home and rapes a teenage daughter, says Feagin. "That story has yet to be told" in history books and mainstream media, says Feagin. "Yet these elderly women and men tell these stories routinely. Some 80-year-old black

Ethnic Humor's No Joke for Amateurs

It gets ugly when aggression overwhelms the humor.

Why did shock-radio host Don Imus call the Rutgers University women's basketball team "nappy-headed hos?" "I was trying to be funny," Imus explained on his April 9 broadcast, several days after the original comment had blown up into a full-fledged national brouhaha over whether racist and sexist jokes have become a blight on American media.

The debate goes on, in the wake of Imus' firing, with critics arguing that stereotyping jokes have explosive potential and should be used only with caution and, perhaps, not at all. But ethnic humor has a long and robust history, among jokers in public and in private, and few expect to see it abandoned any time soon.

In the 19th and early 20th century, ethnic humor was a staple of stage comedy, but its prevalence receded somewhat as radio brought comedy to the mass media, says Leon Rappoport, professor emeritus of psychology at Kansas State University and author of a recent book on ethnic humor.

The vaudeville stage abounded with "dialect humor," with stereotyped characters like "the operatic Italian" and "the money-grubbing Jew" that audiences easily recognized, Rappoport says. And in the early 20th century, when vaudevillians migrated to radio, the stereotyping humor continued. Fred Allen's radio skits, for example, based their humor on stereotyped characters such as a fast-talking Irishman, a Jewish housewife and numerous others.

Gradually, however, radio comedy "got cleaned up," with ethnic humor mainly expunged, Rappoport says. As a new mass medium, supported by advertisers, radio needed to entice many while offending few, and ethnic jokes — "which can be very aggressive" — risked turning off too many in the unseen listening audience. By the mid-20th century, ethnic humor had become much less prevalent, not only on radio but also on the stage, Rappoport says. By the early 1960s, however, ethnic jokes were being heard again in live comedy, by a new breed of edgy comics whose work was based on irony and social criticism, like Lenny Bruce.

Insult humor was briefly banished from public airwaves, but it returned beginning in the 1970s, says Sheri Parks, associate professor of American studies at the University of Maryland, College Park. Physical comedy and slapstick humor, often fairly violent, once abounded in American mass culture, from Charlie Chaplin to the Three Stooges. But when a 1972 U.S. surgeon general's report declared that violence in media leads to real-life violence, comics once again were forced to find non-physically violent ways to make people laugh, says Parks.

And since a key element in much humor is aggression, comics switched from physical to verbal violence — including stereotyping humor, Parks says. Over the past few decades

women live today with their shades pulled down and no lights on. Their fathers told them to do that to protect themselves against white night riders," he says.

"That's why the black reaction and the white reaction to Imus are so different," says Feagin. "Blacks know that" racially charged language that seems innocuous to whites "can be extremely serious. If it's in a police officer's head, it can get you killed," he says.

Americans' typical reactions to visiting Africans further indicate that language like "nappy headed" and "ho" aren't so much a matter of racial stereotyping but stereotyping of African Americans who are slave descendants, says Baugh, at Washington University. For example, Baugh says that when he hosted an African Fulbright scholar from Guinea, the man reported that the desk clerk at his American hotel was hostile until he explained that he was visiting from Africa. Then, the clerk's demeanor "changed immediately" to welcome, showing that the issue is not race but history, Baugh says.

Words that negatively stereotype are dangerous for anyone to use, including African Americans, he says. "It is possible within one's own group to use a derogatory term [for that group] in a positive way," he says. "But when you breach that private world" — which is all too easy to do — "then trouble happens," he says.

For example, "the more you accept these words" for use in your own community, "the more you may be losing your right to claim discrimination" when the words are used against you, says St. John's Law School's Baynes. "If the word loses its currency" as a slur because it's so

"insult has become the dominant mode of comedy."

There may be a serious problem with raising generations of children exposed on a daily basis to insult humor on television, radio and movies, Parks says. Adults believe when children see comedians and sitcom characters insulting each other aggressively "they know that it's unusual behavior that they shouldn't engage in," she says. "But in fact children look to media for normative behaviors, and when they see or hear something, they just go ahead and do it, too."

Adults like Imus may have a similar problem, according to Arthur Asa Berger, professor of broadcast and electronic communication arts at San Francisco State University and author of books on humor and humor writing. "Humor is a very dangerous thing. There's a lot of aggression in it, and when the aggression overwhelms the humor, we don't excuse" the "hostile" joker, he says.

Some professional comedians employ stereotypes "in a mirthful way," using the context of the joke to convince an audience that "they don't actually mean what they're saying" in a stereotyping joke about a drunken Irishman, for example, says Berger.

Lenny Bruce helped bring ethnic humor back to American comedy in the 1950s and 1960s.

AP Photo/John Lindsay

Professional humorists are always aware of their role and develop a sense of how far they can go to get a laugh or make a point without crossing the line into speech that the audience will read as hateful rather than funny or insightful, says Berger. "Comedians work very hard to do that," he says. "But when people who aren't humorists start messing around with humor," most don't even realize what the pitfalls are, he says.

When it comes to ethnic humor, most comedians agree that "anything goes as long as it's funny," says Rappoport. Nevertheless, "context and intent matter, and there has to be a grain of truth to it," he says. Comics like Richard Pryor, Robin Williams and Chris Rock have joked about ethnic groups, their own and other people's, and "the audience finds itself laughing even if they don't want to," Rappoport says.

But ethnic humor can also spell trouble, if the joker leans too heavily on the ethnic and not enough on the humor, he says. "The thing about the Imus statement is simply that it wasn't funny," says Rappoport. In the annals of humor, Imus is "a trivial footnote of somebody who went too far in the wrong context and then got what he deserved."

commonly used by black people, "when somebody uses the word and really means it, then what do you do?"

Shock Value

Risk, danger and excitement all are important components of popular entertainment. Add to that the spontaneity of live radio, and it's easy to see why hosts who "shock" have been a programming staple for decades — and why they sometimes cross the lines of acceptable speech. Nevertheless, media analysts point out that really shocking talk accounts for a small proportion of programming fare.

Shock of various kinds has "always been part of entertainment," so it's no wonder that radio talkers who say shocking things can draw big audiences, says Clarence W. Thomas, associate professor of mass communications

at Virginia Commonwealth University. "A roller coaster, a slasher movie — they carry a shock, and they're beyond the norm of everyday life, and that's what makes them interesting and entertaining."

What puts the shock in shock radio is that "shock jocks pull ideas and images from private spaces and say them out loud," says Parks, at the University of Maryland. Racial and gender insults that most people utter only among friends and family, along with sex talk, are the main types of speech eligible for that treatment.

With radio increasingly segmented to appeal to niche audiences, programmers have determined that shock jocks most appeal to men and younger listeners, says the Library of American Broadcasting's Gomery. That, in turn, draws advertisers seeking to cater to demographically desirable

Getty Images/Bryan Bedder

Many critics of Don Imus' firing contend that a double standard allows black rappers and hip-hop artists — like rapper Snoop Dogg — to use the same kind of offensive comments about women in their lyrics without being held accountable.

niches. So some personalities regularly push the envelope, hoping to touch the hot-button interests of their core audience. Broadcast television networks, in contrast, have always strived to develop programs that appeal to the masses and offend no one, making them a bad fit for shock commentators, Gomery explains.

Shocking talk has existed on radio from its early days.

Father Charles E. Coughlin wielded enormous influence through his on-air commentaries in the 1930s and '40s. But he began to increasingly incense some listeners with anti-Semitic tirades and extreme criticism of President Franklin D. Roosevelt, communism and American involvement in World War II. Both the Roosevelt administration and the National Association

of Broadcasters placed stricter limitations on who could get air time to speak about controversial issues. However, not until Coughlin's bishop ordered him to return to duty as a parish priest was his radio voice finally silenced.

In the 1940s through the '60s, radio host Joe Pyne pushed the envelope on insult speech, calling homeless people "stinky bums" and responding to guests with comments like "Why don't you take your teeth out, put them in backwards, and bite your throat?"

In the 1970s through the '90s, AM radio, in particular, shifted almost entirely away from music to talk formats, while FM became the medium of choice for music because of its better sound quality. The number of commercial news and talk stations swelled from 360 in 1990 to 802 by July 1993, according to Taylor of Inside Radio. Today, of the 10,600 commercial radio stations in the United States, about 1,360 are talk, while many of the 650 non-commercial public radio stations also embrace variants of the news and talk format.

Comedian George Carlin ran into legal troubles more than once over a routine discussing the "seven words you can never say on television," known as the "seven dirty words." In 1973, after a father complained to the FCC that his young son had heard the routine broadcast on a small New York radio station, the station fought the FCC's sanctions on the grounds that they restricted free speech. The legal case went all the way to the Supreme Court, which — in a 5 to 4 decision — upheld the FCC's right to bar broadcast of material the FCC considered "indecent" at times of day when children might hear it. [18]

The rise of talk radio has increased the likelihood of edgy content. This is particularly true during the 6 to 9 a.m. and 4 to 7 p.m. "drive-time" slots, when more males than females are stuck in their cars for long stretches of time, Gomery says. Because radio talk is spontaneous, unedited and generally unplanned, radio is a "hip, edgy, street-y kind of medium," says Harrison of *Talkers* magazine. Nevertheless, Harrison argues that once Imus and Howard Stern "brought radio into the latest chapter of street culture" back in the 1970s, "shock jock" stopped being a very relevant term. Today, "there are bad boys on the radio," he acknowledges. "But how could anything on radio be truly shocking when there's a wild assortment of perversions all over regular television?"

While shock talk is a persistent element in radio, it still doesn't account for much talking time, perhaps only 3 or 4 percent, says Gomery.

Is ethnic and racial humor dangerous?

YES
Arthur Asa Berger
Professor of Broadcast and Electronic Communication Arts San Francisco State University

Written for *CQ Researcher*, May 2007

Ethnic humor divides as it derides. Societies generally contain many ethnic, racial and religious groups, each of which has distinctive cultural traits, beliefs and values. While ethnic humor may seem to be trivial, it corrodes our sense of community and makes it more difficult for us to live together harmoniously. It focuses on our differences and insults, attacks and humiliates its victims. It is based on stereotyping, which suggests that all members of various ethnic or other groups are the same as far as certain traits deemed "undesirable" by those who use ethnic humor are concerned. This humor can lead to feelings of inferiority and even self-hatred by members of groups attacked by it, while it coarsens and desensitizes those who use it.

Humor is an enigmatic matter that has fascinated our greatest philosophers and thinkers from Aristotle's time to the present. Scholars disagree about why we laugh, but two of the dominant theories about humor — Aristotle's view that it is based upon feelings of superiority and Freud's notion that it involves masked hostility and aggression — apply to ethnic humor.

There is an ethnocentric bias reflected in ethnic humor, a feeling held by those who use this humor that they are superior and that their cultural beliefs and values are the only correct ones. While ethnic humor is widespread — it's found in most countries — it varies considerably from mild teasing to terribly insulting and even vicious humor. Every society seems to find some minority "out-group" to ridicule. But sometimes ethnic humor — about Jews and African-Americans, for example — can easily become anti-Semitic and racist.

People who ridicule Jewish-American "princesses" or "dumb Poles" and other ethnic groups think they are just being funny when they tell friends insulting riddles. We might ask "funny to whom?" Such humor isn't amusing to members of the groups that are ridiculed. Those who use ethnic humor feel that they can make fun of ethnic groups with impunity, but in multicultured societies, fortunately, that is no longer the case. The excuse given by people who use ethnic humor, "I was just trying to be funny," isn't acceptable anymore.

Humor can be liberating and has many benefits, but when it is used to ridicule and insult people, it is harmful to members of the ethnic groups that are victimized by this humor and to society at large. Ethnic humor isn't just a laughing matter.

NO
Leon Rappoport
Professor Emeritus of Psychology Kansas State University

Written for *CQ Researcher*, May 2007

It is hard to think of any serious harm associated with ethnic humor if you have ever fallen down laughing at a routine by Whoopi Goldberg, Robin Williams or Chris Rock, or heard Jackie Mason's lines about the differences between Jews and gentiles. Yet controversies over humor based on ethnic, racial or gender stereotypes go all the way back to the plays of Aristophanes (circa 430 B.C.), and subsequent writers and performers, from Shakespeare through Richard Pryor and Mel Brooks, have been catching flak about it ever since.

Modern social-science studies aimed at settling the harm question have not produced any smoking-gun evidence. The cautious conclusion of a 2004 review of experimental research was that exposure to disparagement humor did not reinforce negative images of the targeted group. Relevant field studies have shown that people feel no significant malice when laughing at jokes based on ethnic stereotypes, and common-sense observations support this: Where are all the suffering victims of the Polish jokes, dumb-blonde jokes, Jewish-American mother and princess jokes that have come and gone over recent years, not to mention the Lutherans, Catholics and Unitarians regularly worked over in Garrison Keillor's monologues on "A Prairie Home Companion"?

The prominent ethnic-humor scholar Christie Davies (author of three important books on the subject) maintains that laughter at such jokes has little to do with social attitudes but reflects the powerful surge of pleasure we tend to feel from "playing with aggression." And this includes members of the group being ridiculed, who often are most amused by clever takes on the stereotypes they know best. This was clearly true among the hundreds of diverse college students who took the class on ethnic humor I taught for several years. They would frequently be particularly carried away with laughter when seeing videos of comedians playing with ironic clichés about their own ethnic, racial or gender group. Like most Americans today, these students grew up in our humor-saturated TV culture and are thus well prepared to maintain a healthy sense of critical distance while enjoying satire, parody and ridicule — remember Boris and Natasha on "Bullwinkle"? — in the context of ethnic humor.

Part of what holds our increasingly multiethnic society together is our rich stock of ironic humor. The fact that we can play with our differences, even at the risk of occasionally offending each other, deserves recognition as a matter of pride rather than prejudice.

Getty Images/Alex Wong

Journalist Gwen Ifill — moderator of PBS' "Washington Week" — declined to appear on Don Imus' radio show in 1993 when she was a *New York Times* Washington correspondent. In apparent retaliation, Imus said the *Times* was "wonderful" because "it lets the cleaning lady cover the White House."

Stereotypes Spreading?

Though shock jocks may not be expanding their reach, shocking language, especially racial and gender stereotypes, has been increasingly used in other branches of the media in recent years, including comedy, gangsta-rap lyrics and on some radio shows featuring political talk.

Over the past few decades, for example, stereotyping insults have become a prominent mode of comedy, says Parks of the University of Maryland. Previously, a great deal of comedy in movies and on television was physical comedy, which was usually somewhat violent, she says.

The shift toward insult humor was mainly triggered by a 1972 surgeon general's report citing evidence that violence in media leads to violence in real life, says Parks. When the FCC responded by discouraging violent content, comedians shifted to other forms of humor, mainly opting for insults based on ethnic or racial stereotypes.

The shocking language that's garnered the most attention in the wake of Imus' comment has been racial and, especially, gender stereotypes in gangsta-rap lyrics. As with insult humor, the use of stereotyping in African American music has greatly expanded in recent years.

"In R&B and soul music, African American women were respected, and even when hip-hop got started, it didn't focus on misogynistic lyrics," says Ohio State University's Jewell.

Gradually, however, the top-selling, highest-profile hip-hop shifted toward lyrics that celebrate the "bling" and flash of a "gangsta" lifestyle and heavily feature misogynistic language like "bitch" and "ho."

Hip-hop "started as a radical critique of society" and especially of racism, says Feagin of Texas A&M. "When it became clear to the music industry that music with a beat could sell across racial lines," social criticism in lyrics "wasn't sold aggressively. White people — who buy 70 percent of rap records — don't want to hear about it."

Consequently, the most commercially successful hip-hop has been lowest-common-denominator music portraying women, especially African American women, as wholly sexualized rather than romantic objects, says Jewell. The proliferation of the sexualized stereotypes — and frequent references to women as "hos" and "bitches" — "has some far-reaching consequences" for black women, because they're widely "perceived as having low morals" as well as being powerless, she says.

This has seeped into talk radio and television, says Parry-Giles at the University of Maryland. The racially diverse College Park campus is just outside Washington, where the intersection of media, politics and race is the focus of several academic programs. Stereotyping insults are "pervasive across the right and the left" on talk radio, she says, noting that progressive talk host Stephanie Miller repeatedly uses Asian stereotypes when she discusses North Korea on her program, Parry-Giles says.

Several conservative talk-radio hosts are especially notorious for race and gender stereotypes and insults. Michael Savage, whose San Francisco-based show is nationally syndicated by the independent Talk Radio Network, has frequently labeled countries with non-white populations as "turd world nations" and referred to the May 2000 "Million Mom March" on Washington for gun control as the "Million Dyke March," according to the liberal media-criticism group Fairness & Accuracy In Reporting. [19]

CURRENT SITUATION

New Crackdown

There are comparatively few rules governing broadcast content, and the ones that exist mostly focus on indecent sexual content. While radio stations have occasionally fired or suspended shock jocks for insulting and stereotyping ethnic and racial comments, sex-related antics have triggered much of the disciplinary action, and most fired jocks have been rehired fairly quickly by their old station or a new one.

Today, however, some liberal media critics such as Media Matters for America are focusing public attention on racist and misogynistic comments and insults. While some commentators applaud, others worry that a crackdown on insult speech could prompt an overreaction by advertisers and regulators.

Advertisers quickly pulled out of sponsorships of Imus' program in the wake of the Rutgers University flap, placing economic pressure on MSNBC and then CBS Radio to fire the veteran host. New York shock jocks JV and Elvis were also recently fired after a racist prank call to a Chinese restaurant, and another New York radio personality, comedian Donnell "Ashy" Rawlings, was fired for anti-Semitic comments. [20]

"The striking thing to me is that this was one of the less offensive quotes from Imus," says Robert Entman, professor of media and public affairs at George Washington University and author of books on media and race and media and political discourse. "He's said many anti-Semitic things and things demeaning to black people that he should have gotten into trouble for decades ago."

This time was different, in part because the target of Imus' remarks was a group of admirable student athletes — as opposed to well-known public figures — which made the "nappy-headed hos" comment seem particularly inappropriate. The Internet also gave interest groups a 24-hour medium to air their complaints and criticisms.

"Imus lost his job because of the Internet," says Kelly McBride, ethics group leader at the Poynter Institute in St. Petersburg, Fla., a nonpartisan media-education organization. "The Internet provides a new venue where enough people can learn about events, complain to each other and lobby advertisers. Some people describe it as an Internet lynch mob, and I think that can be a danger. But I also think that it's democracy at its finest."

Among those leading the Internet criticism of Imus' comment was Media Matters for America, a group founded in 2004 by conservative-turned-liberal writer and journalism activist David Brock to combat what Brock calls media misinformation that advances a conservative agenda, including race- and gender-related insults and stereotyping.

Also fueling efforts to get Imus' employers to take action were changing demographics that have given women and African Americans and other ethnic minorities more clout in the workplace and the economy, some analysts say.

NBC weatherman Al Roker, PBS journalist Gwen Ifill and former NAACP President Bruce Gordon, now on the Board of Directors of CBS, were among the African Americans who called for the networks to cancel Imus after his April comments, and their comments apparently carried weight with the networks and advertisers.

"The more you have diverse voices out there, the less likely incidents like this are to happen," says St. John's Law School's Baynes. "Otherwise, people say, 'Well, it's just words.'"

In addition, "women and African Americans are major buyers today, both groups much richer than they used to be," and advertisers "want to attract them," as they may not have in the past, says the Library of American Broadcasting's Gomery. "That's a big part of this story."

As for Imus, two days after the controversial remark, he offered an apology: "My characterization [of the team] was thoughtless and stupid. . . . And we're sorry," he said on his April 6 program. Three days later, he added: "Here's what I have learned: that you can't make fun of everybody, because some people don't deserve it. And because the climate on this program has been what it has been for 30 years doesn't mean that it has to be that way for the next five years or whatever, because that has to change . . . and I understand that." [21]

Fairness Revisited?

Much of the media scrutiny of racist and sexist language immediately turned to hip-hop lyrics. However, some conservatives worry that the activists who helped oust Imus also will seek to silence conservative political talk show hosts by pressing the federal government to revive the Fairness Doctrine. Following Imus' remarks, the main public and media debate quickly turned to criticism of hip-hop and to whether the Rev. Sharpton, the Rev.

Jackson and other black leaders who strenuously called for Imus' firing had spoken out against gangsta rappers.

Imus firing "is so hypocritical because big media groups like CBS — which owns BET and MTV — traffic in bad language and racist language like the N-word" every time they show a gangsta-rap video, says the Media Research Center's Bozell. "I think the criticism of Imus is reverse racism." In music, he adds, "it's supposedly OK because black people say it."

The quick backlash against hip-hop happened "because it was a quick and easy scapegoat," says Brown of Vanderbilt. He says the radio comments and gangsta-rap lyrics aren't comparable because gangsta rap is seldom broadcast uncut. "To get these particular lyrics that people are talking about, you have to buy them," he says. In general, "they aren't even played on radio."

Meanwhile, some conservatives argue that Imus' firing was the first shot in a war aimed at getting conservative voices such as Bill O'Reilly, Limbaugh and Neal Boortz off radio and television.

Although Imus wasn't a conservative, he has been a vocal opponent of Sen. Hillary Rodham Clinton, D-N.Y., and that made him a target of the same groups who want to silence conservatives, says Kincaid of Accuracy in Media.

Some Imus opponents have called for FCC regulation of stereotyping, derogatory remarks over the airwaves, Kincaid notes. He fears any group that feels it was denigrated over the public airwaves will be able to seek redress at the FCC, a move he believes could impinge on free speech.

Others believe the FCC should do more to ensure that more views get aired. "Why not bring back the Fairness Doctrine?" asks Baynes of St. John's Law School. The FCC rule was largely scrapped in 1987 because the commission feared it might violate broadcasters' free-speech rights.

The rule may be difficult to police, given the range of views on some subjects, Baynes acknowledges. "But the question is, 'Do you think now is better?' I think it's worse." Baynes says the doctrine should also be applied to cable systems, which now have to comply with some federal regulations, including ones requiring them to scramble sexually explicit content.

Some Democrats in Congress would like to revive the rule. Rep. Dennis Kucinich, D-Ohio, chairman of the House Oversight and Government Reform subcommittee, plans hearings on the Fairness Doctrine. [22] House Energy and Commerce Chairman John D. Dingell of Michigan told a conference of advertisers in May that he, too, wants to explore reviving the doctrine. [23]

But "the Fairness Doctrine is an absolute abomination," according to Bozell. "In simple words, it says, 'There ought to be liberal voices on talk radio to offset conservative voices,' " he says.

"But there's already National Public Radio, and if there were a market for more then there would be more liberal voices," Bozell, adds. When the doctrine was in place, many radio stations simply stopped airing discussion of public issues altogether because it was too difficult to find representatives for all opposing views — clearly not an outcome that anyone is looking for, he says.

OUTLOOK

Business as Usual?

Will Imus' firing mark an end to ethnic and gender insults and stereotyping in American media? Few think that's likely. The main reason: Edginess attracts viewers.

Case in point: When outspoken TV personality Rosie O'Donnell joined the talk show "The View," the ratings went up, says Accuracy in Media editor Kincaid. "Imus' ratings also had been going up before the Rutgers incident," he adds.

"Every couple of years some controversy erupts over race, and generally everybody goes back to their normal activities soon afterward," says George Washington University's media and public affairs professor Entman. Racial tension in America, which did come to the surface briefly following Imus' remark, is "a low-grade infection whose symptoms are always present but are tolerable to the majority," he says.

Advertisers would probably welcome Imus back to radio after the controversy dies down, but it's not clear whether a suitable radio venue exists, industry experts say.

For example, General Motors, a big sponsor that quickly pulled ads from the Imus show when controversy began building, would not rule out advertising on an Imus program in the future. Since Imus has apologized for his remarks and vowed to change his tone in the future, the automaker is "open to revisiting at some point down the road" a stint as an Imus advertiser, should his show return, a company spokesperson told *AdWeek* magazine. [24]

But "media options for Imus appear to be limited," said Mike Kinosian, a columnist for the industry publication *Inside Radio.* [25]

"There are only a handful of major radio networks, and it is hard to imagine one would step forward and take him," and "it would be problematic for him [to be] on a small, low-level, unfunded network," said Cary Pahigian, president and general manager in the Portland, Maine, office of Michigan-based Saga Communications, which owns and operates radio and television stations. Satellite radio also is likely out, for the time being at least, since the two big satellite networks — XM and Sirius — hope to merge, and with FCC scrutiny heavy on them at present, "this isn't something they would want to tackle," Pahigian said. [26]

As for gangsta rap, a newly formed coalition opposing sexist lyrics will increase the pressure for performers and record companies to halt the use of sexist language like "ho" and "bitch," says Williams, of the National Congress of Black Women (NCBW), which has been urging music companies to drop such language for years. This spring, however, other groups including the National Organization for Women and the National Council of Women's Organizations have joined with NCBW to fight the sexist language. "With all of us working together, it's only a matter of time," she says.

When it comes to radio, even more targeted niche programs will develop as audio migrates from the airwaves to satellite and the Internet, analysts predict.

That inevitable shift means that radio "will find room for Imus and his language again," predicts the Media Research Center's Bozell.

Other changes also are in store for radio as audiences inevitably grow restless with the brand of talk radio that's dominated for a decade and a half, says Harrison of *Talkers* magazine. "We've been at the peak of a trend of political talk" that is mainly right-wing, he says. Now "people are tired of it," and public boredom spells the end of phenomena of popular culture. Progressive and liberal talk could burgeon in that climate, he predicts.

More than an opening for progressives, though, Americans currently have an appetite for non-partisan political talk, Harrison says. The talker who likely will flourish next "can be liberal, can be conservative," he says. "They'll express ideas," but not fervently back either political party, he predicts.

As for damping down the culture of insult and argument, "that's basically up to everyone," says Georgetown's Tannen. Many people do object to stereotyping insults, for example, uttered privately or in public. But "it's up to us to say something when we hear that talk," she says.

NOTES

1. Gwen Ifill, "Trash Talk Radio," *The New York Times*, April 10, 2007.

2. "Imus Has Long Record of Incendiary Remarks," National Association of Black Journalists Web site, April 18, 2007; www.nabj.org.

3. Richard Prince, "NABJ Says It Still Wants Radio Host Out by Monday," *Journal-isms* column, Maynard Institute for Journalism Education, April 6, 2007.

4. "NAHJ Condemns Radio Host Don Imus for Racial Remarks," press release, National Association of Hispanic Journalists, April 9, 2007.

5. "Rallying Around Their Racist Friend," media advisory, Fairness & Accuracy in Media, April 11, 2007; www.fair.org.

6. Steve McClellan, "They Bailed for Now, But Advertisers Forgive," *AdWeek*, April 16, 2007; www.adweek.com.

7. Quoted in Alex Koppelman, "Is Rush Limbaugh Next?" *Salon.com*, April 16, 2007; www.salon.com.

8. Quoted in Richard Prince, "After Imus, Sights Set on Rap Music," Journal-isms, Maynard Institute for Journalism Education, April 14, 2007.

9. Quoted in Adam Graham, "Imus Storm Hits Hip-Hop World," *Detroit News*, April 14, 2007; www.detnews.com.

10. Billy Ingram, "Legendary Broadcaster Joe Pyne," TVParty.com; www.tvparty.com/empyne.html.

11. Charles Haynes, "Imus, Coulter, and the Marketplace for Offensive Speech," *Commentary*, First Amendment Center, April 15, 2007; www.firstamentmentcenter.org.

12. Ted Rall, "First They Came for the Shock Jocks," TedRall.com and Common Dreams News Center, March 11, 2004; www.commondreams.org.

13. Quoted in *ibid.*

14. Quoted in Dipayan Gupta and Thomas Rogers, "Safe Speech," *Salon.com*, May 1, 2007; www.salon.com.

15. For background, see John Michael Kittross and Christopher H. Sterling, *Stay Tuned: A History of American Broadcasting* (2002); William Triplett, "Broadcast Indecency," *CQ Researcher*, April 16, 2004, pp. 321-344; Alan Greenblatt, "Race in America," *CQ Researcher*, July 11, 2003, pp. 593-624; Kenneth Jost, "Talk Show Democracy," *CQ Researcher*, April 29, 1994, pp. 361-384; and M. Costello, "Blacks in the News Media," *CQ Researcher*, Aug. 16, 1972; "First Amendment and Mass Media," *CQ Researcher*, Jan. 21, 1970, both available at *CQ Researcher Plus Archive*; www.cqpress.com.

16. Zine Magubane, "Why 'Nappy' Is Offensive," *The Boston Globe*, April 12, 2007.

17. *Ibid.*

18. The case is *Federal Communications Commission v. Pacifica Foundation*, 438 U.S. 726, 98 S. Ct. 3026 (1978). The seven words are: shit, piss, fuck, cunt, cocksucker, motherfucker and tits.

19. "GE, Microsoft Bring Bigotry to Life," Fairness & Accuracy in Reporting, Feb. 12, 2003; www.fair.org.

20. Gil Kaufman, "Is Shock Radio Dead? More Potty-Mouthed DJs Join Don Imus in Doghouse," *MTV News*, May 15, 2007; www.mtv.com.

21. Imus' April 6 apology is quoted in "Cleaning up the I-Mess," transcript, "Paula Zahn Now," *CNN.com*, April 13, 2007, http://transcripts.cnn.com/TRAN-SCRIPTS/0704/13/pzn.01.html; "Imus Puts Remarks Into Context," transcript, "Imus in the Morning," MSNBC.com, April 9, 2007, www.msnbc.msn.com/id/18022596.

22. Nate Anderson, "Dennis Kucinich: Bring Back the Fairness Doctrine," *Ars Technica blog*, Jan. 17, 2007; http://arstechnica.com.

23. Ira Teinowitz, "Dingell Backs Return of Fairness Doctrine," *TV Week.com*, May 2, 2007; www.tvweek.com/news.cms?newsId=11988.

24. Quoted in McClellan, *op. cit.*

25. Mike Kinosian, "Minus Imus," *Inside Radio*, April 19, 2007; www.insideradio.com.

26. Quoted in *ibid.*

BIBLIOGRAPHY

Books

Kittross, John Michael, and Christopher H. Sterling, *Stay Tuned: A History of American Broadcasting*, Lawrence Erlbaum Associates, 2002.
The editor of *Media Ethics* magazine and a George Washington University professor of media and public affairs chronicle the growth and development of electronic media and broadcasting in the United States, including the development of shock radio and broadcast-content regulation.

Picca, Leslie Houts, and Joe R. Feagin, *Two-Faced Racism: Whites in the Backstage and Frontstage*, Routledge, 2007.
An assistant professor and a professor of sociology from the University of Dayton and Texas A&M University examine the racial attitudes of white college students who chronicled their race-related experiences and thoughts in detailed diaries. They argue that racism has receded from public life in America but that many people still actively engage in racist talk among close friends and family.

Rappoport, Leon, *Punchlines: The Case for Racial, Ethnic, and Gender Humor*, Praeger, 2005.
A professor emeritus of psychology at Kansas State University details the history of stereotyping humor and argues that it can serve important social functions, including as a tool to combat prejudice.

Articles

"What Happens When Shock Jocks Go Too Far?" POV: The Fire Next Time, Public Broadcasting Service Web site, www.pbs.org/pov/pov2005/the-firenexttime/special_casestudies.html, 2005.
This Web article by producers of a PBS documentary on how talk radio divided a Montana community relates stories of shock jocks who transgressed community standards for acceptable speech and faced controversy.

Kinosian, Mike, "Don's Gone: Post Imess," *Inside Radio*, April 26, 2007, www.insideradio.com.
A columnist for a radio trade publication chronicles Don Imus' career and interviews industry insiders about what his firing may mean to broadcasters.

Koppelman, Alex, "Is Rush Limbaugh Next?" *Salon*, April 16, 2007, www.salon.com.
Panelists at an April meeting of the conservative Free Congress Foundation predicted that congressional Democrats will try to revive the Fairness Doctrine requiring broadcasters to air all sides of controversial issues. They discussed strategies to stop revival of the doctrine, which media analysts argued would endanger conservative political commentators like Rush Limbaugh.

Llorente, Elizabeth, "Hispanics Steamed by Shock Radio Stunt," *The Record* [Bergen, N.J.], March 22, 2007.
Hispanic community leaders in New Jersey protested when shock radio hosts Craig Carton and Ray Rossi, known as "The Jersey Guys," launched a show segment called "La Cuca Gotcha," during which they urged listeners to report suspected illegal immigrants either to the station or to immigration authorities. Critics called for a boycott of the show's advertising, saying that the hosts encouraged racial profiling and vigilante activity.

McBride, Sara, and Brian Steinberg, "Finding a Replacement for Imus Won't Be Easy," *The Wall Street Journal*, April 16, 2007, p. B1.
Controversial radio hosts bring in big audiences and ad revenues, but talented shock talkers who can entertain a national audience aren't plentiful, so stations hire, fire and rehire the same people over and over. Increasing the difficulty for broadcast radio are satellite channels that have lured some top talent to the unregulated medium.

McClellan, Steve, "They Bailed for Now, But Advertisers Forgive," *AdWeek*, April 16, 2007, www.adweek.com.
A journalist who covers the advertising industry argues that advertisers who pulled out of Imus' show didn't want the program canceled.

Steinberg, Jacques, "Talk Radio Tries for Humor and a Political Advantage," *The New York Times*, April 20, 2007.
Shock jocks joked about Virginia Tech mass shooter Seung-Hui Cho while conservative radio hosts speculated about how his Korean background may have played into his becoming a murderer.

Walker, Jesse, "Tuning Out Free Speech," *The American Conservative*, April 23, 2007, www.amconmag.com.
The editor of libertarian *Reason* magazine argues that the history of the Federal Communications Commission's Fairness Doctrine shows that the doctrine stifled speech on the public airwaves.

Reports and Studies

Post-Conference Report: Rethinking the Discourse on Race: A Symposium on How the Lack of Racial Diversity in the Media Affects Social Justice and Policy, **The Ronald H. Brown Center for Civil Rights and Economic Development, St. John's University School of Law, October 2006.**
Conferees at a 2006 forum provide updates on ethnic diversity in media organizations and how the media shape Americans' views of race.

For More Information

Accuracy in Media, 4455 Connecticut Ave., N.W., Suite 330, Washington, DC 20008; (202) 364-4401; www.aim .org/index. A conservative media-criticism group that tracks and disseminates information about liberal bias it observes in the media.

Ban the N-Word, http://banthenword.com. An activist group that disseminates information about racist language and stereotypes in media, including detailed reviews of movies and new music releases.

Fairness and Accuracy in Reporting, 112 W. 27th St., New York, NY 10001; (212) 633-6700; www.fair.org/index.php. A liberal media-criticism group that disseminates information about and advocates for diverse opinions in media, especially inclusion of minority viewpoints.

Inside Radio, 365 Union St., Littleton, NH 03561; (603) 444-5720; www.insideradio.com. An insider publication for the radio industry that posts up-to-date news and commentary on radio-related events.

Maynard Institute for Journalism Education, 1211 Preservation Park Way, Oakland, CA 94612; (510) 891-9202; www.maynardije.org. A nonprofit education center for minority journalists that chronicles race-related issues in media such as the Imus controversy on its extensive Web site.

Media Matters for America, 1625 Massachusetts Ave., N.W., Suite 300, Washington, DC 20036; (202) 756-4100; http://mediamatters.org/index. A liberal media-criticism group that tracks factual errors and misleading statements in the media, focusing on misinformation that may advance a conservative political agenda, and urges journalists to issue corrections of the errors.

Media Research Center, 325 S. Patrick St., Alexandria, VA 22314; (703) 683-9733; www.mediaresearch.org. A conservative media-criticism group that tracks and posts commentary on examples of liberal media bias and on events that threaten conservative media.

Talkers Magazine, 650 Belmont Ave., Springfield, MA 01108; (413) 739-8255; www.talkers.com. A publication covering talk radio that posts news and commentary about the industry on its Web site.

TimWise.org, www.timwise.org. An anti-racism educator who posts essays and reports on historical and current racial dilemmas in America.

7

Debating Hip-Hop

Peter Katel

The Rev. Al Sharpton leads a protest march for cleaner hip-hop lyrics on May 3, 2007, in New York City. Sharpton, who criticized shock jock Don Imus in April for using degrading hip-hop lingo to describe female basketball players, has called for equal accountability among hip-hop artists and music-industry executives.

AP Photo/Frank Franklin II

From *CQ Researcher*,
June 15, 2007.

Critics of hip-hop have much to deplore. The posturing about the "gangsta" lifestyle. The ostentatious displays of "bling" — big diamonds, big cars and big houses. And the ever-present young women who are portrayed as rappers' sexual playthings, draping themselves around star performers and shaking their booties through hundreds of near-pornographic videos. Not to mention the incessant use of the N-word.

"They put the word 'nigga' in a song, and we get up and dance to it," actor and comedian Bill Cosby fumed last year. [1]

Anger over hip-hop has been simmering for more than a decade, largely among African Americans. Much of the concern has focused on its glorification of violence, sexual exploitation and crime. At a time when black males are increasingly endangered — six times more likely than white males to die in homicides — critics like Cosby say gangsta rappers are terrible role models for impressionable inner-city youths. [2]

Superstars Tupac Shakur and The Notorious B.I.G. (Christopher Wallace) fell to hitmen's bullets in 1996 and 1997, respectively. A protégé of hip-hop tycoon Sean "P. Diddy" Combs was sentenced to 10 years in prison for a nightclub shooting eight years ago that Combs had fled. Rapper Cam'ron (Cameron Giles) survived getting shot in 2005 in his $250,000 Lamborghini. And a bodyguard for rapper Busta Rhymes (Trevor Smith) was killed last year at a Brooklyn, N.Y., video shoot. [3]

But outside black America, the heat didn't get turned up on gangsta rap until an aging white radio shock jock, Don Imus, unleashing a word from black street vernacular, offhandedly described the Rutgers University women's basketball team as "nappy-headed hos." [4]

Hip-Hop Trails Rock and Country

Despite its popularity among youth, hip-hop/rap music sales in the United States only accounted for 11.4 percent of all music purchased in 2006, trailing both rock and country. Over the past nine years, hip-hop/rap sales essentially have remained constant. The figures do not include illegally downloaded computer files, which are believed to contribute to hip-hop's overwhelming popularity.

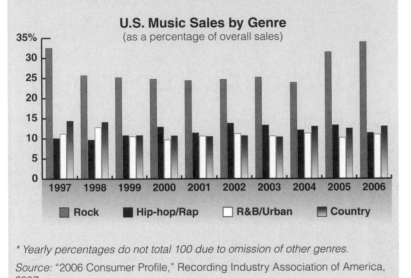

U.S. Music Sales by Genre
(as a percentage of overall sales)

Legend: ■ Rock   ■ Hip-hop/Rap   □ R&B/Urban   ■ Country

Years: 1997, 1998, 1999, 2000, 2001, 2002, 2003, 2004, 2005, 2006

* Yearly percentages do not total 100 due to omission of other genres.

Source: "2006 Consumer Profile," Recording Industry Association of America, 2007

In the uproar that followed, Imus' show was canceled, and critics of gangsta rap intensified their demands for change. Notably, TV talk-show host and communications mogul Oprah Winfrey threw her considerable power into demonstrating that tolerance was eroding for rappers' language and lifestyle.

Winfrey broadcast two programs in which African American writers and entertainers confronted hip-hop magnates. The critics included writer and newspaper columnist Stanley Crouch, who has been thundering for years that hip-hop performers are retailing destructive black stereotypes for the entertainment of a largely white audience. [5]

Entrepreneur Russell Simmons, whose hip-hop empire has been valued at more than $325 million, had defended rappers' artistic freedom in the past. But after Oprah's shows, he changed his tune. "We recommend that the recording and broadcast industries voluntarily remove/bleep/delete the misogynistic words 'bitch' and 'ho' and the racially offensive word 'nigger,' " Simmons and Benjamin Chavis, co-chairmen of the advocacy group Hip-Hop Summit Action Network, said in a statement. Two major performers, Master P (Percy Miller) and Chamillionaire (Hakeem Seriki), took similar stands. [6]

The Rev. Al Sharpton — who helped force Imus off the air — supported the demand. "We plan to continue to march until those three words are gone," he said. [7]

In effect, Sharpton and his allies are trying to return hip-hop to its origins as a street art form that was largely free of violence or sexual exploitation.

Hip-hop emerged in the Bronx in the early 1970s, when the first MCs chanted their raps, and the first DJs spun their vinyl disks, for neighborhood youths who wanted to groove to the music. Hip-hop's venues weren't velvet-roped clubs, or stadiums, but apartment building community rooms, playgrounds and street corners. [8]

"B-boys" and "b-girls" — the 'b' stands for the rhythm-heavy "break" in a song — invented a whole new form of "break" dancing to the new kind of sound. And the so-called graffiti writers who considered themselves radical street artists became part of the hip-hop culture as well. But New Yorkers in general and city government officials saw the graffiti crews as vandals. In retrospect, their activities seem innocent in light of the violence that now seems inseparable from hip-hop. [9]

As they waited to see whether Oprah, Sharpton and other critics had caught a wave of public revulsion, most rappers stayed silent. But not David Banner (Levell Crump), a leading member of the sex-heavy "dirty south" school of rap. He argues that rappers are taking the fall for an entire culture's pathology.

"What does America want?" Banner asks, his voice ringing with outrage. "People go to NASCAR because they want to see somebody crash. They want to see [the movie] 'The Departed,' with people blowing each other's heads off — that's cool, that's trendy. We see what people buy. Gangsta rap is just a reflection of America. America is sick. There's so many other things we should be complaining about, and we're talking about hip-hop."

Banner (the name is borrowed from the comic hero "The Incredible Hulk") agrees with critics that white suburban kids are rappers' biggest audience. "Truth is, there's somebody mad at rap because their son is walking around looking like a black dude. That's what the problem is."

But while Banner expresses contempt for Sharpton and other old-school black political leaders, they are voicing views that have been percolating for years, among ordinary people as well as public figures.

"There's a big correlation between rap and the breakdown of the black community in general," says Chris English, a Web site developer and fledgling rapper and record producer in Pocono Summit, Pa. "Regardless of what people say, it is affecting kids. I still love hip-hop, I still believe in artistic freedom. But I see kids who would rather be on the corner, drinking 40's [40-ounce bottles of malt liquor] and smoking [marijuana] blunts."

Anti-violence educator and filmmaker Byron Hurt explored this territory in his PBS documentary, "Hip-Hop: Beyond Beats and Rhymes." "The more I grew, and the more I learned about sexism and violence and homophobia, the more [rap] lyrics became unacceptable to me," he says in the film. [10]

Other critics within the hip-hop world draw a line between mass-marketed rap and what they consider the real thing. They point to independent-label rappers who disdain the gangsta material, as well as a handful of so-called "conscious" performers who've broken through to the mainstream with songs that reject celebrations of violence and exploitation. Among the latter is Talib Kweli, whose new single includes the line: "I'm stayin' conscious to radio playin' garbage." [11]

T.I.'s "King" Leads Rap Sales

Southern-style rapper T.I., who leads the group Pimp Squad Click — better known by the acronym P$C — led all rappers in album sales in 2006 with "King." The Notorious B.I.G.'s "Duets: The Final Chapter" was No. 5 on the list, nine years after his death.

Top-Selling Rappers, 2006
(by album sales)

Artist	Album	Label
T.I.	"King"	Grand Hustle/Atlantic/AG
Lil Wayne	"Tha Carter II"	Cash Money/Universal Motown/UMRG
Eminem	"Curtain Call: The Hits"	Shady/Aftermath/Interscope
Ludacris	"Release Therapy"	DTP/Def Jam/IDJMG
The Notorious B.I.G.	"Duets: The Final Chapter"	Bad Boy/AG
Chamillionaire	"The Sound of Revenge"	Universal Motown/UMRG
Yung Joc	"New Joc City"	Block/Bad Boy South/AG
Rick Ross	"Port of Miami"	Slip-N-Slide/Def Jam/IDJMG
Juelz Santana	"What the Game's Been Missing!"	Diplomats/Def Jam/IDJMG
Busta Rhymes	"The Big Bang"	Aftermath/Interscope

Source: Billboard, www.billboard.biz

Indeed, rappers who've based their careers on glorifying the thug life might find a censored environment impossible. "For me, don't expect me to compromise myself," rapper 50 Cent (Curtis Jackson) told a hip-hop Web site on June 1. "Fitty" has built his public persona on bullet scars from a drug-dealing past and a (now-settled) gangland-style feud with a rival that included threats of violence and at least one episode of gunplay. [12]

"If it's over then it's over," 50 Cent said. "I'll find something else to do." [13]

Mass-marketed hip-hop may not be over, but rap/hip-hop has slipped to No. 3 in nationwide music sales, accounting for 11.4 percent of a recorded-music market whose total retail value was $11.5 billion in 2006. The country category, which hip-hop had surpassed in 2000, now holds the No. 2 spot. Rock music maintained the lead it has held for years. [14]

The statistics don't reflect the irony of the hip-hop market. "Record executives, if you talk to them privately,

Getty Images/Erik S. Lesser

Gangsta rapper David Banner defends his "dirty south" rap style and misogynistic lyrics, arguing that hip-hop has been used as a scapegoat for society's problems. "Gangsta rap is just a reflection of America," he says.

will say that it's white kids who have the disposable income to buy this stuff," says hip-hop historian Yvonne Bynoe. [15] "Black kids are going to buy bootlegs or dupe songs themselves. But you need young black people to give a rap record the imprimatur of authenticity."

To hip-hop marketers, "authenticity" is a code word for thug culture and a never-ending source of some black intellectuals' contempt for mass-market hip-hop. "There was a time when Malcolm X the liberator was the patron saint of hip-hop," says Chicago-based poet Heru Ofori-Atta, speaking of the assassinated African American leader who earlier in life was a drug dealer named Malcolm Little. "Now it's Malcolm Little the pimp, the hustler, the fool, who is given the microphone."

Indeed, when "60 Minutes" correspondent Anderson Cooper asked Cam'ron if he would tell police if a serial killer lived next door, the rapper declared, "No, I wouldn't call and tell anybody on him. But I'd probably move." After an outcry, the rapper apologized for his remarks. [16]

The retraction reflected the sudden change in tolerance for anti-social behavior. Even pioneer gangsta rapper Ice-T (Tracy Marrow), who now plays a detective on the popular TV show "Law and Order: Special Victims Unit," challenged Cam'ron. "When you and your partner are involved in a crime, and both of y'all get caught and you tell on your partner, that's snitching," Ice-T said in a video interview on the hip-hop Web site, sohh.com.

"Let's get that straight. . . . If I know somebody's in the neighborhood raping little girls — you supposed to tell the police about that sucka. That's not snitching." [17]

As criticism of hip-hop intensifies, here are some of the questions being asked:

Is hip-hop harmful to black America?

Debates over hip-hop have taken place mostly within the black community. Some of hip-hop's fiercest critics, including black intellectuals and entertainers, argue that hip-hop presents a caricature of black America that damages how young black people view themselves and how they're viewed by others.

Author and jazz critic Crouch has decried for years what he calls the ravages of hip-hop. In a 2003 column in the *New York Daily News* — one of dozens he has devoted to the theme — he lamented that ordinary African Americans were bearing the consequences of a genre in which "thugs and freelance prostitutes have been celebrated for a number of years." The result: "Thousands upon thousands . . . have been murdered or beaten up or terrorized. After all, the celebration of thugs and thuggish behavior should not be expected to bring about any other results." [18]

Though white suburban teenagers make up the vast majority of hip-hop fans, Crouch added, the class privileges they enjoy largely shield them and their communities from the outcome. "With black teenagers . . . street behavior is defined these days as being 'authentic' and 'not trying to be white.' Those who take that seriously have been committing intellectual suicide for years by aspiring downward." [19]

Younger cultural critics, even those who partly agree with Crouch, reject such sweeping condemnations. Instead, they insist on distinguishing between mass-marketed hip-hop and what they see as its purer, original form, less tainted by the demands of the marketplace.

"I like conscious hip-hop, and the stuff that you just dance to," says Lisa Fager, a former promotional specialist at commercial radio stations and record labels, "but I don't like stuff that demeans me as a black woman, or a woman, period — or degrades my community. People don't want to be called bitches, niggas and hos." Fager co-founded an advocacy organization in the Washington area, Industry Ears, largely to call attention to the Federal Communications Commission's responsibility to regulate radio content during hours when children may be listening. [20]

Virtually the entire school of hip-hop that focuses on social criticism is kept off commercial radio, Fager contends, making a point that echoes widely in African American intellectual circles. "The gatekeepers don't want us to be politically active," she says, referring to programming and record executives who decide what gets recorded and broadcast. "Hurricane Katrina, you don't think that was something the black community talked about? But there were no songs on the radio about it."

Rapper Banner doesn't dispute Fager on what gets played. "The labels don't want to deal with anything that creative," he says. "They don't want to develop an artist; they want the quickest thing people will buy. And as soon as one feminist gets mad, they back up."

But Banner reacts explosively to African Americans who attack hip-hop as degrading. Hip-hop mogul Simmons' proposal to ban offensive words is "stupid," Banner says. "There was a time in history when we didn't have a choice about being called a nigger. Now that we're making money off it, it's a problem."

He adds, "If I try to change my music, I'm not going to sell my records, and that's the truth. My fans have literally come to me and they say, 'We put you on for pimp [songs]. You put anything else on, you're betraying us.' "

Other blacks argue that rappers who blame profit-motivated companies and the market are copping out. "If what you are doing is not lifting people up to a better day, then I don't think it's valuable and necessary for our people," says poet Heru, a native of Ghana, who practiced law in Florida until he took to poetry full time in 2001.

"For us, and for me, music is more than just music," says Heru. "In Africa-based communities, whether on the continent or in the Western Hemisphere, music is ceremonial and music is used for everything. So what ceremony are we introducing to people? If it's about killing random people in your community or degrading women of your community, that's not a ceremony I want to celebrate."

For others, viewing hip-hop only through the prism of race is simplistic. James McBride, a writer, jazz saxophonist and bandleader, says, "the music has demonstrated that it's bigger than race." In a recent article for *National Geographic*, McBride examined hip-hop's global reach and existential pull: "It's about identity — 'this is what I am, this is what I know.' This is what every 15-year-old kid feels. This music is the music of all young people. White people loved jazz in the '40s, too." [21]

Reflecting hip-hop's international popularity, 20-year-old French "b-boy" Lilou performs during the Red Bull BC One break-dancing tournament in Berlin in 2005. Break-dancing is a core element of hip-hop, along with rapping, DJ-ing and graffiti-writing.

But rappers do get subjected to a higher standard of scrutiny and indignation, McBride says. "If it weren't promoted or initiated by young black men, then I think some of this debate wouldn't even be a debate," he argues. "Alice Cooper used to do disgusting things on stage" without provoking storms of condemnation. In the 1970s and '80s, Cooper's "shock-rock" stage shows depicted a woman being decapitated and Cooper being hanged. [22]

Is hip-hop a genuine artistic/social movement transcending rap and break-dancing?

Cultural critics argue that after evolving for more than 30 years, hip-hop has become an artistic and social movement extending far beyond rapping over rhythm tracks, break-dancing and spray-painting graffiti.

Like blues, jazz and rock, hip-hop has emerged from the underground to be studied in universities, examined in scholarly tomes and celebrated in museum shows. (*See sidebar, p. 150.*) [23]

"Political context, lack of resources and reappropriation . . . provide an aesthetic context from which hip-hop has sprung," writes actor, playwright and director Danny Hoch in a recent anthology of essays on hip-hop. "They have also informed — and continue to inform — our artistic practice, even when the form or genre varies." [24] By "reappropriation," Hoch means "sampling," or taking snippets from other peoples' work and using them in creating something new.

Colleges Embrace Hip-Hop Studies

'It's worthy of scholarship.'

When David Cook submitted his undergraduate thesis — "The Power of Rap" — at the University of California, Berkeley, in 1987, he didn't include sources.

"I handed it in without footnotes," he recalled recently. "I mean, [I was] talking about something I was a part of, something I knew a lot about, and [my professor] was like, 'Footnote something. There's got to be books about hip-hop.' "

But 20 years ago there were few academic works on the subject, so Cook ended up citing Davey D — the alias he still uses as a hip-hop journalist — as somebody quoted in *Bomb* magazine. He received an A on the paper. [1]

Today's students would have no trouble crafting bibliographies — or even taking college courses — on hip-hop and its origins. From "American Protest Literature from Tom Paine to Tupac" at Harvard to "Beginning Hip Hop Funkamentals" — a dance class at UCLA — colleges and universities increasingly are offering courses in tune with the current generation of students. Stanford University's The Hiphop Archive — an educational and artistic repository and research center dedicated to hip-hop culture — estimates 300 such courses are being offered nationwide, with many being taught by professors who themselves were involved in the movement's earlier stages. [2]

Historically black Howard University, in Washington, D.C., became the first college to offer a hip-hop course in 1991 and aims to become the first university to offer a hip-hop minor by 2009. "If you look at the overall impact of hip-hop on youth in the United States and abroad, you see why it's worthy of scholarship," says Howard history graduate student Joshua Kondwani Wright, who is spearheading efforts to establish the minor.

Mark Anthony Neal, an associate professor of black popular culture at Duke University who helped organize Hip-Hop Appreciation Week on campus, adds, "Pop culture, and especially hip-hop now, has a large influence on how people see the world. That demands we take it seriously. We also know that popular culture is a place where ideology is introduced."

Although the study of black culture has been a prominent fixture on college campuses since the end of the civil rights era, the study of hip-hop has been controversial. In 2004, then-Harvard University President Lawrence H. Summers declined to offer tenure to noted hip-hop scholar Marcyliena Morgan despite unanimous support from the Department of African and African-American Studies. Many speculated the decision reflected Summers' lack of respect for hip-hop's presence in the ivory tower.

Morgan eventually accepted a tenured position at Stanford, taking The Hiphop Archive with her. Just last month, an ad hoc committee at Harvard and Interim President Derek C. Bok offered a tenured professorship to Morgan, reversing Summers' decision. [3]

But only a few within academia belittle the study of hip-hop. "It's a continuum of African-American history and African-American culture," says Wright. Moreover, some scholars are using their knowledge of the subject to propose remedies to social ills.

"We cannot ignore the sociological and economic circumstances out of which the hip-hop culture emerges," says James Peterson, assistant professor of English at Bucknell University, who teaches a course on hip-hop culture and composition. "And effectively addressing many societal problems requires an examination of the hip-hop culture." Peterson, who is also an educational consultant, has often been asked to assess the role of hip-hop in issues such as urban crime.

But will hip-hop remain a viable academic pursuit a generation from now, when society's problems are unlikely to be associated with hip-hop and today's regular fixtures on MTV and Black Entertainment Television are reduced to archives in VH1 Classic?

"If anything, it strengthens authenticity within the academy," says Peterson. "If studied from a historical perspective, hip-hop will become similar to what jazz or blues studies are now."

— *Darrell Dela Rosa*

---

[1] See Reyhan Harmanci, "Academic Hip-Hop? Yes, Yes Y'all," *The San Francisco Chronicle*, March 5, 2007, p. F1.

[2] For a list of courses, see www.hiphoparchive.org.

[3] See William Lee Adams, "Ivory Tower: Teachings Of Tupac," *Newsweek*, Oct. 4, 2004, p. 45; Lulu Zhou, "Hip Hop Scholar Offered Tenure," *The Harvard Crimson*, May 25, 2007, www.thecrimson.com.

A fellow essayist, playwright and actress, Eisa Davis, pushes hip-hop's boundaries even further. " 'Scarface,' 'Boiler Room,' 'Ghost Dog' — these are all hip-hop films even though there is nary a graf artist, MC, DJ or b-boy in sight," she writes. "Instead, the protagonists are dealers, schemers and samurai stylists — and through the narrative and the soundtracks comes a stance that reveals hip-hop vision."

But, Davis points out, "The hip-hop stance is not a lifestyle, it's a thinking style, and if you try to define [it], those brain waves will run away from you and set up shop on another corner." [25]

Trying to equate rap music with a samurai film could indeed overload brain circuitry. But even hip-hop artists of less sweeping vision argue that their art form should be seen as expandable. "It's a culture," says Miami-based Mecca aka Grimo (Patrick Marcelin), a Haitian American hip-hop performer. "It expresses views and opinions; it has its own language, fashion, the way we walk — that bop, that swagger. It's a subculture that's evolved in the inner city and has become global."

He adds: "We've got to take the good with the bad. I can't tell you the pants hanging down or the cursing isn't part of the culture. But music can definitely be used as an educational tool to change these things."

Performance poetry, recited without accompaniment and known in its rap-spinoff form as "spoken word," is the clearest example of hip-hop culture extending itself beyond its turntable-spinning roots.

In its original form, hip-hop consisted of DJ-ing, or manipulating turntables, volume levels and other features of music tracks; MC-ing (rapping over an accompaniment); graffiti spray-painting and break-dancing.

"I still believe in hip-hop as its four original elements," says hip-hop historian Bynoe. "When you talk about hip-hop movies, I don't know what that means. Is it a movie about black people? A lot of times, 'hip-hop' is, like 'urban,' a euphemism to mean 'black people.' I don't think 'hip-hop' is a concrete enough definition to make it valid beyond the four elements."

Bynoe doesn't object to using hip-hop as a device to get students interested in academic subjects. And she acknowledges that hip-hop theater may be the one valid extension of the hip-hop genre. But she cautions those involved in such projects against assuming "just because you're poor or of color that hip-hop is the only thing you're interested in." In her own case, she says, "There

Sean "P. Diddy" Combs announces his Citizen Change Campaign schedule for the 2004 election season, with Democratic political consultant James Carville. The campaign is one of several hip-hop-driven efforts to register young voters and promote political awareness.

have been some old, dead white guys whose writing and work were relevant to me."

In May, Chicago's Museum of Contemporary Art hosted the Hip-Hop Theater Festival, which sought to introduce theater to inner-city residents who aren't part of the high-culture scene.

The festival showcased work "that has been embraced by a younger population," says Yolanda Cesta Cursach, the museum's associate director of performance programs. She says hip-hop theater is characterized by "a young attitude toward politics in the urban environment — race, class, getting a job, getting incarcerated. It's really about putting a creative face on the politics of urban life."

The performers included a women's ensemble, "We Got Issues," which presented rhymed tales of women's lives; Jerry Quickley, a performance poet whose antiwar piece, "Live from the Front," tells of his adversarial reporting experiences in Iraq; and "Still Fabulous," a story-telling and singing group that was formed at the Illinois Youth Center, a female juvenile detention center.

Rapping on a stage without music may not be a far cry from MC-ing on a dance floor. But writer-musician McBride argues that trying to extend hip-hop much further from its origins may be a fruitless exercise. For example, he says, "I don't see hip-hop in 'Spider-man 3.' Other than quick cuts, the snap-crackle-pop immediacy of in-your-face imagery — if that's what hip-hop is, then yes, it's in 'Spider-man 3.' But I see hip-hop as a deeper question about identity and purpose and sense of place."

Is hip-hop becoming a political force?

Hip-hop and politics have been entwined since the genre's birth. Musically, hip-hop may have started as good-time dance music, but the spray-painted graffiti art style that "taggers" adopted as the visual counterpart of DJ-ing and MC-ing was illegal. Its practitioners and fans celebrated graffiti "tagging" as a reclaiming of urban space by its marginalized inhabitants. "Graffiti writers had claimed a modern symbol of efficiency and progress and made it into a moving violation," writes hip-hop chronicler Jeff Chang about subway-car taggers. "Authorities took their work as a guerrilla war on civility. They were right." [26]

All of hip-hop was shaped, Chang writes in his definitive history, by the social and political upheavals of its time. These include the end of the civil rights era, the crack epidemic, the incarceration boom and globalization.

Hip-hop stars recognize the political roots of their genre and have lent their talents and checkbooks to a variety of causes. In 2003, hip-hop moguls Combs and Simmons helped organize a movement that campaigned for repeal of New York's harsh Rockefeller drug laws. [27] When the campaign failed, some politicians and activists blamed Simmons for settling for small-scale reforms. [28]

Star power may have worked better in registering young people to vote. In 2004, the Hip-Hop Summit Action Network — Simmons is co-chair and Combs is a director — launched a campaign to sign up 2 million new, young voters. The organization's other directors include the top executives of three major record labels and an ex-president of the powerful Recording Industry Association of America. [29]

Combs ran his own registration-and-turnout campaign as well, under the slogan "Vote or Die!" "When the president is running your country," he said in 2004, "he is running you, closing you out of a hospital, or taking you to war. Not just Bush. Every president." [30]

Perhaps aided by the campaign, the number of overall registrations of Americans under age 30 between the 2000 and 2004 presidential elections increased by 3.1 million, according to George Washington University's Graduate School of Political Management. Measured as a share of the general voting public, the percentage of young registered voters rose from 55 percent of the general population to 60 percent. And turnout among young voters rose by 4.3 million between the two elections — with African Americans and Latinos accounting for more than half the surge. [31]

Youth turnout increased by at least two percentage points in the 2006 midterm elections, compared to 2002 (with Democrats reaping most of the benefits), according to the school's Young Voter Strategies project. [32]

Even so, the question remains whether hip-hop represents a marginalized subculture or a rising tide of political protest.

Some politically minded hip-hop community members argue that to focus on big-scale projects led by entertainment-industry giants is to miss the point, in part because they work with the conventional political structure. "Our country has to change, and I don't think it's going to happen through this Democratic-Republican Party medium we have," says Bakari Kitwana, co-founder of the National Hip-Hop Political Convention. "That's one party to me. Why can't we get money into education the way we've dumped money into Iraq? That would be revolutionary, and it would be hip-hop."

Kitwana, former executive editor of *The Source*, a leading hip-hop magazine, argues that the real power of hip-hop politics can be felt in community organizations that have led fights to improve schools or oppose police brutality. "What I'm talking about is off the radar," he adds. "You're not going to see it on CNN."

But Marc Lamont Hill, an assistant professor of urban education and American studies at Temple University in Philadelphia, cautions against overestimating the power of hip-hop. "If Jay-Z did a song tomorrow criticizing multinational capitalism, that's great," he says, "but even if that happens, it has to be connected to a real struggle. We need people who consume hip-hop culture to think about political conditions they can affect through their activism. If we don't think about it that way, all we're doing is making some cool music. We hip-hop scholars and academics sometimes romanticize cultural politics."

Davey D (David Cook), a radio DJ, blogger and newspaper columnist in Oakland, Calif., suggests hip-hop politics is in flux. Some influential voices in the community, for instance, challenge the usefulness of voting. The rapper Nas (Nasir Bin Olu Dara Jones) "would get on the stage and say, 'Don't vote, they're not counting our votes.' And his message gets reinforced inadvertently by grass-roots people who feel that the system is too corrupt."

The mass-market political side of hip-hop suffers from its own weaknesses, Davey D says. "Russell [Simmons] and them have raised awareness, but they didn't do voter education. There's not a lot of activism with them. I would describe activism as being politically engaged and seeing the system, or various touch points in that system, as something that needs to be dealt with day in and day out."

Still Davey D remains committed to the idea that the hip-hop community represents a political force, whether at the polls or in community matters. On the other hand, Southern-style rapper Banner sees a wave of political disillusionment spreading as a result of the 2004 Republican presidential victory.

"We had all these kids hyped, and when it didn't turn out the way it was supposed to, they're not going to vote for the next 10 years," Banner says. "A lot of people from the Republicans said, 'If it was about vote or die, then most of you people are dead.' "

So far, events haven't borne out Banner's gloomy outlook. But activists who see themselves as part of the political hip-hop community are trying to avoid the outcome he predicts.

"We rap, we utilize the art," says T. J. Crawford, 31, a community organizer whose Chicago Hip-Hop Political Action Committee registered 17,000 young people in 2004 and is now working on voter education. "The most important thing is making voting relevant, so that people understand how the system works."

BACKGROUND

Made in the Bronx

The cradle of hip-hop lies in the Bronx, a borough of New York City that has nurtured generations of middle- and working-class families, many newly arrived in the United States, including Colin L. Powell. The former chairman of the joint chiefs and Secretary of State grew up there in the 1940s and '50s, the son of Jamaican immigrants. [33]

But the engine of upward mobility that propelled Powell and thousands of other Bronxites into college and greater prosperity was sputtering by the late 1970s. New York was shedding its role as a manufacturing center, losing thousands of factory jobs in the process. At the same time, the civil rights and anti-Vietnam War movements had created a current of social rebelliousness that was still running strong. [34]

Amid this sociopolitical heavy weather a new musical style blew in from Jamaica, where many musicians and singers were leaving for jobs in Britain and the United States. The migration of performers forced disc jockeys to take over the top spots in an active song-and-dance culture. "Outfitted with powerful amplifiers and blasting stacks of homemade speakers, one only needed a selector and turntable to transform any yard," writes Chang in *Can't Stop Won't Stop: A History of the Hip-Hop Generation.* [35]

In 1967, the DJ's role expanded even further when a record-spinner happened upon a disk with the vocals missing — the result of an engineer's error. The DJ used the record on his next gig, as a rhythmic foundation for spouting rhymes. Dancers loved it, and the trend took off.

That same year, the emigrés included 12-year-old Clive Campbell, who arrived in New York with powerful memories of Jamaica's sound-system DJs. Clive's father took up DJ-ing as a sideline, buying big speakers and an amplifier to play for house parties.

By the time he reached high school, Clive was following in his father's footsteps. But he rewired the equipment to push more power to the speakers and to mix echo and other effects with his patter as DJ Kool Herc — borrowing from a popular brand of cigarettes and the name of the mythological strongman.

When his sister Cindy threw a dance party on Aug. 11, 1973, in the community room of the family's apartment building on Sedgwick Avenue, Kool Herc made his debut — and so did hip-hop. Cindy used her share of the entrance fee to buy clothes for school.

Going Global

As news of the event spread and demand for Herc's services rose, he came up with a trend-setting innovation. Other DJs were already using two turntables, so that a new song could start when the first one ended. But Herc would put the same tune on each turntable, allowing him to continue the bass-and-drums "break" section of a dance song as it was fading away on the other record. Dancers — who loved the breaks — went wild.

Other Bronx DJs soon adopted the technique, adding the Jamaican technique of rhyming over the beat. "Rapping" spread through other neighborhoods and eventually to clubs. All it took for the national spotlight to hit the localized craze was one record — the Sugar Hill Gang's "Rapper's Delight," which came out in 1979.

CHRONOLOGY

1970s–1980s *Hip-hop is born in the Bronx and spreads throughout New York City before starting to take off elsewhere.*

Aug. 11, 1973 The first recognized hip-hop event takes place in the Bronx at a dance in an apartment building's community room.

October 1979 "Rapper's Delight," by the Sugar Hill Gang, becomes the first hip-hop record to be released.

March 1981 Afrika Bambaataa and the Jazzy Five release "Jazzy Sensation," which fuses dance-funk beats and so-called electronica sounds and helps widen hip-hop's appeal.

1984 Hip-hop powerhouse Def Jam Recordings issues its first record.

1988 Public Enemy releases "It Takes a Nation of Millions to Hold Us Back," which merges hip-hop with black nationalism.

1989 The Los Angeles-based group N.W.A. (Niggaz With Attitude), creates "gangsta rap," characterized by the song "Fuck Tha Police."

1990s *Hip-hop becomes a force in the entertainment industry, even as rap becomes increasingly identified with graphic depictions of sex, misogyny and glorification of violence and drugs; criticism mounts, as do sales.*

1992 Supreme Court lets stand an appeals court's ruling that Miami-based 2 Live Crew's "Nasty As They Want To Be" is not obscene. Bill Clinton, the Democratic presidential nominee, attacks rap performer Sister Souljah (Lisa Williamson) for comments about the Los Angeles riots, calling her remarks racist.

Feb. 23, 1994 Rap lyrics are both attacked and described as reflecting the lives of urban youths at a Senate Judiciary Committee hearing.

Sept. 13, 1996 Gangsta rapper Tupac Shakur dies after a gangland-style hit on the Las Vegas Strip. About six months later, rival rapper The Notorious B.I.G. (Christopher Wallace) dies in a similar shooting in Los Angeles.

Dec. 27, 1999 Sean Combs (then known as "Puff Daddy") is arrested for gun possession outside a New York

nightclub; he is later acquitted, though a bodyguard gets prison time for having opened fire.

2000s *Music industry steadily loses steam; hip-hop magnates and stars diversify and take up politics, while "dirty south" rap, with its raunchy lyrics that many say degrade women, gains in popularity.*

December 2003 Rapper Jay-Z joins a consortium that eventually buys the NBA's New Jersey Nets.

2004 In April, students at Atlanta's Spelman College demand rapper Nelly meet with them to discuss his raunchy "Tip Drill" video, but he refuses and also cancels a charity fundraising appearance at the women's college. . . . The Hip-Hop Summit Action Network and Sean "P. Diddy" Combs each organize national voter-registration campaigns focused at African-American youth. . . . Chicago Hip-Hop Political Action Committee registers 17,000 young voters.

2005 Record and cable TV executives at a Spelman panel discussion try to explain why they market videos that portray women as sex toys.

2006 Hip-hop recordings slip to 11.4 percent of U.S. market share, from 13.3 percent in 2005.

2007 On Jan. 1, Atlanta police raid a major mixtapes production operation. . . . In April, radio shock jock Don Imus is fired for describing the Rutgers women's basketball team as "nappy-headed hos," spurring debate about hip-hoppers' use of similar language. . . . Under pressure from TV personality Oprah Winfrey and other African-American leaders, the Hip-Hop Summit Action Network calls for a ban on "bitch," "ho" and "nigger" in recordings. . . . Rappers Master P and Chamillionaire announce plans to tone down street language in the future. . . . Rapper Cam'ron is criticized after telling "60 Minutes" he wouldn't call the police even to protect neighbors from a serial killer; he later apologizes for the comment. . . . The "Hip-Hop Project" opens; the Bruce Willis-produced documentary depicts young people learning artistic expression through rap. . . . "Dirty south" rapper David Banner transports relief supplies to Hurricane Katrina-ravaged areas and organizes a fundraising concert for hurricane victims.

"Imitations popped up from Brazil to Jamaica," Chang writes. "It became the best-selling 12-inch single ever pressed." [36] The tune's first words: "I said uh hip-hop. . . ."

By 1980, even *The Washington Post* was taking notice of "the newest craze among the 14-to-21-year-olds, the record-buying majority who are putting rap records on the national charts and making money for the nightclub disc jockeys capitalizing on a bit of New York City party culture." [37]

As rap's popularity soared, its home turf was becoming a grittier, tougher place. City government was headed toward bankruptcy. Education, garbage collection and other public services were strained to their limits.

Meanwhile, the election of Ronald Reagan as president in 1980 marked a turn toward conservative policies that hit poor communities across the country. Reagan's first years in office saw a tax cut that he championed swing the country into a recession marked by unemployment and cutbacks in state and local assistance programs. [38]

Although the national economy slowly improved, many poor communities were assaulted by the arrival of a cheap, addictive stimulant — crack cocaine — and barely felt the change. The ensuing crack epidemic devastated inner cities across the country. Crack left users wanting another hit almost immediately. High demand helped make crack a big business in job-starved ghettoes, where local drug sellers served neighborhood customers as well as users driving in from the suburbs. [39]

As addiction and warfare between rival drug-trafficking gangs ravaged poor neighborhoods, law enforcement cracked down. New sentencing laws imposed tougher penalties for crack trafficking than for dealing in powdered cocaine, which didn't make an inroad in inner cities because of its relatively high price. [40]

Inevitably, popular culture, including hip-hop, began to reflect the distressing, new inner-city realities.

Sex and Violence

The lighthearted dance-party flavor that characterized early rap soon took a turn toward hard-edged social commentary with a black-nationalist spin. A key source of inspiration was a pre-hip-hop group of African-nationalist verse writers, The Last Poets, who had released a groundbreaking album of poetry recited over percussion backing in 1970. The Long Island, N.Y., group Public Enemy took the idea into the hip-hop age with an album, "It Takes a Nation of Millions to Hold Us Back," released in 1988. [41]

Public Enemy soon became engulfed in a controversy over anti-Jewish comments by Professor Griff (Richard Griffin), the group's "minister of information." After he blamed Jews for "the majority of wickedness that goes on across the globe," Griff was dropped by the group and then rehired, before it broke up for a time.

Public Enemy's founder, Chuck D (Carlton Douglas Ridenhour) became, and remains, a leading spokesman for rap as a form of social and political commentary and activism. His description of rap as "the black CNN" stands as one of the most widely circulated observations ever coined about hip-hop.

But the comment had a perhaps-unintended consequence — it tended to validate "gangsta" rap. The new hip-hop genre seemed to spin off from Public Enemy's work but departed from its message of social improvement: Violence and the drug trade were glorified; police were threatened; and women were treated purely as sex objects and prostitutes.

The Los Angeles-based group N.W.A. (Niggaz With Attitude) is considered the founder of gangsta rap, though arguably it was depicting the drug war rather than celebrating it, as the group's imitators did. In 1989, sales of N.W.A.'s second album, "Straight Outta Compton," reached gold-record status — 500,000 copies sold — within six weeks and eventually racked up 3 million sales. Its degradation of women and profanity made radio airplay impossible, so the album sold initially through a below-the-radar distribution system of mom-and-pop record stores in black communities, then through word-of-mouth among white teenagers. Once stores in white neighborhoods stocked it, "That's all it took," a record salesman said years later. Eventually, white suburban kids accounted for about 80 percent of sales. [42]

One of the album's cuts, "Fuck Tha Police," was structured as a snapshot of life on the street:

. . . Searchin' my car, lookin for the product
Thinkin' every nigga is sellin narcotics . . .
Just cuz I'm from the CPT [Compton], punk police are afraid of me
A young nigga on a warpath
And when I'm finished, it's gonna be a bloodbath
Of cops, dyin' in LA. [43]

Hip-Hop Stars Are Branching Out

Tycoons have clothing lines, TV shows.

Hip-hop has come a long way from the community rooms and street corners where pioneers in the 1970s and '80s developed the arts of sampling and rapping and sold cassettes out of car trunks.

And in the view of hip-hop tycoon Russell Simmons — who has branched out into fashion, TV and jewelry — the genre still has a long way to go. "Hip-hop is not fully exploited," Simmons said. [1]

He should know. Simmons' hip-hop enterprises are worth upwards of $325 million. But music sales — traditionally hip-hop's top moneymaker — are hurting, as the music business struggles to adjust to a digital world in which consumers can easily and cheaply acquire music over the Internet.

Sales of hip-hop recordings and downloads in the United States reached about $131 million in 2006 — or 11.4 percent of the $11.5 billion U.S. music market — according to the Recording Industry Association of America (RIAA). [2] And while breakdowns by genre aren't available for the $33 billion global recorded-music market, two hip-hop albums — by 50 Cent and Eminem — were among the world's top 10 bestsellers in 2005, the most recent figures available. [3]

But music sales are plunging, both nationally and globally — by 6.2 percent in the United States and 3 percent worldwide in 2005. And sales of "physical" products, such as CDs, are down 6.7 percent, according to the International Federation of the Phonographic Industry. [4]

The diversified Simmons doesn't worry about those problems, however. The co-founder of hip-hop's first record label, Def Jam Recordings, is out of the music business now; his Rush Communications produces movies, TV shows, yoga DVDs and "urban wear."

Simmons' fellow hip-hop pioneers haven't done too shabbily either. Sean "P. Diddy" Combs — a performer as well as entrepreneur — is a designer, actor and international fashion icon. Def Jam co-founder Rick Rubin, whose work ranges far beyond hip-hop, won his fifth producer-of-the-year Grammy in February and is considering an offer to become co-chairman of Columbia Records. And Lyor Cohen, another Def Jam alum, is chairman and CEO of U.S. Recorded Music for Warner Music Group. [5]

A handful of other rappers have also hit it big, though not quite on Simmons' level. Ice Cube (O'Shea Jackson), once a member of the much-condemned N.W.A., has diversified into acting, producing and screenplay writing for mainline Hollywood features. Jay-Z (Shawn Corey Carter) sold his Rocawear clothing line in March for $204 million, owns a chain of upscale clubs and helps promote Budweiser Select beer. He recently bought a minority share of the NBA's New Jersey Nets and is still president and CEO of Def Jam. And Lil Jon (Jonathan Smith), a rapper and producer in the Southern "crunk" style, also produces clothing and has starred in a video game and a Comedy Central cartoon show. [6]

With the push for diversification, it might appear that rappers are hedging their bets on the recording business. Rap album sales dropped 20 percent in 2006, and the top 10 best-selling albums that year included no rap records — an occurrence not seen for more than 10 years. "Hip-Hop Is Dead," declared the title of a late-2006 album by rapper Nas. [7]

No funerals are scheduled, but rap has slipped to third place (after country music) in U.S. music sales — from 13.3 percent of market share in 2005 to 11.4 percent in 2006. "It's not losing popularity," says David Banner (Levell Crump). "Downloading is up, and the music industry is going down." [8]

A top industry-watcher agrees. "I don't have any data that supports that hip-hop, particularly, is down," says Don

"Gangsta, gangsta" was the title of another selection, giving the genre its name.

A pushback against gangsta rap began almost immediately, fueled by black activists and police. An assistant director of the FBI sent the record company a letter accusing the firm of encouraging "violence against and disrespect for the law-enforcement officer.' " The letter stoked consumer interest even more. [44]

Some politically minded hip-hop radio D.J.'s, led by Davey D, in the San Francisco Bay area, organized a boycott of N.W.A., largely because of its repeated use of the N-word. But "progressive" college radio stations refused to take part in what they called censorship of black rappers, whom college kids considered voices of the inner city. "They were fascinated with anger from the ghetto," Davey D says now. "I live in the 'hood, and I'm not fascinated by it."

Gorder, chair of the Music Business/Management Department at Berklee College of Music. In general, he adds, "Demand for music has never been greater. It's a strong market. The business models are having to adjust."

One adjustment may be dealing with "mixtapes" — CD albums with songs not yet officially released, designed to test the market and keep a performer's work before the public between formal releases. The little-known sector of the business — the name is a holdover from the old days of cassettes — came under scrutiny after an Atlanta recording studio was raided in January by police. Accompanied by RIAA officials, the police grabbed two men — along with 25,000 CDs — on charges of illegally producing CDs. (The RIAA later said the police, not the association, had instigated the raid, but industry insiders were skeptical.) [9]

The men, Tyree Simmons and Donald Cannon, turned out to be two of the country's best-known DJs and are well known for producing mixtapes. [10]

Derrick Ewan, an XM Satellite Radio DJ who goes by the name Furious Styles, says the record companies actually help get mixtapes made. "The label wants you to make tapes," Ewan says. "They give you the songs and in some cases pay you to make a mixtape. They don't care if you sell them." Ewan says he hasn't received such payments or run afoul of copyright laws because the CDs he makes showcase unsigned acts — his DJ niche.

Still, mixtapes are easily available at independent record stores and even online, and the business has its own whole-

Hip-hop entrepreneurs Sean "P. Diddy" Combs, Jay-Z and Russell Simmons (from left) have built multi-million-dollar businesses involving street clothing, jewelry, sports, television and film.

Getty Images/Evan Agostini

salers. For all the millions made in hip-hop clothing and jewelry, the old hip-hop hustle is still alive and well at street level — and some mixtapes are even sold out of car trunks.

[1] See Mindy Fetterman, "Russell Simmons can't slow down," *USA Today*, May 14, 2007, p. B1.

[2] "2006 Consumer Profile," Recording Industry Association of America, undated, www.riaa.com/news/marketingdata/pdf/2006RIAAConsumerProfile.pdf.

[3] See Jeff Leeds, "Music Industry's Sales Post Their Sixth Year of Decline," *The New York Times*, April, 1, 2006, p. C2; "Digital formats continue to drive the global music market — World Sales 2005," International Federation of Phonographic Industries, March 31, 2006, www.ifpi.org/content/section_news/20060331a.html.

[4] "The Recording Industry World Sales 2001," International Federation of the Phonographic Industry, April, 2002, www.ifpi.org/content/library/worldsales2001.pdf.

[5] See Fetterman, *op. cit.*; Alana Semuels, "Rappers hear siren song of opportunity,: Los Angeles Times, March 12, 2007; Sia Michel, "A New Sound for Old What's-His-Name," *The New York Times*, Sept. 10, 2006, p. B67; Robert Hilburn, "The Music Industry Titans — Rick Rubin; A balance of rattle and om," *Los Angeles Times*, Feb. 11, 2007, p. F1; Charles Duhigg, "Q&A; Getting Warner Music More Upbeat," *Los Angeles Times*, Aug. 28, 2006, p. C1; "Lyor Cohen," (official biographical sketch) Warner Music Group, undated, www.wmg.com/about/biography/?id=contact400004.

[6] See Yvonne Bynoe, Encyclopedia of Rap and Hip Hop Culture (2006), pp. 178-181; Semuels, *op. cit*; Steve Jones, "Jay-Z is a very busy man," *USA Today*, Nov. 21, 2006, p. D5.

[7] Semuels, *op. cit.*

[8] For market-share statistics, see "2006 Consumer Profile," *op. cit.*

[9] See Samantha M. Shapiro, "Hip-Hop Outlaw (Industry Version)," *The New York Times Magazine*, Feb. 18, 2007, p. 29.

[10] See *ibid.*

Opposition to gangsta rap merged with another current that had been building since 1985. A group of political wives began decrying rock songs' lyrics, especially explicit sexual references. Tipper Gore, wife of then-Sen. Al Gore, D-Tenn., and Susan Baker, wife of then-Treasury Secretary James A. Baker III, a Republican, founded the Parents Music Resource Center to demand ratings and voluntary warnings on albums, which per-

formers and record companies opposed during a congressional hearing. But in 1990, record companies began putting warnings on albums with language that could be considered offensive. [45] That year, with hip-hop's popularity soaring, Gore began echoing African American concerns over gangsta rap lyrics. [46]

At roughly the same time, explicitly sexual lyrics in albums produced by Luther Campbell of Miami led to

Getty Images/Scott Gries (all)

Hip-Hop Pioneers

Kool Herc (top) introduced break-beat DJ-ing in the 1970s, in which the percussive instrumental "breaks" of songs are isolated and repeated during dance parties. Bronx DJ Afrika Bambaataa (middle) pioneered the use of electronic drum machines to create hip-hop beats. In the 1980s, Public Enemy (bottom) became one of the first mainstream hip-hop groups to promote social and political activism.

litigation that reached the U.S. Supreme Court. Campbell was an entrepreneur-turned-rapper who produced and then joined the group 2 Live Crew. Among its songs: "We Want Some Pussy" and "Dick Almighty."

A series of court battles in Florida led eventually to a 1992 ruling by the 11th U.S. Circuit Court of Appeals in Atlanta that one of the group's albums, "Nasty as They Wanna Be," was not obscene. The Supreme Court let the decision stand. The years that followed saw gangsta rappers indulging in vulgarity as enthusiastically — and profitably — as they did in violence.

The Big Time

By the end of the 1990s, rap was a billion-dollar business — much of the revenue generated by gangsta rap purveyors like California-based Death Row Records. [47]

But the boom had been started on the East Coast by Simmons, then a budding rap promoter, and Rick Rubin, a white hip-hop fan with ambitions to manage rappers and produce recordings. In 1979, they founded Def Jam Productions.

Def Jam soon branched out from promoting and producing rap shows to recording rappers. After signing an unknown rapper who became a big-time hitmaker, LL Cool J (James Todd Smith III), the fledgling Def Jam signed a distribution deal with CBS/Columbia records and went on to produce some of the biggest hip-hop acts.

The money rolled in. Simmons and his partners (Rubin had left the firm) sold Def Jam to Universal Music Group for $130 million in 1999.

Another sign of hip-hop's new status was MTV's entry into the rap world, following years in which the channel didn't show black artists' videos. In 1988, the TV show "Yo! MTV Raps," began a swing toward rap that, a year later, had the channel showing rap videos 12 hours a day. Black Entertainment Television (BET) likewise came to rely heavily on hip-hop videos.

Hip-hop's sudden new status grew out of an appeal that reached beyond the inner cities. White suburban appetites for gangsta rap grew all the more intense as some stars began living up to the name, none more than Tupac Shakur. The California rapper reached the heights of hip-hop stardom during a five-year solo career that ended in September 1996 when he died at age 25 in a hail of bullets in Las Vegas. [48]

Shakur, who combined genuine talent with an attraction to the "thug life," was seen by many as a player in an East Coast-West Coast feud between California-based Death Row Records — for which he recorded — and New York-based Bad Boy Entertainment, headed by Combs. The label's biggest star, The Notorious B.I.G., was gunned down in Los Angeles six months later. Both murders remain unsolved. [49]

Controversy

The revulsion to rap engendered by N.W.A. and 2 Live Crew intensified. In New York, columnist Crouch kept up a steady drumbeat of fierce criticism beginning in the 1990s. "Illiterates with gold and diamonds in their teeth" Crouch called hip-hop entertainers. He slammed them for, among other things, marketing a stereotype of inner-city life that both titillated white kids and damaged black inner-city kids by making the thug a hero. [50]

Throughout the '90s, a growing number of African American critics — especially women — joined in the criticism. C. Delores Tucker, a Democratic politician from Philadelphia who had founded the National Political Congress of Black Women, spoke for "many disillusioned, middle-class, middle-aged people of color," writes hip-hop chronicler Chang. [51]

With generational and class fault lines in black America becoming exposed, Democratic presidential candidate Bill Clinton — renowned for his connection to the African American public — harshly criticized popular rapper Sister Souljah (Lisa Williamson) for comments she'd made after the near-fatal beating of a white truck driver by black youths during the Los

Rapper Tupac Shakur was a major player in the feud between California-based Death Row Records — for which Shakur recorded — and New York's Bad Boy Entertainment. Shakur was killed in a Las Vegas drive-by shooting in 1996. The Notorious B.I.G., Shakur's rival and Bad Boy's most popular artist, was killed in a similar shooting in 1997 in Los Angeles.

Angeles riots of 1992. "I mean, if black people kill black people every day, why not have a week and kill white people?" she said. [52]

She went on to indicate that she was describing rioters' state of mind rather than espousing violence. But Clinton pilloried her anyway. Speaking at a meeting of the Rev. Jesse Jackson's Rainbow Coalition, he said: "If you took the words white and black and you reversed them, you might think [former Ku Klux Klan leader] David Duke was giving that speech." Political writers showered Clinton with praise for what they saw as a courageous challenge to an outspoken member of one of the Democratic Party's major constituencies. [53]

New York rapper Nas, who leans toward "conscious" hip-hop, titled his controversial 2006 album "Hip Hop Is Dead" because he thinks the genre has become too commercialized and has lost its street credibility.

In 1994, attacks on gangsta rap converged with growing concern about violence on TV and in video games, prompting House and Senate hearings.

"It is an unavoidable conclusion that gangsta rap is negatively influencing our youth," Tucker told the Senate Judiciary Committee on Feb. 23, 1994. "This explains why so many of our children are out of control and why we have more blacks in jail than we have in college." [54]

Others argued that Tucker and her allies were, in effect, advocating killing the messenger. "Gangsta rappers are an easy target," Michael Eric Dyson, now a professor of humanities at the University of Pennsylvania, told lawmakers. "We should be having a hearing on crime and on economic misery." [55] Dyson authored the provocative 2006 book *Is Bill Cosby Right? Or Has the Black Middle Class Lost its Mind?*

None of the hearings led to legislation. Instead, the debate continued bubbling, especially within the African American community.

The outrage flared in 2004 at Atlanta's Spelman College. Rapper Nelly had been scheduled to visit the prestigious, historically black institution for women to encourage bone-marrow donations. But then students became aware of a Nelly song and video, "Tip Drill" — street slang for a homely woman with a good body. The video, in which David Banner appeared, featured the usual gyrating, bikini-clad women and an offensive scene in which the rapper swipes a credit card between a woman's buttocks. [56]

The students had planned to confront Nelly about the song, but he canceled his appearance. "Spelman is 10 blocks from a strip club," Nelly said. "You're not out in front of the strip club picketing." [57]

A panel discussion held the following year at the school showed that opinions on both sides remained firm. Bryan Lynch, an executive with TVT Records, a leading independent label that's home to some gangsta rappers, told the audience that record companies catered to record buyers' tastes. Panel mediator Michaela Davis, fashion editor of *Essence* magazine, snapped back: "Crack sells, too." [58]

CURRENT SITUATION

Imus Fallout

After the brief outburst of remorse that followed Imus' sudden fall, the captains of the hip-hop industry are keeping their microphones switched off. Calls and e-mails from reporters (including *CQ Researcher*) to top record and radio executives are going unanswered. A press conference that Simmons' Hip-Hop Summit Action Network had announced for a date in May to discuss language in rap songs was canceled. [59]

"I expect them to wait it out," says Don Gorder, chairman of the Music Business/Management Department at Berklee College of Music in Boston. "I would be surprised to see any strong policy statements. In pure business terms, people vote with their pocketbooks. Is it record companies' responsibility to steer them away from [gangsta rap]? I don't think they'd say that."

Should hip-hop artists produce material that is socially uplifting to African-Americans?

YES Heru Ofori-Atta
Poet, author of The Unapologetic African: Inside The Mind of a Frontline Poet

Written for *CQ Researcher*, June 2007

According to the American worldview, an artist should be "free" to do whatever he wants as long as he doesn't disrupt capitalism and/or white supremacy. In an intact African worldview, the village is more important than any one person. As an unapologetic African, I care about my people more than I care about hip-hop. I care about the minds of black children more than I care about my freedom of speech. I care about setting high standards for my people more than I care about capitulating to the low cultural standards set by white culture.

Any art form created by people of African descent must speak to the best of who we are and our aspirations. Art that doesn't must be thrown away. History will show that this is the correct position of a people who are still oppressed — socially, economically, politically and religiously. In fact, history judges a people based on the cultural artifacts they have left behind. In 3007, what would an archaeologist or anthropologist deduce about the African-American culture of today? The conclusion would not make our descendants proud.

I recently appeared on a panel with an artist who said if he wakes up in the morning and feels like writing about having sex with groupies and smoking crack, he would write it and feel "proud" to perform it. After all, that's what freedom of speech is about. Panelists said they didn't want to preach to their fans. I informed them that when an artist sings, raps or performs poetry bragging about shopping for acquisitions of illusory splendor, he is preaching for materialism.

The powers that be, who have always been against the progress of people of African descent in this country, have made sure the only artists to wield power are the village idiot and not the village freedom fighter and sage. The ruling elite saw the effects on the tastes, interests and values of American society when political dissenters were popular musicians in the 1960s and '70s.

As Nigerian musician and activist Fela Anikupalo Kuti said, "Music is a weapon." A weapon can be used to 1) commit suicide, 2) unjustly hurt others or 3) defend oneself, one's family and home. Black artists must ask themselves what are they using this weapon for? I proudly and unequivocally choose No. 3.

NO Marc Lamont Hill
Assistant professor of urban education and American studies, Temple University

Written for *CQ Researcher*, June 2007

More than any other musical genre in history, hip-hop has been linked to the sociopolitical fortunes and futures of African-American and Latino youth. Critics, fans and even artists themselves argue that hip-hop practitioners should produce music that socially uplifts its constituents. Although such efforts are highly valuable, it is both unfair and unrealistic to expect all artists to produce "socially uplifting music."

To be sure, artists have always played a critical role in our collective struggles for freedom, justice and equality. From the plantation to the pulpit, black and brown creative expression has been an indispensable weapon against the most vicious forms of oppression. While hip-hop artists should not be excluded from this tradition, we must expand our understanding of "social uplift" in ways that move us beyond the explicitly political.

From its birth in the streets and parks of post-industrial urban spaces, hip-hop has been more than a reflection of our political predilections. In addition to speaking truth to power, hip-hop, like its cultural forebears, has enabled us to find joy, love and community in the midst of the most absurd circumstances. While songs about a fresh romance, a newborn baby or a fun party may not end sexism, racism or poverty, they allow us to sustain a sense of hope and possibility against the most discouraging odds. Such sensibilities are as important to social-justice struggles as political education or cultural nationalism. From this perspective, Public Enemy's exhortations to "Fight the Power" and dead prez's critiques of the school system are just as valuable as Lupe Fiasco's stories about his skateboard.

Additionally, by placing exorbitant political demands on hip-hop artists, we easily misplace our political hopes in ways that compromise our progress. Despite the importance of an incisive lyrical critique or a provocative slogan, such things cannot replace the critical work of organizing, voting, striking or marching. By overestimating the power of cultural politics, the hip-hop generation absolves itself of the responsibilities of real, on-the-ground engagements with the public and its problems.

Like all human beings, hip-hop artists have moral obligations that necessarily inform their professional and personal lives. As such, they should feel compelled not to create any music that degrades, assaults or otherwise contradicts the values and goals of our respective communities. But they should also feel empowered to produce art that reflects their own feelings, desires and beliefs about the world — uplifting or not.

Some rappers made their own evaluations of how the wind was shifting — or re-examined their consciences — and acted accordingly. Master P founded Take a Stand Records to market "street music without offensive lyrics." [60]

In an open letter to the news media, he said, "Oprah Winfrey is absolutely right. We need to grow up and be responsible for our own actions. . . . Most artists' mission is to sell records. My mission is to help save and change lives." [61]

Best-selling rapper Chamillionaire spoke in similar terms. "On my new album, I don't say the word n***a," he told the hip-hop news site, AllHipHop.com. "I guarantee if I don't go out and say it in the media they're not even gonna realize that. People go back and listen to all of my old mixtapes and don't even realize that I wasn't even doing all that type of stuff. I was saying n***a, but I wasn't saying the F-word or [the] B-word. I was never saying those types of things. . . . I hear that so much, and it restricts your creativity and how far it can go." [62]

Nevertheless, for members of the hip-hop world who had been sounding the alarm for years over rap lyrics, the record and radio executives bear the biggest responsibility. "Nobody is saying that porn stars need to make more substantive and dramatic films," says Industry Ears co-founder Fager. "Why are we looking at rappers to change their content? It's the gatekeeper who allows this stuff to be made and seen."

That take on the matter can be found throughout the loosely knit community of the hip-hop world's internal critics. "Certainly we've heard rap artists make [sexist] comments," says historian Bynoe, "but they don't own record companies, for the most part, or radio stations or cable companies. The decisions about what content will be aired or produced isn't up to rap artists. If tomorrow these entities decide that material is not going to be broadcast, it would end."

Whether broadcasters and cable companies are likely to be forced into that position is another question. "Congress has bigger targets in its sights," says Adam D. Thierer, senior fellow at the Progress & Freedom Foundation, a think tank funded by telecommunications and entertainment giants, including Sony Music Entertainment and Time Warner. "They are so obsessed with regulating violence on cable TV. That has sucked all the oxygen out of the room."

But that picture could change. A hip-hop equivalent of Janet Jackson's breast-baring "wardrobe malfunction"

on live TV during the 2004 Super Bowl halftime show would likely put serious pressure on radio and/or radio executives. "It could lead to them being drug in front of a congressional committee to testify," Thierer says. The Jackson episode led the FCC to fine CBS $550,000. And then Congress raised fines tenfold for broadcasting "indecent" material. [63]

So far, the recent indignation over rap lyrics has the industry avoiding the congressional witness table. But the flare-up that followed Cam'ron's controversial statement on CBS' "60 Minutes" might have blazed brighter if he hadn't beat a retreat.

Days after saying that talking to police about a crime "would definitely hurt my business," Cam'ron acknowledged having refused to help in an investigation in which he himself had been shot. "But my experience in no way justifies what I said," he said. Looking back now, I can see how those comments could be viewed as offensive, especially to those who have suffered their own personal tragedies or to those who put their lives on the line to protect our citizens from crime." [64]

Good Works

It's not just "hos and clothes." That's what an orphaned young Brooklynite tells a group of other hard-luck kids he's brought together at an alternative high school to make a hip-hop record. Chris "Kharma Kazi" Rolle's idea is to show them how to turn their experiences into material.

After considerable struggle, the kids eventually did make their record, and two New York University film students document their progress. The fledgling filmmakers assembled their material into a movie, "The Hip Hop Project," which opened in May. [65]

Both the record and the movie attracted impressive support — from Simmons, Queen Latifah and movie star Bruce Willis. "In five years, hopefully, there'll be 25 programs in 25 other cities in this country" that replicate the New York project's methods, Willis says in a promotional Web video. [66]

In effect, the movie illustrates what some hip-hop advocates have been insisting for years: that the music is a tool for social betterment, not merely a soundtrack for street crime. "If you're just seeing it on TV, you're only going to see the bad hip-hop," says rapper Blitz the Ambassador, who greets the movie as validation. "Hip-hop helps these kids cope with extreme environments they are born into," he says.

In effect, the project also supports the vision of hip-hop theater activists, who argue the art form is made to order for artistically undernourished kids who need to express themselves. "Let's not isolate the voices of these young people," says Clyde Valentín, executive director of the Hip-Hop Theater Festival, which travels from city to city. "Let's encourage them to write their voices."

A native of Brooklyn, Valentín was a break-dancer in the early days of hip-hop. Like others, he argues that using hip-hop as a vehicle of expression also combats the "criminalization" of young people, especially blacks and Latinos, by enabling them to break free of stereotypes.

Miami's Mecca aka Grimo has a contract with Miami-Dade County Public Schools to run poetry workshops, which he describes in terms similar to those that resonate in the new film. "My main purpose is to stimulate their brains," Mecca says. "It's not just putting words together. I want these kids to start making sense. Being able to recite lyrics, come up with messages — that's a beautiful thing."

Paradoxically, the self-expression that Mecca tries to encourage is aimed at combating impressions largely created by mass-marketed hip-hop. "I do believe that the hip-hop culture — rap music and visuals — has definitely gone in a direction that's detrimental to black youth," he says. "You gotta get shot, you got to be a gangsta to be cool in the streets. Hip-hop became part of a system that's implemented in urban communities to keep people down or make money off them."

To be sure, even rappers who do work the seamier side of the hip-hop street get some credit for good works.

After Hurricane Katrina devastated the Gulf Coast, Banner used his tour bus to deliver emergency supplies to southern Mississippi and organized a fund-raising concert in Atlanta starring other much-criticized rappers, including Nelly. [67]

"I am definitely critical of both of them for some of the stuff they do," says Davey D. "But David Banner — I can't write him off. I didn't go to Mississippi. He did."

OUTLOOK

New and Old

No one could have predicted that a Jamaica-born, Bronx-developed combination of turntable music and spontaneous versifying would morph into a global enter-tainment force. Now the people who follow hip-hop's fortunes are fairly cautious about predicting its future.

The starting point for looking toward that future is to recognize the extent of the change already wrought by hip-hop, says writer and musician McBride. "This music has changed the way all of us think about music. It's hard for those of us who grew up listening to music as melody. When rap artists pull samples from different records, there's no tonality, the center of gravity is gone, so it's hard for us listeners of Western music to lock into where the center of the song is."

With those changes in the nature of music has come a break in the chain of musical heritage. "We've had whole generations growing up without hearing the great songs of the '40s," McBride says. "Their idea of an old song is Grandmaster Flash and the Furious Five."

That severing of the link between present and past musical styles might not be as widespread as McBride argues. Some hip-hop fans haven't abandoned what might be termed old-fashioned music, the kind that you play on instruments other than a turntable. Inevitably, that practice links them with musicians of the past.

Among the hip-hop performers who put the old and new together are The Roots, a Philadelphia group, and Wyclef Jean, a Haitian American superstar. Jean, for instance, performs on guitar, playing Santana-style solos and even picking the guitar from behind his head, and then with his mouth, techniques made famous by Jimi Hendrix. And in 2004, Queen Latifah went back even further in musical time, recording an album of standards, (including some from the '40s). This year, Mecca aka Grimo performed in Miami in May with guitar and drums behind him. [68]

Generally speaking, Mecca says, "We need to explore the art form of live music. That will jump us off into a bigger genre of music. Eventually we could be classified as world music if we take to live instruments."

Meanwhile, the debates about lyrics that have dominated discussion of hip-hop for nearly two decades strongly influence others' views of the future. "People are getting tired of gangsta hip-hop," Mecca adds. "In 10 years, you'll see another high point of good, clean, conscious hip-hop."

For others, the lessons of the recent past inspire more caution. "I had no clue in '98 that by 2007 hip-hop would have taken such a blow," says Blitz the Ambassador, describing what he calls the ill effects of

Southern rap. "That whole wave of music just took over and killed the lyrics."

Still, he holds out hope that old-school hip-hop at least will survive. "I really hope we can find a way to positively progress," Blitz says. "And if it's another genre, I hope it's more positive."

English, the fledgling independent record label owner, voices the identical hope. But he adds, "I don't see that happening. The major labels haven't said anything. This is their moneymaking machine."

Meanwhile, English says, he plays non-gangsta hip-hop to his 7- and 11-year-old daughters — but exposes them to soul and disco as well. "They need to know what good music really is."

Davey D, the Oakland-based DJ and writer, sees more room for hope, largely because of his sense that gangsta rap's appeal is fading." I want it to be dead," he says. "If ratings are going down, that's great. I'm not trying to save that manifestation of hip-hop. We're very clear that there's been an enabling of people to just be immature."

But if gangsta rap dies, what will replace it? "We might not even call it hip-hop," says Davey D. But he's sure that whatever kind of music grabs hold of the public will help them better understand their world.

It will be, he says, the "soundtracks to conditions that people are living in."

NOTES

1. Quoted in Brent Jones, "Cosby calls to absent fathers," *Baltimore Sun*, Aug. 23, 2006, p. B1.

2. See "The State of Black America," The National Urban League, 2007, p. 37.

3. See Robert Hilburn and Jerry Crowe, "Rapper Tupac Shakur, 25, Dies 6 Days After Ambush," *Los Angeles Times*, Sept. 14, 1996, p. A1; Chuck Phillips, "Bad Boy II Man," *Los Angeles Times*, May 25, 1997, p. 8 [Calendar section]; Katherine E. Finkelstein, "Combs Protégé is Sentenced to 10 Years in Shooting," *The New York Times*, June 2, 2001, p. B2; Andrew Jacobs, "Security Guard Killed Outside of a Busta Rhymes Video Shoot," *The New York Times*, Feb. 6, 2001, p. B1.

4. For background, see Marcia Clemmitt, "Shock Jocks," *CQ Researcher*, June 1, 2007, pp. 481-504.

See also, Teresa Wiltz and Darragh Johnson, "The Imus Test: Rap Lyrics Undergo Examination," *The Washington Post*, April 25, 2007, p. C1.

5. See "A Hip-Hop Town Hall," April 17, 2007, "The Oprah Winfrey Show," www.oprah.com/tows/slide/200704/20070417/slide_20070417_284_101.jhtml. For a sample of Crouch's views, see Bakari Kitwana, *Why White Kids Love Hip Hop* (2005), pp. 107-109.

6. Quoted in Reuters, "Hip-Hop Mogul Simmons Calls For Ban on 3 Epithets," *The Washington Post*, April 24, 2007, p. C5. See also Kelefa Sanneh, "How Don Imus' Problem Became a Referendum on Rap," *The New York Times*, April 25, 2007, p. B2; Marcus Franklin, "Music Execs Silent as Rap Debate Rages," The Associated Press, May 11, 2007; Wiltz and Johnson, *op. cit.*

7. Franklin, *op. cit.*

8. See Jeff Chang, *Can't Stop Won't Stop: A History of the Hip-Hop Generation* (2005), pp. 67-88.

9. *Ibid.*, pp. 118-125.

10. For information on the film, see Hurt's Web site, www.bhurt.com.

11. See Talib Kweli, "Say Something," Talib Kweli Message Board, April 20, 2007, http://board.talibkweli.com/index.php?showtopic=850.

12. See "AllHipHop Direct 9 — Censorship 2007," *AllHipHop.com* (on YouTube), June 1, 2007, www.youtube.com/watch?v=YzdwISAjdos. For background on 50 Cent, see Stephanie Utrata and Tracy Connor, "The Game Fires Back at 50," *New York Daily News*, March 6, 2005, p. A4.

13. See "AllHipHop Direct 9," *ibid.*

14. "2006 Consumer Profile," Recording Industry Association of America, undated, www.riaa.com/news/marketingdata/pdf/2006RIAAConsumerProfile.pdf.

15. See Yvonne Bynoe, *Encyclopedia of Rap and Hip Hop Culture* (2006).

16. See "Stop Snitchin,' " "60 Minutes," April 22, 2007, www.cbsnews.com/stories/2007/04/19/60minutes/main2704565.shtml.

17. Interview, Ice-T, undated, www.freshflixx.com/channel/sohh-tv/index.php?bcpid=376530222&bclid=440748065&bctid=823328719.

18. See Stanley Crouch, "Hip-Hop's Thugs Hit New Low," *New York Daily News*, Aug. 11, 2003, p. 35.

19. *Ibid.*

20. See Industry Ears Web site, www.industryears.com /index.php.

21. See James McBride, "Hip-Hop Planet," *National Geographic*, April 2007, p. 100.

22. See Jim Sullivan, "When shock art goes too far," *Boston Globe*, Nov. 1, 1989, p. 75.

23. See, for example, Jeff Chang, ed., *Total Chaos: The Art and Aesthetics of Hip-Hop* (2007), which includes Oliver Wang, "Trapped Between the Lines: The Aesthetics of Hip-Hop Journalism;" and Danny Hoch, "Toward a Hip-Hop Aesthetic: A Manifesto for the Hip-Hop Arts Movement."

24. See Hoch, *ibid.*, p. 355.

25. See Eisa Davis, "Found in Translation: The Emergence of Hip-Hop Theater," in Chang, Total Chaos, *op. cit.*, p. 72.

26. Chang, *Can't Stop Won't Stop*, *op. cit.*, p. 122.

27. See John J. Goldman, "Rally Protests N.Y. Drug Laws," *The New York Times*, July 5, 2003, p. A28; Marcus Franklin, "A hip-hop voting bloc," *St. Petersburg Times*, Aug. 31, 2003, p. A1.

28. See Leslie Eaton and Al Baker, "Changes Made to Drug Laws Don't Satisfy Advocates," *The New York Times*, Dec. 9, 2004, p. B1; and Dasun Allah, "Movement Hijacked by Hip-Hop?" *Village Voice* [New York], June 17, 2003, p. 24.

29. See "Hip-hop group announces voter registration drive," The Associated Press, Jan. 19, 2004; and "Hip-Hop Summit Action Network, Board of Directors," www.hsan.org/Content/main.aspx?pageid=10.

30. Quoted in Ann Gerhart, "Citizen Diddy; the Rapper-Designer is Out to Make Voting Hip," *The Washington Post*, Sept. 3, 2004, p. C1.

31. See "The 2004 Youth Vote," Center for Information & Research on Civil Learning & Engagement, University of Maryland, www.civicyouth.org /PopUps/2004_votereport_final.pdf.

32. See "New Lake-Goeas Poll Analysis Shows Iraq, Pocketbook Issues & Candidate Contact Spurred Large 2006 Youth Vote," Dec. 14, 2006, Young Voter Strategies, www.youngvoterstrategies.org/index.php? tg=articles&idx=More&topics=37&article=284.

33. See Rick Hampson, "Memory is all that's left of Powell's South Bronx," *USA Today*, Jan. 22, 2001, p. A8.

34. Except where otherwise indicated, this section is drawn from Chang, *Can't Stop Won't Stop*, *op. cit.*

35. *Ibid.*, p. 29. See also David Gonzalez, "Will Gentrification Spoil the Birthplace of Hip-Hop?" *The New York Times*, May 21, 2007, p. B1.

36. *Ibid.*, p. 131.

37. Quoted in Leah Y. Latimer, "Recording the Rap: Jive Talk at the Top of the Charts," *The Washington Post*, Aug. 31, 1980, p. G1.

38. For background, see Bob Benenson, "Reaganomics on Trial," *CQ Researcher*, Jan. 8, 1982, available at *CQ Researcher Plus Archives*, http://cqpress.com.

39. For background, see Mary H. Cooper, "The Business of Illegal Drugs," *CQ Researcher*, May 20, 1988, available at *CQ Researcher Plus Archives*, http://cqpress.com.

40. For background, see Kenneth Jost, "Sentencing Debates," *CQ Researcher*, Nov. 5, 2004, pp. 925-948.

41. This subsection also draws from Bynoe, op. cit., and David Gates with Peter Katel, "The Importance of Being Nasty," *Newsweek*, July 2, 1990, p. 52; Linda Greenhouse, "Supreme Court Roundup," *The New York Times*, Dec. 8, 1992. p. A22.

42. Quoted in Terry McDermott, "Parental Advisory: No One Was Ready for N.W.A.'s 'Straight Outta Compton,' " *Los Angeles Times*, April 14, 2002.

43. See N.W.A., "Fuck Tha Police," www.lyricsdepot. com/n-w-a/fuck-tha-police.html.

44. See McDermott, *op. cit.*

45. See Dennis McDougal, "Music Group, ACLU Join Forces in Lyric Battle," *Los Angeles Times*, Sept. 16, 1985, Calendar Sect., p. 2; "Industry Offers Voluntary tag for Recordings," The Associated Press, May 9, 1980.

46. See Tipper Gore, "Hate, Rape and Rap," [op-ed], *The Washington Post*, Jan. 8, 1990, p. A15.

47. See Shelley Branch, "Goodbye Gangsta; Can Jimmy Iovine Make Interscope a Mainstream Success?" *Fortune*, July 7, 1997, p. 40.

48. Hilburn and Crowe, *op. cit.*

49. See Chuck Phillips, "Who Killed Tupac Shakur," *Los Angeles Times*, Sept. 6, 2002, p. A1; Chuck Phillips, "Slain Rapper's Family Keeps Pushing Suit," *Los Angeles Times*, Feb. 4, 2007, p. B11; and Phillips, May 25, 1997, *op. cit.*

50. See Stanley Crouch, "Merchants of Filth Have Worthy Foe," *New York Daily News*, April 3, 2006, p. 31.

51. Quoted in Chang, *Can't Stop, Won't Stop, op. cit.*, p. 452.

52. *Ibid.*, p. 394.

53. *Ibid.*, pp. 395-396.

54. Quoted in Linda M. Harrington, "On Capitol Hill, a Real Rap Session," *Chicago Tribune*, Feb. 24, 1994, p. A1.

55. *Ibid.*

56. See Gracie Bonds Staples and Vikki Conwell, "Spelman women dis sex-laden rap videos," *Atlanta Journal-Constitution*, April 21, 2004, p. A1.

57. Quoted in Elliott C. McLaughlin, "Spelman continues its war on hip-hop," The Associated Press, Feb. 25, 2005.

58. *Ibid.*

59. See Franklin, *op. cit.*, May 11, 2007.

60. Quoted from *AllHipHop*, in Franklin, *ibid.* See also Take a Stand Records Web site, www.takeastandrecords.com/index.html.

61. Quoted in Larry "The Blackspot" Hester, "Music News: 50 Cent Pushes Back Release Date, Master P Speaks Out," BET.com, *Music, News & Interviews*, May 25, 2007, www.bet.com/Music/News/musicnews_50_5.25.htm?wbc_purpose=Basic&WBCMODE =PresentationUnpublished.

62. See Danielle Harling and Dove, "Grammy Award-Winning Rapper Chamillionaire Profanity Free," *AllHipHop*, April 27, 2007; www.allhiphop.com /Hiphopnews/?ID=7007.

63. "Bush Signs Broadcast Decency Law," The Associated Press, June 15, 2006.

64. See "Stop Snitchin,' " *op. cit.*

65. See Mark Olsen, "More than words to tell their stories," *Los Angeles Times*, May 11, 2007, p. E6; Teresa Wiltz, "No Rhyme or Rhythm," *The Washington Post*, May 11, 2007, p. WE29.

66. See "The Hip Hop Project," film Web site, http: //pressurepointfilms.com/thehiphopproject.html.

67. See Michael Brick, "Cultural Divisions Stretch to Relief Concerts," *The New York Times*, Sept. 17, 2005, p. B7.

68. See "Wyclef Shreds in Haiti," *MiamiVideo*, Dec. 1, 2006, www.brightcove.com/title.jsp?title=494388358 &channel=474448254&lineup=-1; "Mecca Live From Oxygen," *MiamiVideo*, undated, www.brightcove.com /title.jsp?title=900691975&channel=474448254&line up=-1; Lorraine Ali, "God Save The Queen," *Newsweek*, Oct. 4, 2004, p. 59.

BIBLIOGRAPHY

Books

Bynoe, Yvonne, *Encyclopedia of Rap and Hip Hop Culture*, Greenwood Press, 2006.
A prominent critic of some aspects of hip-hop produced this systematic look at the major players and trends.

Chang, Jeff, *Can't Stop Won't Stop: A History of the Hip-Hop Generation*, Picador, St. Martin's Press, 2005.
A leading hip-hop journalist provides a detailed but fast-moving account of hip-hop in the context of social and political developments.

Chang, Jeff, ed., *Total Chaos: The Art and Aesthetics of Hip-Hop*, Basic Civitas Books, 2007.
A variety of scholars and hip-hop creators examine the artistic significance of hip-hop in its various musical, theatrical and other incarnations.

Cobb, William Jelani, *To the Break of Dawn: A Freestyle on the Hip Hop Aesthetic*, New York University Press, 2007.
A Spelman College historian takes a close look at the messages, imagery and techniques of imaginative and inventive hip-hop songs.

Kitwana, Bakari, *Why White Kids Love Hip Hop*, Basic Books, 2005.
Race and hip-hop, one of the most complicated topics in the field, gets an insider's look by a leader of the political-activism side of the hip-hop world.

Morgan, Joan, *When Chickenheads Come Home to Roost: A Hip-Hop Feminist Breaks it Down*, Touchstone, Simon & Schuster, 1999.
A former staff writer at *Vibe*, a major hip-hop magazine, discusses hip-hop as part of an examination of male-female relations among African Americans.

Articles

Boles, Mark A., "Breaking the 'Hip Hop' Hold: Looking Beyond the Media Hype," in "The State of Black America 2007: Portrait of the Black Males," National Urban League, 2007, p. 239.
A market researcher and member of the Urban League Board of Trustees examines the role of hip-hop — especially music videos — in distorting young African Americans' values.

Davey D, "Why commerce is killing the true spirit of hip-hop," *San Jose Mercury-News*, March 1, 2007, p. M4.
A veteran of the hip-hop world finds "corporate" hip-hop losing ground — and salutes that outcome — given what he calls its vulgarity and perpetuation of racial stereotypes.

Fetterman, Mindy, "Russell Simmons can't slow down," *USA Today*, May 14, 2007, p. B1.
One of hip-hop's biggest success stories radiates confidence to a reporter who looks at Simmons' success in branching out from record sales.

McBride, James, "Hip Hop Planet," *National Geographic*, April, 2007, p. 100.
An author and musician — who'd spent years ignoring hip-hop — travels throughout the country and to Africa to understand its wide appeal.

McDermott, Terry, "Parental Advisory: Explicit Lyrics," *Los Angeles Times Magazine*, April 14, 2002, p. 12.
In a long narrative filled with colorful characters, a *Los Angeles Times* correspondent traces gangsta rap to its very beginnings.

Michel, Sia, "A New Sound for Old What's-His-Name," *The New York Times*, Sept. 10, 2006, Sect. 2, p. 67.
Sean "P. Diddy" Combs gets ready to release a new album and takes a reporter on a tour of his world.

Span, Paula, "The Business of Rap is Business," *The Washington Post*, June 4, 1995, p. G1.
A *Washington Post* reporter takes an early look at rap stars' efforts to turn musical success into something more durable.

Williams, Clarence, "Outreach Group Tries to Foster Greater Cooperation With Police," *The Washington Post*, May 13, 2007, p. C5.
In a violence-plagued Washington, D.C., neighborhood, activists encourage residents to report crime to police — defying the "no-snitching" message of some rap stars.

Video

"Hip Hop: Beyond Beats and Rhymes," Byron Hurt, director-producer, IndependentLens, PBS, 2007.
A college football star turned violence-prevention educator examines hip-hop's role in fostering stereotypes that widen the gulf between men and women.

"Stop Snitchin,' " "60 Minutes," Anderson Cooper, correspondent, April 19, 2007, www.cbsnews.com/sections/ i_video/main500251.shtml?channel=60Sunday.
The CBS TV newsmagazine takes on rap stars — and their record companies — who urge crime victims and witnesses not to cooperate with police.

"Wild Style," Lee Ahearn, director/writer, 1983.
A fictional film starring hip-hop fans who helped found the movement is considered a key document of its early days, with a heavy emphasis on graffiti "taggers."

For More Information

AllHipHop, www.allhiphop.com. Widely consulted site for news, music downloads and video interviews with stars and fans.

Davey D's Hip Hop Corner, http://daveyd.com. A combination news site, collection of essays about hip-hop-related topics and hip-hop history archive.

The Hiphop Archive, Department of Communication, Building 120, McClatchy Hall, 450 Serra Mall, Stanford University, Stanford, CA 94305; (650) 725-2142; http://hiphoparchive.org. Vast trove of material on multiple aspects of hip-hop.

Hip-Hop Association, P.O. Box 1181, New York, NY 10035; (212) 500-5970; http://hiphopassociation.org. Harlem-based community-development organization that uses hip-hop as a tool in educational and leadership-development projects.

Hip-Hop Summit Action Network, www.hsan.org. The organizational home of hip-hop's tycoons, who have involved themselves in voter registration and, more recently, in an effort to clean up rap lyrics.

Hip-Hop Theater Festival, 57 Thames St. #4B, Brooklyn, NY 11237; (718) 497-4240; www.hiphoptheaterfest.org. Organizes hip-hop events in major cities.

Industry Ears, http://industryears.com. Advocacy organization that presses the Federal Communications Commission to regulate radio stations that broadcast hip-hop songs with sexually explicit lyrics.

8

Reparations Movement

David Masci and Alan Greenblat

Environmental Justice Resource Center

Children were among the survivors in April 1945 when Russian soldiers liberated the Nazi concentration camp at Auschwitz, Poland, where hundreds of thousands of Jews were murdered. Billions of dollars have been paid to Holocaust survivors.

From *CQ Researcher,*
June 22, 2001. (Updated September 30, 2008)

Rep. John Conyers Jr. is not a man who gives up easily. Ten times since 1989, the feisty 22-term Michigan Democrat has introduced a measure in the House of Representatives to create a commission to study paying reparations to African American descendants of slaves. Each time, the bill has died. But Conyers is optimistic. He claims that beating the same legislative drum so long has helped bring the reparations issue to the attention of the American people.

"Twelve years ago, most people didn't even know what reparations were, and now it's a front-burner issue," he said in 2001. "It's like those first [unsuccessful] bills making Martin Luther King's birthday a holiday: You have to build up a critical mass of support, or you don't get anyplace."

At that time, the reparations idea captured the public's imagination — or at least part of the public's imagination. Universities admitted that they had profited long ago from slave labor, insurance companies and banks disclosed that their predecessor organizations had benefited from slavery and descendants of slaves filed enormous lawsuits seeking damages.

But the notion of financial compensation has lost momentum in recent years. In its place, there has been a fairly widespread effort by governments to apologize for their role in slavery and the slave trade, from Britain to the U.S. House of Representatives. "When people commit injustices and do bad things, they ought to apologize and ask for forgiveness," said Rep. Steve Cohen, D-Tenn., who sponsored the House resolution, which passed in July 2008. "Countries should operate in the same manner. Slavery is abhorrent." [1]

Seeking Justice for Australia's Aborigines

Australian Olympic gold medal winner Cathy Freeman knew all about the "stolen generation" of Aborigines. Her grandmother was one of the thousands of youngsters taken from their parents by white authorities.

Winning the 400-meter dash at 'the 2000 Summer Games gave Freeman a chance to speak out on the centuries of mistreatment of Australia's indigenous people.

Aborigines have lived in Australia for at least 40,000 years, most likely migrating from Southeast Asia. Their downfall as a people began in 1788, when British ships brought 1,000 settlers, including more than 500 convicts from overcrowded jails. Clashes began almost immediately, but the Aborigines' primitive weapons were no match for British guns and mounted soldiers.

Because the convicts provided free labor, the white settlers treated the Aborigines as little more than useless pests. Those who were not killed were driven away to fenced reservations in the most inhospitable parts of the "outback" territory. Crimes against Aborigines often went unpunished.

Aborigines, who make up 2 percent of Australia's largely white population of 21 million, were not allowed to vote until 1962; they were not counted in the census until 1967.

Olympic gold medalist Cathy Freeman has used her celebrity to call attention to her fellow Aborigines.

AFP Photo/Romeo Gacad

Moreover, Aborigines' life expectancy is 20 years less than the national average and they occupy the lowest rung of the nation's economic ladder.

In 1992, they won a significant victory when courts recognized that the Aborigines had "owned' Australia before whites arrived. By 2001, they owned more than 15 percent of the continent, mostly in the remote northern territory. But in 2007, Prime Minister John Howard rescinded land-rights policies, putting indigenous lands in the Northern Territory back in the hands of the national government. Howard's "emergency intervention" came in response to complaints about widespread violence and child abuse.

For many Aborigines, the new policies of mandatory health checks for children and limiting the spending of welfare money to food and clothes served as reminders of perhaps the worst injustice perpetrated against their group — the state-sponsored abduction of Aboriginal children from their parents.

From the early 1900s until the 1970s, as many as 100,000 Aboriginal children were taken from their parents to be raised among whites in orphanages or foster families. State and federal laws that permitted the practice were based on the belief that full- blooded Aborigines would eventually die out and that assimilating the children into white society was the best way to save them.

The House action came in the wake of a half-dozen states in the old Confederacy apologizing for their role in slavery, and three years after the Senate's apology for not passing an anti-lynching law decades earlier marked the first time that chamber had apologized for the nation's treatment of African Americans. Such actions came amidst a spate of apologies from national leaders ranging from Tony Blair, who apologized as prime minister of Great Britain in 2006 for his nation's part in slavery and the slave trade, to Kevin Rudd, who made an apology for

In 1997, the Australian Human Rights and Equal Opportunity Commission reported that many of the children had been physically and sexually abused and suffered long-term psychological damage from the loss of family and cultural ties.

But Australian Sen. John Herron called the 1997 report "one-sided" and said the stories about removing Aboriginal children from their families was greatly exaggerated."

His comments stung Aden Ridgeway, the only Aborigine senator in Parliament, who angrily compared Herron's statements to "denying the Holocaust."

"They were denying they had done anything wrong, denying that a whole generation was stolen," Freeman said. "The fact is, parts of people's lives were taken away."

Herron recognizes the removal of Aboriginal children as a blemish on Australia's history, but he claims many were taken with their parents' consent and for their own welfare. He believes amends are the responsibility of states and churches and has suggested that reparations claims be filed individually via the courts. Canada has offered compensation to indigenous children removed from their homes, as has the Australian state of Tasmania.

But reparations proponents say it is difficult to prove abuse in the absence of documents and witnesses. They cite the first

At a rally during the 2000 Olympics in Sydney, an Aborigine spokesman calls for the resignation of Prime Minister John Howard, who opposed reparations for mistreated indigenous Australians.

AFP Photo/Torsten Blackwood

stolen-generations case, brought in 2000, which was dismissed for lack of evidence.

Howard refused even to issue an apology, stating that contemporary ' Australians should not be held responsible for the mistakes of past generations.

Howard and his party were turned out of power in 2007, however. In 2008, as the first act of his new government, Prime Minister Kevin Rudd issued an apology for Australia's history of mistreatment of its indigenous people, "for the pain, suffering and hurt" that the government had caused, specifically citing the issue of the so-called stolen generation.

Although many complained that the words should have been backed up with increased spending on health and education and some still advocate for monetary compensation, the long-desired apology did prove a balm for much of the aboriginal population. A song based on a snippet from Rudd's speech became a bestselling download.

---

[1] "Separated, But Not a Generation," *Illawarra Mercury*, Aug. 19, 2000, p. 9.

[2] Mitchell Zuckoff, "Golden Opportunity, Australian Aboriginal Activists Hope to Exploit the Olympics to Publicize Their Demands for an Apology, Cash Reparations and Limited Sovereignty," *The Boston Globe*, Sept. 18, 2000, p. 1E.

[3] Michael Gordon, "Beginning Of The Legend," *Sydney Morning Herald*, Sept. 25, 2000, p. 10.

Australia's mistreatment of the aboriginal population the first order of business when his party took power in 2008.

"At the end of the day, we said three words: 'I am sorry,' " said state Sen. Anthony C. Hill Sr., a Florida Democrat, after the state legislature formally apologized for the state's "shameful" history of slavery in March 2008. "I think now we can begin the healing process of reconciliation." [2]

Some commentators have criticized such resolutions and statements as being politically motivated — a way for political leaders to distance themselves conveniently from the actions of past leaders. "Trading apologies and forgiveness on behalf of dead people sounds phony — especially when the issue is centuries old (such as Viking rape and pillage in Ireland, which Denmark's culture minister Brian Mikkelson bemoaned in 2007)," editorialized *The Economist* in 2008. [3] Even Adam Hochschild, the liberal author of a widely-praised book about the abolition of the slave trade, expressed concern about efforts to atone for past sins, arguing that it would be better to "focus on the clear, glaring injustices of the present. "To feel outrage at a dreadful crime in history is natural and right," Hochschild wrote in 2006. "But does it make sense to extend the principle of guilt and responsibility backward in time over generations? Two centuries ago, scholars estimate, about three-quarters of the people on Earth were slaves, indentured servants, labor-

> "Whites need to realize that we'll have no chance of cohering as a nation in the future unless we deal with this issue now."
>
> — *Randall Robinson, President, TransAfrica*

ers in debt bondage, serfs or in servitude of one sort or another. Add to that grim tally the wars, colonial conquests, genocides, concentration camps and other barbarities human beings have inflicted on each other since then. If we were to take responsibility for everything done by our ancestors, few of us — anywhere in the world — would have clean hands. Few of us, also, would be without victims among our forebears. The entire world would be awash in apologies." [4]

Given that Barack Obama's position on the reparations issue, it seems unlikely that the trend toward expiating sins through apology will lead to cash reparations, as Conyers and others have hoped for years. Alan Keyes, Obama's opponent in his 2004 Illinois Senate race, proposed lifting

federal income taxes for "a generation or two" of African Americans as a form of reparations. Obama has said that slavery's residual damage could not be cured with money. "Rather, we should focus on ensuring that our anti-discrimination laws are vigorously enforced," Obama said, "and that we continue to invest in education, job training and other programs that lift all people out of poverty and improve their opportunities in life." [5]

Obama himself in the presidential race of 2008 has demonstrated the progress African Americans have made, and the lack of need for nursing old wounds, argues Roger Clegg, of the Center for Equal Opportunity, a conservative group opposed to racial preferences. "The success of the Obama candidacy underscores the irrelevance of an apology," Clegg said. "Haven't we moved beyond it?" [6]

But reparations supporters note that the impoverishment of African Americans through slavery and the century of segregation the followed its abolition has not been wiped out even by the most prominent successes. Chester A. Hurdle and his brother Timothy fielded a class action suit in California in 2002, seeking reparations on behalf of their father, who was taken from his parents and sold into bondage in 1856. Hurdle said his action was partially inspired by a commentary written by a reparations opponent who argued that slaves and their immediate descendants were dead. "I guess I'm a ghost," Hurdle said, "and so is my brother and my sister." [7]

Until 50 years ago, debates over reparations for victims of persecution were largely theoretical. But in the wake of World War II, monetary reparations increasingly have been seen as a viable means of addressing past injustices — not just to Jews slaughtered in the Holocaust but to Japanese Americans, Mexican farm workers, Native Americans and Australian aborigines. In fact, the debate over slavery reparations comes on the heels of a string of victories for groups seeking financial restitution.

In 1988, for instance, Congress passed a law authorizing the U.S. government to apologize for interning Japanese Americans during the war and award $20,000 to each surviving victim. More recently, European countries and companies from Bayer AG to Volkswagen paid billions of dollars to victims of Nazi Germany's effort to exterminate Europe's Jews and other "undesirables."

Now it is time for slavery reparations, proponents say. Randall Robinson, author of the bestseller *The Debt: What America Owes to Blacks*, argues that acknowledging the nation's debt to African Americans for slavery and a subsequent century of discrimination will help heal the country's existing racial divide. "We cannot have racial reconciliation until we make the victims of this injustice whole," says Robinson, founder of TransAfrica, a Washington, D.C.-based black advocacy group.

Besides raising a moral question, reparations for slavery is also an economic issue, Robinson says. Many of the problems facing black America are directly linked to slavery and the 100 years of forced segregation that followed emancipation in 1865, he says. "It's foolish to argue that the past has nothing to do with the present," Robinson says. "There's a reason why so many African Americans are poor: It's because a terrible wrong occurred in our history that produced a lasting inequality." Reparations will help right that wrong, advocates say, by helping black Americans reach social and economic parity.

But other black Americans warn that paying reparations for slavery will drive a new wedge between blacks and whites, leading to greater racial polarization. "Doing something like this would create a tremendous amount of resentment among whites," says Walter Williams, former chairman of the Economics Department at George Mason University in Fairfax, Va.

Williams says whites and other Americans would understandably be opposed to paying restitution for a crime that ended more than 135 years ago and to a community now making great social, political and economic strides. "Blacks have come so far; this is nothing but counterproductive," he says.

Opponents also argue that, rather than correcting economic disparity, reparations would take money and attention away from more pressing social and economic issues facing black Americans, such as a substandard education system and high incarceration rates for young African American men. "This would be such a huge waste of resources, at a time when so much needs to be done in education and other areas," Williams says.

To counter such arguments, slavery reparations advocates have begun modeling their efforts on successful techniques used by Holocaust victims. In recent years, Holocaust-related reparations have netted survivors and their families more than $10 billion in compensation for slave labor, recovered bank accounts and unclaimed life insurance policies.

But some argue that compensating victims of injustice cheapens their suffering. Indeed, a group of mostly Jewish American scholars and journalists has criticized some of the efforts to obtain relief for Holocaust survivors. They say the lawyers and Jewish groups involved have turned the legitimate quest for restitution into a shameless money grab that degrades the memory of the millions who perished. "Fighting for money makes it much harder to see a tragedy in the right light," says Melissa Nobles, a professor of political science at the Massachusetts Institute of Technology (MIT) in Boston. "They have hijacked the Holocaust and appointed themselves saviors of the victims — all in the name of money," says Norman Finkelstein, political scientist and author of *The Holocaust Industry: Reflections on the Exploitation of Jewish Suffering.* Finkelstein points out that those representing the victims have used hardball tactics to "blackmail" Germany, Switzerland and other countries

> "I can't think of a better fortification for racism than reparations to blacks."
>
> — *Walter Williams,*
> *Chairman, Economics Department,*
> *George Mason University*

into paying huge sums to satisfy what are often dubious claims. Besides cheapening the historical legacy of the Holocaust, he argues, such actions could potentially trigger an antisemitic backlash in Europe.

Supporters say they are only working aggressively to obtain some small measure of justice for the victims. "We are trying to compensate slave laborers and return the assets of survivors," says Elan Steinberg, former executive director of the World Jewish Congress, one of the groups leading the Holocaust reparations efforts. "In doing this, we must uncover the truth, which is often hard for these countries to confront." He says Holocaust victims should not be denied their assets or rightful compensation just because confronting European countries with their past

For Native Americans, a Different Struggle

Unlike African-Americans, Native Americans are not seeking a huge settlement to right the wrongs of the past. Instead, they're working on the present. "We don't want reparations," says John Echohawk, executive director of the Native American Rights Fund, an Indian advocacy group in Boulder, Colo. "What we do want is the government to honor its duty to us — and we want our land and our water back." They also want up to $40 billion they say the government owes them.

Tribes have been making land claims against the government for more than a century. Today, dozens of claims are being dealt with (see p. 180). But the biggest fight for restitution has come over allegations of government mishandling of a huge trust fund for Native Americans. Indian advocates say the federal government will end up owing between $10 billion and $40 billion to Native Americans when the matter is cleared up. Bush administration officials claim that because payments were made to Indians all along, the number will be in the millions, not billions.

Since 1887, the federal government's Bureau of Indian Affairs (BIA) has managed many of the natural resources on Indian lands, such as oil and mineral deposits and grazing and water rights. Proceeds from the sale or use of these resources are, in theory at least, put into a trust fund admin-

istered by the government on behalf of members of the tribes who own the assets — some 500,000 Native Americans throughout the country.

In the 1970s, Elouise Cobell, a member of the Blackfoot tribe, began to question the government's management of these accounts. Other Indians had long suspected mismanagement, but no one had challenged the BIA officials who controlled the fund. Over the next two decades, Cobell, who has an accounting background, concluded that billions of dollars had been lost, and that many Indians were being cheated out of money that was rightfully theirs. Her efforts to get BIA officials to pay attention to the problem came to naught. "They tried to belittle me and intimated that I was a dumb Indian," she says.

In 1996, after years of what Cobell calls stonewalling by federal officials, she and four other Native Americans filed a class action suit in federal court against the Department of the Interior, which controls BIA. "The suit was a last resort, because no one would listen to us," Echohawk says. "No one did anything."

The plaintiffs charged that many records had been destroyed; that officials had improperly invested much of the money coming into the trust; and that no effort was made to keep individual Indians informed about the individual accounts the government kept for them. [1]

might lead to an anti-Jewish backlash. "Survivors have a right to pursue legitimate claims," he insists. "This is about justice." "It is good that we try to make some effort to acknowledge someone's suffering, even if it is inadequate," says Tim Cole, a professor of 20th century European history at the University of Bristol in England. At the very least, reparations are important symbolic gestures to the victims from the victimizers, he adds.

As the debate over reparations continues, here are some of the questions experts are asking:

Should the United States pay reparations to African American descendants of slaves?

For much of its 250-year history on these shores, slavery was America's most divisive and controversial issue. The

Founders fought over the status of African slaves when drafting both the Declaration of Independence and the Constitution. And of course, in 1861 slavery helped trigger the nation's most costly conflict, the four-year Civil War that tore the country apart.

Today, few Americans of any race would disagree that slavery was the most shameful and tragic episode in American history. Many would also agree that African Americans as a whole, including the descendants of slaves, are still suffering from its effects.

Reparations proponents say compensation is justified on a variety of levels, beginning with the fact that African Americans remain severely handicapped by the legacy of slavery, lagging behind the nation as a whole in virtually every measure. As a result, supporters say, they need and

Even before the suit was filed, the federal government had made some attempts to address the problem. In 1994, Congress passed the Native American Trust Fund Accounting and Management Reform Act, authorizing the appointment of a special trustee to manage and reform the fund. But the first such trustee, former Riggs Bank President Paul Homan, resigned in protest in 1999, complaining that the Interior Department was not adequately committed to reform.

Meanwhile, Cobell's suit against the government succeeded. In 2000, a federal court ruled against the Interior Department and took control of the trust fund. "The government kept arguing that they were doing the best they could, but that just wasn't true," Echohawk says.

Penny Manybeads stands beside her hogan at the Navajo Indian reservation in Tuba City. Ariz., in 1993. Native Americans want the government to pay for the mismanagement of their natural resources trust fund.

AP Photo/Jeff Robbins

"Fortunately, the court didn't believe them."

The government lost a subsequent appeal. Most recently, the new Bush administration decided not to continue to appeal the ruling, ending resistance to a court-administered solution. Although the presiding judge has ordered the administration to admit that its own records are not reliable, the sides continue to debate how much the government owes the trust fund "We hope we can avoid a protracted legal battle over damages and settle out of court," Echohawk says'. But that hasn't been the case.

And Echohawk remains wary. "I'm cautious because until now, the government has fought us every inch of the way," he says. "Federal stonewalling and neglect are part of the story of the American Indian."

---

[1] Colman McCarthy, "Broken Promises Break Trust," *The Baltimore Sun*, March 7, 1999.

---

deserve extra help to overcome the economic and social disadvantages they face. "Our entire economic sector has been and remains truncated because of slavery," says Ronald Walters, a political science professor at the University of Maryland. "We need something to help reverse this terrible harm done to blacks in this country." "You have an enormous, static and fixed inequality in America due to a 350-year human-rights crime," Robinson agrees. "We have an obligation to compensate the people still suffering for the wrong that occurred."

Robinson, Walters and others argue that reparations are justified by the fact that the United States grew prosperous largely through the toil of unpaid African Americans. "Exports of cotton, rice and tobacco swelled the coffers of the U.S. Treasury, yet the people who pro-

duced it were never paid," Robinson says.

However, an overwhelming majority of Americans do not believe the nation owes black Americans reparations. A CNN/Gallup Poll in 2002 found that 90 percent of whites opposed cash reparations payments, compared with 55 percent support among African Americans. [8]

Some Americans feel that the nation has already paid reparations for slavery by passing civil rights and affirmative action laws and by funding myriad social programs designed to help African Americans and other disadvantaged peoples. "Since the War on Poverty in the 1960s, the nation has spent $6 trillion on fighting poverty," Williams says. Others dismiss the whole idea of reparations for slavery out of hand, citing the potentially astronomical cost. Compensating for slavery's injustices could cost as much as $10 trillion, according to some estimates, dwarfing the estimated $60 billion paid to Holocaust victims so far.

Nevertheless, supporters say, reparations would ease African Americans' feeling that the nation cares little about their plight. "The socio-economic inequality that exists today because of slavery means that the American promise of egalitarianism remains unfulfilled for blacks," Walters says. "It would make the idea of America and American democracy meaningful to blacks." Paying reparations would benefit the entire nation by creating a more conducive environment for racial reconciliation, supporters say. "We'll never have any harmony or stability between the races until there is commitment to make the victim whole," Robinson says. "Whites need to realize that we'll have no chance of cohering as a nation in the future unless we deal with this issue now." Conyers agrees that paying reparations would encourage racial healing — for both blacks and whites. "This could create a bridge that unlocks understanding and compassion between people," he says.

But opponents say compensating slavery victims will have exactly the opposite effect — creating new grounds for racial polarization. "I can't think of a better fortification for racism than reparations to blacks," says George Mason University's Williams. "To force whites today, who were not in any way responsible for slavery, to make payments to black people — many of whom may be better off [than the whites] — will create nothing but great resentment." "It would create a huge backlash against black people, which is something they don't really need," says Glenn Loury, an author and economics professor at Brown University. "It would also be seen as just another example of black people's inability 'to get over it and move on.' "

Indeed, opponents say, reparations might even have the reverse effect: They could significantly weaken the nation's commitment to lifting poor black Americans out of poverty. "This would be a Pyrrhic victory for African Americans," says Loury, who is black. "It would undermine the claim for further help down the road, because the rest of America will say: 'Shut up: You've been paid.' " In addition, Loury says, pushing for restitution detracts from the real issues facing the black community. "This whole thing takes the public's attention away from important issues, like failing schools and the fact that so many African Americans are in jail."

Have efforts to collect reparations for Holocaust victims gone too far?

In the last decade, efforts to compensate and recover stolen property for Holocaust victims and their heirs increased dramatically. What started in the mid-1990s as an action to recover money in long-dormant Swiss bank accounts snowballed into a host of lawsuits and settlements against European insurance companies, German and American manufacturers and art galleries around the world. [9]

By and large, these actions have been hailed as a great victory for victims of oppression. Yet a small but growing circle of critics questions the efforts. They charge the lawyers working on behalf of Holocaust victims — as well as the World Jewish Congress, the International Commission on Holocaust Era Insurance Claims and the Conference on Jewish Material Claims Against Germany (known as the Claims Conference) and other groups — with exploiting a historical tragedy for monetary gain.

"This whole thing has gone way too far," says Gabriel Shoenfeld, senior editor of *Commentary*, a conservative opinion magazine that examines issues from a Jewish perspective. "This is a case of a just cause that has been traduced by overzealous organizations and some rather unscrupulous lawyers." Finkelstein goes further, branding those who work on behalf of survivors as "the Holocaust industry" and their actions "nothing short of a shakedown racket." Shoenfeld and Finkelstein are troubled by the fact that Jewish groups and attorneys working on the cases have taken it upon themselves to represent Holocaust survivors. "Groups like the World Jewish Congress don't really represent anyone," Finkelstein says. "They weren't elected by anyone to do this, and most Jews don't even know who they are." He argues that such groups are using the survivors' high moral status as a cudgel to beat countries and corporations into submission. "They've wrapped themselves in the mantle of the needy Holocaust victims against the greedy, fat Swiss bankers and Nazi industrialists," Finkelstein says. "They are out of control and reckless."

Shoenfeld says the claims often are either overblown, dubious or simply not valid. "It's clear that they're trying to humiliate these countries into giving in," he says. Shoenfeld cites a case against Dutch insurers, who had already settled with the Netherlands' Jewish community for unpaid wartime insurance policies. "These guys then came in and tried to unfairly blacken Holland's reputation by painting their behavior during the war in an unfavorable light, without acknowledging all of the good things Dutch people did for Jews during that time," he says. "It was all an effort to blackmail them, to extract more money from them."

Even the much-publicized victory against the Swiss banks was marred by unscrupulous tactics, Finkelstein contends. After forcing the banks to set up a commission headed by former U.S. Federal Reserve Chairman Paul A. Volcker to investigate claims, they demanded a settlement before the commission finished its work, he says. The Swiss caved in and paid $1.25 billion, Finkelstein says, because the groups were creating public hysteria and had American politicians threatening an economic boycott. "They honed this strategy against the Swiss and then turned to the French, Germans and others and used it successfully against them."

Such heavy-handed tactics create unnecessary ill will against European Jews, critics say. "By bludgeoning the Europeans into submission, the Holocaust industry is fomenting anti-Semitism," Finkelstein says. Shoenfeld says the tactics have already spurred an antisemitic backlash in Germany and Switzerland. "Don't Jews have enough problems in the world without bringing upon themselves the wrath of major European powers?" he asks.

But groups pursuing Holocaust reparations say their opponents are misguided. "How can anyone ask [if] we are going too far in attempting to get restitution for people who were driven from their homes, forced into hiding, persecuted and forced to work?" asks Hillary Kessler-Godin, director of communications for the Claims Conference in New York City.

Supporters also argue that their tactics are not "heavy-handed" or designed to blackmail European countries. "We're not out to humiliate anyone," says the World Jewish Congress' Steinberg. "But sometimes the truth is hard and difficult for everyone to accept." For instance, it would not serve the truth or the victims to sugarcoat Holland's dismal record of protecting Jews during the Holocaust, Steinberg says. "Holland had the worst record of any Western European country," he argues. "Eighty percent of its Jews were wiped out."

He also points out that his group rushed to settle the Swiss case before the Volcker commission finished its work in order to begin repaying survivors before they died. "Many survivors are very old and dying at such a

rapid rate — some 10,000 to 15,000 a year. We had to move on this," he said in 2001. Proponents also counter the criticism that their actions foment antisemitism. "Antisemitism is not caused by Jewish actions, but by people who don't like Jews," Kessler-Godin says. "To temper our actions on behalf of people who have suffered the worst form of antisemitism possible in the name of not causing antisemitism defies logic."

"Holocaust survivors should not have to abrogate their rights simply for political expediency," Steinberg adds, pointing out that most people, regardless of their religious background, understand and support his group's efforts. "At the end of the day, most non-Jews — except those who represent the banks or insurance companies — see this as an act of justice."

Does putting a price tag on suffering diminish that suffering?

On Dec. 7, 1998, the leader of one of the preeminent Jewish organizations in the United States shocked many American Jews by publicly questioning efforts to obtain reparations for Holocaust survivors. In a *Wall Street Journal* editorial, Abraham Foxman, national director of the Anti-Defamation League, argued that when "claims become the main focus of activity regarding the Holocaust, rather than the unique horror of 6 million Jews, including 1.5 million children, being murdered simply because they were Jewish, then something has gone wrong." [10] Foxman worried that the drive to obtain restitution would shift modern attitudes about the Holocaust from one of reverence for the victims and their suffering to an accounting of their material losses. "I fear that all the talk about Holocaust-era assets is skewing the Holocaust, making the century's last word on the Holocaust that the Jews died, not because they were Jews, but because they had bank accounts, gold, art and property," he wrote. "To me that is a desecration of the victims, a perversion of why the Nazis had a Final Solution, and too high a price to pay for a justice we can never achieve." [11]

Foxman's editorial provoked an immediate response from many prominent Jews. Nobel Peace Prize winner Elie Wiesel argued that compensating Holocaust survivors does not sully their memory but is the right thing to do.

"It is wrong to think of this as about money," said Wiesel, a Holocaust survivor himself. "It is about justice, conscience and morality." [12]

1945-1980 *After World War II, West Germany moves to pay restitution to Jewish survivors of the Holocaust.*

1948 Congress passes the Japanese American Evacuations Claims Act to compensate Japanese Americans who lost property as a result of their World War II internment.

1951 West German Chancellor Konrad Adenauer proposes assistance to Israel and reparations to Jewish Holocaust survivors.

1956 Swiss government asks banks and insurers to reveal their Holocaust-related assets. The companies say such "dormant accounts" hold less than 1 million Swiss francs.

1962 A second request for an accounting of Holocaust-related assets uncovers about 10 million Swiss francs in dormant accounts.

1965 West Germany ends state-to-state payments to Israel. Holocaust survivors continue to receive payments from German government through the present.

1980s-Present *Oppressed groups seek reparations.*

1980 Congress creates a commission to study possible reparations for Japanese American internees.

1987 National Coalition of Blacks for Reparations in America (N'COBRA) is founded.

1988 Congress passes the Civil Liberties Act, which apologizes for the wartime internment of Japanese Americans and authorizes the payment of $20,000 to surviving internees. Eventually, 80,000 Japanese Americans receive an apology and a check.

1989 Rep. John Conyers Jr., D-Mich., introduces legislation to create a commission to study the African American reparation issue. He will reintroduce the bill five more times in the coming years.

1995 European and American media document the role of Swiss banks in financing the Nazi war effort and in failing to make restitution to Holocaust survivors.

1996 Class action suit is filed in New York federal court against Swiss banks, seeking funds from "dormant accounts" of Holocaust victims.

1998 Though not an apology, President Clinton says in a speech at a Ugandan village school that it was wrong for European Americans to have received "the fruits of the slave trade." *Aug.:*

Swiss government agrees to pay $1.25 billion to settle claims against Swiss banks. *Dec.:* In a *Wall Street Journal* op-ed piece, Anti-Defamation League national director and Holocaust survivor Abraham Foxman questions the tactics employed by those seeking reparations for Holocaust survivors.

December 1999 The German government and corporations that used slave labor during the war establish a $4.3 billion fund to compensate surviving slave laborers.

2000 TransAfrica founder Randall Robinson publishes *The Debt: What America Owes to Blacks*, arguing for reparations for slavery.

2001 Conservative commentator David Horowitz creates controversy when he tries to publish an ad in American college newspapers entitled "Ten Reasons Why Reparations for Slavery is a Bad Idea — and Racist, Too."

2002 California's Department of Insurance identifies six insurance companies that issued policies covering slaves as property. Descendants of slaves hold a rally on the National Mall to demand reparations from the federal government.

2003 Chicago requires that city contractors disclose whether their businesses had ever profited from slavery.

2004 A federal judge in Chicago dismisses a $1 billion lawsuit brought by descendants of slaves against several corporations, noting that the plaintiffs had not themselves been injured by slavery but were "trying to assert the legal rights of their ancestors."

2005 The U.S. Senate apologizes for not having passed an anti-lynching law. Bank of America argues that none of its predecessor institutions benefited from slavery, but it donates $5 million to African American history institutions and programs. J.P. Morgan and Wachovia apologize for corporate histories that included putting hundreds of slaves to work and accepting others as collateral.

2006 British Prime Minister Tony Blair expresses "deep sorrow" for Britain's role in slavery and the slave trade.

2007 Virginia is the first state to express "profound regret" over slavery; five other states formally apologize over the following year. Brown University announces a $10 million donation to local schools to atone for its role in the slave trade.

2008 The U.S. House apologizes for slavery and segregation. In Australia, Prime Minister Kevin Rudd apologizes for historic mistreatment of the aboriginal population.

But critics point out that reparations, almost by their nature, are tainted, because they mix the sacredness of a people's suffering and pain with the world's greatest source of corruption: money. "Although there might be a way to handle this whole thing with dignity, it inexorably becomes a sordid business," Finkelstein says. "I believe money always corrupts things."

"There is a real danger here that most people will say: Hey wait a minute. This is all really about money," says MIT's Nobles. "Money can profoundly obscure the nature of a tragedy."

Some critics also contend that monetary reparations can do victims more harm than good. "People who have been victimized need to become free internally in order to move beyond the tragedy that has occurred," says Ruth Wisse, a professor of Yiddish and comparative literature at Harvard University. "In this sense, reparations can be harmful because they make victims less dependent on themselves." Instead of monetary payments, she says, nations should take steps to resolve the political problems that led to the suffering in the first place. "Reparations should be made on political terms, not economic terms," she says.

But advocates for reparations argue that the money is more a powerful symbol than a primary motive. "We're really talking about justice," says the University of Bristol's Cole. "It's a symbolic act, a gesture." Although, Cole says, "no amount of money can ever compensate for the suffering of history's victims," restitution can aid them in some small way. "There are things we can do to ease people's suffering or bring them some sense that justice is being done." "Of course you can't put a price tag on suffering," says the University of Maryland's Walters. "But what you can do is ask: What will bring the victims a measure of dignity? Isn't that the most important thing?"

Proponents also contend that, in the real world where victims of past oppression may still be suffering, monetary compensation can make a huge difference in their lives. For instance, says Kessler-Godin, many Eastern European Holocaust survivors live in poverty and need assistance. "It's OK for Abraham Foxman, living his comfortable American life, to say that it cheapens the memory of victims, but there are people who are living hand to mouth who don't have that luxury." Her group's top priority, Kessler-Godin said in a 2008 interview, is securing property restitution for them. In September of that year, Congress approved a resolution that urges Central and Eastern European governments to pass fair and comprehensive property restitution legislation that would enable citizens and groups to file claims on property once owned by themselves or their ancestors.

Finally, supporters say, forgoing reparations allows the victimizers to retain their financial wealth. "When you argue that a victim shouldn't pursue restitution, you are essentially rewarding the oppressors," Steinberg says.

BACKGROUND

Ancient Notion

The payment of reparations for genocide or other injustices is a relatively new phenomenon, which began with Germany's 1951 pledge to aid Israel and to compensate individual victims of the Holocaust. "Before World War II, nations saw what they did to other people during wartime as a natural byproduct of war," MIT's Nobles says. "The vanquished simply had to accept what had happened to them."

But while the use of reparations may be a relatively new remedy, the ideas behind them have a long, if circuitous, intellectual pedigree stretching back for millennia. For instance, the ancient Greeks and Romans explored the notion that the weak and oppressed deserve sympathy and possibly assistance. The 4th century B.C. Athenian philosopher Plato addressed this issue in his most famous dialogue, *The Republic.* A generation later Aristotle, another Athenian philosopher, wrote that the best kind of government was one that helped those who had been deprived of happiness. [13] Judeo-Christian doctrine also grappled with what individuals and society owe to the downtrodden and oppressed. For instance, in the New Testament, Jesus Christ singled out the persecuted as being particularly deserving of compassion and assistance. [14]

The first modern articulation of these principles came in the 18th century during the Enlightenment. Ironically, it was the intellectual father of free market economics — Scottish philosopher Adam Smith — who wrote most forcefully and eloquently about guilt and the resulting sympathy it causes. In his 1759 treatise, *The Theory of Moral Sentiments*, he wrote: "How selfish soever man may be supposed, there are evidently some principles in his nature, which interest him in the fortunes of others, and render their happiness necessary to

THE WHITE HOUSE
WASHINGTON

A monetary sum and words alone cannot restore lost years or erase painful memories; neither can they fully convey our Nation's resolve to rectify injustice and to uphold the rights of individuals. We can never fully right the wrongs of the past. But we can take a clear stand for justice and recognize that serious injustices were done to Japanese Americans during World War II.

In enacting a law calling for restitution and offering a sincere apology, your fellow Americans have, in a very real sense, renewed their traditional commitment to the ideals of freedom, equality, and justice. You and your family have our best wishes for the future.

Sincerely,

GEORGE BUSH
PRESIDENT OF THE UNITED STATES

OCTOBER 1990

In October 1990, Japanese Americans interned during World War II received this letter of apology from President George Bush, in addition to a check for $20,000.

him, though he derives nothing from it, except the pleasure of seeing it. Of this kind is pity or compassion, the emotion we feel for the misery of others, when we either see it, or are made to conceive it in a very lively manner." [15] Smith argued further that this sympathy is a cornerstone of justice. It is necessary for creating and maintaining general social order, he believed.

Native Americans

In the 18th and 19th centuries, compassion for the plight of others — whether out of Christian duty or to promote the greater good — fueled movements to abolish slavery and the slave trade in Europe and the United States. Later, these impulses led the United States, albeit very slowly, to consider compensating Native Americans for the government's taking of their land and the resulting destruction of much of their population and culture.

The expansion of the American frontier during the 19th century resulted in American Indians being forcibly moved to reservations, where many remain today. Millions of acres, primarily in the Great Plains, were taken from tribes with little or minimal compensation.

But the U.S. government did not consider compensating Native Americans for the loss of this property until 1946, when Congress established a Claims Commission to handle Indian land claims. The body soon became bogged down in the flood of claims, many of which were substantial. When the commission was eliminated in 1978, it had adjudicated only a fraction of the disputes between tribes and the government and had paid Native Americans only token compensation for the lost land. [16] Meanwhile, the courts became much more sympathetic to Indian claims. In 1980, for instance, the Supreme Court awarded the Sioux $122 million for the theft of lands in South Dakota's Black Hills. It remains the largest award for a Native American land claim in U.S. history. (*See story, p. 174.*)

Today, Native Americans are still pressing land claims, particularly in the Eastern United States. "Many of these claims revolve around treaties made between states and Indian nations early in the country's history," says John Echohawk, executive director of the Native American Rights Fund, an Indian advocacy group in Boulder, Colo. Since the U.S. Constitution leaves the power to negotiate Indian treaties with the federal government, many of these agreements with the states are now being challenged, he adds.

Restitution to 'Comfort Women'

On the other side of the globe, victims of a more recent tragedy — Japan's sexual enslavement of thousands of Asian women during World War II — are also seeking restitution. An estimated 200,000 "comfort women" were forced to serve the Japanese military at its far-flung outposts. They claim they were kidnapped or tricked into working as sexual slaves for the Japanese soldiers, who beat and raped them.

In 1995, then Japanese Prime Minister Tomiichi Murayama officially apologized for the practice, but the government has yet to pay any reparations to the surviving women. In 2007, the U.S. House passed a resolution calling on Japan to apologize for the sexual enslavement. "Only by honoring the memory of these atrocities will we be able to continue challenging nations of today to abide by shared human rights norms," said Rep. Mike Honda, D-Calif., the resolution's sponsor. "I sincerely hope that the government of Japan will formally, officially, and unambiguously apologize to the comfort women with an open mind and an open heart."

Other groups that have been victimized, like Armenians, also want restitution. And still others — like Latinos, Chinese Americans and women in the United States — who suffered varying degrees of discrimination over the years, have not organized significant reparations movements, in part because their suffering is perceived as being different from the official policies that led to genocide or slavery.

Japanese Americans

On Feb. 19, 1942, less than three months after the Japanese bombing of Pearl Harbor, President Franklin Delano Roosevelt signed Executive Order 9066, authorizing the removal of Japanese immigrants and their children from the western half of the Pacific coastal states and part of Arizona.

Within days, the government began removing 120,000 Japanese Americans — two-thirds of them U.S.

South Korean "comfort women" who were forced to provide sex for Japanese soldiers in World War II demand compensation during a protest at the Japanese Embassy in Seoul last April.

citizens — from their homes and businesses. Many were forced to sell their property at far below market value in the rush to leave. All were eventually taken to hastily built camps in Western states such as California, Idaho and Utah, where most remained until the war was almost over. Some young Japanese American men were allowed to leave the camps to serve in the armed forces — and many did so with valor — and a handful of mostly young internees were also permitted to relocate to Midwestern or Eastern states. The camps were Spartan, but in no way resembled Nazi concentration camps or Stalinist Russia's gulags. Still, the internees were denied their freedom and, in many cases, their property.

During this time, internee Fred Korematsu and several other Japanese Americans challenged the constitutionality of the internment. Korematsu's case ultimately found its way to the Supreme Court, which ruled that during national emergencies like war Congress and the president had the authority to imprison persons of certain racial groups. After the war, Congress passed the Japanese American Evacuations Claims Act of 1948 to compensate those who had lost property because of their internment. Over the next 17 years, the government paid $38 million to former internees. [17] But efforts to make the government apologize for its wartime actions and pay reparations to internees over and above the property claims remained on a back burner until the 1970s. During that decade, Japanese American activists — led

Japanese Americans wait for housing after being sent to the Manzanar, Calif., internment camp in March 1942 following the Japanese attack on Pearl Harbor. The U.S. later paid $20,000 to each person confined.

by the community's main civic organization, the Japanese American Citizens League (JACL) — began building support for redress.

Initially, only about a third of Japanese Americans favored reparations. Many felt the painful war years should be forgotten. Others worried that vocal demands, coupled with growing fears among the U.S. public over the rising economic power of Japan, would provoke another backlash against Japanese Americans. [18] But by the end of the decade, a majority of Japanese Americans supported the effort, and the JACL began effectively lobbying Congress for redress. In 1980, Congress created the Commission on Wartime Relocations and Internment of Civilians to study the issue.

During public hearings over the next two years, the commission heard emotional testimony as former internees shared their personal sagas. Publicity generated by the hearings helped awaken the American public to the injustice done to the internees. One former internee, Kima Konatsu, told about her family's experience while incarcerated near Gila River, Ariz. "During that four years we were separated [from my husband] and allowed to see him only once," Konatsu told the commission. Eventually he became ill and was hospitalized, she said. "He was left alone, naked, by a nurse after having given him a sponge bath. It was a cold winter and he caught pneumonia. After

two days and two nights, he passed away. Later on, the head nurse told us that this nurse had lost her two children in the war and that she hated Japanese." [19]

In 1983, the commission concluded that there had been no real national security reason to justify relocating or incarcerating the Japanese Americans, and that the action had caused the community undue hardship. A second report four months later recommended that the government apologize for the internment and appropriate $1.5 billion to pay each surviving internee $20,000 in reparations. [20]

That same year, a new National Council for Japanese American Redress (NCJAR) emerged, which opposed what it saw as the JACL's accommodationist approach to reparations. NCJAR filed a class action suit against the government on behalf of the internees, demanding $27 billion in damages. But the suit was dismissed in 1987 on procedural grounds. [21]

Nevertheless, the lawsuit created restitution momentum in Congress, where support had been building since issuance of the commission's 1983 reports. Because many former internees were elderly, proponents argued that something should be done quickly, before most of the intended beneficiaries died. [22]

In 1988, Congress passed the Civil Liberties Act, which authorized $1.25 billion over the next 10 years to pay each internee $20,000. The law also contained an apology to Japanese Americans who had been incarcerated [23] (see p. 180).

On Oct. 9, 1990, the government issued its first formal apologies and checks to Japanese Americans in a moving ceremony in Washington, D.C. A tearful Sen. Daniel K. Inouye, D-Hawaii — a Japanese American who lost an arm fighting for the United States during World War II — told the internees and assembled guests that day: "We honor ourselves and honor America. We demonstrated to the world that we are a strong people — strong enough to admit our wrongs." [24] Since then, some 80,000 former internees have received compensation. [25]

The Holocaust

In many ways, the modern debate over reparations began on Sept. 27, 1951. On that day West German Chancellor Konrad Adenauer appeared before the country's legislature, or Bundestag, and urged his fellow Germans to make some restitution for the "unspeakable

Italian Americans Were Also Mistreated

Japanese Americans were not the only ethnic group to suffer from discrimination during World War II. Many Italian-Americans also were victimized in the name of national security.

The United States was at war with Italy from the end of 1941 until it surrendered to the Allies in 1943. During that time, some 600,000 Italian immigrants were classified as "enemy aliens," even though many had sons fighting for the United States against Italy, Germany and Japan. Tens of thousands were subjected to search and arrest, and 250 were interned in camps. In California, an evening curfew was imposed on more than 50,000 Italian-Americans. Some 10,000 were forced to move away from areas near military installations. Authorities even impounded the boats of Italian American fishermen.

While generally recognized as a gross violation of civil liberties, the federal government's mistreatment of Italians was much less far-reaching than the internment suffered by 120,000 Japanese. Indeed, more German-Americans were interned — about 11,000 in Texas, North Dakota and elsewhere. Perhaps that's why Italian-American groups have not demanded reparations. Instead, they asked the government to "acknowledge" what happened.

In 2000, Congress agreed, passing legislation authorizing the Justice Department to conduct an investigation into the episode. In November 2001, the Department reported that the FBI had drawn up "a list of those thought to be security risks to the nation," including leaders of ethnic and cultural organizations.

Coming as it did on the heels of the terrorist bombings of Sept. 11, 2001, the report drew attention mainly as fodder for a debate between those who felt that its lessons dictated greater sensitivity in the treatment of Arab Americans, and those who argued that harsh treatment of "internal enemies" is sometimes necessary. "People have become more realistic since September 11 about what a wartime government must do to deal with internal threats, and less inclined to apologize about it," wrote Stephen Schwartz in *The Weekly Standard*. "The Italian Americans who came under scrutiny during the war were mainly those suspected of fascist sympathies — a topic omitted from the debate." [1]

---

[1] Stephen Schwartz, "The Right Way to Lock Up Aliens," *The Weekly Standard*, Dec. 10, 2001, p. 12.

---

crimes" Germany had committed against the Jewish people before and during World War II. His proposal — to provide assistance to the newly founded state of Israel as well as restitution to individual Holocaust survivors — was supported by both his own Christian Democratic party and the opposition Social Democrats.

Ironically, West Germany's offer of reparations was much more controversial in Israel, where a sizable minority, led by then opposition politician Menachem Begin, opposed taking "blood money" from Holocaust perpetrators. Begin and others argued that by receiving compensation from the Germans, Israel would literally be selling the moral high ground. [26] But Israeli Prime Minister David Ben Gurion argued forcefully that Israel had a duty to see that Germany did not profit from its heinous crimes. "He understood that we are obligated to ensure that murderers are not inheritors," says the World Jewish Congress' Steinberg. Ben Gurion prevailed, in part because Israel desperately needed funds to resettle European Jews who had survived the Holocaust. The German government began paying restitution to Holocaust survivors around the world in 1953 and has since paid out about $60 billion for both individual claims and aid to Israel. The state-to-state payments ended in 1965, but the German government still sends monthly pension checks to about 100,000 Holocaust survivors.

After West Germany's agreement with Israel, little was done to obtain further restitution for Holocaust victims. Many who had survived the camps were more concerned with getting on with their new lives and wanted to forget about the past. In addition, the Soviet Union and its Eastern bloc allies — where most Holocaust victims had come from — made no effort to aid the quest for restitution. Even the United States was content to let the issue lie, partly in order to focus on integrating West Germany and other Western allies into a Cold War alliance. [27]

Still, the issue did not disappear entirely. In Switzerland — a banking and finance mecca and a neutral country dur-

Rep. John Conyers Jr., D-Mich., wants Congress to create a commission on reparations for descendents of slaves. "Twelve years ago, most people didn't even know what reparations were, and now it's become a front-burner issue," he says.

ing the war — the government was taking small, inadequate steps to discover the extent of Holocaust-related wealth. Many Jews killed by the Germans had opened accounts in Swiss banks and taken out insurance policies from Swiss companies before the war as a hedge against the uncertainty created by the Nazi persecution. In 1956, the Swiss government surveyed its banks and insurance companies to determine the value of accounts held by those who had died or become refugees as a result of the Holocaust. The companies replied that there were less than a million Swiss francs in those accounts. In 1962, the government once again requested an accounting of Holocaust-related assets. This time, the companies came up with about 10 million francs, some of which was paid to account holders or their heirs. In the 1960s, '70s and '80s, other efforts by individuals seeking to recover Swiss-held assets were largely unsuccessful because the banks and insurers required claimants to have extensive proof of account ownership, proof that often had been lost or destroyed during the war.

But in the 1990s the situation changed dramatically. First, the collapse of communist regimes throughout Eastern Europe opened up previously closed archives containing Holocaust-related records. In addition, many Holocaust survivors lost their reticence about pursuing claims, in part because films like Schindler's List brought greater attention to their plight and made it easier to go public. In the mid-1990s, journalists and scholars began uncovering evidence that Switzerland had been a financial haven for Nazi officials, who had deposited gold looted from Holocaust victims in Swiss banks. The investigation stimulated new interest in dormant bank accounts and insurance policies. In 1996 a class action on behalf of victims and their heirs was filed in New York against Swiss banks and insurance companies. Swiss efforts to get the suit dismissed failed. Meanwhile, pressure from the U.S. Congress and local officials threatening economic sanctions against the companies forced the banks and insurers to acknowledge the existence of a large number of dormant accounts. By 1999, the Swiss had negotiated a settlement to set aside $1.25 billion to pay out dormant accounts and fund other Holocaust-related philanthropies.

The Swiss case prompted other Holocaust claims. For instance, in 1998 U.S. and European insurance regulators, Jewish groups and others formed a commission — headed by former Secretary of State Lawrence Eagleburger — to investigate claims against European insurance companies outside Switzerland. The commission was an attempt to bypass lawsuits and to get the insurers — which include some of Europe's largest, like Italy's Generali and Germany's Allianz — to pay elderly claimants before they died. So far, the companies have paid out very little in compensation, because of bureaucratic wrangling at the commission and unwillingness on the part of survivors to accept what have in many cases been only small offers of restitution from the companies. [28]

Meanwhile, former prisoners who had been forced to work without pay for German manufacturers during the war began seeking restitution for their labor. The Nazis had drafted an estimated 12 million people — including 6 million mostly Jewish concentration camp inmates — to provide unpaid labor for some of the biggest names in German industry, including giant automaker Volkswagen. Many were worked to death. [29] Initially Germany and then-Chancellor Helmut Kohl resisted efforts to pay reparations to slave laborers, citing the 1953 settlement with

Should the U.S. government apologize to African Americans for slavery?

YES — Rep. Alcee Hastings, D-Fla.

Excerpted from a floor statement
U.S. House of Representatives, July 29, 2008

This is a significant moment in our nation's history when the nearly 20-year fight to consider federal legislation that apologizes for slavery has at last become a reality. Indeed, it is fitting that we consider legislation of this content and caliber at this time. A global trend has emerged within the 21st Century in which governments have apologized for slavery and discriminatory laws and promised to work toward a better future.

Within the past year, states that were once members of the former Confederacy and were a cesspool for racist and bigoted laws and practices did something that no state had done before: they apologized for the enslavement of black people in this country. More than 240 years after the abolition of slavery and more than four decades after the abolition of Jim Crow, it is time for the federal government to do the same.

In 1988, Congress apologized to Japanese Americans for holding them in concentration camps during World War II. Congress expressed regret for its policies on Hawaii a century after the native Hawaiian kingdom was overthrown. And just [three] years ago, the Senate apologized for not enacting anti-lynching legislation that would have saved the lives of thousands of black people across the South.

Sadly, there are some who continue to oppose Congress apologizing for slavery and segregation. They see apologizing as a futile action that is too little too late. Others contend that an official apology would do more harm that good and would conjure painful images from the past that would fuel resentment. These assertions miss the point.

Failure to pass this resolution that acknowledges the wrongness of slavery and segregation would send the dangerous message that America is unwilling to come to terms with one of the first and last great atrocities that it placed on its citizens through the rule of law. Slavery and racial segregation were permitted through federal law and our government must express the appropriate and long-overdue remorse for its tolerance of this injustice.

In passing this resolution, the House will send a message to the American people and others that the most powerful nation in the world is willing to look honestly at some of the most shameful parts of its history, accept responsibility, and apologize for its actions.

NO — Rep. Steve King, R-Iowa

Excerpted from a floor statement
U.S. House of Representatives, July 29, 2008

H. Res. 194 appropriately reminds us of the horrors of slavery. Slavery was a stain on our original Constitution. It took the blood of hundreds of thousands of Americans who died in the Civil War to erase that stain and to pave the way for passage of the Civil War amendments to our Constitution. We must never forget that.

As I read through this resolution, I pick out some pieces that don't fit my sense of history. I would add that the Civil War is often taught to being fought over slavery. The people on the south side of the Mason-Dixon line would say it was fought over States' rights. I would say among those States' rights was the argument that the Southern States could declare their policy with regard to slavery.

Slavery has put a scar upon the United States that was a component of history as it arrived here, and it has been a component of most of the history within the continents. It has not, as it says here, imposed a rigid system of officially sanctioned racial segregation in virtually all areas of life. Subsequent to the Civil War and the emancipation, there were many areas in the North that were integrated, socially, economically, with a heart to do so, and I think they deserve some credit here as well.

I brought with me, this is my great, great, five times great uncle's Bible. This is the Bible that he carried in his shirt pocket for 3 years during the Civil War. This remains as a connection to me, to my family members who were strong and powerful and committed abolitionists, and some of them gave their lives to free the slaves.

So as I read this resolution today, I don't see a reference of gratitude for all the blood that was given by people to end slavery. I think that needs to be part of this record as well. The horrible price that was paid to pay back in blood drawn by the sword for every drop of blood drawn by the bondsmen's lash. That is a point, too, that the next generations need to learn and need to hear.

I just would emphasize that this Nation threw off the yoke of slavery. We rose above it because we had a strong conviction as a people, we had a strong religious faith that rejected slavery as a sin against this Nation. We can be proud of the price that was paid to free the slaves. And it was a struggle of 100 years to pass the Civil Rights Act that lifted another level. And here we are today at a point where I look forward to the time when we can say we are fully integrated and there is no vestige of slavery and no vestige of racism, and an understanding that we are all God's children created in his image.

South Carolina Gov. Jim Hodges helps to break ground for an African-American monument last year in Columbia. In spite of efforts by several states to come to terms with the history and contributions of black Americans, many advocates for slavey reparations say that only restitution will close the racial divide.

AP Photo/Lou Krasky

Israel. But in 1998 the country elected a new leader, Gerhard Schröeder, who authorized negotiations to settle the issue. In 2000, the German government and companies that had used slave labor established a $4.3 billion fund to compensate an estimated 1.5 million survivors. The deal, negotiated with German and American lawyers for the slave laborers and ratified in the Bundestag in May 2001, indemnifies German industry from further lawsuits on behalf of slave laborers.

CURRENT SITUATION

Reparations for Slavery

Efforts to compensate African Americans for slavery began formally on Jan. 16, 1865, months before the Civil War ended. On that day, Union General William Tecumseh Sherman issued Special Field Order 15, directing his soldiers — who were then marching through the South — to divide up confiscated Confederate farms into 40-acre plots and redistribute the land to slaves. Farm animals were also to be redistributed.

But Sherman's promise of "40 acres and a mule" was never realized. Four months after the order was signed,

President Abraham Lincoln was assassinated. His successor, Southerner Andrew Johnson, largely opposed reconstruction and quickly rescinded Sherman's order. More than 40,000 slaves were removed from farms they had recently occupied.

In the years since Special Field Order 15, the idea of compensating African Americans arose only occasionally in the public arena and attracted little attention. But lately the idea has gained considerable steam, propelled by several high-profile events, such as academic conferences on the subject and the threat of reparations lawsuits by prominent black attorneys.

In addition, Chicago, Detroit and Washington, D.C., have passed resolutions supporting federal reparations legislation. And slavery reparations has become a hot topic on college campuses, as more and more scholars study the idea. "This is the fourth paper I've delivered on reparations this year alone," University of San Diego Law Professor Roy Brooks said at a 2001 conference on the issue. "That suggests there's much to say about the subject and that reparations is a hot issue internationally." [30]

Among the reparations lawsuits were some prepared by prominent black attorneys and advocates, including ' Randall Robinson, O.J. Simpson's late attorney Johnnie Cochran, Harvard University Law School Professor Charles Ogletree and Alexander Pires, who won a $1 billion settlement from the Department of Agriculture on behalf of black farmers who were denied government loans. "The history of slavery in America has never been fully addressed in a public forum," Ogletree said. "Litigation will show what slavery meant, how it was profitable and how the issue of white privilege is still with us. Litigation is a place to start, because it focuses attention on the issue." [31]

But reparations litigation has never gotten far in the courts. U.S. District Judge Charles Norgle dismissed the most prominent case in both 2004 and 2005, arguing that the plaintiffs had failed to show that they had been harmed by slavery and instead were "trying to assert the legal rights of their ancestors."

Estimates vary wildly over how much black Americans are owed for slavery. Larry Neal, an economics professor at the University of Illinois at Urbana-Champaign, has calculated that the United States owes African Americans $1.4 trillion in back wages for work completed before emancipation. Georgetown University Business School Professor Richard America, however, estimates the debt is closer to $10 trillion. 32 "Even in a friendly court, there are going to be statute of limitations problems," Tulane University Law School Professor Robert Wesley says. [33] Moreover, experts point out, under the doctrine of sovereign immunity governments are protected from most legal actions.

Research by New York City lawyer and activist Deadria Farmer-Paellmann revealed that several insurance companies — including Aetna and New York Life — insured slave owners against the loss of their "property." "If you can show a company made immoral gains by profiting from slavery, you can file an action for unjust enrichment," she said. [34] Her work coincided with a 2000 California law requiring all insurance companies in the state to research past business records and disclose any connections to slavery.

Several other institutions have acknowledged historic ties to slavery in recent years, including Brown University, Aetna, Wachovia, JP Morgan and the Episcopal Church. Many of the corporate disclosures were prompted by a Chicago ordinance, passed in 2002, that requires companies seeking to do business with the city to research their histories and disclose whether they had once profited from slavery. In addition, a chorus of civil rights leaders, including the Rev. Jesse L. Jackson, has called on insurers to pay some form of restitution. "We call on the insurance companies to search their national files and disclose any and all policies issued to insure slave owners during the period of slavery," Jackson said. [35] Some black leaders have suggested that culpable corporations establish scholarship funds for underprivileged black students. But, while Aetna has publicly apologized for insuring owners against the loss of slaves, it has refused to provide compensation, arguing that slavery was legal when the policies were issued. New York Life in 2005 sponsored a four-part documentary series on PBS called "Slavery and the Making of America" as part of a broad educational initiative.

OUTLOOK

Starting a Dialogue

Those working to obtain reparations for slavery often compare the fight with the long, uphill struggle faced by civil rights activists in the 1950s and '60s. "The relative powerlessness of our community is not a new thing for African Americans," the University of Maryland's Walters says. "We've been here before and have won, and I think we're going to win this time, too." "The uneasiness that some express about reparations is the same uneasiness that we had about integration and about a woman's right to choose," Harvard's Ogletree said. "We've gained some important mainstream viability, but these things take time." [36]

For now, reparations proponents say that they hope to get the government to consider the issue, just as it did for Japanese American internees and Holocaust survivors. "Right now this is about process," Walters says. "With Japanese Americans, nothing really happened until after the government took some time to study the issue." Some hoped that the apologies from the U.S. House and several states in 2007 and 2008 would lead to financial restitution. Florida Governor Charlie Crist, a Republican expressed openness to that idea, but quickly noted that the state couldn't afford it, given a budget deficit. In other jurisdictions, lawmakers quickly concluded that the idea would not win broad public support.

A claim based on an injustice that occurred so long ago is simply too nebulous to warrant serious consideration by lawmakers or judges, MIT's Nobles says. "This isn't like the case of Japanese Americans, where you had direct survivors of the act in question. [The former internees'] suffering was identifiable and for a specific period of time — four years — making it much less complicated."

NOTES

1. Darryl Fears, "Slavery Apology: A Sincere Step or Mere Politics?", *The Washington Post*, Aug. 2, 2008, p. C1.

2. Damien Cave and Christine Jordan Sexton, "Florida Legislature Apologizes for State's History of Slavery," *The New York Times*, March 27, 2008, p. A18.

3. "Who's Sorry Now?", *The Economist*, Oct. 4, 2008.

4. Adam Hochschild, "The False Justice of Reparations," *Los Angeles Times*, Dec. 9, 2006, p. A31.

5. John Chase, "Obama, Keyes Concur on Little," *Chicago Tribune*, Oct. 18, 2004, p. 1.

6. Wendy Koch, "Legislators to Push for U.S. Apology for Slavery," *USA Today*, Feb. 28, 2008, p. 6A.

7. Darryl Fears, "Aging Sons of Slaves Join Reparations Battle," *The Washington Post*, Sept. 30, 2002, p. A3.

8. Peter Viles, "Suit Seeks Billions in Slave Reparations," CNN.com, March 27, 2002, http://archives.cnn.com/2002/LAW/03/26/slavery.reparations/.

9. For background, see Kenneth Jost, "Holocaust Reparations," *CQ Researcher*, March 26, 1999, pp. 257-280.

10. Quoted in Abraham H. Foxman, "The Dangers of Holocaust Restitution," *The Wall Street Journal*, Dec. 7, 1998.

11. Quoted in *Ibid.*

12. Mortimer Adler, *Aristotle for Everybody* (1978), p. 126.

13. Quoted in Arthur Spiegelman, "Leaders of Fight for Holocaust Reparations Under Attack," *The Houston Chronicle*, Dec. 27, 1998.

14. Matthew 5:10.

15. Adam Smith, *The Theory of Moral Sentiments* (1759), pp. 47-48.

16. Elazar Barkan, *The Guilt of Nations: Restitution and Negotiating Historical Injustices* (2000), p. 183.

17. Mitchell T. Maki, *et al.*, *Achieving the Impossible Dream: How Japanese Americans Obtained Redress* (1999), p. 54.

18. Barkan, *op. cit.*, p. 34.

19. Maki, *op. cit.*, p. 107.

20. *Ibid.*

21. *Ibid.*, pp. 121-128.

22. Christine C. Lawrence, ed., *1988 CQ Almanac* (1988), p. 80.

23. *Ibid.*

24. Maki, *op. cit.*, p. 213.

25. *Ibid.*, p. 214.

26. Barkan, *op. cit.*

27. Jost, *op. cit.*

28. Henry Weinstein, "Spending by Holocaust Claims Panel Criticized," *Los Angeles Times*, May 17, 2001.

29. "Key Dates in Nazi Slave Labor Talks," *The Jerusalem Post*, May 21, 2001.

30. Quoted in Erin Texeira, "Black Reparations Idea Builds at UCLA Meeting," *Los Angeles Times*, May 12, 2001.

31. Quoted in Tamar Lewin, "Calls for Slavery Restitution Getting Louder," *The New York Times*, June 4, 2001.

32. Kevin Merida, "Did Freedom Alone Pay a Nation's Debt?" *The Washington Post*, Nov. 28, 1999.

33. Quoted in Tovia Smith, "Legal Scholars Considering Class Action Lawsuit to Seek Restitution for Descendants of African Slaves," Weekend Edition Saturday, National Public Radio, April 1, 2001.

34. Quoted in Lewin, *op. cit.*

35. Quoted in Tim Novak, "Jackson: Companies Owe Blacks," *The Chicago Sun Times*, July 29, 2000.

36. Quoted in Lewin, *op. cit.*

BIBLIOGRAPHY

Books

Barkan, Elazar, *The Guilt of Nations: Restitution and Negotiating Historical Injustices*, W.W. Norton, 2000.
A professor of history at Claremont Graduate University has written an excellent and thorough history of restitution efforts in the 20th century, from attempts by Holocaust survivors to recover stolen property to the campaign to compensate "comfort women" forced to provide sex to Japanese soldiers. Barkan also examines the intellectual origins of the reparations movement.

Finkelstein, Norman G., *The Holocaust Industry: Reflections on the Exploitation of Jewish Suffering*, Verso, 2000.
Finkelstein, a political scientist, charges lawyers and Jewish groups with exploiting the Holocaust for financial and political gain, using unethical and immoral tactics. He contends that much of the money "extorted" from European companies and countries is not going to survivors, and that the entire process is degrading the historical legacy of the Holocaust.

Berthold, S. Megan, *Achieving the Impossible Dream: How Japanese Americans Obtained Redress*, University of Illinois Press, 1999.
The authors trace the history of efforts to get the U.S. government to pay reparations to Japanese Americans interned during World War II.

Robinson, Randall, *The Debt: What America Owes to Blacks,* **Plume, 2000.**

The founder of TransAfrica argues for reparations for African Americans, writing: "If . . . African Americans will not be compensated for the massive wrongs and social injuries inflicted upon them by their government, during and after slavery, then there is no chance that America can solve its racial problems — if solving these problems means, as I believe it must, closing the yawning economic gap between blacks and whites in this country."

Articles

Bivis, Larry, "Debate on Reparations for Slavery Gaining Higher Profile," Gannett News Service, April 21, 2001.

The article examines African Americans' growing call for reparations.

Dyckman, Martin, "Our Country has Paid the Bill for Slavery," *St. Petersburg Times,* **June 25, 2000.**

Dyckman makes a strong case against reparations to black Americans, arguing that the Union soldiers who died in the Civil War to free the slaves paid the country's debt to African Americans.

Fears, Darryl, "Slavery Apology: A Sincere Step or Mere Politics?", *The Washington Post,* **Aug. 2, 2008, p. C1.**

The reporter examines the House resolution apologizing for slavery and wonders whether it will lead to further steps such as financial reparations, or was merely a symbolic act undertaken for political reasons.

Hochschild, Adam, "The False Justice of Reparations," *Los Angeles Times,* **Dec. 9, 2006, p. A31.**

The author of a book about the slave trade argues that apologizing for past atrocities offers false comfort, noting both the widespread guilt of nations when it comes to slavery and war and the need to concentrate on present injustices.

Jost, Kenneth, "Holocaust Reparations," *CQ Researcher,* **March 26, 1999.**

Jost gives an excellent overview of the debate over reparations for the survivors of the Nazi Holocaust. His description of the fight over dormant bank accounts and insurance policies in Switzerland is particularly illuminating.

McTague, Jim, "Broken Trusts: Native Americans Seek Billions They Say Uncle Sam Owes Them," *Barron's,* **April 9, 2001.**

McTague examines the Native American lawsuit against the federal government for decades of mishandling of the trust fund derived from the lease and sale of natural resources on Indian lands. The tribe recently won a judgment against the federal government, and the suit may result in native tribes receiving up to $10 billion.

Merida, Kevin, "Did Freedom Alone Pay a Nation's Debt?" *The Washington Post,* **Nov. 28, 1999.**

Merida examines the movement to obtain reparations for the African American descendants of slaves, providing a good historical overview of efforts to compensate newly freed slaves after the Civil War.

Schoenfeld, Gabriel, "Holocaust Reparations — A Growing Scandal," *Commentary Magazine,* **September 2000.**

The magazine's senior editor takes Jewish groups to task for their hardball tactics against Germany and other European countries in their Holocaust reparations efforts. He worries they will foment bad feeling in Europe against Jews and Israel.

Trounson, Rebecca, "Campus Agitator," *Los Angeles Times,* **April 10, 2001.**

The article chronicles the controversy surrounding recent attempts by conservative commentator David Horowitz to place ads in college newspapers that argue against reparations for African Americans.

"Who's Sorry Now?", *The Economist,* **Oct. 4, 2008.**

The British magazine examines the wave of apologies coming from world leaders for past atrocities.

Zipperstein, Steven J., "Profit and Loss," *The Washington Post,* **p. Sept. 24, 2000.**

A professor of Jewish studies at Stanford University accuses author Norman G. Finkelstein of making wild and unsubstantiated charges in The Holocaust Industry (*see above*). "Imagine an old-style rant, with its finely honed ear for conspiracy, with all the nuance of one's raging, aging, politicized uncle," he writes.

For More Information

Anti-Defamation League, 823 United Nations Plaza, New York, N.Y. 20017; (212) 490-2525; www.adl.org. Fights anti-Semitism and represents Jewish interests worldwide.

Conference on Jewish Material Claims Against Germany, 1359 Broadway, Room 2020, New York, N.Y., 10018; (646) 536-9100; www.claimscon.org. Pursues reparations claims on behalf of Jewish victims of the Nazi Holocaust.

Japanese American Citizens League (JACL), 1765 Sutter St., San Francisco, Calif. 94115; (415) 921-5225; www.jacl.org. The nation's oldest Asian American civil rights group fights discrimination of Japanese Americans.

Joint Center for Political and Economic Studies, 090 Vermont Ave., N.W., Suite 1100, Washington, D.C. 20005; (202) 789-3500; www.jointcenter.org. Researches and analyzes issues of importance to African Americans.

National Coalition of Blacks for Reparations in America, P.O. Box 90604, Washington, D.C. 20090; (202) 291-8400; www.ncobra.com. Lobbies for reparations for African Americans.

Native American Rights Fund, 1712 N St., N.W., Washington, D.C. 20036; (202) 785-4166; www.narf.org. Provides Native Americans with legal assistance for land claims.

TransAfrica, 1629 K St., N.W., Washington D.C. 20006; (202) 223-1960; www.transafricaforum.org. Lobbies on behalf of Africans and people of African descent around the world.

U.S. Holocaust Memorial Museum, 100 Raoul Wallenberg Place, S.W., Washington, D.C. 20024; (202) 488-0400; www.ushmm.org. Preserves documentation and encourages research about the Holocaust.

World Jewish Congress, PO Box 90400, Washington, D.C. 20090; (212) 755-5770; www.worldjewishcongress.org. An international federation of Jewish communities and organizations that has been at the forefront of negotiations over Holocaust reparations.

9

Immigration Debate

Alan Greenblatt

A Mexican farmworker harvests broccoli near Yuma, Ariz. With the number of illegal immigrants in the U.S. now over 12 million — including at least half of the nation's 1.6 million farmworkers — tougher enforcement has become a dominant theme in the 2008 presidential campaign. Meanwhile, with Congress unable to act, states and localities have passed hundreds of bills cracking down on employers and illegal immigrants seeking public benefits.

From *CQ Researcher*,
February 1, 2008.

John McCain, the senior senator from Arizona and the leading Republican candidate for president, has been hurt politically by the immigration issue.

McCain would allow illegal immigrants to find a way eventually to become citizens. The approach is seen by many Republican politicians and voters (and not a few Democrats) as akin to "amnesty," in effect rewarding those who broke the law to get into this country. Legislation that he helped craft with Sen. Edward M. Kennedy, D-Mass., and the White House went down to defeat in both 2006 and 2007.

McCain rejects the approach taken by House Republicans during a vote in 2005 and favored by several of his rivals in the presidential race — namely, classifying the 12 million illegal immigrants already in this country as felons and seeking to deport them. This wouldn't be realistic, he says, noting not only the economic demands that have brought the foreign-born here in the first place but also the human cost such a widespread crackdown would entail.

On the stump, McCain talks about an 80-year-old woman who has lived illegally in the United States for 70 years and has a son and grandson serving in Iraq. When challenged at Clemson University last November by a student who said he wanted to see all illegal immigrants punished, McCain said, "If you're prepared to send an 80-year-old grandmother who's been here 70 years back to some other country, then frankly you're not quite as compassionate as I am." [1]

As the issue of illegal immigrants reaches the boiling point, however, and as he gains in the polls, even McCain sounds not quite so compassionate as before. In response to political pressures, McCain now shares the point of view of hard-liners who say stronger border security must come before allowing additional work permits or the

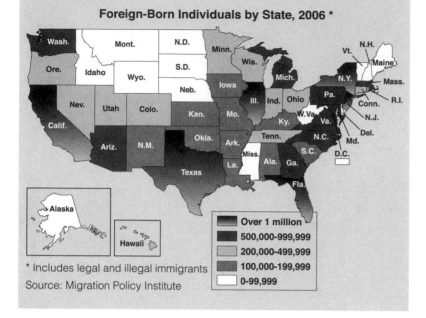

California Has Most Foreign-Born Residents

California's nearly 10 million foreign-born residents represented about one-quarter of the national total in 2006 and more than twice as many as New York.

Foreign-Born Individuals by State, 2006 *

Legend:
- Over 1 million
- 500,000-999,999
- 200,000-499,999
- 100,000-199,999
- 0-99,999

* Includes legal and illegal immigrants

Source: Migration Policy Institute

about two suspects in a triple murder in New Jersey who turned out to be illegal immigrants. He argued that President Bush should call Congress into special session to address the matter, calling himself "sickened" by Congress being in recess "while young Americans are being massacred by people who shouldn't be here."

Gingrich said Bush should be more serious about "winning the war here at home, which is more violent and more dangerous to Americans than Iraq or Iran." [4]

Concerns about terrorism have also stoked fears about porous borders and unwanted intruders entering the country.

"Whenever I'm out with a [presidential] candidate at a town hall meeting, it's the exception when they do not get a question about immigration — whether it's a Democratic event or a Republican event," says Dan Balz, a veteran political reporter at *The Washington Post.*

"path to citizenship" that were envisioned by his legislation.

"You've got to do what's right, OK?" McCain told *The New Yorker* magazine recently. "But, if you want to succeed, you have to adjust to the American people's desires and priorities." [2]

Immigration has become a central concern for a significant share of the American public. Immigrants, both legal and illegal, are now 12.6 percent of the population — more than at any time since the 1920s.

Not only is the number of both legal and illegal immigrants — now a record 37.9 million — climbing rapidly but the foreign-born are dispersing well beyond traditional "gatekeeper" states such as California, New York and Texas, creating social tensions in places with fast-growing immigrant populations such as Georgia, Arkansas and Iowa. [3]

Complaints about illegal immigrants breaking the law or draining public resources have become a daily staple of talk radio programs, as well as CNN's "Lou Dobbs Tonight."

In a high-profile speech in August 2007, Newt Gingrich, a former Republican House Speaker, railed

With no resolution in sight to the immigration debate in Congress, the number of immigrant-related bills introduced in state legislatures tripled last year, to more than 1,500. Local communities are also crafting their own immigration policies. (*See sidebar, p. 202.*)

In contrast to the type of policies pursued just a few years ago, when states were extending benefits such as in-state tuition to illegal immigrants, the vast majority of current state and local legislation seeks to limit illegal immigrants' access to public services and to crack down on employers who hire them.

"For a long time, the American public has wanted immigration enforcement," says Ira Mehlman, media director of the Federation for American Immigration Reform (FAIR), which lobbies for stricter immigration limits.

"Is there a rhetorical consensus for the need for immigration control? The answer is clearly yes," Mehlman says. "When even John McCain is saying border security and enforcement have to come first before the amnesty he really wants, then there is really a consensus."

While most of the Republican presidential candidates are talking tougher on immigration today than two or three years ago, Democrats also are espousing the need for border security and stricter enforcement of current laws. But not everyone is convinced a majority of the public supports the "enforcement-only" approach that treats all illegal immigrants — and the people that hire them — as criminals.

"All through the fall, even with the campaign going on, the polls consistently showed that 60 to 70 percent of the public supports a path to citizenship," says Tamar Jacoby, a senior fellow at the Manhattan Institute who has written in favor of immigrant absorption into U.S. society.

There's a core of only about 20 to 25 percent of Americans who favor wholesale deportation, Jacoby says. "What the candidates are doing is playing on the scare 'em territory."

But over the last couple of years, in the congressional and state-level elections where the immigration issue has featured most prominently, the candidates who sought to portray themselves as the toughest mostly lost.

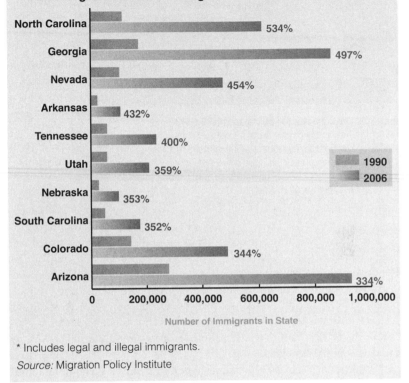

Fastest-Growing Foreign-Born Populations

Foreign populations at least tripled in 10 states since 1990. In North Carolina foreign-born residents increased by a record 534 percent.

Percentage Increases in Foreign-Born Individuals, 1990-2006

Number of Immigrants in State

* Includes legal and illegal immigrants.

Source: Migration Policy Institute

Some analysts believe that, despite the amount of media attention the issue has attracted, anti-immigrant hard-liners may have overplayed their hand, ignoring the importance of immigrant labor to a shifting U.S. economy.

"To be energized we need new workers, younger workers, who are going to be a part of the whole economy. We don't have them here in the United States," Sen. Kennedy told National Public Radio in 2006.

"We need to have the skills of all of these people," he continued. "The fact is, this country, with each new wave of immigrants, has been energized and advanced, quite frankly, in terms of its economic, social, cultural and political life. I don't think we ought to fear it, we ought to welcome it." [5]

Polls have made it clear that the Republican Party, which is seen as generally tougher on the issue, is losing support among Hispanics — the fastest-growing segment of the population.

"The Bush strategy — enlightened on race, smart on immigration — developed in Texas and Florida with Jeb Bush — has been replaced by the Tancredo-Romney strategy, which is demonizing and scapegoating immigrants," said Simon Rosenberg, a Democratic strategist, "and that is a catastrophic event for the Republican Party." [6] Jeb Bush, the president's brother, served two terms as governor of Florida, while Colorado Rep. Tom Tancredo and former Massachusetts Gov. Mitt Romney each sought this year's GOP presidential nomination. *

---

* Tancredo dropped out in December, and Romney had been trailing McCain in the primaries.

A prospective employer in Las Vegas holds up two fingers indicating how many day laborers he needs. One of the few pieces of immigration legislation still considered to have a chance in Congress this year is the SAVE Act, which would require all employers to use an electronic verification system to check the legal status of all workers.

There is a well-known precedent backing up Rosenberg's argument. In 1994, Pete Wilson, California's Republican governor, pushed hard for Proposition 187, designed to block illegal immigrants from receiving most public services. The proposition passed and Wilson won reelection, but it turned Hispanic voters in California against the GOP — a shift widely believed to have turned the state solidly Democratic.

"While there might be some initial appeal to trying to beat up on immigrants in all different ways, it ultimately isn't getting to the question of what you do with 12 million people," says Angela Kelley, director of the Immigration Policy Center at the American Immigration Law Foundation, which advocates for immigrants' legal rights. "It isn't a problem we can enforce our way out of."

But it's not a problem politicians can afford to ignore. There will be enormous pressure on the next president and Congress to come up with a package that imposes practical limits on the flow of illegal immigrants into the United States. Doing so while balancing the economic interests that immigrant labor supports will remain no less of a challenge, however.

That's in part because the immigration debate doesn't fall neatly along partisan lines. Pro-GOP business groups, for example, continue to seek a free flow of labor, while unions and other parts of the Democratic coalition fear just that.

"The Democrats tend to like immigrants, but are suspicious of immigration, while the Republicans tend to like immigration but are suspicious of immigrants," says Frank Sharry, executive director of the National Immigration Forum, a pro-immigration lobby group.

"Republicans want to deport 12 million people while starting a guest worker program," he says. "With Democrats, it's the reverse."

During a Republican debate in Florida last December, presidential candidate and former Massachusetts Gov. Mitt Romney took a less draconian position, moving away from his earlier calls to deport all illegals. "Those who have come illegally, in my view, should be given the opportunity to get in line with everybody else," he said. "But there should be no special pathway for those that have come here illegally to jump ahead of the line or to become permanent residents or citizens." [7]

One of the loudest anti-immigration voices belongs to Republican Oklahoma state Rep. Randy Terrill, author of one of the nation's toughest anti-immigration laws, which went into effect in December 2007. "For too long, our nation and our state have looked the other way and ignored a growing illegal immigration crisis," he said. "Oklahoma's working families should not be forced to subsidize illegal immigration. With passage of House bill 1804, we will end that burden on our citizens." [8] Among other things, the law gives state and local law enforcement officials the power to enforce federal immigration law.

As the immigration debate rages on, here are some of the specific issues that policy makers are arguing about:

Should employers be penalized for hiring illegal immigrants?

For more than 20 years, federal policy has used employers as a checkpoint in determining the legal status of workers. It's against the law for companies to knowingly hire illegal immigrants, but enforcement of this law has been lax, at best.

Partly as a result — but also because of the growing attention paid to illegal immigrants and the opportunities that may attract them to this country — the role of business in enforcing immigration policy has become a major concern.

"I blame 90 percent on employers," says Georgia state Sen. Chip Rogers. "They're the ones that are profiting by breaking the law."

The Immigration and Customs Enforcement agency has pledged to step up its efforts to punish employers who knowingly hire undocumented workers. In response, an Electrolux factory in Springfield, Tenn., fired more than 150 immigrant workers in December after Immigration and Customs Enforcement (ICE) agents arrested a handful of its employees.

Last year, ICE levied $30 million in fines and forfeitures against employers, but arrested fewer than 100 executives or hiring managers, compared with 4,100 unauthorized workers. [9]

One of the few pieces of immigration legislation still considered to have a chance in Congress this year is the SAVE Act (Secure America With Verification Enforcement), which would require all employers to use an electronic verification system to check the legal status of all workers. The House version of the bill boasts more than 130 cosponsors.

Employers are also being heavily targeted by state and local lawmakers. More than 300 employment-related laws addressing illegal immigrants have been recently passed by various levels of government, according to the U.S. Chamber of Commerce.

"There is still this general consensus that although the current employer-sanctions regime hasn't worked, the point of hire is the correct place to ensure that the employee before you is legally here," says Kelley, of the American Immigration Law Foundation.

But for all the efforts to ensure that businesses check the legal status of their workers — and to impose stiffer penalties on those who knowingly hire illegal immigrants — there is still considerable debate about whether such measures will ultimately resolve the problem.

Critics contend there is no easy way for employers to determine legal status. For one thing, documents often

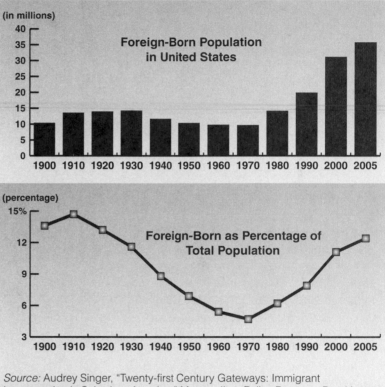

Immigration Is on the Rise

The number of foreign-born people in the United States has nearly quadrupled since 1970, largely because of changes in immigration laws and increasing illegal immigration (top). The increase has pushed the foreign-born percentage of the population to more than 12 percent (bottom).

Number and Percentage of Foreign-Born Individuals in the U.S., 1900-2005

Source: Audrey Singer, "Twenty-first Century Gateways: Immigrant Incorporation in Suburban America," Metropolitan Policy Program, Brookings Institution, April 2007

are faked. Dan Pilcher, spokesman for the Colorado Association of Commerce and Industry, notes that during a high-profile ICE raid on the Swift meatpacking plant in Greeley in December 2006, many of the arrests were for identity theft, not immigration violations, since so many illegal immigrants were using Social Security numbers that belonged to other people.

"Even when those numbers are run through the system, the computers didn't pick up anything," Pilcher says. "Until that system [of verification] is bulletproof, it

Legal Immigration Has Steadily Increased

The number of legal immigrants has risen steadily since the 1960s, from about 320,000 yearly to nearly 1 million. The largest group was from Latin America and the Caribbean. (In addition to legal entrants, more than a half-million immigrants arrive or remain in the U.S. illegally each year.)

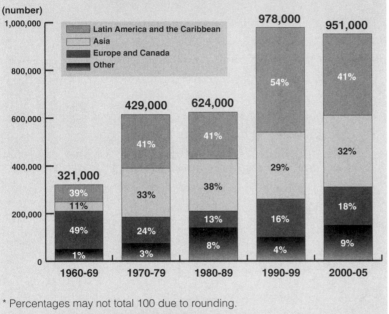

Average Annual Number of Legal U.S. Immigrants by Region of Origin, 1960-2005

(number)

Legend:
- Latin America and the Caribbean
- Asia
- Europe and Canada
- Other

Year	Total	Latin America and the Caribbean	Asia	Europe and Canada	Other
1960-69	321,000	39%	11%	49%	1%
1970-79	429,000	41%	33%	24%	3%
1980-89	624,000	41%	38%	13%	8%
1990-99	978,000	54%	29%	16%	4%
2000-05	951,000	41%	32%	18%	9%

* Percentages may not total 100 due to rounding.

Source: "Economic Mobility of Immigrants in the United States," Economic Mobility Project, Pew Charitable Trusts, 2007

do is give me a program so I can make sure the person is legal for me to hire," says Bryan R. Tolar, director of marketing, education and environmental programs for the Georgia Agribusiness Council.

So far, though, there is no such system. The Department of Homeland Security's E-Verify system, which grew out of a pilot program, is the new checking point of choice. In fact, federal contractors will soon be required to check the residency status of employees using E-Verify. As of Jan. 1, a new state law requires all employers in Arizona to use the E-Verify system.

But such requirements have drawn lawsuits from both business groups and labor unions, who complain that E-Verify is based on unreliable databases. Tom Clark, executive vice president of the Denver Metro Chamber of Commerce, complains that E-Verify is not accurate and worries therefore that the employer sanctions contained in the Arizona law could lead to serious and unfair consequences.

Under the law, companies found guilty of hiring an illegal worker can lose their business licenses for 10 days; for second offenses they are at risk of forfeiting their licenses entirely. "Do you know the [power] that gives you to take out your competitors?" Clark asks.

doesn't work to try to mandate that businesses be the front line of enforcement."

Concerns about the verification systems in place are shared across the ideological spectrum. "We're now 21 years after the enactment of employer sanctions, and we still haven't come up with a system that allows for instant verification," says Mehlman, at the Federation for American Immigration Reform. "If Visa and MasterCard can verify literally millions of transactions a day, there's no reason we can't have businesses verify the legal status of their employees."

"When you look to employers to be the ones that are going to have damages imposed for hiring someone who is not properly documented, the first thing you have to

Supporters of tougher employer sanctions say the databases are getting better all the time. Mark Krikorian, executive director of the Center for Immigration Studies, says E-Verify needs to be made into a requirement for all American employers. Once they are handed a working tool, he says, all businesses need to follow the same rules.

"Legal status is a labor standard that needs to be enforced just like other labor standards," he says. "Holding business accountable to basic labor standards is hardly revolutionary."

The National Immigration Forum's Sharry agrees that employers "need to be held to account for who they hire." But he warns that imposing stiff penalties against them at a juncture when verification methods remain in doubt could create greater problems.

"Until you create an effective verification system, employer sanctions will drive the problem further underground and advantage the least scrupulous employers," Sherry says.

Can guest worker programs be fixed?

The United States has several different programs allowing foreigners to come into the country for a limited time, usually to work for specific "sponsoring" employers, generally in agriculture. But most of these programs have been criticized for being ineffective — both in filling labor demands and ensuring that temporary workers do not become permanent, illegal residents.

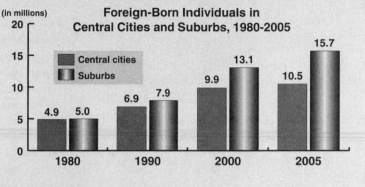

More Immigrants Moving to Suburbs

The gap between the number of immigrants who live in inner cities and suburbs widened significantly from 1980-2005. By 2005 more than 15 million foreign-born people were in suburbs, or three times as many in 1980. The number in cities doubled during the same period. Demographers attribute the popularity of the suburbs to their relative lack of crime, lower cost and better schools.

Foreign-Born Individuals in Central Cities and Suburbs, 1980-2005

(in millions)

Central cities / Suburbs

- 1980: 4.9 / 5.0
- 1990: 6.9 / 7.9
- 2000: 9.9 / 13.1
- 2005: 10.5 / 15.7

Source: Audrey Singer, "Twenty-first Century Gateways: Immigrant Incorporation in Suburban America," Metropolitan Policy Program, Brookings Institution, April 2007

The best-known guest worker program, the H-2A visa program for visiting agricultural workers, has been derided by farmers as cumbersome and time-consuming, preventing them from timing their hiring of workers to growing and harvesting seasons. Farmers use H-2A visas only to cover an estimated 2 percent of farmworkers.

Instead, growers turn to the black market for undocumented workers. At least half of the nation's 1.6 million farmworkers — and as many as 70 percent by some estimates — are immigrants lacking documentation. [10]

Still, growers' groups have complained about labor shortages as border security and regulation of employers are tightening. Some growers in the Northwest last fall let cherries and apples rot because of a shortage of workers, and some in North Carolina did not plant cucumbers because of a fear they wouldn't find the workers to harvest them. [11]

Three federal agencies — Homeland Security, State and Labor — have been working in recent months to craft regulations to speed the H-2A visa process. But farmworker advocates worry that the sort of changes the administration has been contemplating could weaken labor protections for workers. Some critics of lax immigration policy complain, meanwhile, that the H-2A

changes would allow employers to skirt a process designed to limit the flow of immigrant workers.

Changes adopted by or expected from the administration could weaken housing and wage standards that have traditionally been a part of temporary-worker programs, which date back to World War II, according to Bruce Goldstein, executive director of Farmworker Justice, a group that provides legal support to migrant workers.

Those changes would make a bad situation for farmworkers worse, Goldstein contends. "The government has failed to adopt policies that adequately protect workers from abuses and has failed to enforce the labor protections that are on the books," Goldstein says.

The Federation for American Immigration Reform's Mehlman criticizes the proposed changes for "trying to tip the balance in favor of employers.

"There's no evidence that we have a labor shortage in this country," Mehlman says. "You have businesses that have decided they don't want to pay the kind of wages American workers want in order to do these kinds of jobs."

Whether there is an overall labor shortage or not, clearly the numbers don't add up in agriculture. Officials with several immigration-policy groups note that the

After living in Clarion, Iowa, for nine years, undocumented Mexican immigrant Patricia Castillo, right, and her family were deported for entering the country illegally. Townspeople like Doris Holmes and her daughter Kelli threw a fund-raiser to help the Castillos pay their legal bills.

number of people coming to work in this country outnumber the visas available to new, full-time workers by hundreds of thousands per year.

"The only way we can provide for the labor needs of a growing and very diverse agriculture industry is to make sure there's an ample workforce to do it," says Tolar, at the Georgia Agribusiness Council. "Americans have proven that they're not willing to provide the work that needs doing at a wage agriculture can support."

Five years ago, a bipartisan group of congressmen, working with farmworkers, growers and church groups, proposed a piece of legislation known as the AgJobs bill. The attempt at a compromise between the most directly interested players has been a part of the guest worker and immigration debates ever since.

The bill would allow some 800,000 undocumented workers who have lived and worked in the U.S. for several years to register, pay a fine and qualify for green cards (proof of legal residency) by working in agriculture for three to five more years. It would also streamline the H-2A visa application process.

Although it won Senate passage as part of a larger immigration bill in 2006, the current version of AgJobs has not gained traction due to complaints that it would reward illegal immigrants and employers with what amounts to "get out of jail free" cards.

In November 2007, Sen. Dianne Feinstein, D-Calif., announced that she would not seek to attach AgJobs as an amendment to a larger farm bill, due to strong opposition to legislation seen as helping illegal immigrants. "We know that we can win this," Feinstein said in a statement. But, she conceded, "When we took a clear-eyed assessment of the politics . . . it became clear that our support could not sustain these competing forces."

Feinstein vows to try again this year. But Krikorian, of the Center for Immigration Studies, which favors reduced immigration, counters that guest worker programs in any form are not the right solution. "They still imagine there's a way of admitting low-wage illegals and not have immigration consequences," he says. "It's a fantasy.

"Guest worker programs don't work anyway," he adds. "There's nothing as permanent as a temporary worker."

The American Immigration Law Foundation's Kelley speaks for many on the other side of the debate who argue that it's not enough to conclude that guest worker programs are problematic. Workers from other countries are going to continue to come into this country, she notes.

"We need somehow to replace what is an illegal flow with a legal flow," Kelley says. "We have a guest worker program now — it's called illegal immigration."

Should illegal immigrants be allowed to attend public colleges and universities?

Miami college students Juan Gomez, 18, and his brother Alex, 20, spent a week in jail in Fort Lauderdale last summer. They were both students at Miami Dade College but faced deportation as illegal immigrants. They had come to the United States from Colombia when they were toddlers.

In handcuffs while riding to the detention center, Juan managed to type out a text message to a friend on his cell phone. The friend set up a Facebook group that in turn led 3,000 people to sign petitions lobbying Congress on the brothers' behalf.

In response, Rep. Lincoln Diaz-Balart, R-Fla., and Sen. Christopher Dodd, D-Conn., introduced legislation to prevent their deportation. As a courtesy to Congress, immigration officials delayed their deportation for two more years. [12]

But the brothers may still face deportation, because Congress failed to pass the DREAM (Development, Relief and Education for Alien Minors) Act. The bill would protect students from deportation and allow young adults (up to age 30) to qualify for permanent legal status if they completed high school and at least two years of college or military service.

On Oct. 24, 2007, the Senate voted 52-48 to end debate and move to a vote on final passage — eight votes short of the 60 needed under Senate rules to end a filibuster. Opponents of the measure claimed it was an unfair plan to grant amnesty to illegal immigrants.

The debate over illegal immigration has regularly and heatedly intersected with questions about education for illegal immigrants: Do young people deserve a break even if their parents skirted the law in bringing them to this country? Should illegal immigrants be barred from publicly supported colleges?

The courts have made it clear that states must provide elementary and secondary educations to all comers, including illegal immigrants. But higher education is another matter entirely.

Ten states have passed legislation in recent years granting in-state tuition to children of illegal immigrants. Most passed their laws during the early years of this decade, before immigration had become such a heated political topic.

Similar proposals in other states have died recently, with critics charging that it would be wrong to reward people who are in the country illegally with one of American society's dearest prizes.

"It is totally unfair if you're going to grant in-state tuition to illegal aliens in Georgia and charge out-of-state tuition to someone from Pennsylvania," says Phil Kent, national spokesman for Americans for Immigration Control.

Katherine "Kay" Albiani, president of the California Community Colleges board, stepped down last month along with two other board members in response to criticism from Republican legislators. The board had voted unanimously last year to support legislation that would have allowed illegal immigrants to qualify for student financial aid and community-college fee waivers.

"We have the best benefit package of any state for illegal immigrants, so they come here," complained California Senate GOP leader Dick Ackerman. [13]

Some argue that illegal immigrants should be barred not only from receiving tuition breaks but also from attending public colleges and universities altogether. Public institutions of higher education, after all, are subsidized by taxpayers, and therefore all students — including illegal immigrants — receive an indirect form of aid from state or local governments.

"Every college student is subsidized to the tune of thousands of dollars a year," says Krikorian, of the Center for Immigration Studies. "They are taking slots and huge amounts of public subsidies that would otherwise go to Americans or legal immigrants."

"Our view is that they shouldn't be there in the first place, and they certainly shouldn't be subsidized by taxpayers," says Mehlman of FAIR. "The typical illegal immigrant isn't coming to the U.S. for higher education. But once you're here, if the state says we'll subsidize your college education, that's a pretty good incentive to stay here."

Others argue that banning students because their parents chose to break the law would be a mistake. "We are a better country than to punish children for what their parents did," former Arkansas Gov. Mike Huckabee said during the Nov. 28 CNN/YouTube GOP presidential debate. Huckabee says he opposes the congressional DREAM Act, but his opponents in the primary campaign have pointed out his former support as governor for in-state tuition for longtime illegal residents.

Beyond the question of whether it's fair to punish students for decisions their parents made, some argue it would be a mistake to deprive illegal immigrants of educational opportunities. A college education may be an extra inducement for them to stay in this country, but the vast majority are likely to remain in this country anyway.

"If these are people who are going to live here for the rest of their lives, we want them to be as educated as possible," says the Manhattan Institute's Jacoby.

The American Immigration Law Foundation's Kelley agrees. She describes the DREAM Act as a reasonable compromise, saying it would protect students but wouldn't give illegal immigrants access to scholarships or grants. She argues that states that do offer in-state tuition rates to illegal immigrant students have not seen "a huge influx" of them.

"Saying to students who have been raised here and by all accounts are American and are graduating in high numbers and are doing well — 'You can't advance and go any further' — doesn't make sense," Kelley says. "It would be helpful to our economy to have these kids get college degrees."

BACKGROUND

Earlier Waves

The United States was created as a nation of immigrants who left Europe for political, religious and economic rea-

CHRONOLOGY

1920s *Hard economic times and public concern about the nation's changing ethnic makeup prompt Congress to limit immigration.*

1921-1929 Congress establishes immigration quota system, excluding Asians and Southern and Eastern Europeans.

1924 U.S. Border Patrol is created to block illegal immigrants, primarily Mexicans.

1940s-1950s *Expansion of U.S. economy during World War II attracts Mexican laborers. U.S. overhauls immigration laws, accepts war survivors and refugees from communist countries.*

1942 Controversial Bracero guest worker program allows Mexicans to work on American farms.

1952 Landmark Immigration and Nationality Act codifies existing quota system favoring Northern Europeans but permitting Mexican farmworkers in Texas.

1960s-1970s *Civil Rights Movement spurs U.S. to admit more Asians and Latin Americans.*

1965 Congress scraps national quotas, gives preference to relatives of immigrants.

1980s *Rising illegal immigration sparks crackdown.*

1986 Apprehension of a record 1.7 million illegal Mexican immigrants prompts lawmakers to legalize undocumented workers and for the first time impose sanctions on employers.

1990s-2000s *Congress again overhauls immigration laws amid national-security concerns.*

1993 Middle Eastern terrorists bomb World Trade Center; two had green cards.

1994 California voters pass Proposition 187, blocking illegal immigrants from receiving most public services; three years later it is largely declared unconstitutional.

1996 Number of illegal immigrants in U.S. reaches 5 million.

Sept. 11, 2001 Attacks on World Trade Center and Pentagon focus new attention on porous U.S. borders.

2004 The 9/11 Commission points to "systemic weaknesses" in border-control and immigration systems.

2005 Congress passes Real ID Act, requiring proof of identity for driver's licenses. . . . President Bush calls for a "temporary worker" program excluding "amnesty" for illegal immigrants. . . . House passes bill to classify illegal immigrants as felons and deport them.

2006 On April 20, Homeland Security Secretary Michael Chertoff announces a federal crackdown on employers who hire illegal aliens. . . . On May 1, hundreds of thousands of immigrants demonstrate across the country to call for legal status. . . . On Nov. 7, 69 percent of Hispanic voters support Democrats in congressional races, according to exit polls.

2007 On May 9, churches in coastal cities provide "sanctuaries" for undocumented families. . . . On May 17, President Bush and a bipartisan group of senators announce agreement on a comprehensive bill to strengthen border protection and allow illegal immigrants eventual access to citizenship. . . . On Aug. 10, the administration calls for more aggressive law enforcement, screening of new employees by federal contractors and firing of workers whose Social Security numbers don't match government databases. . . . On Oct. 24, the Senate fails to end debate on a proposal to protect illegal immigrants who are attending college from deportation. . . . On Dec. 26, Bush signs spending bill calling for 700 miles of "reinforced fencing" along U.S.-Mexico border.

Jan. 1, 2008 Arizona law holding employers responsible for checking legal status of workers is the most recent of hundreds of punitive, new state immigration laws. . . . On Jan. 22, Michigan stops issuing driver's licenses to illegal immigrants. . . . Implementation of Real ID Act, slated to go into effect in May, is postponed.

sons. After independence, the new nation maintained an open-door immigration policy for 100 years. Two great waves of immigrants — in the mid-1800s and the late-19th and early-20th centuries — drove the nation's westward expansion and built its cities and industrial base. [14]

But while the inscription on the Statue of Liberty says America accepts the world's "tired . . . poor . . . huddled masses," Americans themselves vacillate between welcoming immigrants and resenting them — even those who arrive legally. For both legal and illegal immigrants, America's actions have been inconsistent and often racist.

In the 19th century, thousands of Chinese laborers were brought here to build the railroads and then were excluded — via the Chinese Exclusion Act of 1882 — in a wave of anti-Chinese hysteria. Other Asian groups were restricted when legislation in 1917 created "barred zones" for Asian immigrants. [15]

The racist undertones of U.S. immigration policy were by no means reserved for Asians. Describing Italian and Irish immigrants as "wretched beings," *The New York Times* on May 15, 1880, editorialized: "There is a limit to our powers of assimilation, and when it is exceeded the country suffers from something very like indigestion."

Nevertheless, from 1880 to 1920, the country admitted more than 23 million immigrants — first from Northern and then from Southern and Eastern Europe. In 1890, Census Bureau Director Francis Walker said the country was being overrun by "less desirable" newcomers from Southern and Eastern Europe, whom he called "beaten men from beaten races."

In the 1920s, public concern about the nation's changing ethnic makeup prompted Congress to establish a national-origins quota system. Laws in 1921, 1924 and 1929 capped overall immigration and limited influxes from certain areas based on the share of the U.S. population with similar ancestry, effectively excluding Asians and Southern and Eastern Europeans, such as Greeks, Poles and Russians. [16]

But the quotas only swelled the ranks of illegal immigrants — particularly Mexicans, who needed only to wade across the Rio Grande River. To stem the flow, the United States in 1924 created the U.S. Border Patrol to guard the 6,000 miles of U.S. land bordering Canada and Mexico.

After World War II, Congress decided to codify the scores of immigration laws that had evolved over the years. The landmark Immigration and Nationality Act of 1952 retained a basic quota system that favored immigrants from Northern Europe — especially the skilled workers and relatives of U.S. citizens among them. At the same time, it exempted immigrants from the Western Hemisphere from the quota system — except for the black residents of European colonies in the Caribbean.

Mass Deportation

The 1952 law also attempted to address — in the era's racist terms — the newly acknowledged reality of Mexican workers who crossed the border illegally. Border Patrol agents were given more power to search for illegal immigrants and a bigger territory in which to operate.

"Before 1944, the illegal traffic on the Mexican border . . . was never overwhelming," the President's Commission on Migratory Labor noted in 1951, but in the past seven years, "the wetback traffic has reached entirely new levels. . . . [I]t is virtually an invasion." [17]

In a desperate attempt to reverse the tide, the Border Patrol in 1954 launched "Operation Wetback," transferring nearly 500 Immigration and Naturalization Service (INS) officers from the Canadian perimeter and U.S. cities to join the 250 agents policing the U.S.-Mexican border and adjacent factories and farms. More than 1 million undocumented Mexican migrants were deported.

Although the action enjoyed popular support and bolstered the prestige — and budget — of the INS, it exposed an inherent contradiction in U.S. immigration policy. The 1952 law contained a gaping loophole — the Texas Proviso — a blatant concession to Texas agricultural interests that relied on cheap labor from Mexico.

"The Texas Proviso said companies or farms could knowingly hire illegal immigrants, but they couldn't harbor them," said Lawrence Fuchs, former executive director of the U.S. Select Commission on Immigration and Refugee Policy. "It was a duplicitous policy. We never really intended to prevent illegals from coming."

Immigration Reform

The foundation of today's immigration system dates back to 1965, when Congress overhauled the immigration rules, scrapping national-origin quotas in favor of immigration limits for major regions of the world and giving preference to immigrants with close relatives living in the United States. By giving priority to family reunification as a basis for admission, the amendments repaired "a deep and painful flaw in the fabric of American justice," President Lyndon B. Johnson declared at the time.

States Racing to Pass Restrictive Immigration Laws

Arizona, Georgia and Oklahoma seek to outdo Colorado.

Andrew Romanoff, the speaker of the Colorado House, offers a simple explanation for why his state enacted a sweeping immigration law in 2006.

"The immigration system is, by all accounts, broken," he says, "and the federal government has shown very little appetite for either enforcing the law or reforming the law."

In the absence of federal action on immigration, in 2007 every state in the nation considered legislation to address the issue, according to the National Conference of State Legislatures (NCSL). It released a study in November showing that states considered "no fewer than 1,562 pieces of legislation related to immigrants and immigration," with 244 passed into law in 46 states. [1] Both the number of bills and the number of new laws were three times higher than the totals in 2006.

When Colorado's law was enacted in 2006, it was considered perhaps the toughest in the country. It requires anyone older than 18 who is seeking state benefits to show identification proving legal status and requires employers to verify the legal status of workers. But it provides exemptions for certain types of medical care and was designed to hold harmless the children of illegal immigrants.

Colorado's approach has since been superseded by states such as Arizona, Georgia and Oklahoma, which have taken an even harder line. In fact, if there's one clear trend in state and local legislation, it's toward a stricter approach.

In Hazelton, Pa., a controversial set of laws has been held up by the courts. The ordinances would require businesses to turn employee information over to the city, which would then verify documents with the federal government.

Prospective tenants would have to acquire a permit to rent by proving their legal right to be in the country.

"It used to be that state and local activity was all over the map," says Mark Krikorian, executive director of the Center for immigration Studies, which advocates reduced immigration. "Those that are loosening the rules now are the exception."

Georgia's law touches on every facet of state policy that relates to illegal immigrants. Under its provisions, state and local government agencies have to verify the legal residency of benefit recipients. Many employers will have to do the same whenever they make a hiring decision. And law enforcement agencies are given authority to crack down on human trafficking and fake documents.

Thousands of immigrants, both legal and illegal, have left Oklahoma following the November enactment of a law (HB 1804) that makes it a felony to knowingly transport illegal immigrants and requires employers to verify the immigration status of workers. It also limits some government benefits to those who can produce proof of citizenship.

Employers in numerous sectors, including hotels, restaurants and agriculture, have complained about labor shortages. But Republican state Rep. Randy Terrill, who wrote the law, says it will save the state money due to the abolition of public subsidies for illegal immigrants. "There's significant evidence that HB 1804 is achieving its intended purpose," he said. [2]

States just a few years ago were debating the expansion of benefits for illegal immigrants, such as in-state tuition

However, the law also dramatically changed the immigration landscape. Most newcomers now hailed from the developing world — about half from Latin America. While nearly 70 percent of immigrants had come from Europe or Canada in the 1950s, by the 1980s that figure had dropped to about 14 percent. Meanwhile, the percentage coming from Asia, Central America and the Caribbean jumped from about 30 percent in the 1950s to 75 percent during the '70s.

In 1978, the select commission concluded that illegal immigration was the most pressing problem facing

immigration authorities, a perception shared by the general public. [18] The number of border apprehensions peaked in 1986 at 1.7 million, driven in part by a deepening economic crisis in Mexico. Some felt the decade-long increase in illegal immigration was particularly unfair to the tens of thousands of legal petitioners waiting for years to obtain entry visas.

"The simple truth is that we've lost control of our own borders," declared President Ronald Reagan, "and no nation can do that and survive." [19]

rates for college. But now politicians in most locales who appear to be aiding illegal immigrants in any way are widely castigated.

New York Gov. Eliot Spitzer, a Democrat, proposed in fall 2007 that illegal immigrants should be eligible for driver's licenses, arguing that would make them more likely to buy insurance. But the idea touched off a political firestorm not only in his state but also within the Democratic presidential campaign and he quickly backed down.

Early this year, Maryland Democratic Gov. Martin O'Malley called for his state to stop issuing driver's licenses to undocumented immigrants. (It's one of seven that currently do so.) "When you've got a New York governor getting clubbed over the head for trying to institute what Maryland has . . . you realize we are out of sync with the rest of the nation," said state House Republican leader Anthony J. O'Connell.[3]

Legislatures in at least a dozen states are already considering bills modeled on the get-tough approaches taken elsewhere. Legislators in states neighboring Oklahoma,

A demonstrator in Tucson supports Proposition 200 on Dec. 22, 2004. The voter-approved Arizona law denies some public benefits to illegal immigrants.

AP Photo/John Miller

for instance, say that they feel pressure to introduce restrictive legislation, particularly from constituents in areas where immigrants who had lived in Oklahoma have relocated.

The fact that there's a sort of legislative arms race going on, with states trying to outdo each other on the immigration issue, has many people worried. A patchwork approach, with tough laws in scattered places driving some immigrants toward more lenient jurisdictions, is clearly not the way to resolve a national or even international issue such as immigration.

"Obviously, 50 different state immigration policies is ultimately unworkable," says Romanoff. "All of us much prefer a federal solution.

"The question is, how long should we wait? In Colorado we decided we could wait no longer."

---

[1] "2007 Enacted State Legislation Related to Immigrants and Immigration," National Conference of State Legislatures, Nov. 29, 2007, www.ncsl.org/print/immig/2007Immigrationfinal.pdf.

[2] Emily Bazar, "Strict Immigration Law Rattles Okla. Businesses," *USA Today*, Jan. 10, 2008, p. 1A.

[3] Lisa Rein, "Immigrant Driver ID Rejected by O'Malley," *The Washington Post*, Jan. 16, 2008, p. B1.

In the mid-1980s, a movement emerged to fix the illegal-immigration problem. Interestingly, the debate on Capitol Hill was marked by bipartisan alliances described by Sen. Alan K. Simpson, R-Wyo., as "the goofiest ideological-bedfellow activity I've ever seen."[20] Conservative, anti-immigration think tanks teamed up with liberal labor unions and environmentalists favoring tighter restrictions on immigration. Pro-growth and business groups joined forces with longtime adversaries in the Hispanic and civil rights communities to oppose the legislation.

After several false starts, Congress passed the Immigration Reform and Control Act (IRCA) in October 1986 — the most sweeping revision of U.S. immigration policy in more than two decades. Using a carrot-and-stick approach, IRCA granted a general amnesty to all undocumented aliens who were in the United States before 1982 and imposed monetary sanctions — or even prison — against employers who knowingly hired undocumented workers for the first time.

detention centers but provide fiscal relief and bed space to state and local governments housing such prisoners. Last year, ICE sent 276,912 people back to their home countries, including many who were not arrested for crimes but had violated civil immigration statutes. [38]

OUTLOOK

Tough Talk

Immigration will clearly remain an important part of the political conversation in this country. The factors that have made it so prominent — the record number of immigrants, both legal and illegal, and their dispersal into parts of the country that had not seen large influxes of immigrants in living memory — show little sign of abating.

The course that any policy changes will take will depend on who wins the presidency. Attempts at addressing the issue in a comprehensive way in Congress failed, due to concerted opposition to the compromise package brokered between the Bush White House and a bipartisan group of senators. Since that time, more modest bills have not been able to advance.

That means the issue will not be resolved as a policy matter until 2009, at the earliest. Instead, it will remain a major theme of the presidential campaign. Immigration has become, perhaps, the dominant issue among the Republican candidates, as well as one that Democrats have had to address in several particulars.

In a December interview with The Boston Globe, Illinois Sen. Barack Obama, one of the Democratic front-runners, predicted that any Republican candidate, save for McCain, would center his race on two things — fear of terrorism and fear of immigration. [39]

But the immigration issue has not broken along strictly partisan lines. Krikorian of the Center for Immigration Studies predicts that even if the election results in a Democratic president and Congress, the broad policy trajectory will be toward further tightening of immigration policy.

"I don't care whether it's a new Democratic or a new Republican president, they're going to have to address it," says Kent, of Americans for Immigration Control. "The new president will have to toughen up the border."

Politicians of all stripes indeed now pay homage to the idea that border security must be tightened and that current laws need more rigorous enforcement. But debate is still hot over questions of how much to penalize illegal immigrants and employers — and whether efforts to do just that may ultimately prove counterproductive.

Mehlman of the Federation for American Immigration Reform says "the forces that have been trying to promote amnesty and lots of guest workers are not going to go away." Mehlman says that even if current campaign rhetoric generally supports the tough approach his organization favors, the dynamic of actually changing policies in 2009 and after may not change that much.

"It wouldn't be the first time a politician said one thing during the campaign and acted differently once in office," he says.

He notes that the business groups that encourage immigration have deep pockets, but he believes that "this is an issue that the American public is making a stand on."

The National Immigration Forum's Sharry counters that the policy debate has been hijacked by heated political rhetoric and that it's become difficult to discuss what would be the best solutions without accusations being hurled if a proposal sounds at all "soft" on illegal immigrants.

Nevertheless, he notes, most people do not support the toughest proposals that would treat illegal immigrants as felons and seek their mass deportation. "I suspect it's going to take one or perhaps two election cycles to figure out who does it help and who does it hurt," Sharry says. "My prediction is that the Republican embrace of the extreme anti-immigrant groups will be seen in retrospect as an act of slow-motion suicide."

Douglas S. Massey, a Princeton University sociologist, agrees that the politics of this issue may play out poorly over the long term for those proposing a serious crackdown. He notes that there have been many occasions in American history when "beating on immigrants" has been an expedient strategy, but he argues it's never played well successfully as a sustained national issue.

"It's not a long-term strategy for political success, if you look at the future composition of America," Massey says, alluding in particular to the growth in foreign-born populations.

The political debate clearly will have a profound influence on the policy decisions made on immigration in the coming years. But the underlying demographic trends are likely to continue regardless. "With the baby boomers retiring, we will need barely skilled workers more than ever," says Jacoby, of the Manhattan Institute, referring in part to health-care aides.

She argues that growth in immigration is simply an aspect of globalization. Although people are uncomfortable with change and tend to see its downsides first, she believes that people will eventually realize large-scale migration is an inevitable part of the American future.

"We're in a bad time, and our politics are close to broken," she says, "but eventually American pragmatism will come to the surface."

NOTES

1. Quoted in Ryan Lizza, "Return of the Nativist," *The New Yorker*, Dec. 17, 2007, p. 46. For more on immigrant families that face being split up, see Pamela Constable, "Divided by Deportation: Unexpected Orders to Return to Countries Leave Families in Anguish During Holidays," *The Washington Post*, Dec. 24, 2007, p. B1.

2. Quoted in Lizza, *op. cit.*

3. Ellis Cose, "The Rise of a New American Underclass," *Newsweek*, Jan. 7, 2008, p. 74.

4. William Neikirk, "Gingrich Rips Bush on Immigration," *Chicago Tribune*, Aug. 15, 2007, p. 3.

5. Jennifer Ludden, "Q&A: Sen. Kennedy on Immigration, Then & Now," May 9, 2006, NPR.org, www.npr.org/templates/story/story.php?storyId=5393857.

6. Lizza, *op. cit.*

7. "GOP Hopefuls Debate Immigration on Univision," www.msnbc.msn.com/id/22173520/.

8. David Harper, "Terrill Leads Way on Issue," *Tulsa World*, Oct. 30, 2007, www.TulsaWorld.com.

9. Julia Preston, "U.S. to Speed Deportation of Criminals Behind Bars," *The New York Times*, Jan. 15, 2008, p. A12.

10. "Rot in the Fields," *The Washington Post*, Dec. 3, 2007, p. A16.

11. Steven Greenhouse, "U.S. Seeks Rules to Allow Increase in Guest Workers," *The New York Times*, Oct. 10, 2007, p. A16.

12. Kathy Kiely, "Children Caught in the Immigration Crossfire," *USA Today*, Oct. 8, 2007, p. 1A.

13. Patrick McGreevy, "Gov's Party Blocks His College Board Choice," *Los Angeles Times*, Jan. 15, 2008, p. B3.

14. Unless otherwise noted, material in the background section comes from Rodman D. Griffin, "Illegal Immigration," April 24, 1992, pp. 361-384; Kenneth Jost, "Cracking Down on Immigration," Feb. 3, 1995, pp. 97-120; David Masci, "Debate Over Immigration," July 14, 2000, pp. 569-592; and Peter Katel, "Illegal Immigration," May 6, 2005, pp. 393-420, all in *CQ Researcher*.

15. For background, see Richard L. Worsnop, "Asian Americans," *CQ Researcher*, Dec. 13, 1991, pp. 945-968.

16. For background, see "Quota Control and the National-Origin System," Nov. 1, 1926; "The National-Origin Immigration Plan," March 12, 1929; and "Immigration and Deportation," April 18, 1939, all in *Editorial Research Reports*, available from *CQ Researcher Plus Archive*, http://cqpress.com.

17. Quoted in Ellis Cose, *A Nation of Strangers: Prejudice, Politics and the Populating of America* (1992), p. 191.

18. Cited in Michael Fix, ed., *The Paper Curtain: Employer Sanctions' Implementation, Impact, and Reform* (1991), p. 2.

19. Quoted in Tom Morganthau, *et al.*, "Closing the Door," *Newsweek*, June 25, 1984.

20. Quoted in Dick Kirschten, "Come In! Keep Out!" *National Journal*, May 19, 1990, p. 1206.

21. Ann Chih Lin, ed., *Immigration*, CQ Press (2002), pp. 60-61.

22. William Branigin, "Congress Finishes Major Legislation; Immigration; Focus is Borders, Not Benefits," *The Washington Post*, Oct. 1, 1996, p. A1.

23. David Johnston, "Government is Quickly Using Power of New Immigration Law," *The New York Times*, Oct. 22, 1996, p. A20.

24. William Branigin, "INS Shifts 'Interior' Strategy to Target Criminal Aliens," *The Washington Post*, March 15, 1999, p. A3.

25. Deborah Meyers and Jennifer Yau, "US Immigration Statistics in 2003," Migration Policy Institute, Nov. 1, 2004, www.migrationinformation.org/USfocus/display.cfm?id=263; and Homeland Security Department, "2003 Yearbook of Immigration Statistics," http://uscis.gov/graphics/shared/statistics/yearbook/index.htm.

26. Jeffrey S. Passel, "Estimates of the Size and Characteristics of the Undocumented Population," Pew Hispanic Center, March 21, 2005, p. 8.

Border-town Life Becomes More Difficult

Cross-border exchanges may be in jeopardy.

On clear afternoons, Tony Zavaleta sometimes stands on the porch of his home outside Brownsville, Texas, gazes across the Rio Grande and watches one of his cousins working his farm on the other side of the river.

"I've got all kinds of family across the river," says Zavaleta, vice president for external affairs at the University of Texas, Brownsville. "In fact, at 3 o'clock today I'm going to the bridge to pick up a cousin, and we're going to Starbucks to have coffee."

The U.S.-Mexico border looks like a clearly drawn line on a map, but up close the delineation is blurred. The two nations are connected by history, economy and, most significantly, a border population with extensive and often deep roots in both nations.

"We have family business, family dealings, intermarriages, social events on both sides of the border, and that is the case for literally hundreds of thousands of people," says Zavaleta, whose family traces its heritage on both sides of the river back to the 18th century.

These strong relationships have created what many describe as a unique border culture — one they believe is threatened by the new border fence. "We're one community, and we've historically operated as one community," says Chad Foster, mayor of Eagle Pass, Texas, about his city's relationship with Piedras Negras, immediately across the border. "We have individuals who live in Piedras Negras but pay tuition so their kids can go to school in Eagle Pass. We have people who live in Eagle Pass and run plants in Piedras Negras. We've always gone back and forth."

The border between the United States and Mexico remains the busiest in the world, with more than 220 million legal crossings a year. But casual interchange between the two nations, the lifeblood of border culture, has been growing more difficult in recent years, particularly with the beefed-up border security since the Sept. 11 terrorist attacks. Now, many fear a further stifling of the relationship.

"You wouldn't think it would affect everyday, legal crossing," says Zavaleta, "but it has already done that."

Foster says the fence sends a signal: "You're not welcome."

When combined with longer waits at the legal ports of entry due to tighter security and inadequate staffing, they say, the fence creates the sense that crossing the border is best avoided — a feeling that could have serious economic implications for border communities.

Tom Fullerton, an economics professor at the University of Texas, El Paso, has studied the financial relationships between cities located across from each other on the border. In El Paso, he attributes an average of $900 million annually in retail sales to Mexicans crossing the border

of labor shortage followed by massive restrictions and deportations," writes Katherine Fennelly, a member of the League of Women Voters' Immigration Study Committee. [34]

When joblessness rose during the Depression in the late 1920s, thousands of Mexican immigrants were deported. But when World War II left the United States with another labor shortage, the country reversed course and created the Bracero Program — Spanish for "laborer" — to bring in Mexicans, mainly to work in agriculture and on the railroads.

The program brought in more than 400,000 workers a year during its 22-year history. [35] But illegal immigration grew at the same time, particularly in the late-1940s and '50s as Mexicans came north to take advantage of America's postwar economic boom. In reaction, Immigration and Naturalization Commissioner Gen. Joseph Swing initiated "Operation Wetback" in 1954, with federal and local authorities sweeping through Mexican American barrios looking for illegal immigrants. Thousands were deported. [36]

When the Bracero Program ended in 1965, legal entry became more difficult for Mexican farmworkers. But work in U.S. fields and orchards remained plentiful, so many Mexicans began to travel into the United States seasonally without legal documents.

to shop in the United States.

Business also travels the other way. "I don't know the number of people I've met who routinely go to the dentist in Nogales [Mexico] because it's cheaper," says folklorist Maribel Alvarez, an assistant professor at the University of Arizona's Southwest Center.

Betty Perez, who operates a small ranch a couple of miles from the border near Roma, Texas, says many ranchers go across the border "to buy a good bull or sell a good bull or a horse. There's a lot of horse business down there."

Fullerton says it's difficult to estimate the economic consequences of the border fence, but with trade liberalization, Mexicans now can find almost anything they might buy in the United States at home. "It's possible they'll say, 'We'll just stay here and not worry about going into this country where we're not really welcome,' " he notes.

That would be just fine for many fence supporters, including those living along the border. Ed Williams, a retired University of Arizona political science professor, points out the existence of a border culture does not imply universal mutual appreciation. "While many borderlands people have been sympathetic to their brethren across the line, others have always been suspicious," he says. "There are people in the border communities who say, 'Build that damn wall.' "

Patricia Escobar, left, of Los Angeles, visits through the fence with her daughter Rosa, who lives in Tijuana, Mexico.

But opinion does not necessarily divide strictly along racial lines. "You can find a lot of people with Spanish surnames who will say, 'Keep those Mexicans out,' " says Zavaleta. "And a lot of Anglos feel that's bad for business."

But Alvarez, who edits the center's "Borderlore" blog, notes the breadth of the population whose lives have been lived on both sides of the border. "You have the ranchers. You have the Native Americans. You have the bohemians that come to the desert to write and paint," she says. "You have a very grounded working class that crosses back and forth almost daily."

Border towns even have shared fire departments and other civic institutions. "Laredo and Nuevo Laredo, prior to the 1980s, was essentially like a spot on the Canadian border or between two Scandinavian countries," says Fullerton. "That's how closely intertwined they were. They even shared a minor league baseball team."

But when people living on the border reminisce about earlier, less-security-conscious days, they most often cite the personal exchanges that built a sense of a shared land. "I remember when my grandfather decided he wanted to give me a horse as a gift," says Zavaleta. "He just had a ranch hand ride it across the river. I was 14, and I remember standing on the riverbank and watching that horse come across from my grandfather. You wouldn't do that today."

'Tortilla Curtain' Rises

As illegal immigration grew, certain border cities became the favorites for border crossers. By 1978 the problem had become bad enough in El Paso, Texas, that the government erected 12.5 miles of chain-link fence — the "Tortilla Curtain" — along the border. The Border Patrol has expanded infrastructure along the border since, with lighting and more agents on the ground, but the fence remains in place, says Tom Fullerton, an economist at the University of Texas, El Paso. "You can't go more than 30 feet without finding spots where either holes have been cut or repaired," he says.

Some see the Tortilla Curtain as the primitive forerunner of today's fence. Before the U.S. government embraced the idea, however, policy would once again veer in a different direction. During the Reagan administration, "Congress allowed people who had been in the United States illegally for a number of years to apply for citizenship," says Staudt, of the University of Texas, El Paso. [37]

But the Immigration Reform and Control Act of 1986 — what some call the "amnesty bill" — did little to stem the flow of illegal immigrants, so anti-immigration sentiment continued to grow in Border States. The Clinton administration reacted with operations "Hold

Critics Say Fence Disrupts Wildlife

Border fence is 'stopping wildlife in their tracks.'

The San Pedro River in Arizona — one of only two major rivers that flow north from Mexico into the United States — provides habitat to an astonishing variety of birds and small mammals. It also serves as a watering hole for deer, mountain lions, bobcats and possibly even jaguars as they range across the arid Sonoran Desert in Mexico and the United States.

The U.S. government recognized the importance of the San Pedro and the surrounding landscape when it created the San Pedro Riparian National Conservation Area — a 57,000-acre refuge for the animals and plants of the region's fragile desert riparian ecosystem, one of the few remaining in the American Southwest.

But today the area is also home to a section of the new border fence, slicing the desert landscape in half as it stretches east from the riverbank. Much of America's new fencing is being built on environmentally sensitive public lands, which critics fear could have disastrous consequences, especially for wildlife.

"You can call this a fence, but to animals it's an impenetrable barrier," says Matt Clark, Southwest representative for Defenders of Wildlife, an organization dedicated to the preservation of wild animals and native plants. "It's between 14 and 18 feet tall; it goes on for miles; it's not something they can jump over or circumvent. It might not be very effective at stopping people, but it's stopping wildlife in their tracks."

Border barriers are being built or are planned for portions of Arizona's Cabeza Prieta National Wildlife Refuge and the Organ Pipe National Monument. In Texas, new fencing is planned near Big Bend National Park and on the Lower Rio Grande Valley National Wildlife Refuge. In California, the federal government is even filling in a canyon, Smuggler's Gulch, with more than 2 million cubic yards of dirt so it can run a fence across it.

Environmental concerns differ by area, but in general the fence divides the breeding and hunting territories of many species, separating animals from food, water or potential mates, according to wildlife advocates. Sometimes the animals have already had their habitat reduced or disrupted by development, and their populations cannot afford to be split in two.

"With isolation comes a lack of genetic exchange — a lack of genetic diversity, which makes these populations less fit to survive," says Clark.

The impact of new border barriers could be particularly acute in the Lower Rio Grande Valley refuge, according to Scott Nicol, a member of the Texas-based No Border Wall citizens' coalition.

The 90,000-acre refuge consists of 115 separate plots along the Rio Grande River, designed so wildlife can use the river as a corridor to move from one plot to another. But they would be blocked if the government builds new barriers along the river levees as now planned, Nicol says. "You

the Line" in El Paso in 1993 and "Gatekeeper" in San Diego the following year. Border Patrol agents and technology were concentrated in these areas, and fencing was either built or reinforced. [38]

Both operations dramatically reduced illegal immigration in the targeted locations, although illegal crossings did not fall significantly overall. But Congress seemed to judge the approach a success. A series of bills then expanded the Border Patrol, increased money for security measures and, after 9/11, gave the new Homeland Security secretary the authority to ignore laws that might slow fence construction.

Although President Bush pushed for a comprehensive immigration-reform package that would have included guest-worker and limited-amnesty programs, Congress remained focused on enforcement. The Secure Fence Act of 2006 mandated double-layer security fencing along significant parts of the border. That requirement was later modified to give Secretary Chertoff more latitude, but the message was clear: America was building a border fence.

Facing the Fence

In 2006, more than 90 percent of the 1.2 million illegal migrants apprehended by the Border Patrol were caught

put a wall there that keeps animals from getting to the river," he explains, "and the individual plots are not large enough to support them."

Among the rare or endangered species threatened by the fence, says Clark, are jaguars, Sonoran pronghorn antelopes, ocelots, jaguarundi, flat-tailed horned lizards and the Cactus Ferruginous Pygmy Owl. A bird may seem an unlikely victim of a 14-foot fence, but wildlife advocates say the fence threatens the habitat for many birds. "You have barriers that can catch debris and sediment, create artificial dams, shifting water flows, impacting the vegetation," Clark says. "All of this does damage."

The ability of the jaguar and other animals to range between Mexico's Sonoran Desert and the Southwestern United States may be blocked by the border fence.

AFP/Getty Images/Elmer Martinez

we need to do to mitigate risk to the environment. Our goal is to make sure we leave the environment in better condition than we found it."

The border fence is being built in several different styles. Some of the most recent, described as "bollard" fencing, is made of round, concrete-filled poles spaced six inches apart in a staggered pattern. In Arizona, bollard fencing is being constructed in the washes, which run with water in the rainy season. Border Patrol officials believe bollard fences are more eco-friendly, because water can flow around the poles and because small animals and reptiles can pass between them. But environmentalists doubt this will be enough to prevent erosion and habitat damage.

Department of Homeland Security Secretary Michael Chertoff has used authority granted by Congress to waive compliance with environmental laws in several areas as he proceeds with the fence, a move that upset local officials and led to a lawsuit by Defenders of Wildlife and the Sierra Club. (See "Current Situation," p. 232.)

Customs and Border Protection officials say they are still working to protect native plants and animals. "Even though the secretary used his waiver authority to keep moving this process forward, we're not disregarding environmental considerations at all," says Jason Ahern, Customs and Border Protection deputy commissioner. "We're looking at what

The fence's advocates point out that illegal immigrants are already damaging fragile desert lands. "When hundreds of thousands of people are hiking through pristine ecosystems, setting fires, dumping trash and abandoning vehicles, building a fence that can drastically reduce that destruction is a good thing," says Rosemary Jenks, governmental affairs director for NumbersUSA, which supports reducing both legal and illegal immigration.

But trails and trash can be cleaned up, Clark says. "The wall has significantly more impact," he adds, "because of its magnitude and because it's permanent."

along the border with Mexico — nearly 88 percent of them Mexicans. But U.S. authorities also picked up nearly 150,000 people from 197 other countries. (See graphic, p. 215.)

The largest number, after Mexicans, came from Central America. In 2006, there were 46,329 illegal immigrants from El Salvador, 33,365 from Honduras and 25,135 from Guatemala. Many were twice illegal, having first entered Mexico without papers and then the United States.

The arduous and dangerous effort to enter the United States is a sign of border-crossers' determination. In *Enrique's Journey, The Story of a Boy's Dangerous Odyssey*

to Reunite with His Mother, journalist Sonia Nazario traced the 1,600-mile cross-Mexico migration made by thousands of Central American children following their mothers to the United States. Many were turned back repeatedly but refused to quit. Enrique, the boy she followed, finally succeeded in making it all the way into the United States on his eighth attempt. [39]

Nazario's book also illuminated a little-noticed trend: An increasing number of women have been making the journey alone, followed by an increasing number of their children. Nazario estimates about 48,000 children a year enter the United States illegally. Mexican railroad workers report children as young as 7 trying to cross their country alone traveling to the United States. [40]

With little or no knowledge of what they are facing, these illegal migrants seem unlikely to give up their journey because of the fence. The Center for Comparative Immigration Studies found similar determination. Briseida, a 24-year-old woman from Oaxaca, recounted being caught six times in a single month before making it into the United States. [41]

Research also indicates that most illegal immigrants had jobs in Mexico but thought the United States offered greater opportunity. "Ninety-three percent of undocumented Mexican immigrants left jobs in Mexico," says Robert Pastor, director of the Center for North American Studies at American University in Washington. "They're not coming to the United States for jobs. They're coming because they can earn six to 10 times more."

CURRENT SITUATION

Local Blowback

America's new border fence may represent a national commitment by the Bush administration, but it's also a matter of local politics. For many who live on the border, the fence isn't being built along some abstract line, it's going through their community, or neighborhood or even backyard.

In the Rio Grande Valley in Texas, in particular, local concerns are sparking a battle that pits communities in President Bush's home state against his administration. The Texas Border Coalition, made up of mayors, economists and business leaders from 19 municipalities and 10 counties in the valley, in May sued the Department of Homeland Security, alleging it is ignoring due process and abusing private property rights in its rush to put up the fence.

"We didn't want to file this lawsuit, but we felt we had no choice," says coalition Chairman Chad Foster, the mayor of Eagle Pass, a border town of about 22,000. "We just want the government to follow the law."

The anti-fence blowback has been triggered by tactics adopted by the Department of Homeland Security to speed construction. When some property owners refused to give the Corps of Engineers permission to survey for the fence on their land, the Corps sent landowners letters threatening a lawsuit and raising the possibility of seizing their property through eminent domain. [42]

Landowners responded by challenging the government in court. "I don't think they counted on anybody standing up to them," says Eloisa Tamez, who lives on a three-acre plot along the Rio Grande that has been in her family for nearly 250 years. "We're not big, powerful people here. We respect our government. But we're not just going to lay down and let the bulldozer roll over us."

In January, a federal judge ordered 10 property owners along the border — including Tamez — to permit the surveying, but only after denying the government the right to take the land without a hearing. [43] The government's actions against individual landowners, however, are not the only ones provoking indignation.

In Eagle Pass, for example, the City Council met with Homeland Security in 2006 over the department's plans to leave a city park and golf course south of the proposed barrier. "They were going to cede our municipal golf course and a city park to Mexico," he says. "We had a resolution to oppose it, and they said they would allow us to delete the fence. But they came back a year later and sued us. We can't trust them."

Because the fence is being located on or outside of flood control levees, in several Texas locations the preliminary site is inside the U.S. border. In the small town of Granjeno, for instance, about 35 landowners found they might end up on the wrong side of the border fence. [44] In Brownsville, the proposed fence will run through the University of Texas campus, leaving some facilities south of the barrier. Campus officials say they are working with Homeland Security to resolve the situation. [45]

Homeland Security said it places a high priority on feedback from local residents. Since May 2007, the agency has held 100 meetings with local officials and 600 with individual property holders along the Southwest border. [46]

CBP Deputy Commissioner Ahern says siting the fence has been a painstaking process. "We looked at enforcement data," he says. "We looked at geography. We looked at landscape. We looked at alternatives. This was a thoughtful and detailed analysis by both local and national Border Patrol leadership."

But some Texans believe politics plays a role. The Texas Border Coalition lawsuit asserts that Homeland Security is violating the Fifth Amendment's Equal Protection provision by "giving certain politically well-connected property owners a pass on having the border fence built on their property," according to the coalition's Web site.

Is a border fence the answer to the illegal immigration problem?

YES Rep. Duncan Hunter, R-Calif.

Written for *CQ Researcher*, September 2008

A battle is being waged for control of the U.S.-Mexican border between the U.S. Border Patrol and criminals who utilize this largely unprotected land corridor to carry narcotics and other contraband into the United States. Citizens on both sides of the border, whose safety is seriously threatened by escalating violence, are caught in the middle.

Last year drug-war violence claimed least 2,500 lives in Mexico, and numerous U.S. citizens reportedly have been kidnapped and murdered by Mexican criminals linked to the drug trade. The local sheriff in the Laredo, Texas, border community compared conditions there to a "war zone" and said his officers appear "outgunned" by the drug cartels.

Border Patrol agents are also at risk, because they often are the first to encounter these criminals. Since 2001, assaults against agents have nearly tripled, from 335 to 987 in 2007. Four agents and three other border security officials were killed last year, and two agents have been killed so far in 2008.

The land corridor between Tijuana, Mexico, and San Diego, Calif., has been overrun by smugglers and criminals. It wasn't until my legislation mandating construction of the San Diego border fence that the armed gangs and drug cartels lost control of this smuggling route. Since then, conditions on both sides of the border have improved.

Since construction of the border fence began in 1996, San Diego County has become one of the most secure and responsibly enforced border regions. Smuggling of people and narcotics in this area has decreased by more than 90 percent, and violent crime has declined by 53 percent.

Such a high level of effectiveness illustrates that fencing — supported with the right mix of personnel and technology — is an excellent border enforcement tool.

The Department of Homeland Security (DHS) is accelerating fence construction in several areas along the border, rightly utilizing its broad waiver authority to expedite completion in locations subject to unnecessary delays and litigation. DHS expects to meet its goal of 670 miles of new fence by the end of this year, but overall a lot of work remains in creating an enforceable border.

Moving forward, it would be wise to extend this infrastructure to other smuggling routes and heavily transited areas of the U.S.-Mexican border. Not only is it the quickest and easiest way to control the border, but it's also proven to be the most effective.

NO Rep. Silvestre Reyes, D-Texas
Former El Paso Sector Chief, U.S. Border Patrol

Written for *CQ Researcher*, September 2008

I am acutely aware of the challenges of securing our borders, having served for more than 26 years with the U.S. Border Patrol. I have not only patrolled the U.S.-Mexican border but also supervised thousands of hard-working, dedicated Border Patrol agents and initiated a successful deterrence strategy called Operation Hold the Line. I also supported fencing certain strategic areas to augment enforcement. I strongly feel, however, that erecting nearly 700 miles of fencing on our Southern border is wasteful, irresponsible and unnecessary, and I voted against the Secure Fence Act.

Hundreds of miles of fencing will do little to curb the flow of undocumented immigrants and could even increase demand for human smuggling. It will only provide a false sense of security for supporters of a hard line on immigration reform. With construction expected to exceed $1.2 billion and lifetime maintenance of up to $50 billion, the exorbitant cost of this border fence would be better invested in additional Border Patrol agents, equipment and technology.

As the only member of Congress with a background in border control, I have worked to educate my colleagues that existing policies and the border fence will do little to honor our legacy as a nation of immigrants and will threaten our nation's security. I have worked with the Department of Homeland Security (DHS), hosted many leaders at annual border conferences and have emphasized that border communities must be consulted in fencing decisions.

Unfortunately, DHS Secretary Michael Chertoff recently made the troubling announcement that he intends to waive more than 30 federal environmental laws to expedite construction of the fence. This approach continues DHS's continued disregard for border communities and undermines decades-old policies that have preserved many of our region's most valuable environmental assets, cultural sites and endangered wildlife.

After Secretary Chertoff's decision, I joined 13 of my colleagues in submitting an *amicus* brief to the U.S. Supreme Court, asking the justices to hear an appeal challenging the secretary's waiver authority.

Our nation needs comprehensive immigration reform with three main components: strengthened border security; an earned path to legalization along with tough, strictly enforced sanctions against employers who hire undocumented immigrants; and a guest worker program. Hundreds of miles of border fencing is not the answer.

Specifically, the coalition refers to media reports the fence is being built through city and county-owned land while bypassing land owned by Dallas billionaire Ray Hunt, a close friend of President Bush who recently donated $35 million to help build the George W. Bush Memorial Library at Southern Methodist University.

The coalition's allegations brought a sharp response from Ahern. "I reject the idea out of hand," he says. "Our analysis of where to locate the fence was based on the operational and tactical requirements in a given area, not on who owned the land or whether they were influential individuals."

Legal Challenges

Even as construction continues, however, Chertoff faces another challenge that has the active support of several members of Congress. Last spring Chertoff used the broad authority granted him by Congress to waive more than 30 environmental-, historical- and cultural-protection laws and regulations to enable fence construction to proceed.

"Criminal activity at the border does not stop for endless debate or protracted litigation," Chertoff said in the statement announcing the decision. [47]

The Sierra Club and Defenders of Wildlife already had sued Homeland Security over an earlier, more limited waiver allowing fence construction to continue in the San Pedro Riparian National Conservation Area in Arizona, home to many rare and endangered species of plants and animals. The environmental groups feared that the fence would block migratory patterns and access to water and habitat for several endangered animals and that construction could harm certain rare plants. (*See sidebar, p. 226.*)

A federal judge ruled against their claim, which challenged the constitutionality of the secretary's waiver authority. The fence is now up in the conservation area. After Chertoff expanded his use of waivers to cover construction of the entire fence, the environmental groups asked the Supreme Court to hear their case; in July the court refused to take the case.

Before the court's decision, however, the lawsuit had been joined by 14 Democratic House members, including Mississippi Rep. Bennie Thompson, chairman of the Homeland Security Committee, and several lawmakers from border districts. Their friend-of-the-court briefs argued that Congress overstepped its constitutional bounds when it allowed the secretary to ignore laws.

On the other side, Rep. Peter King, R-N.Y., ranking minority member of the House Homeland Security Committee, backed Chertoff's use of waivers. "He's acting entirely within the law, and any attempts to impede the fence's progress through frivolous litigation will only serve to lessen the security of our country," King said. 48

Noah Kahn, an expert on federal lands at Defenders of Wildlife, says Chertoff's decision to bypass laws intended to provide a thorough review of environmental and cultural impacts makes it impossible to determine whether there were other options, such as better use of surveillance technology in environmentally sensitive areas. "One of the basic problems is the complete lack of transparency in the way the Department of Homeland Security has carried out this entire process," says Kahn. "They've completely ignored not just communities and other public partners but even other federal agencies in their deliberations."

Cindy Alvarez, who oversaw an environmental assessment of the fence in the San Pedro conservation area, defends the agencies building the fence. "Once the waiver came into play, it took it out of our hands," says Alvarez, assistant field manager of the U.S. Bureau of Land Management's Tucson office. "But that said, the Border Patrol and the Corps of Engineers are continuing to try to be good land stewards while meeting the nature of their missions. They are continuing to work with us."

Homeland Security's critics are skeptical. "The only reason you waive the laws is because you're planning on breaking them," says Scott Nicol, a member of the No Border Wall Coalition, a citizens' group in Texas.

The Tohono O'odham Indian Nation, which straddles the border, has also been concerned about Chertoff's use of waivers. The tribe has so far agreed to allow vehicle barriers, but not pedestrian fencing, on tribal lands but is weighing its options concerning the waivers, says Pete Delgado, a tribal spokesman. With more fencing planned for environmentally and culturally sensitive areas in both Texas and California, further legal challenges to Chertoff's authority and the fence's route seem almost inevitable.

Straddling the Fence

Nothing illustrates the complicated political fault lines that run through the border fence debate better than the way the presidential nominees have straddled the issue.

By voting for the Secure Fence Act of 2006, both GOP candidate Sen. John McCain, R-Ariz., and Democratic contender Sen. Barack Obama, D-Ill., voted to authorize the dramatic expansion of border fencing now under way. A year later, presumably busy campaigning, they missed the key votes on the Consolidated Appropriations Act, which gave the Homeland Security secretary more latitude on when and where to locate the fencing.

Since then, McCain and Obama have sent conflicting messages about what they think now that the fence is actually being built. Obama's campaign Web site calls for preserving "the integrity of our borders" and says the candidate supports "additional personnel, infrastructure and technology on the border and at our ports of entry."

But when a question about the border fence came up during a primary campaign debate with Sen. Hillary Rodham Clinton, D-N.Y., in Texas, Obama struck a skeptical note about the fence now being built. After Clinton criticized the Bush administration's approach and called for more personnel and better technology instead of a physical barrier, Obama agreed. "There may be areas where it makes sense to have some fencing," Obama said. "But for the most part, having [the] border patrolled, surveillance, deploying effective technology, that's going to be the better approach." [49]

McCain's campaign Web site calls for "securing the border through physical and virtual barriers." But the word "fence" can't be found on McCain's Border Security Web page. In interviews, however, McCain has said he supports building a border fence in areas where it's necessary, while he believes technology can more effectively do the job in others.

Anti-immigrant groups have criticized McCain for supporting President Bush's failed comprehensive immigration reform package, which included a path for many illegal immigrants in the United States to gain citizenship. The sensitive nature of the issue in Republican circles was clear at a town meeting in Texas, when McCain was asked how he would balance individual property rights with border security.

"This meeting is adjourned," McCain joked, before saying he would look into the issue. [50] Earlier, he said he hoped federal and local officials could work together to resolve their differences over the fence.

Neither candidate's campaign press office responded to requests for further information clarifying their candidate's position.

OUTLOOK

Demographic Solution

What goes up can always come down — even if it is 670 miles long and built by the U.S. government of double-layered steel. And many critics of the border fence say that's just what will happen.

"The United States eventually will have to tear down the wall they built because the forces of globalization drawing us together are much stronger than the forces trying to tear us apart," says Payan, at the University of Texas, El Paso.

Others, particularly those concerned with the fence's impact on the environment, place their faith in technology. "Ultimately, we're going to be a lot less dependent on physical infrastructure," says Bob Barnes, a senior policy adviser at the Nature Conservancy. "Particularly in open country, virtual fencing — sensors, cameras and other surveillance technology — is a lot more mobile and can react to changing patterns of immigration more easily."

Customs and Border Protection Deputy Commissioner Ahern says the agency will continue using sensors, remote-controlled cameras, unmanned surveillance planes and other high-tech hardware. But he believes there will always be a need for fencing.

"No matter how good our technology is, in some of these areas of the border [illegal crossings are] going to be too easy," he says. "So, especially in urban environments, we're always going to need that tactical infrastructure, some kind of physical barrier."

But illegal immigration is about more than the border. It also reflects economic and political conditions in two countries, and that's where some experts believe the most significant changes will be seen, Payan suggests. Rodriguez, at the University of Houston's Center for Immigration Research, notes that the rapidly growing U.S. Latino population is likely to make anti-immigrant political posturing less acceptable in the future. [51]

At the same, he says, a little noticed demographic trend within Mexico could also shift the equation. The Mexican birthrate has been falling for decades and, Rodriguez says, is expected to decline to the replacement rate by 2050. [52] Then, the country will no longer have the surplus labor it now exports to the United States. "If you think there are too many Mexicans," he says, "the problem eventually is that there's not going to be enough Mexicans to do the dirty work."

Other analysts believe further economic integration between the two nations will regularize the labor flow. "I can't help but think that in the future there will be a time when the North American continent will resemble the European Union," says Staudt, at the University of Texas.

Meanwhile, what happens to the border fence? Back in Eagle Pass, Texas, Mayor Foster had the most cynical view. Given the estimates of up to $47 billion to maintain it over the next 25 years, he believes it will simply be abandoned. "I think it gets turned into barbecue grills on both sides of the border," Foster says.

NOTES

1. The Associated Press poll, conducted by Ipsos Public Affairs, of 1,103 adults on March 3-5, 2008. The poll had a margin of error of +/- 3.1 percent.

2. From the Department of Homeland Security Web site, border fence update page, www.dhs.gov/xprev prot/programs/border-fence-southwest.shtm.

3. Testimony of Department of Homeland Security Secretary Michael Chertoff before the House Subcommittee on Homeland Security Appropriations, April 10, 2008. The text is available at www.dhs .gov/xnews/testimony/testimony_1207933887848 .shtm.

4. See Arthur H. Rotstein, "US scraps $20 million prototype of virtual fence," The Associated Press, April 23, 2008, www.cbsnews.com/stories/2008/04/23/ tech/main4037342.shtml?source=related_story. Also see Brady McCombs, " 'Virtual fence' work is halted," *Arizona Daily Star*, Aug. 19, 2008, www.azstarnet. com/metro/253456.

5. See the Border Fence Project Web site, www.borderfenceproject.com/index.shtml, one of several citizens' groups that propose fencing the entire border.

6. See the Humane Borders Web site, www.humane borders.org/, one of several organizations that object to the fence.

7. Estimates of the annual number of illegal border crossers and the total illegal population vary widely. But an analysis of Census Bureau data by the Pew Hispanic Center in March 2006 seems to provide the best, impartial estimate of annual illegal migration. The report, "The Size and Characteristics of the Unauthorized Migrant Population in the United States," also estimated the total illegal immigrant population in the United States at 11.5 million to 12 million.

8. "Homeland Security — DHS Has Taken Actions to Strengthen Border Security Programs and Operations, but Challenges Remain," testimony before the Subcommittee on Homeland Security, House Committee on Appropriations, Government Accountability Office, pp. 16, March 6, 2008.

9. "Secure Border Initiative, The Importance of Applying Lessons Learned to Future Projects," Government Accountability Office, testimony before House Homeland Security Subcommittees on Management, Investigations and Oversight and Border, Maritime and Global Counterterrorism, Feb. 27, 2008, p. 2.

10. Blas Nuñez-Neto and Yule Kim, "Border Security: Barriers along the U.S. International Border, Congressional Research Service, May 13, 2008, p. 33.

11. *Ibid.*, pp. 14-15.

12. *Ibid.*, p. 2.

13. Ray Koslowski, "Immigration Reforms and Border Security Technologies," Social Science Research Council, July 31, 2006. For background, see Mary H. Cooper, "Rethinking NAFTA," *CQ Researcher*, June 7, 1996, pp. 481-504, and David Masci, "U.S.-Mexico Relations," *CQ Researcher*, Nov. 9, 2001, pp. 921-944.

14. "Modes of Entry for the Unauthorized Migrant Population," Pew Hispanic Center, Fact Sheet, May 22, 2006, http://pewhispanic.org/files/factsheets /19.pdf.

15. Wayne Cornelius, *et al.*, "Controlling Unauthorized Immigration from Mexico: The Failure of Prevention through Deterrence and the Need for Comprehensive Reform," Center for Comprehensive Immigration Studies, June 10, 2008, pp. 2-3.

16. Becky Pallack and Mariana Alvarado Avalos, "Employer-sanctions law starting to have the intended effect," *Arizona Daily Star*, Dec. 23, 2007.

17. Howard Fischer, "Some who voted for sanctions seek rollback," *Arizona Daily Star*, Jan. 18, 2008, p. A1.

18. For background, see Peter Katel, "Prison Reform," *CQ Researcher*, April 6, 2007, pp. 289-312, and Charles S.

Clark, "Prison Overcrowding," *CQ Researcher*, Feb. 4, 1994, pp. 97-120.

19. "The Cost to Local Taxpayers for Illegal or 'Guest' Workers," Federation for American Immigration Reform, 2006, www.fairus.org.

20. Melissa Merrell, "The Impact of Unauthorized Immigrants on the Budgets of State and Local Governments," Congressional Budget Office, December 2007, p. 3.

21. *Ibid.*, p. 3.

22. Steven Camarota, "The High Cost of Cheap Labor, Illegal Immigration and the Federal Budget," Center for Immigration Studies, August 2004, p. 1.

23. Robert McNatt and Frank Benassi, Standard & Poor's Ratings Direct, as cited in *Business Week*, "Econ 101 on Illegal Immigrants," April 2006, www.businessweek.com/investor/content/apr2006/pi20060407_072803.htm.

24. "US border fence plan 'shameful' " BBC News (online), Dec. 19, 2995, http://news.bbc.co.uk/2/hi/americas/4541606.stm.

25. Nuñez-Neto and Kim, *op. cit.*, p. 40.

26. Wayne Cornelius, "Death at the Border: The Efficacy and 'Unintended' Consequences of U.S. Immigration Control Policy 1993-2000," Center for Comparative Immigration Studies, *Working Paper 27*, December 2001.

27. "President Bush Meets with President Calderon of Mexico," White House press release, April 21, 2008, www.whitehouse.gov/news/releases/2008/04/20080421-6.html.

28. "Joint Statement by President Bush, President Calderon, Prime Minister Harper," White House press release, April 22, 2008, www.whitehouse.gov/news/releases/2008/04/20080422-4.html.

29. *Journal of the Southwest*, Vol. 50, No. 3, University of Arizona, autumn 2008.

30. Derek Williams, *The Reach of Rome, A History of the Roman Imperial Frontier, 1st-5th Centuries AD* (1996), p. 111.

31. Tom Tancredo, "Mexico's Lawless Border Poses Huge Test for Washington," *Human Events*, Feb. 6, 2006.

32. Mary Beard, "Don't Blame Hadrian for Bush's Wall," *Times Literary Supplement*, April 30, 2007, http://timesonline.typepad.com/dons_life/2007/04/dont_blame_hadr.html.

33. Williams, *op. cit.*, p. 108.

34. Katherine Fennelly, "U.S. Immigration, A Historical Perspective," *The National Voter*, February 2007, p. 5.

35. Andorra Bruno, "Immigration: Policy Considerations Related to Guest Worker Programs," Congressional Research Service, June 27, 2007, p. 1.

36. PBS Interactive Border Timeline, www.pbs.org/kpbs/theborder/history/timeline/20.html.

37. For background, see Hank Donnelly, "Immigration," *Editorial Research Reports*, June 13, 1986, available at *CQ Researcher Plus Archive*. Also see Kenneth Jost, "Cracking Down on Immigration," *CQ Researcher*, Feb. 3, 1995, pp. 97-120; and Alan Greenblatt, "Immigration Debate," *CQ Researcher*, Feb. 1, 2008, pp. 97-120.

38. "Border Patrol History," U.S. Customs and Border Protection, www.cbp.gov/xp/cgov/border_security/border_patrol/border_patrol_ohs/history.xml.

39. Sonia Nazario, *Enrique's Journey, The Story of a Boy's Dangerous Odyssey to Reunite With his Mother* (2006).

40. *Ibid.*, pp. 5-6.

41. Cornelius, *et al.*, *op. cit.*, June 10, 2008, p. 2.

42. Ralph Blumenthal, "In Texas, Weighing Life with a Border Fence," *The New York Times*, Jan. 13, 2008. For background, see Kenneth Jost, "Property Rights," *CQ Researcher*, March 4, 2005, pp. 197-220.

43. "Opponents of Border Fence Lose Round in Court," The Associated Press, *The New York Times*, Jan. 29, 2008.

44. Alicia Caldwell, The Associated Press, "Border Fence Could Cut through Backyards," *USA Today*, Nov. 11, 2007.

45. See "Updated Border Fence Information," University of Texas, Brownsville, www.utb.edu.

46. "DHS Exercises Waiver Authority to Expedite Advancement in Border Security," Department of Homeland Security press release, April 1, 2008.

47. *Ibid.*

48. "Key House Democrats Join Suit Against Use of Waivers for Border Fence," *Congressional Quarterly Today*, April 16, 2008.

Conditions on Reservations Improved

Socioeconomic conditions improved more on reservations with gambling than on those without gaming during the 1990s, although non-gaming reservations also improved substantially, especially compared to the U.S. population. Some experts attribute the progress among non-gaming tribes to an increase in self-governance on many reservations.

Socioeconomic Changes on Reservations, 1990-2000*
(shown as a percentage or percentage points)

	Non-Gaming	Gaming	U.S.
Real per-capita income	+21.0%	+36.0%	+11.0%
Median household income	+14.0%	+35.0%	+4.0%
Family poverty	-6.9	-11.8	-0.8
Child poverty	-8.1	-11.6	-1.7
Deep poverty	-1.4	-3.4	-0.4
Public assistance	+0.7	-1.6	+0.3
Unemployment	-1.8	-4.8	-0.5
Labor force participation	-1.6	+1.6	-1.3
Overcrowded homes	-1.3	-0.1	+1.1
Homes lacking complete plumbing	-4.6	-3.3	-0.1
Homes lacking complete kitchen	+1.3	-0.6	+0.2
College graduates	+1.7	+2.6	+4.2
High school or equivalency only	-0.3	+1.8	-1.4
Less than 9th-grade education	-5.5	-6.3	-2.8

* The reservation population of the Navajo Nation, which did not have gambling in the 1990s, was not included because it is so large (175,000 in 2000) that it tends to pull down Indian averages when it is included.

Source: Jonathan B. Taylor and Joseph P. Kalt, "Cabazon, The Indian Gaming Regulatory Act, and the Socioeconomic Consequences of American Indian Governmental Gaming: A Ten-Year Review, American Indians on Reservations: A Databook of Socioeconomic Change Between the 1990 and 2000 Censuses," Harvard Project on American Indian Economic Development, January 2005

of Sinte Gleska University, on the Rosebud Sioux Reservation in South Dakota. "We're at the bottom rung of the ladder in all areas, whether it's education levels, economic achievement or political status." [2]

National statistics aren't much better:

- Indian unemployment on reservations nationwide is 49 percent — 10 times the national rate. [3]
- The on-reservation family poverty rate in 2000 was 37 percent — four times the national figure of 9 percent. [4]

- Nearly one in five Indians age 25 or older in tribes without gambling operations had less than a ninth-grade education. But even members of tribes with gambling had a college graduation rate of only 16 percent, about half the national percentage. [5]
- Death rates from alcoholism and tuberculosis among Native Americans are at least 650 percent higher than overall U.S. rates. [6]
- Indian youths commit suicide at nearly triple the rate of young people in general. [7]
- Indians on reservations, especially in the resource-poor Upper Plains and West, are the nation's third-largest group of methemphetamine users. [8]

The immediate prognosis for the nation's 4.4 million Native Americans is bleak, according to the Harvard Project on American Indian Economic Development. "If U.S. and on-reservation Indian per-capita income were to continue to grow at their 1990s' rates," it said, "it would take half a century for the tribes to catch up." [9]

Nonetheless, there has been forward movement in Indian Country, though it is measured in modest steps. Among the marks of recent progress:

- Per-capita income rose 20 percent on reservations, to $7,942, (and 36 percent in tribes with casinos, to $9,771), in contrast to an 11 percent overall U.S. growth rate. [10]
- Unemployment has dropped by up to 5 percent on reservations and in other predominantly Indian areas. [11]
- Child poverty in non-gaming tribes dropped from 55 percent of the child population to 44 percent (but the Indian rate is still more than double the 17 percent average nationwide). [12]

More than two centuries of court decisions, treaties and laws have created a complicated system of coexistence between tribes and the rest of the country. On one level, tribes are sovereign entities that enjoy a government-to-government relationship with Washington. But the sovereignty is qualified. In the words of an 1831 Supreme Court decision that is a bedrock of Indian law, tribes are "domestic dependent nations." [13]

The blend of autonomy and dependence grows out of the Indians' reliance on Washington for sheer survival, says Robert A. Williams Jr., a law professor at the University of Arizona and a member of North Carolina's Lumbee Tribe. "Indians insisted in their treaties that the Great White Father protect us from these racial maniacs in the states — where racial discrimination was most developed — and guarantee us a right to education, a right to water, a territorial base, a homeland," he says. "Tribes sold an awful lot of land in return for a trust relationship to keep the tribes going."

Today, the practical meaning of the relationship with Washington is that American Indians on reservations, and to some extent those elsewhere, depend entirely or partly on federal funding for health, education and other needs. Tribes with casinos and other businesses lessen their reliance on federal dollars.

Unlike other local governments, tribes don't have a tax base whose revenues they share with state governments. Federal spending on Indian programs of all kinds nationwide currently amounts to about $11 billion, James Cason, associate deputy secretary of the Interior, told the Senate Indian Affairs Committee in February.

But the abysmal conditions under which many American Indians live make it all too clear that isn't enough, Indians say. "This is always a discussion at our tribal leaders' meetings," says Cecilia Fire Thunder, president of the Oglala Sioux Tribe in Pine Ridge, S.D. "The biggest job that tribal leaders have is to see that the government lives up to its responsibilities to our people. It's a battle that never ends."

Indeed, a decades-old class-action suit alleges systematic mismanagement of billions of dollars in Indian-owned assets by the Interior Department — a case that has prompted withering criticism of the department by the judge (*see p. 253*).

Government officials insist that, despite orders to cut spending, they've been able to keep providing essential services. Charles Grim, director of the Indian Health

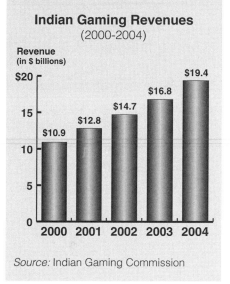

Revenues From Casinos Almost Doubled

Revenue from Indian gaming operations nearly doubled to $19.4 billion from 2000-2004. The number of Indian casinos increased from 311 to 367 during the period.

Indian Gaming Revenues
(2000-2004)

Revenue
(in $ billions)

Year	Revenue
2000	$10.9
2001	$12.8
2002	$14.7
2003	$16.8
2004	$19.4

Source: Indian Gaming Commission

Service, told the Indian Affairs Committee, "In a deficit-reduction year, it's a very strong budget and one that does keep pace with inflationary and population-growth increases."

In any event, from the tribes' point of view, they lack the political muscle to force major increases. "The big problem is the Indians are about 1 percent of the national population," says Joseph Kalt, co-director of the Harvard Project. "The voice is so tiny."

Faced with that grim political reality, Indians are trying to make better use of scarce federal dollars through a federally sponsored "self-governance" movement. Leaders of the movement say tribes can deliver higher-quality services more efficiently when they control their own budgets. Traditionally, federal agencies operate programs on reservations, such as law enforcement or medical services.

But since the 1990s, dozens of tribes have stepped up control of their own affairs both by building their own

AP Photo/William Lauer

Controversial Whiteclay, Neb., sells millions of cans of beer annually to residents of the nearby Pine Ridge Reservation in South Dakota. Alcohol abuse and unemployment continue to plague the American Indian community.

businesses and by signing self-governance "compacts" with the federal government. Compacts provide tribes with large chunks of money, or block grants, rather than individual grants for each service. Then, with minimal federal oversight, the tribes develop their own budgets and run all or most services.

The self-governance trend gathered steam during the same time that Indian-owned casinos began booming. For many tribes, the gambling business provided a revenue stream that didn't flow from Washington.

According to economist Alan Meister, 228 tribes in 30 states operated 367 high-stakes bingo halls or casinos in 2004, earning an estimated $19.6 billion. [14]

The gambling houses operate under the 1988 Indian Gaming Regulatory Act (IGRA), which was made possible by a U.S. Supreme Court ruling upholding tribes' rights to govern their own activities. [15] A handful of tribes are doing so well that $80 million from six tribes in 2000-2003 helped fuel the scandal surrounding onetime Washington super-lobbyist Jack Abramoff, whose clients were among the most successful casino tribes. [16]

If the Abramoff scandal contributed to the notion of widespread Indian wealth, one reason may be the misimpression that tribes don't pay taxes on their gambling earnings. In fact, under the IGRA, federal, state and local governments took in $6.3 billion in gambling-generated

tax revenues in 2004, with 67 percent going to the federal government. In addition, tribes paid out some $889 million in 2004 to state and local governments in order to get gambling operations approved. [17]

The spread of casinos has prompted some cities and counties, along with citizens' groups and even some casino-operating tribes, to resist casino-expansion plans.

The opposition to expansion is another reason tribal entrepreneur Morgan doesn't think gaming is a good long-range bet for Indians' future. His vision involves full tribal control of the Indians' main asset — their land. He argues for ending the "trust status" under which tribes can't buy or sell reservation property — a relic of 19th-century protection against rapacious state governments.

Indian Country needs a better business climate, Morgan says, and the availability of land as collateral for investments would be a big step in that direction. "America has a wonderful economic system, probably the best in the world, but the reservation tends to be an economic black hole."

As Indians seek to improve their lives, here are some of the issues being debated:

Is the federal government neglecting Native Americans?

There is wide agreement that the federal government bears overwhelming responsibility for Indians' welfare, but U.S. and tribal officials disagree over the adequacy of the aid Indians receive. Sen. John McCain, R-Ariz., chairman of the Senate Indian Affairs Committee, and Vice Chairman Byron L. Dorgan, D-N.D., have been leading the fight for more aid to Indians. "We have a full-blown crisis . . . particularly dealing with children and elderly, with respect to housing, education and health care," Dorgan told the committee on Feb. 14. He characterized administration proposals as nothing more than "nibbling around the edges on these issues . . . making a few adjustments here or there.' "

Administration officials respond that given the severe federal deficit, they are focusing on protecting vital programs. "As we went through and prioritized our budget, we basically looked at all of the programs that were secondary and tertiary programs, and they were the first ones on the block to give tradeoffs for our core programs in maintaining the integrity of those," Interior's Cason told the committee.

For Indians on isolated reservations, says Bordeaux of the Rosebud Sioux, there's little alternative to federal money. He compares tribes' present circumstances to those after the buffalo had been killed off, and an Army general told the Indians to eat beef, which made them sick. "The general told them, 'Either that, or you eat the grass on which you stand.' "

But David B. Vickers, president of Upstate Citizens for Equality, in Union Springs, N.Y., which opposes Indian land claims and casino applications, argues that accusations of federal neglect are inaccurate and skirt the real problem. The central issue is that the constitutional system is based on individual rights, not tribal rights, he says. "Indians are major recipients of welfare now. They're eligible. They don't need a tribe or leader; all they have to do is apply like anybody else."

Pat Ragsdale, director of the Bureau of Indian Affairs (BIA), acknowledges that Dorgan's and McCain's criticisms echo a 2003 U.S. Commission on Civil Rights report, which also called underfunding of Indian aid a crisis. "The government is failing to live up to its trust responsibility to Native peoples," the commission concluded. "Efforts to bring Native Americans up to the standards of other Americans have failed in part because of a lack of sustained funding. The failure manifests itself in massive and escalating unmet needs." [18]

"Nobody in this government disputes the report, in general," says Ragsdale, a Cherokee. "Some of our tribal communities are in real critical shape, and others are prospering."

The commission found, for example, that in 2003 the Indian Health Service appropriation amounted to $2,533 per capita — below even the $3,803 per capita appropriated for federal prisoners.

Concern over funding for Indian programs in 2007 centers largely on health and education. Although 90 percent of Indian students attend state-operated public schools, their schools get federal aid because tribes don't pay property taxes, which typically fund public schools. The remaining 10 percent of Indian students attend schools operated by the BIA or by tribes themselves under BIA contracts.

"There is not a congressman or senator who would send his own children or grandchildren to our schools," said Ryan Wilson, president of the National Indian Education Association, citing "crumbling buildings and outdated structures with lead in the pipes and mold on the walls." [19]

Cason told the Indian Affairs Committee the administration is proposing a $49 million cut, from $157.4 million to $108.1 million, in school construction and repair in 2007. He also said that only 10 of 37 dilapidated schools funded for replacement by 2006 have been completed, with another 19 scheduled to finish in 2007. Likewise, he said the department is also behind on 45 school improvement projects.

McCain questioned whether BIA schools and public schools with large Indian enrollments would be able to meet the requirements set by the national No Child Left Behind Law. [20] Yes, replied Darla Marburger, deputy assistant secretary of Education for policy. "For the first time, we'll be providing money to . . . take a look at how students are achieving in ways that they can tailor their programs to better meet the needs of students." Overall, the Department of Education would spend about $1 billion on Indian education under the administration's proposed budget for 2007, or $6 million less than in 2006.

McCain and Dorgan are also among those concerned about administration plans to eliminate the Indian Health Service's $32.7 million urban program, which this year made medical and counseling services available to some 430,000 off-reservation Indians at 41 medical facilities in cities around the nation. (*See Sidebar, p. 250.*) The administration argues that the services were available through other programs, but McCain and Dorgan noted that "no evaluation or evidence has been provided to support this contention." [21]

Indian Health Service spokesman Thomas Sweeney, a member of the Citizen Potawatomi Nation of Oklahoma, says only 72,703 Indians used urban health centers in 2004 and that expansion of another federal program would pick up the slack. [22]

In Seattle, elimination of the urban program would cut $4 million from the city's Indian Health Board budget, says Executive Director Ralph Forquera. "Why pick on a $33 million appropriation?" he asks. In his skeptical view, the proposal reflects another "unspoken" termination program. You take a sub-population — urban Indians — and eliminate funding, then [you target] tribes under 1,000 members, and there are a lot of them. Little by little, you pick apart the system."

The IHS's Grim told the Senate committee on Feb. 14 the cuts were designed to protect funding that "can be used most effectively to improve the health status of American Indian and Alaskan Native people."

Have casinos benefited Indians?

Over the past two decades, Indian casinos have become powerful economic engines for many tribal economies. But the enthusiasm for casinos is not unanimous.

"If you're looking at casinos in terms of how they've actually raised the status of Indian people, they've been an abysmal failure," says Ted Jojola, a professor of planning at the University of New Mexico and a member of Isleta Pueblo, near Albuquerque. "But in terms of augmenting the original federal trust-responsibility areas — education, health, tribal government — they've been a spectacular success. Successful gaming tribes have ploughed the money either into diversifying their economies or they've augmented funds that would have come to them anyway."

Tribes with casinos near big population centers are flourishing. The Coushatta Tribe's casino near Lake Charles, La., generates $300 million a year, enough to provide about $40,000 to every member. [23] And the fabled Foxwoods Resort Casino south of Norwich, Conn., operated by the Mashantucket Pequot Tribe, together with Connecticut's other big casino, the Mohegan Tribe's Mohegan Sun, grossed $2.2 billion just from gambling in 2004. [24]

There are only about 830 Coushattas, so their benefits also include free health care, education and favorable terms on home purchases. [25] The once poverty-stricken Mashantuckets have created Connecticut's most extensive welfare-to-work program, open to both tribe members and non-members. In 1997-2000, the program helped 150 welfare recipients find jobs. [26]

Most tribes don't enjoy success on that scale. Among the nation's 367 Indian gambling operations, only 15 grossed $250 million or more in 2004 (another 40 earned $100 million to $250 million); 94 earned less than $3 million and 57 earned $3 million to $10 million. [27]

"We have a small casino that provides close to $3 million to the tribal nation as a whole," says Bordeaux, on the Rosebud Sioux Reservation. The revenue has been channeled into the tribe's Head Start program, an emergency home-repair fund and other projects. W. Ron Allen, chairman of the Jamestown S'Klallam Tribe in Sequim, Wash., says his tribe's small casino has raised living standards so much that some two-dozen students a year go to college, instead of one or two.

Efforts to open additional casinos are creating conflicts between tribes that operate competing casinos, as well as with some of their non-Indian neighbors. Convicted lobbyist Abramoff, for example, was paid millions of dollars by tribes seeking to block other tribal casinos. [28]

Some non-Indian communities also oppose casino expansion. "We firmly believe a large, generally unregulated casino will fundamentally change the character of our community forever," said Liz Thomas, a member of Tax Payers of Michigan Against Casinos, which opposes a casino planned by the Pokagon Band of Potawotami Indians Tribe in the Lake Michigan town of New Buffalo, where Taylor and her husband operate a small resort.

"People are OK with Donald Trump making millions of dollars individually," says Joseph Podlasek, executive director of the American Indian Center of Chicago, "but if a race of people is trying to become self-sufficient, now that's not respectable."

Nevertheless, some American Indians have mixed feelings about the casino route to economic development. "I don't think anyone would have picked casinos" for that purpose, says the University of Arizona's Williams. "Am I ambivalent about it? Absolutely. But I'm not ambivalent about a new fire station, or Kevlar vests for tribal police fighting meth gangs."

"There's no question that some of the money has been used for worthwhile purposes," concedes Guy Clark, a Corrales, N.M., dentist who chairs the National Coalition Against Legalized Gambling. But, he adds, "If you do a cost-benefit analysis, the cost is much greater than the benefit." Restaurants and other businesses, for example, lose customers who often gamble away their extra money.

Even some Indian leaders whose tribes profit from casinos raise caution flags, especially about per-capita payments. For Nebraska's Winnebagos, payments amount to just a few hundred dollars, says CEO Morgan. What bothers him are dividends "that are just big enough that you don't have to work or get educated — say, $20,000 to $40,000."

But there's no denying the impact casinos can have. At a January public hearing on the Oneida Indian Nation's attempt to put 17,000 acres of upstate New York land into tax-free "trust" status, hundreds of the 4,500 employees of the tribe's Turning Stone Resort and Casino, near Utica, showed up in support. "When I was a kid, people worked for General Motors, General Electric, Carrier and Oneida Ltd.," said casino Human Resources Director Mark Mancini. "Today, people work for the Oneida Indian Nation and their enterprises." [29]

For tribes that can't build independent economies any other way, casinos are appealing. The 225,000-member Navajo Nation, the biggest U.S. tribe, twice rejected gaming before finally approving it in 2004. [30] "We need that infusion of jobs and revenue, and people realize that," said Duane Yazzie, president of the Navajos' Shiprock, N.M., chapter. [31]

But the Navajos face stiff competition from dozens of casinos already in operation near the vast Navajo reservation, which spreads across parts of Arizona, New Mexico and Utah and is larger than the state of West Virginia.

Would money alone solve American Indians' problems?

No one in Indian Country (or on Capitol Hill) denies the importance of federal funding to American Indians' future, but some Indians say it isn't the only answer.

"We are largely on our own because of limited financial assistance from the federal government," said Joseph A. Garcia, president of the National Congress of American Indians, in his recent "State of Indian Nations" speech. [32]

Fifty-two tribal officials and Indian program directors expressed similar sentiments in March before the House Appropriations Subcommittee on the Interior. Pleading their case before lawmakers who routinely consider billion-dollar weapons systems and other big projects, the tribal leaders sounded like small-town county commissioners as they urged lawmakers to increase or restore small but vital grants for basic health, education and welfare services.

"In our ICWA [Indian Child Welfare Act] program, currently we have a budget of $79,000 a year," said Harold Frazier, chairman of the Cheyenne River Sioux, in South Dakota. "We receive over 1,300 requests for assistance annually from 11 states and eight counties in South Dakota. We cannot give the type of attention to these requests that they deserve. Therefore, we are requesting $558,000."

To university President Bordeaux, federal funding is vital because his desolate reservation has few other options for economic survival. "What's missing is money," he says.

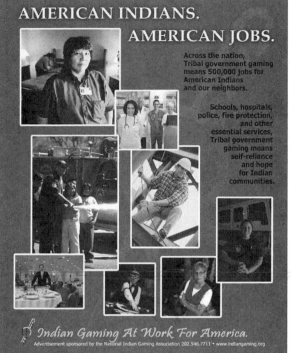

A National Indian Gaming Association advertisement touts the benefits of tribal gaming operations to American Indian communities. Some 228 tribes in 30 states operated 367 high-stakes bingo halls or casinos in 2004.

Money is crucial to improving Indians' health, says Dr. Joycelyn Dorscher, director of the Center of American Indian and Minority Health at the University of Minnesota-Duluth. Especially costly are programs to combat diabetes and other chronic diseases, says Dorscher, a Chippewa. While health programs have to be carefully designed to fit Indian cultural patterns, she says, "Everything comes down to time or money in the grand scheme of things."

But with funding from Washington never certain from year to year, says the Harvard Project's Kalt, "The key to economic development has not been federal funding" but rather "tribes' ability to run their own affairs."

For tribes without self-government compacts, growing demands for services and shrinking funding from Washington make keeping the dollars flowing the highest priority. "We're always afraid of more cutbacks," says Oglala Sioux President Fire Thunder.

But an Indian education leader with decades of federal budgetary negotiations acknowledges that problems go beyond funding shortfalls. "If you ask students why they dropped out, they say, 'I don't see a future for myself,' " says David Beaulieu, director of Arizona State University's Center for Indian Education. "Educators need to tie the purposes of schooling to the broad-based purposes of society. We're more successful when we tie education to the meaning of life."

The University of Arizona's Williams says a tribe's success and failure may be tied more to the way its government is organized than to how much funding it gets.

Williams says the first priority of tribes still using old-style constitutions should be reorganization, because they feature a weak executive elected by a tribal council. "That's what the BIA was used to," he explains. "It could play off factions and families, and the economic system would be based on patronage and taking care of your own family." Under such a system, he adds, "there's not going to be any long-term strategic planning going on." [33]

Yet other needs exist as well, says the American Indian Center's Podlasek. "It's so difficult for us to find a place to do a traditional ceremony," he says. "We had a traditional healer in town last month, and he wanted to build a sweat lodge. We actually had to go to Indiana. Doing it in the city wasn't even an option."

BACKGROUND

Conquered Homelands

Relations between Indian and non-Indian civilizations in the Americas began with the Spanish Conquistadors' explorations of the 1500s, followed by the French and British. By turns the three powers alternated policies of enslavement, peaceful coexistence and all-out warfare against the Indians. [34]

By 1830, with the Europeans largely gone, white settlers moved westward into Georgia, Mississippi and Alabama. Unwilling to share the rich frontier land, they pushed the Indians out. President Andrew Jackson backed the strategy, and Congress enacted it into the Indian Removal Act of 1830, which called for moving the region's five big tribes into the Oklahoma Territory.

If the law didn't make clear where Indians stood with the government, the treatment of Mississippi's Choctaws provided chilling evidence. Under a separate treaty, Choctaws who refused to head for Oklahoma could remain at home, become citizens and receive land. In practice, none of that was allowed, and Indians who stayed in Mississippi lived marginal existences.

Georgia simplified the claiming of Cherokee lands by effectively ending Cherokee self-rule. The so-called "Georgia Guard" reinforced the point by beating and jailing Indians. Jackson encouraged Georgia's actions, and when Indians protested, he said he couldn't interfere. The lawsuit filed by the Cherokees eventually reached the Supreme Court.

Chief Justice John Marshall's 1831 majority opinion, *Cherokee Nation v. Georgia*, would cast a long shadow over Indians' rights, along with two other decisions, issued in 1823 and 1832. "Almost all Indian policy is the progeny of the conflicting views of Jackson and Marshall," wrote W. Dale Mason, a political scientist at the University of New Mexico. [35]

In concluding that the court couldn't stop Georgia's actions, Marshall defined the relationship between Indians and the U.S. government. While Marshall wrote that Indians didn't constitute a foreign state, he noted that they owned the land they occupied until they made a "voluntary cession." Marshall concluded the various tribes were "domestic dependent nations." In practical terms, "Their relations to the United States resembles that of a ward to his guardian." [36]

Having rejected the Cherokees' argument, the University of Arizona's Williams writes, the court "provided no effective judicial remedy for Indian tribes to protect their basic human rights to property, self-government, and cultural survival under U.S. law." [37]

Along with the *Cherokee* case, the other two opinions that make up the so-called Marshall Trilogy are *Johnson v. M'Intosh* (also known as *Johnson v. McIntosh*), and *Worcester v. State of Georgia.* [38]

In *Johnson*, Marshall wrote that the European empires that "discovered" America became its owners and had "an exclusive right to extinguish the Indian title of occupancy, either by purchase or by conquest. The tribes of Indians inhabiting this country were fierce savages. . . . To leave them in possession of their country was to leave the country a wilderness." [39]

However, Marshall used the 1832 *Worcester* opinion to define the limits of state authority over Indian tribes, holding that the newcomers couldn't simply eject Indians.

"The Cherokee nation . . . is a distinct community occupying its own territory . . . in which the laws of Georgia can have no force," Marshall wrote. Georgia's conviction and sentencing of a missionary for not swearing allegiance to the state "interferes forcibly with the relations established between the United States and the Cherokee nation." [40] That is, the federal government — not states — held the reins of power over tribes.

According to legend, Jackson remarked: "John Marshall has made his decision — now let him enforce it." Between Jackson's disregard of the Supreme Court and white settlers' later manipulation of the legal system to vacate Indian lands, the end result was the dispossession of Indian lands.

Forced Assimilation

The expulsions of the Native Americans continued in the Western territories — especially after the Civil War. "I instructed Captain Barry, if possible to exterminate the whole village," Lt. Col. George Green wrote of his participation in an 1869 campaign against the White Mountain Apaches in Arizona and New Mexico. "There seems to be no settled policy, but a general policy to kill them wherever found." [41]

Some military men and civilians didn't go along. But whether by brute force or by persuasion, Indians were pushed off lands that non-Indians wanted. One strategy was to settle the Indians on reservations guarded by military posts. The strategy grew into a general policy for segregating Indians on these remote tracts.

Even after the Indians were herded onto lands that no one else wanted, the government didn't respect reservation boundaries. They were reconfigured as soon as non-Indians saw something valuable, such as mineral wealth.

The strategy of elastic reservation boundaries led to the belief — or rationalization — that reservations served no useful purposes for Indians themselves. That doctrine led to a policy enshrined in an 1887 law to convert reservations to individual landholdings. Well-meaning advocates of the plan saw it as a way to inculcate notions of private property and Euro American culture in general.

All tribal land was to be divided into 160-acre allotments, one for each Indian household. The parcels wouldn't become individual property, though, for 25 years.

Indian consent wasn't required. In some cases, government agents tried persuading Indians to join in; in others, the divvying-up proceeded even with many Indians opposed. In Arizona, however, the government backed off from breaking up the lands of the long-settled Hopis, who resisted attempts to break up their territory. The vast Navajo Nation in Arizona, Utah and New Mexico was also left intact.

While widely reviled, the "forced assimilation" policy left a benign legacy for the affected Indians: the grant of citizenship. Beyond that, the era's Indians were restricted to unproductive lands, and with little means of support many fell prey to alcoholism and disease.

The bleak period ended with President Franklin D. Roosevelt. In his first term he appointed a defender of Indian culture, John Collier, as commissioner of Indian affairs. Collier pushed for the Indian Reorganization Act of 1934, which ended the allotment program, financed purchases of new Indian lands and authorized the organization of tribal governments that enjoyed control over revenues.

Termination

After World War II, a new, anti-Indian mood swept Washington, partly in response to pressure from states where non-Indians eyed Indian land.

Collier resigned in 1945 after years of conflict over what critics called his antagonism to missionaries proselytizing among the Indians and his sympathies toward the tribes. The 1950 appointment of Dillon S. Myer — fresh from supervising the wartime internment of Japanese Americans — clearly reflected the new attitude. Myer showed little interest in what Indians themselves thought of the new policy of shrinking tribal land holdings. "I realize that it will not be possible always to obtain Indian cooperation. . . . We must proceed, even though [this] may be lacking." [42]

Congress hadn't authorized a sweeping repeal of earlier policy. But the introduction of dozens of bills in the late 1940s to sell Indian land or liquidate some reservation holdings entirely showed which way the winds were blowing. And in 1953, a House Concurrent Resolution declared Congress' policy to be ending Indians' "status as wards of the United States, and to grant them all of the rights and privileges pertaining to American citizenship." A separate law granted state jurisdiction over Indian reservations in five Midwestern and Western states and extended the same authority to other states that wanted to claim it. [43]

CHRONOLOGY

1800s *United States expands westward, pushing Indians off most of their original lands, sometimes creating new reservations for them.*

1830 President Andrew Jackson signs the Indian Removal Act, forcing the Cherokees to move from Georgia to Oklahoma.

1832 Supreme Court issues the last of three decisions defining Indians' legal status as wards of the government.

1871 Congress makes its treaties with tribes easier to alter, enabling non-Indians to take Indian lands when natural resources are discovered.

Dec. 29, 1890 U.S. soldiers massacre at least 150 Plains Indians, mostly women and children, at Wounded Knee, S.D.

1900-1950s *Congress and the executive branch undertake major shifts in Indian policy, first strengthening tribal governments then trying to force cultural assimilation.*

1924 Indians are granted U.S. citizenship.

1934 Indian Reorganization Act authorizes expansion of reservations and strengthening of tribal governments.

1953 Congress endorses full assimilation of Indians into American society, including "relocation" from reservations to cities.

1960s-1980s *In the radical spirit of the era, Native Americans demand respect for their traditions and an end to discrimination; federal government concedes more power to tribal governments, allows gambling on tribal lands.*

1969 American Indian Movement (AIM) seizes Alcatraz Island in San Francisco Bay to dramatize claims of injustice.

July 7, 1970 President Richard M. Nixon vows support for Indian self-government.

Feb. 27, 1973 AIM members occupy the town of Wounded Knee on the Pine Ridge, S.D., Sioux Reservation, for two months; two Indians die and an FBI agent is wounded.

1988 Indian Gaming Regulatory Act allows tribes to operate casinos under agreements with states.

1990s *Indian-owned casinos boom; tribal governments push to expand self-rule and reduce Bureau of Indian Affairs (BIA) supervision.*

1994 President Bill Clinton signs law making experimental self-governance compacts permanent.

March 27, 1996 U.S. Supreme Court rules states can't be forced to negotiate casino compacts, thus encouraging tribes to make revenue-sharing deals with states as the price of approval.

June 10, 1996 Elouise Cobell, a member of the Blackfeet Tribe in Montana, charges Interior Department mismanagement of Indian trust funds cheated Indians out of billions of dollars. The case is still pending.

Nov. 3, 1998 California voters uphold tribes' rights to run casinos; state Supreme Court later invalidates the provision, but it is revived by a 1999 compact between the tribes and the state.

2000s *Indian advocates decry low funding levels, and sovereignty battles continue; lobbying scandal spotlights Indian gambling profits.*

2000 Tribal Self-Governance Demonstration Project becomes permanent.

2003 U.S. Commission on Civil Rights calls underfunding for Indians a crisis, saying federal government spends less for Indian health care than for any other group, including prison inmates.

Feb. 22, 2004 *Washington Post* reports on Washington lobbyist Jack Abramoff's deals with casino tribes.

March 29, 2005 U.S. Supreme Court blocks tax exemptions for Oneida Nation of New York on newly purchased land simply because it once owned the property.

April 5, 2006 Tribal and BIA officials testify in Congress that methamphetamine addiction is ravaging reservations.

The following year, Congress "terminated" formal recognition and territorial sovereignty of six tribes. Four years later, after public opposition began building (spurred in part by religious organizations), Congress abandoned termination. In the meantime, however, Indians had lost 1.6 million acres.

At the same time, though, the federal government maintained an associated policy — relocation. The BIA persuaded Indians to move to cities — Chicago, Denver and Los Angeles were the main destinations — and opened job-placement and housing-aid programs. The BIA placed Indians far from their reservations to keep them from returning. By 1970, the BIA estimated that 40 percent of all Indians lived in cities, of which one-third had been relocated by the bureau; the rest moved on their own. [44]

Activism

Starting in the late 1960s, the winds of change blowing through American society were felt as deeply in Indian Country as anywhere. Two books played a crucial role. In 1969, Vine Deloria Jr., member of a renowned family of Indian intellectuals from Oklahoma, published his landmark history, *Custer Died For Your Sins*, which portrayed American history from the Indians' viewpoint. The following year, Dee Brown's *Bury My Heart at Wounded Knee* described the settling of the West also from an Indian point of view. The books astonished many non-Indians. Among young Indians, the volumes reflected and spurred on a growing political activism.

It was in this climate that the newly formed American Indian Movement (AIM) took over Alcatraz Island, the former federal prison site in San Francisco Bay (where rebellious Indians had been held during the Indian Wars), to publicize demands to honor treaties and respect Native Americans' dignity. The takeover lasted from Nov. 20, 1969, to June 11, 1971, when U.S. marshals removed the occupiers. [45]

A second AIM-government confrontation took the form of a one-week takeover of BIA headquarters in Washington in November 1972 by some 500 AIM members protesting what they called broken treaty obligations. Protesters charged that government services to Indians were inadequate in general, with urban Indians neglected virtually completely.

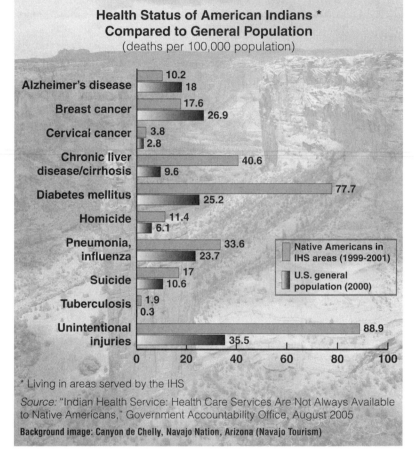

Disease Toll Higher Among Indians

American Indians served by the Indian Health Service (IHS) — mainly low-income or uninsured — die at substantially higher rates than the general population from liver disease, diabetes, tuberculosis, pneumonia and influenza as well as from homicide, suicide and injuries. However, Indians' death rates from Alzheimer's disease or breast cancer are lower.

Health Status of American Indians *
Compared to General Population
(deaths per 100,000 population)

	Native Americans in IHS areas (1999-2001)	U.S. general population (2000)
Alzheimer's disease	10.2	18
Breast cancer	17.6	26.9
Cervical cancer	3.8	2.8
Chronic liver disease/cirrhosis	40.6	9.6
Diabetes mellitus	77.7	25.2
Homicide	11.4	6.1
Pneumonia, influenza	33.6	23.7
Suicide	17	10.6
Tuberculosis	1.9	0.3
Unintentional injuries	88.9	35.5

* Living in areas served by the IHS

Source: "Indian Health Service: Health Care Services Are Not Always Available to Native Americans," Government Accountability Office, August 2005

Background image: Canyon de Chelly, Navajo Nation, Arizona (Navajo Tourism)

Budget Cuts Target Health Clinics

When Lita Pepion, a health consultant and a member of the Blackfeet Nation, learned that her 22-year-old-niece had been struggling with heroin abuse, she urged her to seek treatment at the local Urban Indian Clinic in Billings, Mont.

But the young woman had so much trouble getting an appointment that she gave up. Only recently, says Pepion, did she overcome her addiction on her own.

The clinic is one of 34 federally funded, Indian-controlled clinics that contract with the Indian Health Service (IHS) to serve urban Indians. But President Bush's 2007 budget would kill the $33-million program, eliminating most of the clinics' funding.

Indians in cities will still be able to get health care through several providers, including the federal Health Centers program, says Office of Management and Budget spokesman Richard Walker. The proposed budget would increase funding for the centers by nearly $2 billion, IHS Director Charles W. Grim told the Senate Indian Affairs Committee on Feb. 14, 2006. [1]

But Joycelyn Dorscher, president of the Association of American Indian Physicians, says the IHS clinics do a great job and that, "It's very important that people from diverse backgrounds have physicians like themselves."

Others, however, including Pepion, say the clinics are poorly managed and lack direction. Ralph Forquera, director of the Seattle-based Urban Indian Health Institute, says that while the clinics "have made great strides medically, a lack of resources has resulted in services from unqualified professionals." In addition, he says, "we have not been as successful in dealing with lifestyle changes and mental health problems."

Many Indian health experts oppose the cuts because Indians in both urban areas and on reservations have more health problems than the general population, including 126 percent more chronic liver disease and cirrhosis, 54 percent more diabetes and 178 percent more alcohol-related deaths. [2]

Indian health specialists blame the Indians' higher disease rates on history, lifestyle and genetics — not just on poverty. "You don't see exactly the same things happening to other poor minority groups," says Dorscher, a North Dakota Chippewa, so "there's something different" going on among Indians.

In the view of Donna Keeler, executive director of the South Dakota Urban Indian Health program and an Eastern Shoshone, historical trauma affects the physical wellness of patients in her state's three urban Indian clinics.

Susette Schwartz, CEO of the Hunter Urban Indian Clinic in Wichita, Kan., agrees. She attributes Indians' high rates of mental health and alcohol/substance abuse to their long history of government maltreatment. Many Indian children in the 19th and early 20th centuries, she points out, were taken from their parents and sent to government boarding schools where speaking native languages was pro-

---

Another protest occurred on Feb. 27, 1973, when 200 AIM members occupied the village of Wounded Knee on the Oglala Sioux's Pine Ridge Reservation in South Dakota. U.S. soldiers had massacred at least 150 Indians at Wounded Knee in 1890. AIM was protesting what it called the corrupt tribal government. And a weak, involuntary manslaughter charge against a non-Indian who had allegedly killed an Indian near the reservation had renewed Indian anger at discriminatory treatment by police and judges.

The occupation soon turned into a full-blown siege, with the reservation surrounded by troops and federal law-enforcement officers. During several firefights two AIM members were killed, and an FBI agent was wounded. The occupation ended on May 8, 1973.

Self-Determination

Amid the surging Indian activism, the federal government was trying to make up for the past by encouraging tribal self-determination. [46]

In 1975, Congress passed the Indian Self-Determination and Education Assistance Act, which channeled federal contracts and grants directly to tribes, reducing the BIA role and effectively putting Indian communities in direct charge of schools, health, housing and other programs.

And to assure Indians that the era of sudden reversals in federal policy had ended, the House in 1988 passed a resolution reaffirming the "constitutionally recognized government-to-government relationship with Indian tribes." Separate legislation set up a "self-governance

hibited. "Taking away the culture and language years ago," says Schwartz, as well as the government's role in "taking their children and sterilizing their women" in the 1970s, all contributed to Indians' behavioral health issues.

Keeler also believes Indians' low incomes cause their unhealthy lifestyles. Many eat high-fat, high-starch foods because they are cheaper, Pepion says. Growing up on a reservation, she recalls, "We didn't eat a lot of vegetables because we couldn't afford them."

Native Americans in downtown Salt Lake City, Utah, demonstrate on April 21, 2006, against the elimination of funding for Urban Indian Health Clinics.

AP Photo/Salt Lake Tribune

uncomfortable for me," she says.

But Schwartz believes a great benefit of the urban clinics are their Indian employees, "who are culturally competent and sensitive and incorporate Native American-specific cultural ideas." Because of their history of cultural abuse, it takes a long time for Native Americans to trust non-Indian health providers, says Schwartz. "They're not just going to go to a health center down the road."

Opponents of the funding cuts for urban Indian health centers also cite a recent letter to President Bush from Daniel R. Hawkins Jr., vice president for federal, state and local government for the National Association of Community Health Centers. He said the urban Indian clinics and community health centers are complementary, not duplicative.

While Pepion does not believe funding should be cut entirely, she concedes that alternative health-care services are often "better equipped than the urban Indian clinics." And if American Indians want to assimilate into the larger society, they can't have everything culturally separate, she adds. "The only way that I was able to assimilate into an urban society was to make myself do those things that were

Dorscher and Schwartz also say the budget cuts could lead to more urban Indians ending up in costly emergency rooms because of their reluctance to trust the community health centers. "Ultimately, it would become more expensive to cut the prevention and primary care programs than it would be to maintain them," Dorscher says.

— *Melissa J. Hipolit*

[1] Prepared testimony of Director of Indian Health Service Dr. Charles W. Grim before the Senate Committee on Indian Affairs, Feb. 14, 2006.

[2] Urban Indian Health Institute, "The Health Status of Urban American Indians and Alaska Natives," March 16, 2004, p. v.

demonstration project" in which eligible tribes would sign "compacts" to run their own governments with block grants from the federal government. [47]

By 1993, 28 tribes had negotiated compacts with the Interior Department. And in 1994, President Bill Clinton signed legislation that made self-governance a permanent option.

For the general public, the meaning of newly strengthened Indian sovereignty could be summed up with one word: casinos. In 1988, Congress enacted legislation regulating tribal gaming operations. That move followed a Supreme Court ruling (*California v. Cabazon*) that authorized tribes to run gambling operations. But tribes could not offer a form of gambling specifically barred by the state.

The law set up three categories of gambling operations: Class I, traditional Indian games, controlled exclusively by tribes; Class II, including bingo, lotto, pull tabs and some card games, which are allowed on tribal lands in states that allow the games elsewhere; and Class III, which takes in casino games such as slot machines, roulette and blackjack, which can be offered only under agreements with state governments that set out the size and types of the proposed casinos.

Limits that the Indian Gaming Regulatory Act put on Indian sovereignty were tightened further by a 1996 Supreme Court decision that the Seminole Tribe couldn't sue Florida to force negotiation of a casino compact. The decision essentially forced tribes nation-

Native American children and adults in the Chicago area keep in touch with their cultural roots at the American Indian Center. About two-thirds of the nation's Indians live in urban areas.

wide to make revenue-sharing deals with states in return for approval of casinos. [48]

Meanwhile, particularily on reservations from Minnesota to the Pacific Northwest, a plague of methamphetamine addiction and manufacturing is leaving a trail of death and shattered lives. By 2002, Darrell Hillaire, chairman of the Lummi Nation, near Bellingham, Wash., said that members convicted of dealing meth would be expelled from the tribe. [49]

But the Lummis couldn't stop the spread of the scourge on other reservations. National Congress of American Indians President Garcia said early in 2006: "Methamphetamine is a poison taking Indian lives, destroying Indian families, and razing entire communities." [50]

CURRENT SITUATION

Self-Government

Some Indian leaders are advocating more power for tribal governments as the best way to improve the quality of life on reservations.

Under the Tribal Self-Governance Demonstration Project, made permanent in 1994, tribes can replace program-by-program grants by entering into "compacts" with the federal government, under which they receive a single grant for a variety of services. Some 231 tribes and

Alaskan Native villages have compacts to administer a total of about $341 million in programs. Of the Indian communities now living under compacts, 72 are in the lower 48 states. [51]

Under a set of separate compacts, the Indian Health Service has turned over clinics, hospitals and health programs to some 300 tribes and Alaskan villages, 70 of them non-Alaskan tribes.

The self-governance model has proved especially appropriate in Alaska, where the majority of the native population of 120,000 is concentrated in 229 villages, many of them remote, and compact in size, hence well-suited to managing their own affairs, experts say.

Another advantage of Alaska villages is the experience they acquired through the 1971 Alaska Native Claims Settlement Act, which granted a total of $962 million to Alaska natives born on or before Dec. 18, 1971, in exchange for giving up their claims to millions of acres of land. Villages formed regional corporations to manage the assets. In addition, all Alaska residents receive an annual dividend ($946 in 2005) from natural-resource royalty income. [52]

"The emergence of tribal authority is unprecedented in Indian Country's history," says Allen, of the Jamestown S'Klallam Tribe, one of the originators of the self-governance model. "Why not take the resources you have available and use them as efficiently as you can — more efficiently than currently being administered?" [53]

But the poorer and more populous tribes of the Great Plains and the Southwest have turned down the self-governance model. "They can't afford to do it," says Michael LaPointe, chief of staff to President Rodney Bordeaux of the Rosebud Sioux Tribe. "When you have a lot of poverty and not a lot of economic activity to generate tribal resources to supplement the unfunded mandates, it becomes impossible."

In contrast with the Jameston S'Klallam's tiny membership of 585 people, there are some 24,000 people on the Rosebud Siouxs' million-acre reservation. The tribe does operate law enforcement, ambulances and other services under contracts with the government. But it can't afford to do any more, LaPointe says.

A combined effect of the gambling boom and the growing adoption of the self-governance model is that much of the tension has gone out of the traditionally strained relationship between the BIA and tribes. "BIA people are getting pushed out as decision-makers," Kalt

American Indian Center/Warren Perlstein

says. Some strains remain, to be sure. Allen says he senses a growing reluctance by the BIA to let go of tribes. "They use the argument that that the BIA doesn't have the money [for block grants]," he says.

BIA Director Ragsdale acknowledges that tougher financial-accounting requirements sparked by a lawsuit over Interior Department handling of Indian trust funds are slowing the compact-approval process. (*See "Trust Settlement" below.*) But, he adds, "We're not trying to hinder self-governance."

Limits on Gambling

Several legislative efforts to limit Indian gaming are pending. Separate bills by Sen. McCain and House Resources Committee Chairman Richard Pombo, R-Calif., would restrict tribes' ability to acquire new land for casinos in more favorable locations.

More proposals are in the pipeline. Jemez Pueblo of New Mexico wants to build a casino near the town of Anthony, though the pueblo is 300 miles away. [54]

In eastern Oregon, the Warm Springs Tribe is proposing an off-reservation casino at the Columbia River Gorge. And in Washington state, the Cowlitz and Mohegan tribes are planning an off-reservation casino near Portland. [55] The process has been dubbed "reservation shopping."

Under the Indian Gaming Regulatory Act of 1988, a tribe can acquire off-reservation land for casinos when it is:

- granted as part of a land claim settlement;
- granted to a newly recognized tribe as its reservation;
- restored to a tribe whose tribal recognition is also restored; or
- granted to a recognized tribe that had no reservation when the act took effect.

The most hotly debated exemption allows the secretary of the Interior to grant an off-reservation acquisition that benefits the tribe without harming the community near the proposed casino location. Both Pombo and McCain would repeal the loophole created by this so-called "two-part test." Under Pombo's bill, tribes acquiring land under the other exemptions would have to have solid historic and recent ties to the property. Communities, state governors and state legislatures would have to approve the establishment of new casinos, and tribes would reimburse communities for the effects of casinos on transportation, law enforcement and other public services.

McCain's bill would impose fewer restrictions than Pombo's. But McCain would give the National Indian Gaming Commission final say over all contracts with outside suppliers of goods and services.

The bill would also ensure the commission's control over big-time gambling — a concern that arose from a 2005 decision by the U.S. Court of Appeals for the District of Columbia that limited the agency's jurisdiction over a Colorado tribe. The commission has been worrying that applying that decision nationwide would eliminate federal supervision of casinos.

McCain told a March 8 Senate Indian Affairs Committee hearing that the two-part test "is fostering opposition to all Indian gaming." [56]

If the senator had been aiming to soften tribal opposition to his bill, he didn't make much headway. "We believe that it grows out of anecdotal, anti-Indian press reports on Indian gaming, the overblown issue of off-reservation gaming, and a 'pin-the-blame-on-the-victim' reaction to the Abramoff scandal," Ron His Horse Is Thunder, chairman of the Standing Rock Sioux Tribe of North Dakota and South Dakota, told the committee. He argued that the bill would amount to unconstitutional meddling with Indian sovereignty.

But the idea of restricting "reservation-shopping" appeals to tribes facing competition from other tribes. Cheryle A. Kennedy, chairwoman of the Confederated Tribes of the Grand Ronde Community of Oregon, said her tribe's Spirit Mountain Casino could be hurt by the Warm Springs Tribes' proposed project or by the Cowlitz and Mohegan project. [57]

Pombo's bill would require the approval of new casinos by tribes that already have gambling houses up and running within 75 miles of a proposed new one.

The House Resources Committee heard another view from Indian Country at an April 5 hearing. Jacquie Davis-Van Huss, tribal secretary of the North Fork Rancheria of the Mono Indians of California, said Pombo's approval clause would doom her tribe's plans. "This provision is anti-competitive," she testified. "It effectively provides the power to veto another tribe's gaming project simply to protect market share."

Trust Settlement

McCain's committee is also grappling with efforts to settle a decade-old lawsuit that has exposed longstanding federal mismanagement of trust funds. In 1999, U.S.

Urban Indians: Invisible and Unheard

Two-thirds of the nation's 4.4 million American Indians live in towns and cities, but they're hard to find.[1] "Indians who move into metropolitan areas are scattered; they're not in a centralized geographical area," says New Mexico Secretary of Labor Conroy Chino. "You don't have that cohesive community where there's a sense of culture and language, as in Chinatown or Koreatown in Los Angeles."

Chino's interest is professional as well as personal. In his former career as a television journalist in Albuquerque, Chino, a member of the Acoma Pueblo, wrote an independent documentary about urban Indians. His subjects range from a city-loving San Franciscan who vacations in Hawaii to city-dwellers who return to their reservations every vacation they get. Their lives diverge sharply from what University of Arizona anthropologist Susan Lobo calls a "presumption that everything Indian is rural and long, long ago."[2]

Indian society began urbanizing in 1951, when the Bureau of Indian Affairs (BIA) started urging reservation dwellers to move to cities where — it was hoped — they would blend into the American "melting pot" and find more economic opportunity and a better standard of living.[3]

But many found the urban environment oppressive and the government assistance less generous than promised. About 100,000 Indians were relocated between 1951 and 1973, when the program wound down; unable to fit in, many fell into alcoholism and despair.[4]

Still, a small, urban Indian middle class has developed over time, partly because the BIA began systematically hiring Indians in its offices. Indians keep such a low profile, however, that the Census Bureau has a hard time finding them. Lobo, who consulted for the bureau in 1990, recalls that the agency's policy at the time was to register any household where no one answered the door as being in the same ethnic group as the neighbors. That strategy worked with urban ethnic groups who tended to cluster together, Lobo says, but not with Native Americans because theirs was a "dispersed population."

By the 2000 census that problem was resolved, but another one cropped up. "American Indians are ingenious at keeping expenses down — by couch-surfing, for instance," Lobo says. "There's a floating population that doesn't get counted because they weren't living in a standard residence."

But other urban Indians live conventional, middle-class lives, sometimes even while technically living on Indian land. "I am highly educated, a professor in the university, and my gainful employment is in the city of Albuquerque," says Ted Jojola, a professor of planning at the University of New Mexico (and a member of the Census Bureau's advisory committee on Indian population). "My community [Isleta Pueblo] is seven minutes south of Albuquerque. The reservation has become an urban amenity to me."

Some might see a home on Indian land near the city as a refuge from discrimination. "There have been years where you couldn't reveal you were native if you wanted to get a job," says Joseph Podlasek, executive director of the American Indian Center of Chicago.

Joycelyn Dorscher, president of the Association of American Indian Physicians, recalls a painful experience several years ago when she rushed her 6-year-old daughter to a hospital emergency room in Minneapolis-St. Paul, suspecting appendicitis. The young intern assigned to the case saw an Indian single mother with a sick child and apparently assumed that the daughter was suffering from neglect. "She told me if I didn't sit down and shut up, my daughter would go into the [child-protective] system," recalls Dorscher, who at the time was a third-year medical student.

Even Chino, whose mainstream credentials include an M.A. from Princeton, feels alienated at times from non-Indian city dwellers. He notes that Albuquerque officials ignored Indians' objections to a statue honoring Juan de Oñate, the 16th-century conqueror who established Spanish rule in what is now New Mexico. "Though native people protested and tried to show why this is not a good idea," Chino says, "the city went ahead and funded it."[5]

In the long run, Chino hopes a growing presence of Indian professionals — "we're not all silversmiths, or weavers" — will create more acceptance of urban Indians and more aid to combat high Indian dropout rates and other problems. "While people like having Indians in New Mexico and like visitors to get a feel for the last bastion of native culture," he says, "they're not doing that much for the urban Indian community, though we're paying taxes, too."

---

[1] Urban Indians were 64 percent of the population in 2000, according to the U.S. Census Bureau. For background, see, "We the People: American Indians and Alaska Natives in the United States," U.S. Census Bureau, 2000, p. 14, www.census.gov/prod/2006pubs/censr-28.pdf.

[2] "Looking Toward Home," *Native American Public Telecommunications,* 2003, www.visionmaker.org.

[3] Donald L. Fixico, *The Urban Indian Experience in America* (2000), pp. 9-11.

[4] *Ibid.*, pp. 22-25.

[5] Oñate is especially disliked at Acoma, Chino's birthplace, where the conqueror had the feet of some two-dozen Acoma men cut off in 1599 after Spanish soldiers were killed there. For background, see Wren Propp, "A Giant of Ambivalence," *Albuquerque Journal,* Jan. 25, 2004, p. A1; Brenda Norrell, "Pueblos Decry War Criminal," *Indian Country Today,* June 25, 2004.

Should tribes open casinos on newly acquired land?

YES

Ernest L. Stevens, Jr.
Chairman, National Indian Gaming Association

From statement before U.S. House Committee on Resources, Nov. 9, 2005

Indian gaming is the Native American success story. Where there were no jobs, now there are 553,000 jobs. Where our people had only an eighth-grade education on average, tribal governments are building schools and funding college scholarships. Where the United States and boarding schools sought to suppress our languages, tribal schools are now teaching their native language. Where our people suffer epidemic diabetes, heart disease and premature death, our tribes are building hospitals, health clinics and wellness centers.

Historically, the United States signed treaties guaranteeing Indian lands as permanent homes, and then a few years later, went to war to take our lands. This left our people to live in poverty, often on desolate lands, while others mined for gold or pumped oil from the lands that were taken from us.

Indian gaming is an exercise of our inherent right to self-government. Today, for over 60 percent of Indian tribes in the lower 48 states, Indian gaming offers new hope and a chance for a better life for our children.

Too many lands were taken from Indian tribes, leaving some tribes landless or with no useful lands. To take account of historical mistreatment, the Indian Gaming Regulatory Act (IGRA), provided several exceptions to the rule that Indian tribes should conduct Indian gaming on lands held on Oct. 17, 1988.

Accordingly, land is restored to an Indian tribe in trust status when the tribe is restored to federal recognition. For federally recognized tribes that did not have reservation land on the date IGRA was enacted, land is put into trust. Or, a tribe may apply to the secretary of the Interior. The secretary consults with state and local officials and nearby Indian tribes to determine whether an acquisition of land in trust for gaming would be in the tribe's "best interest" and "not detrimental to the surrounding community."

Now, legislation would require "newly recognized, restored, or landless tribes" to apply to have land taken in trust through a five-part process. Subjecting tribes to this new and cumbersome process discounts the fact that the United States mistreated these tribes by ignoring and neglecting them, taking all of their lands or allowing their lands to be stolen by others.

We believe that Congress should restore these tribes to a portion of their historical lands and that these lands should be held on the same basis as other Indian lands.

NO

State Rep. Fulton Sheen, R-Plainwell
Michigan House of Representatives

From statement to U.S. House Committee on Resources, April 5, 2006

The rampant proliferation of tribal gaming is running roughshod over states' rights and local control and is jeopardizing everything from my own neighborhood to — as the Jack Abramoff scandal has demonstrated — the very integrity of our federal political system.

In 1988, Congress passed the Indian Gaming Regulatory Act (IGRA) in an effort to control the development of Native American casinos and, in particular, to make sure that the states had a meaningful role in the development of any casinos within their borders. At that time, Native American gambling accounted for less than 1 percent of the nation's gambling industry, grossing approximately $100 million in revenue.

Since that time, the Native American casino business has exploded into an $18.5 billion industry that controls 25 percent of gaming industry revenue. Despite this unbridled growth, IGRA and the land-in-trust process remain basically unchanged.

When Congress originally enacted IGRA, the general rule was that casino gambling would not take place on newly acquired trust land. I believe Congress passed this general rule to prevent precisely what we see happening: a mad and largely unregulated land rush pushed by casino developers eager to cash in on a profitable revenue stream that is not burdened by the same tax rates or regulations that other businesses have to incur. "Reservation shopping" is an activity that must be stopped. And that is just one component of the full legislative overhaul that is needed.

IGRA and its associated land-in-trust process is broken, open to manipulation by special interests and in desperate need of immediate reform. It has unfairly and inappropriately fostered an industry that creates enormous wealth for a few select individuals and Las Vegas interests at the expense of taxpaying families, small businesses, manufacturing jobs and local governments.

Our research shows that while local and state governments receive some revenue-sharing percentages from tribal gaming, the dollars pale in comparison to the overall new costs to government and social-service agencies from increased infrastructure demands, traffic, bankruptcies, crime, divorce and general gambling-related ills.

I do not think this is what Congress had in mind. Somewhere along the way, the good intentions of Congress have been hijacked, and it is time for this body to reassert control over this process. It is imperative that Congress take swift and decisive steps today to get its arms around this issue before more jobs are lost and more families are put at risk.

District Judge Royce Lamberth said evidence showed "fiscal and governmental irresponsibility in its purest form." [58]

The alternative to settlement, McCain and Dorgan told the Budget Committee, is for the case to drag on through the courts. Congressional resolution of the conflict could also spare the Interior Department further grief from Lamberth. In a February ruling, he said Interior's refusal to make payments owed to Indians was "an obscenity that harkens back to the darkest days of United States-Indian relations." [59]

Five months later, Lamberth suggested that Congress, not the courts, may be the proper setting for the conflict. "Interior's unremitting neglect and mismanagement of the Indian trust has left it in such a shambles that recovery may prove impossible." [60]

The court case has its roots in the 1887 policy of allotting land to Indians in an effort to break up reservations. Since then, the Interior Department has been responsible for managing payments made to landholders, which later included tribes, for mining and other natural-resource extraction on Indian-owned land.

But for decades, Indians weren't receiving what they were owed. On June 10, 1996, Elouise Cobell, an organizer of the Blackfeet National Bank, the first Indian-owned national bank on a reservation, sued the Interior Department charging that she and all other trust fee recipients had been cheated for decades out of money that Interior was responsible for managing. "Lands and resources — in many cases the only source of income for some of our nation's poorest and most vulnerable citizens — have been grossly mismanaged," Cobell told the Indian Affairs Committee on March 1.

The mismanagement is beyond dispute, said John Bickerman, who was appointed to broker a settlement. Essentially, Bickerman told the Senate Indian Affairs Committee on March 28, "Money was not collected; money was not properly deposited; and money was not properly disbursed."

As of 2005, Interior is responsible for trust payments involving 126,079 tracts of land owned by 223,245 individuals — or, 2.3 million "ownership interests" on some 12 million acres, Cason and Ross Swimmer, a special trustee, told the committee.

Bickerman said a settlement amount of $27.5 billion proposed by the Indian plaintiffs was "without foundation." But the Interior Department proposed a settlement of $500 million based on "arbitrary and false assumptions," he added. Both sides agree that some $13 billion should have been paid to individual Indians over the life of the trust, but they disagree over how much was actually paid.

Supreme Court Ruling

Powerful repercussions are expected from the Supreme Court's latest decision in a centuries-long string of rulings involving competing claims to land by Indians and non-Indians.

In 2005, the high court said the Oneida Indian Nation of New York could not quit paying taxes on 10 parcels of land it owns north of Utica. [61]

After buying the parcels in 1997 and 1998, the tribe refused to pay property taxes, arguing that the land was former tribal property now restored to tribal ownership, and thereby tax-exempt. [62]

The court, in an opinion written by Ruth Bader Ginsburg, concluded that though the tribe used to own the land, the property right was too old to revive. "Rekindling the embers of sovereignty that long ago grew cold" is out of the question, Ginsburg wrote. She invoked the legal doctrine of "laches," in which a party who waits too long to assert his rights loses them. [63]

Lawyers on both sides of Indian law cases expect the case to affect lower-court rulings throughout the country. "The court has opened the cookie jar," Williams of the University of Arizona argues. "Does laches only apply to claims of sovereignty over reacquired land? If a decision favoring Indians is going to inconvenience too many white people, then laches applies — I swear that's what it says." Tribes litigating fishing rights, water rights and other assets are likely to suffer in court as a result, he argues.

In fact, only three months after the high court decision, the 2nd U.S. Circuit Court of Appeals in New York invoked laches in rejecting a claim by the Cayuga Tribe. Vickers of Upstate Citizens for Equality says that if the 2nd Circuit "thinks that laches forbids the Cayugas from making a claim because the Supreme Court said so, you're going to find other courts saying so."

In Washington, Alexandra Page, an attorney with the Indian Law Resource Center, agrees. "There are tribes in the West who have boundary disputes on their reservations; there are water-law cases where you've got people looking back at what happened years ago, so the

Supreme Court decision could have significant practical impact. The danger is that those with an interest in limiting Indian rights will do everything they can to expand the decision and use it in other circumstances."

OUTLOOK

Who Is an Indian?

If advocates of Indian self-governance are correct, the number of tribes running their own affairs with minimal federal supervision will keep on growing. "The requests for workshops are coming in steadily," says Cyndi Holmes, self-governance coordinator of the Jamestown S'Klallam Tribe.

Others say that growth, now at a rate of about three tribes a year, may be nearing its upper limit. "When you look at the options for tribes to do self-governance, economics really drives whether they can," says LaPointe of the Rosebud Sioux, whose tribal government doesn't expect to adopt the model in the foreseeable future.

But the longstanding problems of rural and isolated reservations are not the only dimension of Indian life. People stereotypically viewed as tied to the land have become increasingly urban over the past several decades, and the view from Indian Country is that the trend will continue.

That doesn't mean reservations will empty out or lose their cultural importance. "Urban Indian is not a lifelong label," says Susan Lobo, an anthropologist at the University of Arizona. "Indian people, like everyone else, can move around. They're still American Indians."

For Indians, as for all other peoples, moving around leads to intermarriage. Matthew Snipp, a Stanford University sociologist who is half Cherokee and half Oklahoma Choctaw, notes that Indians have long married within and outside Indian society. But the consequences of intermarriage are different for Indians than for, say, Jews or Italians.

The Indian place in American society grows out of the government-to-government relationship between Washington and tribes. And most tribes define their members by what's known as the "blood quantum" — their degree of tribal ancestry.

"I look at it as you're kind of USDA-approved," says Podlasek of the American Indian Center. "Why is no other race measured that way?"

Harvard Law School graduate Lance Morgan, a member of Nebraska's Winnebago Tribe, used seed money from his tribe's small casino to create several thriving businesses. He urges other tribes to use their casino profits to diversify. "Gaming is just a means to an end," he says.

Podlasek is especially sensitive to the issue. His father was Polish American, and his mother was Ojibway. His own wife is Indian, but from another tribe. "My kids can be on the tribal rolls, but their kids won't be able to enroll, unless they went back to my tribe or to their mother's tribe to marry — depending on what their partners' blood quantum is. In generations, you could say that, by government standards, there are no more native people."

Snipp traces the blood-quantum policy to a 1932 decision by the Indian Affairs Commission, which voted to make one-quarter descent the minimum standard. The commissioners were concerned, Snipp says, reading from the commission's report, that thousands of people "more white than Indian" were receiving "shares in tribal estates and other benefits." Tribes are no longer bound by that decision, but the requirement — originally inserted at BIA insistence — remains in many tribal constitutions.

On the Indian side, concern over collective survival is historically well-founded. Historian Elizabeth Shoemaker of the University of Connecticut at Storrs calculated that the Indian population of what is now the continental United States plummeted from a top estimate of 5.5 million in 1492 to a mere 237,000 in 1900. Indian life expectancy didn't begin to rise significantly until after 1940. [64]

Now, Indians are worrying about the survival of Indian civilization at a time when Indians' physical survival has never been more assured.

Even as these existential worries trouble some Indian leaders, the living conditions that most Indians endure also pose long-term concerns.

Conroy Chino, New Mexico's Labor secretary and a member of Acoma Pueblo, says continuation of the educational disaster in Indian Country is dooming young people to live on the margins. "I'm out there attracting companies to come to New Mexico, and these kids aren't going to qualify for those good jobs."

Nevertheless, below most non-Indians' radar screen, the Indian professional class is growing. "When I got my Ph.D. in 1973, I think I was the 15th in the country," says Beaulieu of Arizona State University's Center for Indian Education. "Now we have all kinds of Ph.D.s, teachers with certification, lawyers." And Beaulieu says he has seen the difference that Indian professionals make in his home state of Minnesota. "You're beginning to see an educated middle class in the reservation community, and realizing that they're volunteering to perform lots of services."

In Albuquerque, the University of New Mexico's Jojola commutes to campus from Isleta Pueblo. Chairman of an advisory committee on Indians to the U.S. Census Bureau, Jojola shares concerns about use of "blood quantum" as the sole determinant of Indian identity. "A lot of people are saying that language, culture and residence should also be considered," he says.

That standard would implicitly recognize what many Indians call the single biggest reason that American Indians have outlasted the efforts of those who wanted to exterminate or to assimilate them. "In our spirituality we remain strong," says Bordeaux of the Rosebud Sioux. "That's our godsend and our lifeline."

NOTES

1. For background, see "The Administration of Indian Affairs," *Editorial Research Reports 1929* (Vol. II), at *CQ Researcher Plus Archive*, CQ Electronic Library, http://library.cqpress.com.

2. For background see Phil Two Eagle, "Rosebud Sioux Tribe, Demographics," March 25, 2003, www.rosebudsiouxtribe-nsn.gov/demographics.

3. "American Indian Population and Labor Force Report 2003," p. ii, Bureau of Indian Affairs, cited in John McCain, chairman, Senate Indian Affairs Committee, Byron L. Dorgan, vice chairman, letter to Senate Budget Committee, March 2, 2006, http://indian.senate.gov/public/_files/Budget5.pdf.

4. Jonathan B. Taylor and Joseph P. Kalt, "American Indians on Reservations: A Databook of Socioeconomic Change Between the 1990 and 2000 Censuses," Harvard Project on American Indian Economic Development, January 2005, pp. 8-13; www.ksg.harvard.edu/hpaied/pubs/pub_151.htm. These data exclude the Navajo Tribe, whose on-reservation population of about 175,000 is 12 times that of the next-largest tribe, thus distorting comparisons, Taylor and Kalt write.

5. *Ibid.*, p. 41.

6. McCain and Dorgan, *op. cit.*

7. "Injury Mortality Among American Indian and Alaska Native Youth, United States, 1989-1998," Morbidity and Mortality Weekly Report, Centers for Disease Control and Prevention, Aug. 1, 2003, www.cdc.gov/mmwr/preview/mmwrhtml/mm5230a2.htm#top.

8. Robert McSwain, deputy director, Indian Health Service, testimony before Senate Indian Affairs Committee, April 5, 2006.

9. *Ibid.*, p. xii.

10. Taylor and Kalt, *op. cit.*

11. *Ibid.*, pp. 28-30.

12. *Ibid.*, pp. 22-24.

13. The decision is *Cherokee Nation v. Georgia*, 30 U.S. 1 (1831), http://supreme.justia.com/us/30/1/case.html.

14. Alan Meister, "Indian Gaming industry Report," Analysis Group, 2006, p. 2. Publicly available data can be obtained at, "Indian Gaming Facts," www.indiangaming.org/library/indian-gaming-facts; "Gaming Revenues, 2000-2004," National Indian Gaming Commission, www.nigc.gov/TribalData/GamingRevenues2004 2000/tabid/549/Default.aspx.

15. The ruling is *California v. Cabazon Band of Mission Indians*, 480 U.S. 202 (1987), http://supreme.justia.com/us/480/202/case.html.

16. For background, see Susan Schmidt and James V. Grimaldi, "The Rise and Steep Fall of Jack Abramoff," *The Washington Post*, Dec. 29, 2005, p. A1. On March 29, Abramoff was sentenced in Miami to 70 months in prison after pleading to fraud, tax evasion and conspiracy to bribe public officials in charges growing out of a Florida business deal. He is cooperating with the Justice Department in its Washington-based political-corruption investigation. For background see Peter Katel, "Lobbying Boom," *CQ Researcher*, July 22, 2005, pp. 613-636.

17. Meister, op. cit., pp. 27-28. For additional background, see John Cochran, "A Piece of the Action," *CQ Weekly*, May 9, 2005, p. 1208.

18. For background, see, "A Quiet Crisis: Federal Funding and Unmet Needs in Indian Country," U.S. Commission on Civil Rights, July, 2003, pp. 32, 113. www.usccr.gov/pubs/na0703/na0731.pdf.

19. Ryan Wilson, "State of Indian Education Address," Feb. 13, 2006, www.niea.org/history/SOIEAddress 06.pdf.

20. For background see, Barbara Mantel, "No Child Left Behind," *CQ Researcher*, May 27, 2005, pp. 469-492.

21. McCain and Dorgan, *op. cit.*, pp. 14-15.

22. According to the Health and Human Services Department's budget proposal, recommended funding of $2 billion for the health centers would allow them to serve 150,000 Indian patients, among a total of 8.8 million patients. For background, see "Budget in Brief, Fiscal Year 2007," Department of Health and Human Services, p. 26, www.hhs.gov/budget/07budget/2007BudgetInBrief.pdf.

23. Peter Whoriskey, "A Tribe Takes a Grim Satisfaction in Abramoff's Fall," *The Washington Post*, Jan. 7, 2006, p. A1.

24. Meister, *op. cit.*, p. 15.

25. Whoriskey, *op. cit.*

26. For background see Fred Carstensen, *et al.*, "The Economic Impact of the Mashantucket Pequot Tribal National Operations on Connecticut," Connecticut Center for Economic Analysis, University of Connecticut, Nov. 28, 2000, pp. 1-3.

27. "Gambling Revenues 2004-2000," National Indian Gaming Commission, www.nigc.gov/TribalData/GamingRevenues20042000/tabid/549/Default.aspx.

28. Schmidt and Grimaldi, *op. cit.*

29. Alaina Potrikus, "2nd Land Hearing Packed," *The Post-Standard* (Syracuse, N.Y.), Jan. 12, 2006, p. B1.

30. For background see "Profile of the Navajo Nation," Navajo Nation Council, www.navajonationcouncil.org/profile.

31. Leslie Linthicum, "Navajos Cautious About Opening Casinos," *Albuquerque Journal*, Dec. 12, 2004, p. B1.

32. For background, see "Fourth Annual State of Indian Nations," Feb. 2, 2006, www.ncai.org/News_Archive.18.0.

33. For background see Theodore H. Haas, *The Indian and the Law* (1949), p. 2; thorpe.ou.edu/cohen/tribalgovtpam2pt1&2.htm#Tribal%20Power%20Today.

34. Except where otherwise noted, material in this section is drawn from Angie Debo, *A History of the Indians of the United States* (1970); see also, Mary H. Cooper, "Native Americans' Future," *CQ Researcher*, July 12, 1996, pp. 603-621.

35. W. Dale Mason, "Indian Gaming: Tribal Sovereignty and American Politics," 2000, p. 13.

36. *Cherokee Nation v. Georgia, op. cit.*, 30 U.S.1, http://supct.law.cornell.edu/supct/html/historics/USSC_CR_0030_0001_ZO.html.

37. Robert A. Williams Jr., *Like a Loaded Weapon: the Rehnquist Court, Indians Rights, and the Legal History of Racism in America* (2005), p. 63.

38. *Johnson v. M'Intosh*, 21 U.S. 543 (1823), www.Justia.us/us21543/case.html; *Worcester v. State of Ga.*, 31 U.S. 515 (1832), www.justia.us/us/31/515/case.html.

39. *Johnson v. M'Intosh, op. cit.*

40. *Worcester v. State of Ga., op. cit.*

41. Quoted in Debo, *op. cit.*, pp. 219-220.

42. Quoted in *ibid.*, p. 303.

43. The specified states were Wisconsin, Minnesota (except Red Lake), Nebraska, California and Oregon (except the land of several tribes at Warm Springs). For background, see Debo, *op. cit.*, pp. 304-311.

44. Cited in Debo, *op. cit.*, p. 344.

45. For background see Troy R. Johnson, *The Occupation of Alcatraz Island: Indian Self-Determination and the Rise of Indian Activism* (1996).

46. For background, see Mary H. Cooper, "Native Americans' Future," *CQ Researcher*, July 12, 1996, pp. 603-621.

47. For background see "History of the Tribal Self-Governance Initiative," Self-Governance Tribal Consortium, www.tribalselfgov.org/Red%20Book/SG_New_Partnership.asp.

48. Cochran, *op. cit.*

49. For background see Paul Shukovsky, "Lummi Leader's Had It With Drugs, Sick of Substance Abuse Ravaging the Tribe," *Seattle Post-Intelligencer*, March 16, 2002, p. A1.

50. "Fourth Annual State of Indian Nations," *op. cit.*

51. Many Alaskan villages have joined collective compacts, so the total number of these agreements is 91.

52. For background see Alexandra J. McClanahan, "Alaska Native Claims Settlement Act (ANCSA)," Cook Inlet Region Inc., http://litsite.alaska.edu/aktraditions/ancsa.html; "The Permanent Fund Dividend," Alaska Permanent Fund Corporation, 2005, www.apfc.org/alaska/dividendprgrm. cfm?s=4.

53. For background see Eric Henson and Jonathan B. Taylor, "Native America at the New Millennium," Harvard Project on American Indian Development, Native Nations Institute, First Nations Development Institute, 2002, pp. 14-16, www.ksg.harvard.edu/hpaied/pubs/pub_004.htm.

54. Michael Coleman, "Jemez Casino Proposal At Risk," *Albuquerque Journal*, March 10, 2006, p. A1; Jeff Jones, "AG Warns Against Off-Reservation Casino," *Albuquerque Journal*, June 18, 2005, p. A1.

55. For background see testimony, "Off-Reservation Indian Gaming," House Resources Committee, Nov. 9, 2005, http://resourcescommittee.house.gov/archives/109/full/110905.htm.

56. Jerry Reynolds, "Gaming regulatory act to lose its 'two-part test,' " *Indian Country Today*, March 8, 2006.

57. Testimony before House Resources Committee, Nov. 9, 2005.

58. Matt Kelley, "Government asks for secrecy on its lawyers' role in concealing document shredding," The Associated Press, Nov. 2, 2000.

59. "Memorandum and Order," Civil Action No. 96-1285 (RCL), Feb. 7, 2005, www.indiantrust.com/index.cfm?FuseAction=PDFTypes.Home&PDFType_id=1&IsRecent=1.

60. "Memorandum Opinion," Civil Action 96-1285 (RCL), July 12, 2005, www.indiantrust.com/index.cfm?FuseAction=PDFTypes.Home&PDFType_id=1&IsRecent=1.

61. Glenn Coin, "Supreme Court: Oneidas Too Late; Sherrill Declares Victory, Wants Taxes," *The Post-Standard* (Syracuse), March 30, 2005, p. A1.

62. *Ibid.*

63. *City of Sherrill, New York, v. Oneida Indian Nation of New York*, Supreme Court of the United States, 544 U.S._(2005), pp. 1-2, 6, 14, 21.

64. Elizabeth Shoemaker, *American Indian Population Recovery in the Twentieth Century* (1999), pp. 1-13.

BIBLIOGRAPHY

Books

Alexie, Sherman, *The Toughest Indian in the World*, Grove Press, 2000.
In a short-story collection, an author and screenwriter draws on his own background as a Spokane/Coeur d'Alene Indian to describe reservation and urban Indian life in loving but unsentimental detail.

Debo, Angie, *A History of the Indians of the United States*, University of Oklahoma Press, 1970.
A pioneering historian and champion of Indian rights provides one of the leading narrative histories of the first five centuries of Indian and non-Indian coexistence and conflict.

Deloria, Vine Jr., *Custer Died For Your Sins: An Indian Manifesto*, University of Oklahoma Press, 1988.
First published in 1969, this angry book gave many non-Indians a look at how the United States appeared through Indians' eyes and spurred many young Native Americans into political activism.

Mason, W. Dale, *Indian Gaming: Tribal Sovereignty and American Politics*, University of Oklahoma Press, 2000.
A University of New Mexico political scientist provides the essential background on the birth and early explosive growth of Indian-owned gambling operations.

Williams, Robert A., *Like a Loaded Weapon: The Rehnquist Court, Indians Rights, and the Legal History of Racism in America*, University of Minnesota Press, 2005.
A professor of law and American Indian Studies at the University of Arizona and tribal appeals court judge delivers a detailed and angry analysis of the history of U.S. court decisions affecting Indians.

Articles

Bartlett, Donald L., and James B. Steele, "Playing the Political Slots; How Indian Casino Interests Have Learned the Art of Buying Influence in Washington," *Time*, Dec. 23, 2002, p. 52.
In a prescient article that preceded the Jack Abramoff lobbying scandal, veteran investigative journalists examine the political effects of some tribes' newfound wealth.

Harden, Blaine, "Walking the Land with Pride Again; A Revolution in Indian Country Spawns Wealth and Optimism," *The Washington Post*, Sept. 19, 2004, p. A1.
Improved conditions in many sectors of Indian America have spawned a change in outlook, despite remaining hardships.

Morgan, Lance, "Ending the Curse of Trust Land," *Indian Country Today*, March 18, 2005, www.indiancountry.com/content.cfm?id=1096410559.
A lawyer and pioneering tribal entrepreneur lays out his vision of a revamped legal-political system in which Indians would own their tribal land outright, with federal supervision ended.

Robbins, Ted, "Tribal cultures, nutrition clash on fry bread," "All Things Considered," National Public Radio, Oct. 26, 2005, transcript available at www.npr.org/templates/story/story.php?storyId=4975889.
Indian health educators have tried to lower Native Americans' consumption of a beloved but medically disastrous treat.

Thompson, Ginger, "As a Sculpture Takes Shape in New Mexico, Opposition Takes Shape in the U.S.," *The New York Times*, Jan. 17, 2002, p. A12.
Indian outrage has clashed with Latino pride over a statue celebrating the ruthless Spanish conqueror of present-day New Mexico.

Wagner, Dennis, "Tribes Across Country Confront Horrors of Meth," *The Arizona Republic*, March 31, 2006, p. A1.
Methamphetamine use and manufacturing have become the scourge of Indian Country.

Reports and Studies

Cornell, Stephen, *et al.*, "Seizing the Future: Why Some Native Nations Do and Others Don't," Native Nations Institute, Udall Center for Studies in Public Policy, University of Arizona, Harvard Project on American Indian Economic Development, John F. Kennedy School of Government, Harvard University, 2005.
The authors argue that the key to development lies in a tribe's redefinition of itself from object of government attention to independent power.

"Indian Health Service: Health Care Services Are Not Always Available to Native Americans," Government Accountability Office, August 2005.
Congress' investigative arm concludes that financial shortfalls combined with dismal reservation conditions, including scarce transportation, are stunting medical care for many American Indians.

"Strengthening the Circle: Interior Indian Affairs Highlights, 2001-2004," Department of the Interior (undated).
The Bush administration sums up its first term's accomplishments in Indian Country.

For More Information

Committee on Indian Affairs, U.S. Senate, 838 Hart Office Building, Washington, DC 20510; (202) 224-2251; http://indian.senate.gov/public. A valuable source of information on developments affecting Indian Country.

Harvard Project on American Indian Economic Development, John F. Kennedy School of Government, 79 John F. Kennedy St., Cambridge, MA 02138; (617) 495-1480; www.ksg.harvard.edu/hpaied. Explores strategies for Indian advancement.

Indian Health Service, The Reyes Building, 801 Thompson Ave., Suite 400, Rockville, MD 20852; (301) 443-1083; www.ihs.gov. One of the most important federal agencies in Indian Country; provides a wide variety of medical and administrative information.

National Coalition Against Legalized Gambling, 100 Maryland Ave., N.E., Room 311, Washington, DC 20002; (800) 664-2680; www.ncalg.org. Provides anti-gambling material that touches on tribe-owned operations.

National Indian Education Association, 110 Maryland Ave., N.E., Suite 104, Washington, DC 20002; (202) 544-7290; www.niea.org/welcome. Primary organization and lobbying voice for Indian educators.

National Indian Gaming Association, 224 Second St., S.E., Washington, DC 20003; (202) 546-7711; www.indiangaming.org. Trade association and lobbying arm of the tribal casino industry.

Self-Governance Communication and Education Tribal Consortium, 1768 Iowa Business Center, Bellingham, WA 98229; (360) 752-2270; www.tribalselfgov.org. Organizational hub of Indian self-governance movement; provides a wide variety of news and data.

Upstate Citizens for Equality, P.O. Box 24, Union Springs, NY 13160; http://upstate-citizens.org. Opposes tribal land-claim litigation.

12

Gang Crisis

William Triplett

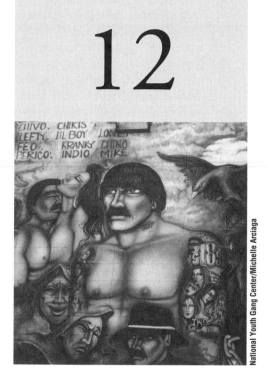

CHIVO. CHIKIS
LEFTY JIL BOY LONEY
FEO. KRANKY CHINO
PERICO: INDIO MIKE

National Youth Gang Center/Michelle Arciaga

A wall mural in East Los Angeles marks the 18th Street gang's turf. At least 21,500 gangs are active nationwide, in small communities as well as cities. Recent immigration has energized violent Latino and Asian gangs like Mara Salvatrucha and the Oriental Playboys.

From *CQ Researcher*,
May 14, 2004.

In June 2001, Fredy Reyes-Castillo met four fellow Latino immigrants at a gas station in Reston, an affluent Northern Virginia suburb. With its upscale malls and subdivisions, it's what drug dealers call a "green area" — full of kids with money.

The four were members of Mara Salvatrucha, or MS-13, a nationwide Latino street gang infamous for its drug dealing and violence. Reyes-Castillo, 22, was not a member, but that day he pretended to be. When the real gangsters realized he didn't understand MS-13 slang or sport gang tattoos, they beat him to death so brutally it took weeks to identify his body. [1]

Three months later, in nearby Alexandria, MS-13 members walked into a McDonald's and spotted an acquaintance, Joaquim Diaz, 19. Diaz was not an MS-13 member and didn't pretend to be.

However, one of the gang members, Denis Rivera, suspected Diaz had joined a rival gang. Rivera and another gang member convinced Diaz to accompany them to Washington to buy marijuana. But Diaz soon found himself in a remote area where he was slashed, stabbed, run over and then mutilated.

Rivera's girlfriend, Brenda Paz, later told police Rivera had bragged that he had tried to behead Diaz, comparing it to "preparing a chicken." But his knife had been too dull, so he had cut out Diaz's larynx instead. Paz entered the federal Witness Protection Program but left before Rivera went on trial. Weeks later her pregnant body was found on the banks of the Shenandoah River, stabbed to death. Police believe MS-13 was responsible. [2]

Newspapers across the country report scores of similar crimes in places like Reston that, until now, have not known gang violence. Even Utah, which historically has enjoyed a relatively low crime

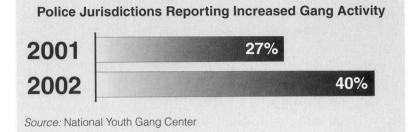

Gang Activity Jumped 50 Percent in 2002

Forty percent of police agencies reported an increase in local gang activity in 2002, a 50 percent rise over 2001, according to a research agency funded by the Department of Justice. Nationwide, there were some 21,500 gangs and 731,000 gang members in 2002.

Police Jurisdictions Reporting Increased Gang Activity

2001	27%
2002	40%

Source: National Youth Gang Center

the climactic rise at the end of the decline almost always sets a record." [7]

Moreover, authorities say, today's gangs are surprisingly well organized. The organizational chart of Chicago's 7,000-member Gangster Disciples — recovered during execution of a search warrant — was described by a federal prosecutor as "more sophisticated than many corporations." More than half the size of the Chicago Police Department, the gang had formed a political action committee, bought legitimate businesses and even sponsored community events, the prosecutor said. [9]

rate, has at least 250 gangs with 3,000 members operating in the Salt Lake City region alone. [3]

Gang experts say the U.S. gang problem, which had diminished in the 1990s, has worsened dramatically in recent years. In 2001, for instance, 27 percent of police agencies polled by the National Youth Gang Center (NYGC), a research agency funded by the Department of Justice (DOJ), said gang activity was increasing in their jurisdictions. In 2002, however, the figure had jumped to more than 40 percent, with at least 21,500 gangs — and more than 731,000 members — active nationwide. [4] In addition to MS-13, the major groups include the Bloods, Crips, Black Gangster Disciples Nation, Almighty Latin Kings Nation and various so-called Jamaican posses, as well as outlaw motorcycle gangs and prison gangs.

Perhaps most alarmingly, the National Alliance of Gang Investigators Associations (NAGIA) says gangs have morphed from an urban scourge into a nationwide threat. "Gang membership has crossed all socioeconomic, ethnic and racial boundaries and now permeates American society," said an NAGIA report. "The gang problem today is much more pervasive and menacing than at any [other] time in history." [5]

Wesley McBride, president of the California Gang Investigators Association, told a Senate Judiciary Committee hearing on gang violence in September 2003 that while gang activity may wane periodically, it usually roars back at record levels. "While there have been occasional declines in gang activity over the years," McBride said, "the declines never seem to establish a record low [and]

In the wake of the Sept. 11, 2001, terrorist attacks on the United States, gangs have even drawn the attention of the State Department and the Department of Homeland Security. Having already diversified from drug dealing into auto theft, extortion, property crimes and home invasion, some East Coast gangs have begun trafficking in fraudulent identification papers that could be used by terrorists trying to enter the country illegally.

While experts agree gangs are a serious problem, few agree on the causes or remedies. Even the definition of a gang is controversial. Some law enforcement officials say a youth gang is three or more 14-to-24-year-olds associating mainly, if not exclusively, to commit crimes. Others, like David Rathbun, a juvenile probation official in Fairfax County, Va., have simpler criteria for identifying gangs: "If it walks like a duck and quacks like a duck, it's probably a duck."

Because different authorities define gangs differently, national figures on gang activity and membership are often only "informed estimates," says NYGC Executive Director John Moore. But according to his organization's "fairly reliable" estimates, he says, 49 percent of U.S. gang members are Latino, 34 percent are black, 10 percent are white and 6 percent are Asian. While Latino and Asian gangs tend to be the most violent, white gangs have expanded into the most new territory over the last decade. [10]

Gangs also commit a disproportionate amount of urban violence. In Rochester, N.Y., for example, gang members who participated in a survey represented only 30 percent of the violent offenders in the region but committed 68 percent of the violent offenses. In Denver, gang members were only 14 percent of those surveyed but admitted to 79 percent of all violent, adolescent offenses committed in the city. [11] In fact, Moore says, 35 percent of Denver's homicides are gang-related.

Many gang victims are potential witnesses, police say. When not killing witnesses, gangs routinely intimidate them, usually through assault or rape. The U.S. attorney in New Orleans recently told Congress that witness intimidation had increased 50 percent in the previous year. [12] "Gangs have even been known to kill police officers who serve as witnesses against them," McBride said. [13]

Yet, the statistics can be tricky. For instance, the data show that overall gang membership and activity in smaller communities have decreased somewhat, but remain as high as ever — if not higher — in large cities and surrounding suburbs, Moore says. "They have decreased in smaller areas, but that's not where their strength ever was," he says.

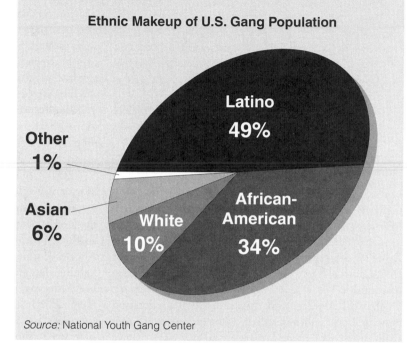

Most Gang Members Are Latino, Black

Nearly half of all U.S. gang members are Latino, and more than a third are black, according to a research agency funded by the Department of Justice. White gangs reportedly have expanded into the most new territory over the last decade, while Asian gangs have moved into the Northeast, and Latino, black and Asian gangs have migrated into the South.

Ethnic Makeup of U.S. Gang Population

Latino 49%
African-American 34%
White 10%
Asian 6%
Other 1%

Source: National Youth Gang Center

As law enforcement officials and policymakers try to assess America's gang problem, here are some of the questions under debate:

Is government doing enough to combat the problem?

Traditionally, state and local authorities have dealt with gangs, since they were not considered a federal problem. In addition to law enforcement, policymakers have tried a variety of prevention programs, such as midnight basketball, designed to give adolescents socially acceptable alternative activities. Other programs, such as vocational training, have offered at-risk youth the promise of legitimate jobs, since unemployment is a major reason kids join gangs.

As gangs migrated — or "franchised" themselves, as some officials describe it — from Los Angeles and other major cities, many police departments set up special gang units. Authorities felt they were keeping pace with the

problem until gangs began increasing in the late 1980s and early '90s, when insufficient resources prevented police from keeping up. Since then, state and local authorities say they haven't been able to keep up with the increase. If the federal government would provide more resources, local law enforcement authorities say they could do more.

Several federal agencies assist in the fight against gangs. Since gang crime often involves guns, the Bureau of Alcohol, Tobacco, Firearms and Explosives (BATFE) investigates gangs. Similarly, gangs' frequent involvement with illegal drugs draws attention from the Drug Enforcement Administration (DEA).

Perhaps foremost among federal anti-gang agencies are the 75 FBI Safe Streets Gang Task Forces (SSGTFs) operating around the country. The SSGTFs emphasize "identification of the major violent street gangs [and] drug enterprises [that] pose significant threats," Grant D.

Bloods gang members from Los Angeles display their gang signs and colors. Gang members generally don't wear their colors in public nowadays to avoid trouble from police or rival gangs.

Ashley, assistant director of the FBI's Criminal Investigative Division, told the Senate Judiciary Committee. [14]

"SSGTFs operate under the premise of cooperation between local, state and federal agencies," says Jeff Riley, chief of the FBI's Safe Streets and Gang Unit. "Once established, the SSGTFs are charged with bringing the resources of all the participating agencies to bear on the area's gang problem. This includes using sensitive investigative techniques, with an emphasis on long-term, proactive investigations into the violent criminal activities of the gang's leadership and hierarchy."

Moreover, when appropriate, U.S. attorneys "actively and creatively" prosecute gang crimes in federal courts, according to three U.S. attorneys who testified last September before the Judiciary Committee. In addition to using traditional narcotics and firearms statutes, federal prosecutors are using the Racketeer Influenced and Corrupt Organizations (RICO) law — successfully used to weaken the Mafia — against gangs. The U.S. attorney in Southern California recently convicted 75 members of the 18th Street and Mexican Mafia gangs under the RICO law. [15]

The DOJ also administers the Office of Juvenile Justice and Delinquency Prevention (OJJDP) and the Gang Resistance Education and Training (GREAT) program, which tries to develop positive relationships among local law enforcement, families and at-risk youths.

But McBride says federal law enforcement efforts have been ineffective because they have not been properly coordinated with state and local efforts. For instance, he says Los Angeles law enforcement agencies "hardly ever hear from" the FBI task force on gangs based in Los Angeles.

"You can almost compare [the situation] to the 9/11 hearings," says McBride, referring to the recent commission hearings that revealed a crucial lack of communication between various intelligence agencies before the terrorist attacks. "That's much like what's happening in the gang world."

Riley responds that the SSGTF in Los Angeles is located near the heart of the Watts section and focuses on inner-city gang activity, rather than on the more suburban activity McBride has been battling.

Fairfax County's Rathbun says the FBI task force in Northern Virginia, as well as U.S. immigration officials, works well with local officials, but he acknowledges that the level of cooperation varies from region to region.

But McBride, who recently retired from the Los Angeles County Sheriff's Department after 28 years of fighting gangs, contends that federal prosecution has not been effective. "You'd think they're prosecuting gang members right and left," says McBride, referring to the testimony at last September's Senate Judiciary Committee hearing. "I can tell you that U.S. attorneys don't want to see a gang case. They're very hard to prosecute, very labor-intensive and in their [U.S. attorneys'] defense, they simply can't handle all the cases — we probably arrest 40,000 gang members a year just in L.A. But don't say the feds are doing a great job of prosecuting gang members."

Many state and local authorities say they are best equipped to prosecute gangs, if the federal government would provide the necessary funding. Robert McCulloch, prosecuting attorney of St. Louis County, Mo., and president of the National District Attorneys Association, says 180 gangs with about 4,000 members are fighting a violent turf war in St. Louis. But he says most cases will never be prosecuted because he can't offer witness protection.

"Prosecutors across the county believe witness intimidation is the single, biggest hurdle facing successful gang prosecution," he said. In Denver, a defendant allegedly ordered a sexual assault on a female witness scheduled to testify in a gang homicide. In Savannah, a gang murder occurred in front of 300 people, but no one would identify the assailant. [16]

Most state and local jurisdictions cannot afford witness-protection programs or the training and overtime needed for gang investigations. The state budget crisis and tax cuts have sapped local funds, and the war on terrorism has forced the redeployment of anti-gang units. [17]

"There are already plenty of laws to prosecute gangs," says Beryl Howell, a former legislative director for Sen. Patrick J. Leahy, D-Vt., who worked on anti-juvenile-crime legislation in the mid-1990s. The obstacles to pursuing gangs effectively, she says, are "resource issues, not legal issues."

Sens. Orrin G. Hatch, R-Utah, and Dianne Feinstein, D-Calif., hope to remedy that with the Gang Prevention and Effective Deterrence Act of 2003. The bill would authorize approximately $100 million in federal funds annually for five years to underwrite area law enforcement efforts in jurisdictions with "high-intensity interstate gang activity." Another $40 million a year would fund prevention programs.

The Hatch-Feinstein bill would do more than provide desperately needed funds, says Bill Johnson, executive director of the National Association of Police Organizations and a former Florida prosecutor. It would also make participation in a "criminal street gang" and recruiting people to commit "gang crimes" federal offenses, punishable by 10 to 30 years in prison.

"It won't be the only solution, by any stretch of the imagination," he continues. "But if used properly, it'll help crush some of these gangs that really do overrun neighborhoods and communities."

But others are concerned that the bill would expand the federal role in fighting gangs, and in the process hamper local prosecutions. For instance, by redefining some state offenses as federal crimes, the bill could curtail state prosecutors' discretion in bringing charges and negotiating plea agreements, because defendants would be facing federal as well as state prosecution for gang crimes.

"We should be wary of making a federal crime out of everything," said Sen. Leahy. [18]

But Feinstein argues: "It used to be that gangs were local problems, demanding local, law-enforcement-based solutions. But over the last 12 years, I have seen the problem go from small to large and from neighborhood-based to national in scope. What were once loosely organized groups . . . are now complex criminal organizations whose activities include weapons trafficking, gambling, smuggling, robbery, and, of course, homicide. This is why we need a strong federal response."

Is There a Gang in Your 'Hood?

The following quiz can help neighborhoods measure potential gang activity. A score of 50 points or more indicates the need for a gang-prevention and intervention program:

In your community:

- Is there graffiti? (5 points)
- Is the graffiti crossed out? (10)
- Do the young people wear colors, jewelry, clothing, flash hand signs or display other behaviors that may be gang related? (10)
- Are drugs available? (10)
- Has there been a significant increase in the number of physical confrontations? (5)
- Is there an increasing presence of weapons? (5)
- Are beepers, pagers or cell phones used by the young people? (10)
- Has there been a "drive-by" shooting? (15)
- Have you had a "show-by" display of weapons? (10)
- Are truancies and/or daytime burglaries increasing? (5)
- Have racial incidents increased? (5)
- Is there a history of local gangs? (10)
- Is there an increasing presence of "informal social groups" with unusual names containing words like: kings, disciples, queens, posse, crew? (15)

Scoring Key

0-20 points = No Problem	50-65 points = You Have Problems
25-45 points = Emerging Problems	70+ points = You Have Serious Problems

Source: Tennessee Gang Investigators Association

The Violence of Mara Salvatrucha

David Rathbun has seen a lot of youngsters come through the juvenile justice system in Fairfax County, Va., near Washington, D.C. But he can't shake the memory of the 11-year-old charged with murder.

The boy and his 16-year-old brother belonged to Mara Salvatrucha, a Latino gang known for its violence. The two boys were out early one morning, "looking for trouble," says Rathbun, a juvenile-probation official. When they thought a youth across the street flashed a rival gang's sign at them — a gesture of disrespect — they crossed the street and stabbed him to death.

Violence is a gang's normal stock-in-trade, but gang experts say Mara Salvatrucha — or MS-13 — has made shootings, stabbings, hackings, beatings and rapes its brazen specialties. The gang originated in Los Angeles among refugees of El Salvador's civil war of the 1980s and rapidly spread around the country. The gang was formed in Los Angeles to protect Salvadoran immigrants from other, hostile Latino immigrants, according to veteran gang investigator Wesley McBride. The theory was: strike back twice as violently as you were attacked, and they'll leave you alone. Many MS-13s had been guerrilla fighters in El Salvador's bloody civil war.

MS-13 began as a merger between immigrants who'd been involved with La Mara — a street gang in El Salvador — and former members of the FMNL, a paramilitary group of Salvadoran guerrilla fighters called "Salvatruchas."

MS-13's victims have included innocent people caught in the middle as well as other gang members. In 2002, MS-13's Los Angeles cell reportedly dispatched several members to Fairfax County with instructions to kill a county police officer "at random." They didn't succeed. [1]

The Justice Department says MS-13 now has about 8,000 members in 27 states and the District of Columbia, and 20,000 more members in Central and South America, particularly El Salvador. The gang is involved in smuggling and selling illegal drugs, but different cells (or cliques, as they're sometimes called) may be involved in other activities, including providing "protection" to houses of prostitution, Rathbun says.

The independent National Gang Crime Research Center (NGCRC) ranks gangs by their violence level, with 1 being least dangerous and 3 the most dangerous. MS-13 is ranked a 3. Center Director George W. Knox describes MS-13's level of violence as "extraordinary." [2]

An investigator with the Orange County, Calif., district attorney's office says the gang participates in a broad range of criminal activities across the country. "MS members have been involved in burglaries, auto thefts, narcotic sales, home-invasion robberies, weapons smuggling, car jacking, extortion, murder, rape, witness intimidation, illegal firearm sales, car theft and aggravated assaults. . . . [C]ommon drugs sold by MS members include cocaine, marijuana, heroin, and methamphetamine. Mara Salvatrucha

Others are concerned about the historic conflicts between federal and state/local investigations and prosecutions. While SSGTFs are designed to work cooperatively with local authorities, differences remain in their investigative priorities. For instance, federal investigators' concentration on building cases over time will usually net more convictions, but local authorities often need to respond more quickly to community complaints, usually with street sweeps that can interfere with federal investigations.

Should gun laws be tightened to combat gang violence?

More than 350,000 incidents of gun violence, including 9,369 homicides, were committed in 2002, according to Michael Rand, chief of victimization statistics at the Justice

Department's Bureau of Justice Statistics. But no one knows what percentage of those murders were committed by gang members, partly because of disagreement over what constitutes gang-related crime. To some officials, if two gang members commit an armed robbery, the crime can only be considered gang-related if they share the proceeds with the rest of the gang. To others, any armed robbery committed by gang members qualifies as gang-related.

According to the BATFE, 41 percent of the 88,570 guns used in crimes in 46 large cities in 2000 were traced to people age 24 or younger. [19] Of course, no one knows how many of them were gang members.

But as a recent Justice Department survey concluded: "Although both gang members and at-risk youths admitted

gang members have even placed a 'tax' on prostitutes and non-gang member drug dealers who are working in MS 'turf.' Failure to pay up will most likely result in violence." [3]

One of the gang's signatures is a military-style booby trap used to protect a stash of illegal drugs. The trap usually consists of a tripwire rigged to an anti-personnel grenade.

Joining the gang requires potential members to be "jumped in." Several gangs observe this ritual, which involves a group-administered beating. Typically, gang members surround the candidate and then attack him; other gang members evaluate how well he defends himself and his ability to endure punches. MS-13's jumping-in lasts for 13 seconds.

Most MS-13 members are between ages 11 and 40, but leaving the gang is often difficult. The father of the two

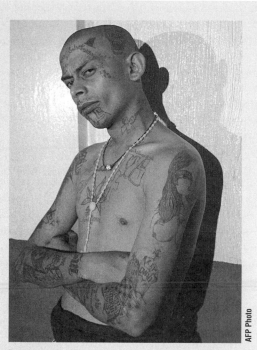

Police arrested this Mara Salvatrucha leader last year in San Salvador, El Salvador. Thousands of the gang's most violent U.S. members have been deported.

AFP Photo

boys who stabbed the suspected rival gang member to death is also an MS-13 member; the mother wholeheartedly supports her husband's and sons' memberships, Rathbun says.

The 16-year-old was tried as an adult and sentenced to a maximum-security prison, but Rathbun has hope for the 11-year-old, who took school classes when he was in the county's juvenile system. "He had a probation officer that worked very closely with him, and his sense of self-worth increased as he did better academically. He stayed in touch with the gang, but he wasn't participating any more. I don't think his father will ever be out of MS-13, but, knock wood, I think we may have changed the son's course."

[1] "Focus on Gangs: Salvadoran MS-13 Rated Among Most Violent," *Emergency Net News*, Aug. 24, 2002; http://www.emergency.com/polcpage.htm.

[2] *Ibid.*

[3] Al Valdez, "A South American Import," National Alliance of Gang Investigators Associations, 2000; http://www.nagia.org/mara_salvatrucha.htm.

significant involvement with guns, gang members were far likelier to own guns, and the guns they owned were larger caliber." More than 80 percent of gang members surveyed said either they or their fellow members had carried concealed guns into school, while only one-third of at-risk youths said they or their friends had done the same. [20] The most popular weapons were 9mm semiautomatic pistols. [21]

"Gangs, like any criminals, can never be as effective without firearms," says Joe Vince, a retired BATFE analyst. "Absolutely, guns are a tool of the trade for gangs — you've never heard of a drive-by with a knife."

Vince regularly investigated gangs' gun-show purchases, where unlicensed firearms dealers are exempt from the Brady Handgun Violence Prevention Act, which requires licensed sellers to perform a criminal background check before selling a weapon. Since it is illegal for anyone to sell a firearm to a buyer with a criminal record, gangs often send buyers who don't have criminal records to gun shows. [22]

Such "straw purchases" are also illegal, but unscrupulous unlicensed dealers pretend not to recognize a suspicious purchase, even when an 18-year-old is trying to buy a dozen guns at once, Vince says. "We found a lot of gangs sending someone who didn't have a record to gun shows, and he'd be on a cell phone talking to the gang leaders and saying, 'Hey, this guy's offering this, and that guy's offering that,' " Vince says.

"Some dealers even advertise that they're not licensed, so you can buy from them no-questions-asked," says Garen Wintemute, director of the Violence Prevention Research Program at the University of California, Davis.

In Chicago — which now may have the nation's largest and most active gang population — gangs are blamed for 45 percent of last year's 598 homicides. [23] Authorities also believe Chicago has more illegal firearms than any other city: In 2003, Chicago police seized more than 10,000 illegal guns; Los Angeles police recovered just under 7,000 and New York City under 4,000. [24]

Gun control advocates maintain that tougher gun laws and more stringent enforcement of them could cut gang violence. "Wherever you can reduce the availability and accessibility of firearms to criminals, you reduce violent crime," Vince says. "People just cannot be as violent without a gun."

However, Erich Pratt, communications director for Gun Owners of America (GOA), says, "We've yet to discover any gun control legislation that successfully keeps guns out of the wrong hands. Washington, D.C., is certainly the epitome of that — you have a draconian gun ban there that doesn't let anybody own any guns, and yet the bad guys continue to get firearms."

Data compiled by the Bureau of Justice Statistics show that handgun homicides started decreasing in 1993 — a year before Congress enacted the Brady law — and continued to fall through 2000.

But a study in the *Journal of the American Medical Association* suggests no link between the decrease and the Brady law. "We find no differences in homicide or firearms homicide rates in the 32 . . . states directly subject to the Brady Act provisions compared with the remaining [18] states," the researchers wrote. [25]

Wintemute says the results could be interpreted in two equally valid ways: "One is that the Brady law never went far enough from the beginning," he says, "or that the Brady law is a failure and we should get rid of it."

Supporters of the law say that at the least it has prevented the crime rate from worsening. But Andrew Arulanandam, public affairs director for the National Rifle Association (NRA), says the law's stringent record-keeping provisions make that unlikely.

"You mean to tell me that some guy who's going to commit a heinous crime is going to leave a paper trail?" Arulanandam asks. Gang members are "not going to be deterred by a firearm law. More often than not, they'll obtain the firearm by illegal means."

But record-keeping is diminishing. Because of a provision in the Omnibus Appropriations bill, passed last January, federal authorities who run criminal background checks on gun buyers are no longer required to keep a record of the check for 90 days. In fact, they must now destroy the record within 24 hours.

Moreover, Eric Howard, spokesman for the Brady Campaign to Prevent Gun Violence, says the Department of Justice recently found that Brady background checks blocked more than a million potential purchasers from buying guns. "This flies in the face of what [the NRA] says all the time: That these guys aren't going to get background checks, they'll get guns elsewhere," Howard says. "Well, these guys aren't the sharpest knives in the drawer." The Brady law could very well have kept the nation's crime rate lower than it might otherwise have been in the past decade, Howard argues. [26]

Nonetheless, some states enforce the Brady law less stringently, so gangs go to those states. For instance, gangs in Chicago have established a gun-running pipeline into Mississippi, where Brady enforcement and local gun laws are generally more relaxed. [27]

Opponents of gun control say this proves their point: Regardless of how many prohibited purchases are blocked, criminals will always find a way to get firearms. The best deterrent, they say, is not to limit the number of guns on the street but to increase them — by allowing law-abiding citizens to carry concealed weapons. "States that have adopted concealed-carry legislation are seeing the greatest and most dramatic decreases in the murder rate," Pratt says.

The gun problem is like the drug problem, says the NRA's Arulanandam. "Drugs are outlawed, but people get their hands on them."

The BATFE's Vince agrees with the comparison, but he and other gun control advocates want to close the gun-show loophole, which the gun lobby says would penalize law-abiding, unlicensed dealers.

"If you focus law enforcement only on gun users but not on dealers," he says, "that's like saying we're going to go after everyone that shoots heroin but not the cartel."

Should more minors be tried as adults for gang crimes?

An undercover Chicago police officer working a drug deal in the depressed Humboldt Park neighborhood in April noticed two young men run into an alley. Seconds later, he heard gunshots and saw the men running out. A third man lay dying in the alley.

As the cop chased the suspects, they turned and fired at him. He continued chasing them and eventually caught them. One was 18, the other 15. Both were members of the Maniac Latin Disciples. "I wanted to shoot a Cobra" — a rival gang — "to prove how tough I was," the 15-year-old reportedly said. He was charged as an adult with first-degree murder. [28]

In colonial days, children sometimes faced adult charges and just as often were incarcerated with adults; sometimes they were executed. [29] In the late 19th century, however, social reformers argued that juveniles were developmentally different from adults and could be rehabilitated. The nation established a juvenile justice system — with separate statutes and penalties — at the beginning of the 20th century.

But in cases involving violent crimes, prosecutors sometimes try minors as adults, triggering debate over the tactic's effectiveness and justification. A surge in juvenile crime beginning in the late 1980s — largely triggered by a crack epidemic — led many minors to be charged as adults. A 1989 Supreme Court ruling allowing states to execute juvenile offenders 16 and older has kept the debate alive.

Currently, state prosecutors decide whether minors charged with violent felonies should be charged as adults. But the proposed Hatch-Feinstein bill would allow federal prosecutors to try any gang member 16 or older as an adult.

The legislation has triggered debates over whether more minors should be tried as adults, and whether the federal government should be trying minors at all. "We're always uncomfortable when furthering policies that take things that should be state matters and throw them into federal courts," the GOA's Pratt says. "We agree that if you do an adult crime, you do the adult time, but we think the states [should] handle it."

"The feds don't have any infrastructure set up to deal with juveniles, so they usually defer to the states, and wisely so," says Rathbun of Fairfax County. "We've had a couple of murder cases where the feds got involved, and it was useful because [the accused] got harsher sentences. But that's just a handful of our cases."

However, former legislative director Howell believes that federal authorities can more effectively prosecute gangs than state or local authorities. "The gang problem warrants federal attention because it quickly overtakes local and state boundaries," she says. "It can overtake national boundaries, too."

For example, as a federal prosecutor Howell once went after members of the Flying Dragons, which ran gambling and Mah Jong parlors in New York's Chinatown. But the gang also smuggled heroin from Hong Kong. The investigation had to contend with the respective requirements and laws affecting New York and Hong Kong authorities, not to mention language and cultural complications between both cities.

But prosecuting juveniles as adults won't solve the gang problem, she says. "Where does that get you?" she asks. "The younger you send kids to prison, the better-educated they become at being criminals. Adult prisons have lost much pretense, if they ever had any, of being rehabilitative. With the juvenile system, there's at least a pretense of rehabilitation."

Federal prosecution of minors as adults would be "a good law to have on the books and threaten with, but it's not going to help much," adds McBride, of the California Gang Investigators Association. States have tougher provisions on minors and gangs than federal agencies, he notes, and states aren't making any demonstrable headway against gangs by prosecuting minors as adults.

Trying minors as adults "is an effective tool the same way a sledge hammer is an effective tool," says the National Association of Police Organizations' Johnson. "It ought to be used sparingly, but in those cases where it's necessary, then it ought to be used."

More than 60 child-advocacy organizations oppose the Senate bill's provision to prosecute juveniles as adults for gang crimes. "I understand the desire to respond to gang violence," said Marc Schindler, a staff attorney for the Youth Law Center. "But this is the wrong way to do it. It's basically going to throw kids away to the adult system." [30]

Even law-and-order hard-liners acknowledge that the threat of severe punishment alone will not deter gangs. "A lot of gang members are in gangs because their parents didn't give a rat's behind about them," says McBride, echoing experts on all sides of the issue. "How do you make a momma care for her kid? You can't legislate that."

The best deterrent to gangs, many experts say, is to have parents involved with their children's lives, but in today's economy, that's often nearly impossible. Some observers attribute the rise in immigrant gangs to the fact that both parents often work multiple jobs and have little time to spend with their kids.

CHRONOLOGY

1950s *Southern blacks migrate to Northern inner cities; classic era of teen street gangs; wave of Puerto Rican immigrants arrives in New York City.*

Sept. 26, 1957 Leonard Bernstein's hit musical "West Side Story" opens on Broadway. It looks unflinchingly at the growing menace of gang warfare.

1960s *Gangs take on traits from civil rights, Black Muslim and radical youth movements; government channels some gangs into anti-poverty work.*

1961 President John F. Kennedy signs Juvenile Delinquency and Youth Offenses and Control Act, creating a federal committee to address youth crime.

1967 President's Task Force on Juvenile Delinquency calls for community efforts to curb youth crime. . . . Senate probes fraud in federal grant program for Chicago's Blackstone Rangers gang.

1970s *Police officials and academics shift their strategies on gangs from social work to suppression and control.*

Aug. 21, 1974 Congress creates Office of Juvenile Justice and Delinquency Prevention.

1975 Justice Department launches first national gang survey.

1980s *Latino and Asian immigrants make Los Angeles the nation's gang capital; crack cocaine arrives in inner cities; Reagan administration declares war on drugs.*

1982 FBI designates motorcycle gangs as national investigative priority within its organized-crime program.

1985 California creates State Task Force on Youth Gang Violence; L.A. Police Chief Daryl F. Gates vows to eliminate gangs in five years.

Late 1980s Highly profitable crack cocaine becomes the product of choice for drug-dealing gangs, sparking fights over the most profitable turf and a spike in violent crime.

1988 President Ronald Reagan signs Anti-Drug Abuse Act. . . . California convenes State Task Force on Gangs and Drugs; Los Angeles police crack down on gang neighborhoods.

May 15, 1989 Administration of first President George Bush bans imports of semiautomatic assault weapons used by street gangs.

1990s *Gangs expand out from inner cities; government, police and academics coordinate comprehensive approach to the gang problem.*

1995 Gang homicides in Los Angeles hit a record 809 deaths . . . more than half of all violent crime in Buffalo, N.Y., is gang related.

1997 FBI estimates that 50,000 gang members are active in Chicago. . . . Congress attempts to overhaul the U.S. juvenile justice system, but the bill deadlocks over juvenile sentencing and gun control.

1999 Congress again addresses juvenile justice, but House and Senate negotiators again stall over gun control.

2000s *Police say gang violence begins to rise; Asian and Latino gangs account for most juvenile violence; Congress again attempts to pass anti-gang legislation.*

Sept. 11, 2001 Terrorist strikes against the U.S. cause many police departments to reassign special gang units to counter-terrorist duties.

Jan. 2004 Congress passes Omnibus Appropriations bill, which contains a provision voiding the Brady law's requirement that the National Instant Criminal Background Check system maintain records of criminal checks for 90 days; gun control advocates claim this will make it harder for authorities to trace crime guns to gang members and other criminals.

April 2004 Senate Judiciary Committee begins consideration of the Gang Prevention and Effective Deterrence Act, sponsored by Sens. Dianne Feinstein, D-Calif., and Orrin Hatch, R-Utah. Committee approval is expected in May.

Whatever the causes, the rise in gang crime has made some authorities open to anything that might help. Los Angeles County's sheriff recently estimated that the 96,000 gang members in his jurisdiction commit half the violent offenses each year. "We believe there are teenagers close to 18 who are committing heinous adult acts, and they should be treated as an adult," said Steve Whitmore, a spokesman for the L.A. sheriff's office. [31]

BACKGROUND

Early Gangs

The youth gang phenomenon dates back at least to the days of St. Augustine (A.D. 354-430), who wrote in his *Confessions* of the pleasures of stealing pears with adolescent accomplices: "My pleasure was not in those pears, it was in the offense itself, which the company of fellow sinners occasioned." [32]

In 17th-century London, youth gangs with such names as the Mims, the Bugles and the Dead Boys terrorized the citizenry by breaking windows, destroying taverns and fighting, each group wearing different-colored ribbons. And Charles Dickens often wrote about gangs in the 19th century, perhaps most famously the gang of boy orphans run by the money-grubbing Fagin in the classic *Oliver Twist*.

In the United States, the first recorded youth gang was the Forty Thieves, founded in about 1825 in Lower Manhattan. Others appeared in Philadelphia in the 1840s, such as the Bouncers, the Rats and the Skinners. Mostly they defaced walls with graffiti and carried pistols and knives.

Immigrants usually formed gangs for self-protection. Often not speaking the language of their new country and unfamiliar with its customs, they found assimilation extremely difficult. Discrimination added a sense of victimization to their existing feelings of alienation, and they saw gangs as a refuge from a hostile environment.

Waves of Irish immigrants in New York in the 19th century soon begat such gangs as the Bowery Boys and the Dead Rabbits, who waged three-day rumbles that

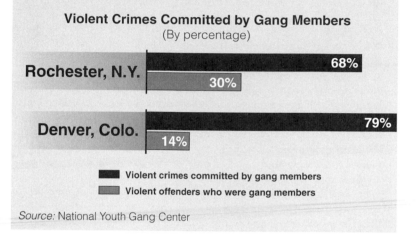

Gangs Commit Most Violent Teen Crimes

Gang members make up a small percentage of violent offenders but commit a disproportionate amount of teenage violent crime, as shown by statistics from Rochester, N.Y., and Denver, Colo.

Violent Crimes Committed by Gang Members
(By percentage)

Rochester, N.Y. 68% / 30%

Denver, Colo. 79% / 14%

■ Violent crimes committed by gang members
■ Violent offenders who were gang members

Source: National Youth Gang Center

forced helpless police to call in the Army. Their nonchalance toward violence was remarkable: A member of the Plug Uglies is said to have attacked a stranger and cracked his spine in three places just to win a $2 bet. [33] Female gang members also were known in the mid-19th century, among them the celebrated street fighters Hellcat Annie and Battle Annie. [34]

Early New York gangs, as brutally portrayed in the 2002 movie "Gangs of New York," often sold their services to labor unions and company operators maneuvering in the rough and tumble world of politics. "By 1855," a city historian wrote, "it was estimated that the Metropolis contained at least 30,000 men who owed allegiance to gang leaders and through them to the leaders of Tammany Hall and the Know Nothing, or Native American Party." [35] During the Civil War, Irish gang members were blamed for the anti-conscription riots in which many blacks were lynched.

The German and Italian immigrants who arrived in the late 19th century produced equally violent gangs. Some would commit crimes for hire: A slash on the cheek with a knife cost $10; throwing a bomb, $50; murder, $100. "It might be inferred that the New York tough is a very fierce individual [but] it is only when he hunts with the pack that he is dangerous," noted social reformer and photographer Jacob Riis. [36]

When Girls Join Gangs

In Augusta, Ga., six members of an all-girl gang corner a 22-year-old woman on the street and savagely beat her. [1] In San Antonio, Texas, two girls slash a rival gang girl's face with a broken bottle. [2] In Buffalo, N.Y., female members of a mixed gang transport narcotics and sometimes sell drugs on the streets. [3]

Gang members are usually seen as young men wearing distinctive clothes or colors, using a common slang and hand signals and fighting with gangs from other neighborhoods. If females are in the picture at all, they're usually viewed as supporting players — girlfriends, perhaps, or maybe sisters, but never gang members in their own right. Yet, female gangs have existed in America at least since the 19th century.

Relatively little is known about female gangs, however, and most of the knowledge has been acquired only in the last 20 years. Sexist stereotyping has largely been responsible for the lack of awareness, according to the Justice Department's Office of Juvenile Justice and Delinquency Prevention (OJJDP). Researchers historically perceived gangs in terms of vandalism, theft and assault — generally considered male provinces.

"It was often assumed that females did not take part in such behavior, so early researchers were not interested in the delinquency of female gang members," wrote sociologist Joan Moore and criminologist John Hagedorn in an issue of the Juvenile Justice Bulletin devoted to female gangs. [4]

When gang activity escalated in the 1980s and '90s, researchers began noticing that female gangs were either autonomous entities or affiliates of male gangs. With names like Latin Queens, the female counterpart to Latin Kings, and Sisters of the Struggle, they usually had their own identities and structures.

No one knows how many female gangs exist. Law enforcement surveys tend to show that between 4 and 11 percent of gang members are female, but social-service surveys show higher numbers.

Although little is known about female gang activity, some research and anecdotal reports show that most girl gangs are involved in delinquency or non-violent crimes, with drug offenses ranking near the top of the list. Female gang members commit fewer violent crimes than male gang members and in general are more prone to property crime. [5]

"The biggest difference between female gangs and male gangs is violence," says Hagedorn, a professor of criminal justice at the University of Illinois. "Girls are very seldom involved in homicide. The difference between males and females on this issue is massive."

Still, he acknowledges, female gang members can sometimes be just as violent as males. In the mid-1990s, an 11-city survey of eighth-graders revealed that more than 90 percent of male and female gang members admitted to having commit-

The most notorious of the early immigrant gangs in New York was, of course, the Mafia, or La Cosa Nostra ("Our Thing"), which originated as a criminal organization in Sicily. The Mafia rose to power by extorting neighborhood shopkeepers for "protection" money against arson. It consolidated its power during Prohibition, when it controlled the illegal distribution of liquor in many U.S. cities.

By the turn of the century, Jewish gangs and Chinese gangs had been added to the ethnic stew in New York's Bowery, Chinatown and in such rough neighborhoods as Hell's Kitchen on the West Side. During Prohibition, many youth gangs became involved with adult bootleggers. In Southern California, waves of Mexican immigrants arrived to form the first so-called barrio gangs.

But the worst gang problems plagued Chicago. In 1927 criminologist Frederick M. Thrasher published the

first major book on the problem, *The Gang: A Study of 1,313 Gangs in Chicago*, in which he analyzed gangs of every ethnic and racial stripe: Polish, Irish, Anglo American, Jewish, Slavic, Bohemian, German, Swedish, Lithuanian, black, Chinese and Mexican. "The gang is a conflict group," Thrasher wrote. "It develops through strife and warfare."

The ethnic character of American gangs continued to manifest itself. In the 1930s, the rising numbers of blacks migrating from the South to New York, as well as new immigrants from the British West Indies, set up the first rivalries among black gangs. In the early 1940s, gangs of Latino youths in Southern California frequently clashed with U.S. servicemen stationed in the area, eventually provoking the so-called Zoot Suit Riots, named for a flashy clothing style then popular among Latinos.

ted one or more violent acts in the previous 12 months. Moreover, 78 percent of female gang members reported having been in a gang fight, 65 percent acknowledged carrying a weapon and 39 percent said they had attacked someone with a weapon. [6]

Within mixed gangs, males commonly boast that the females are their sex objects, a claim that has perpetuated the "sex slave" stereotype of female gang members. But OJJDP research done in conjunction with the National Youth Gang Center shows that females deny this, insisting that females of any position or authority in the gang are respected precisely because they do not allow the males to exploit them sexually. Sexual exploitation does occur, they say, but almost always involving girls or young women who are not members of the gang.

Currently, most female gangs are Latina and African-American, though the numbers of Asian and white female gangs have been increasing.

Regardless of ethnicity or race, many girls join gangs for the same reasons as males — seeking friendship and self-affirma-

Female gang members commit fewer violent crimes than male gang members, primarily property and drug offenses.

tion. Sometimes the lack of job opportunities pushes girls and young women to join gangs, as it does boys and young men. But many female gang members share a common pain of childhood, which they have tried to escape by seeking refuge in a gang. "Research consistently shows that high proportions of female gang members have experienced sexual abuse at home," Hagedorn and Moore write.

There's another important difference between female and male gang members: Females tend to leave a gang sooner because they get pregnant, usually by age 18.

[1] See "Woman Reports Gang Assault," *The Augusta Chronicle*, Feb. 22, 2004, p. B3.

[2] See Elda Silva, "'Homegirls' Gets Personal, Introspective," *The San Antonio Express-News*, Jan. 29, 2004, p. 1F.

[3] See Lou Michel, "The Bloods, Settling Debts with Death," *Buffalo News*, Dec. 16, 2003, p. A1.

[4] See Joan Moore and John Hagedorn, "Female Gangs: A Focus on Research," *Juvenile Justice Bulletin*, March 2001, p. 1.

[5] *Ibid*, p. 5.

[6] *Ibid*, p. 6.

Seeking Respectability

The classic youth-gang era began after World War II, when Americans migrated from the farms to the cities. The first "teenage" subculture emerged in the postwar period, and gangs severed their earlier ties to adult organized crime.

In Los Angeles, two black gangs appeared — the Businessmen and the Home Street Gang. In the 1950s, CBS News correspondent Edward R. Murrow drew nationwide attention to the conditions that produce gangs with the documentary "Who Killed Michael Farmer?" about the death of a handicapped young man at the hands of a Bronx street gang.

Society responded to gangs by trying to build long-term relationships with gang members and by sponsoring dances or athletic contests, such as a New York City Youth Board program that sought to reduce gang tensions. "Participation in a street gang or club," a 1950 Youth Board document read, "like participation in any natural group, is part of the growing-up process. . . . Within the structure of the group the individual can develop such characteristics as loyalty, leadership and community responsibility. . . . Some gangs . . . have developed patterns of anti-social behavior . . . [but] members can be reached and will respond to sympathy, acceptance, affection and understanding when approached by adults who possess those characteristics and reach out to them on their own level." [37]

In the 1960s, the Hell's Angels motorcycle gang gained national exposure and greatly influenced the younger, more ethnic urban gangs. "By 1965," wrote counterculture journalist Hunter S. Thompson, later of

The Rev. Greg Boyle, a Jesuit priest, runs a jobs program in East Los Angeles for gang members who want to stop being criminals.

Rolling Stone fame, "[gangs] were firmly established as All-American bogeymen." Meanwhile, the decade's civil rights movement, urban riots and radical politics spilled over into the world of gangs, particularly among blacks, many of whom would become attracted to revolutionary groups like the Black Panthers.

With President Lyndon B. Johnson's War on Poverty pouring millions of federal grant dollars into inner cities, some criminal youth gangs decided to join the Establishment, heralding either an optimistic or opportunistic approach to addressing social problems, depending on one's viewpoint.

In New York City in 1967, for example, leaders of the Puerto Rican gang Spartican Army decided they wanted a role in bettering the social and economic conditions of their Lower East Side neighborhoods. Borrowing from Johnson's Great Society rhetoric, they took the name the Real Great Society and applied for a grant from the federal Office of Economic Opportunity (OEO). They were turned down, but their well-publicized efforts (profiled in *Life* magazine) attracted private foundation money. They opened a Real Great Society nightclub, a child-care service and a leather-goods store, all of which blossomed briefly but failed within a year. [38] They then organized summer classes for inner-city youths and finally won an OEO grant.

In Chicago, meanwhile, another experiment in gang respectability was under way. In 1967, the Blackstone Rangers, led by a fervent black nationalist, Jeff Fort, began toying with the notion of doing anti-poverty work

with a radical white clergyman, John Fry, who was affiliated with a community-organizing group named for Chicago's Woodlawn neighborhood. Because the group opposed Chicago's powerful mayor, Richard J. Daley, its anti-poverty programs had never received federal grant money, over which Daley had de facto control.

But the possible turnaround of the Blackstone Rangers was too tempting to Washington. In June, the OEO awarded the Woodlawn Organization and the Blackstone Rangers $927,000 to operate anti-poverty programs for a year.

Daley was furious at fellow Democrats in the Johnson administration, but he did not have to fume for long. The Woodlawn program quickly became known as a monumental boondoggle: Only 76 of 800 participants in its jobs program got jobs; bookkeeping was lax; gang members encouraged each other to quit school and be paid from the federal grant; by autumn, Fort had been arrested on murder charges. [39]

In Washington, Sen. John L. McClellan, D-Ark., chairman of the Government Operations Committee, held widely publicized hearings into the Woodlawn grant. Many blamed the OEO for poor judgment. While under indictment, Fort appeared as a witness but refused to speak. (The murder charges against him were later dismissed.)

In May 1968, OEO shut down the Woodlawn project, just weeks after the Blackstone Rangers were given credit for keeping Chicago relatively calm during the urban riots that followed the assassination of the Rev. Dr. Martin Luther King, Jr. The idealistic notion of giving government money to reformed gang members had suffered a crippling blow.

The impact of Chicago's gang experiment during the days of the War on Poverty would be felt for decades. Chicago gang members continued to receive foundation money for nearly 20 years. Fort was sentenced to prison in the early 1970s for fraud committed with the OEO grant. In prison, he converted to Islam and changed the Rangers' name to El Rukns (Arabic for "the foundation").

When he and some fellow gang members emerged from prison in the late 1970s, they threw themselves into the violent drug trade. Dozens of El Rukns members were sent to prison in the early 1980s. In 1987, Fort was sentenced to 75 years in prison for soliciting money from Libya to fund terrorist operations in the U.S. [40]

In the 1980s, crack cocaine became the product of choice for drug-dealing gangs: Highly addictive and inexpensive, crack provided a profit margin greater than powdered cocaine. Gangs soon were fighting over the most profitable turf — markets — giving rise to drive-by shootings and a spike in violent crime.

War Refugees

In El Salvador, civil war in the early 1980s prompted many refugees — and former guerrillas — to flee to the United States. The Mara Salvatrucha, or MS-13, gang emerged from a rapidly swelling population of Salvadoran immigrants in Los Angeles. Other gangs with roots in the Central American immigrant communities of Southern California also formed, and violence frequently erupted between them and the area's long-established Mexican gangs.

Asian gangs began appearing around the same time, mostly as a result of massive Asian immigration, including the "boat people," refugees from war-ravaged Southeast Asia. The gangs of Vietnamese, Cambodian and Laotian refugees had roots in the region's refugee camps following the Vietnam War and the post-war atrocities committed by the Khmer Rouge in Cambodia. [41] By the late 1980s and early '90s, Asian gangs had footholds from West Valley City, Utah, to Manhattan. "When I was a prosecutor in New York," Howell recalls, "the Vietnamese gangs were as violent as anybody."

Throughout the late 1980s and early '90s, many Latino gang members in L.A. headed north to Chicago, already teeming with black, white and mixed-race gangs. In 1991, the city's homicide rate hit a record 609 deaths. In response, Mayor Richard M. Daley recalled the gang-grant scandal from the era when his famous father had run city hall. The younger Daley lashed out at the liberal "social workers" of the 1960s and '70s who had "coddled" the teenage gang members who were now, as adults, Chicago's drug kingpins.

In an effort to reduce the nation's crime rate, Congress in 1996 enacted a law that allows deportation of non-citizens sentenced to a year or more in prison for anything ranging from petty theft to murder. Since then, in what constitutes the largest dragnet in the country's history, more than 500,000 "criminal aliens" have been deported to more than 130 countries, including many gang members who originally immigrated to the United States with their parents to escape poverty or civil war. [42]

While the tactic has effectively reduced the number of criminals in the United States, it has overwhelmed the receiving countries, particularly in Latin America and the Caribbean, which have seen crime rates skyrocket since 1996.

Many of the deported have joined local gangs — often home-country versions of the gangs they belonged to in the United States. El Salvador and Honduras have suffered particularly sharp rises in violent gang crime, with beheadings, shootings, rapes and hackings now commonplace, police say. Moreover, vigilante groups often hunt down gang members and murder them on sight — a practice both U.S. and Latin American officials say only causes retaliation and escalation. [43]

By 1997, the chief of the FBI's violent-crime section estimated that Chicago had 50,000 active gang members — more than the combined area membership of the Moose, the Elks, the Knights of Columbus and the Shriners. [44] Meanwhile, in the previous 16 years approximately 7,300 people had died in gang violence in Los Angeles.

But Chicago and L.A. were not alone. In 1995, police blamed gangs for 41 percent of Omaha's homicides, and more than half of all violent crime in Buffalo. In Phoenix, gang-related homicides jumped 800 percent between 1990 and '94. [45] While the overall violent-crime rate across the country was dropping, violent juvenile crime remained high.

In response, lawmakers drafted the Violent and Repeat Juvenile Justice Act of 1997. The House passed its version of the bill, but the Senate's version — opposed by countless advocacy groups — never made it to a floor vote. Liberals felt it was too harsh, citing its intention to prosecute juveniles as adults and house them with adults in prison. Conservatives felt it penalized law-abiding gun merchants and owners.

Congress tried again in early 1999 with Democrats and Republicans apparently determined to compromise on the issue. But the bipartisan spirit was shattered in April, when two teenagers in Littleton, Colo., went on a shooting rampage at Columbine High School, killing 13 people before turning the guns on themselves. [46] Both the House and Senate passed juvenile crime bills, but liberals and conservatives deadlocked over gun control, effectively killing the bills in conference.

Starting in 1995, juvenile violent crime began falling, and continued falling through 2001, but in 2002 authorities began seeing an upsurge in gang violence. [47] Latino and Asian gangs were committing the most violent offenses, particularly along the Northeast Corridor. Of the two, the Latinos have drawn the most attention because their numbers are currently the largest. And among the Latinos, MS-13 is widely considered the most dangerous.

CURRENT SITUATION

Invisible Crisis

If many Americans are unaware of the country's gang crisis, it may be because some police departments don't want them to know about it. The National Alliance of Gang Investigators Associations says many law enforcement agencies have refused to cooperate with its nationwide survey of gang activities.

"We're getting so many of those forms back from [police] departments refusing to fill them out," McBride says. "The local authorities say, 'We don't want to ruin our economy, because companies won't move here if they know we have gangs!' " McBride says. "I even had one executive tell me that people don't have a right to know, and no sense scaring them. I was flabbergasted. People absolutely have a right to know and need to know how many gangs are out there."

But sometimes the agencies don't respond because of poor record keeping, he says. In Denver, for example, police records show that the city's 17,000 gang members committed only 89 of the 59,581 crimes in 2002. "I heard that figure, and I just wanted to laugh," said a member of the metropolitan police department's gang crimes unit. [48] Moore, of the National Youth Gang Center, says officers often do not know immediately that a crime is gang related; when they find out, they rarely revise the initial police report.

Another problem is the cyclical nature of gangs and gang prevention. Police departments often set up gang units and then dissolve them once they believe the situation is under control, only to see the problem worsen again. "There's just no continuity of incident reporting," Moore says, so police records on gangs are "notoriously slack."

Four years ago, when acknowledging a gang problem carried less stigma than it does today, the NAGIA assembled a national picture of gangs and gang activities that many say is still essentially accurate. Starting in the late 1990s, gangs began penetrating into suburban areas in the Northeast and Mid-Atlantic regions, particularly in upstate New York, eastern Pennsylvania and Northern Virginia. Increasing numbers of Asian gangs were migrating into the Northeast, while two Latino gangs — the

Latin Kings and the Netas — had become involved in political and social causes to establish some legitimacy. [49]

Along with the increase in gangs has come an increase in crime. Last September, for instance, Christopher Christie, U.S. attorney for Newark, N.J., reported that for the third straight year, the city's murder rate had risen, as well as the number of handguns recovered by police. "The rise in violence and unlawful gun possession corresponds directly to a substantial increase in documented gang activity beginning in 1999," he said. [50]

The South also has seen increased activity among established Asian and Latino gangs, and several Latino and black gangs from Chicago have expanded into the region, particularly in drug dealing. [51] In Charlotte, N.C., authorities have been fighting white motorcycle gangs along with the black Kings, but as in Northern Virginia, the most violent and visible gang is MS-13. [52]

In the Chicago area, gangs have been growing more sophisticated and organized. Asian and Latino gangs account for the greatest growth throughout the region, with the latter expanding in direct relation to a widening of the methamphetamine market. Chicago-based gangs have also extended their reach into various regions of the West, where the epicenter of gang activity continues to be Los Angeles.

National Gang Policy?

Investigating gangs that appear to be operating in several regions is complicated, because different gang factions often have different interests. "Gangs are, more often than not, locally based, geographically oriented criminal associations," Sen. Leahy recently said. "Even gangs that purportedly have the same name on the East and West coast are not necessarily affiliated with one another." [53]

What is needed, McBride says, is a national gang policy that spells out an accepted definition of a gang and gang-related activity and a national gang intelligence center, similar to the Department of Justice's National Drug Intelligence Center.

"We need massive federal aid to local government in a multifaceted approach — it can't be just cops," he continues, adding that the approach should coordinate probation, corrections and community-based programs, as well as prevention and intervention programs. Coordination and communication among all relevant authorities, which currently is lacking, also must be beefed up, he says. "And it all has to be long term. The

Would the Gang Prevention and Effective Deterrence Act proposed by Sens. Orrin Hatch and Dianne Feinstein help in the fight against gangs?

YES   Sen. Orrin G. Hatch, R-Utah

From a statement before the U.S. Senate, Oct. 15, 2003

Mr. President, I rise today to introduce a comprehensive, bipartisan bill to increase gang prosecution and prevention efforts.

The Gang Prevention and Effective Deterrence Act of 2003 also increases funding for the federal prosecutors and FBI agents needed to conduct coordinated enforcement efforts against violent gangs.

Additionally, this bill will create new, criminal, gang-prosecution offenses, enhance existing gang and violent-crime penalties to deter and punish illegal street gangs, propose violent-crime reforms needed to prosecute effectively gang members and propose a limited reform of the juvenile-justice system to facilitate federal prosecution of 16- and 17-year-old gang members who commit serious acts of violence.

Once thought to be only a problem in our nation's largest cities, gangs have invaded smaller communities. Gangs now resemble organized-crime syndicates who readily engage in gun violence, illegal gun trafficking, illegal drug trafficking and other serious crimes.

Recent studies confirm that gang violence is an increasing problem in all of our communities. The most current reports indicate that in 2002 alone, after five years of decline, gang membership has spiked nationwide.

While we all are committed to fighting the global war on terrorism, we must redouble our efforts to ensure that we devote sufficient resources to combating this important national problem — the rise in gangs and gang violence in America.

We must take a proactive approach and meet this problem head on if we wish to defeat it. If we really want to reduce gang violence, we must ensure that law enforcement has adequate resources and legal tools, and that our communities have the ability to implement proven intervention and prevention strategies, so that gang members who are removed from the community are not simply replaced by the next generation of new gang members.

Federal involvement is crucial to control gang violence and to prevent new gang members from replacing old gang members. I strongly urge my colleagues to join with me in promptly passing this important legislation.

NO   Jeralyn Merritt
Criminal Defense Attorney, Denver, Colo.

From talkleft.com: the politics of crime, Dec. 21, 2003

Sens. Diane Feinstein, D-Calif., and Orrin Hatch, R-Utah, have teamed up to sponsor a terrible bill — one that panders to irrational fear but resonates politically.

It is rife with new categories of crimes, added punishments for having a gun or being a gang member and myriad "think twice" measures hoping gang members will reconsider before committing a crime.

Anyone who knows gangs knows that lawmakers cannot conceive of a law that would lead a hard-core gang member to "think twice." We already have enough gang- and gun-related sentencing "enhancements" to send a 17-year-old who has never been in trouble with the law to prison for 35 years to life. And that's without his ever touching a gun or ever being an actual member of a gang. We need to overhaul these enhancements, not add to them.

Gangs are not all that mysterious. Reformers know what works with them and what doesn't. Gang experts, intervention practitioners, social scientists, researchers and enlightened law enforcement officials all agree. What works is prevention, intervention and enforcement.

You prevent kids from joining gangs by offering after-school programs, sports, mentoring and positive engagement with adults. You intervene with gang members by offering alternatives and employment to help redirect their lives. You deal with areas of high gang-crime activity with real community policing.

There are ways that money could make a difference in curbing gangs — but the Feinstein-Hatch bill doesn't acknowledge them.

Law enforcement doesn't need more tools; it needs more officers. Real community policing requires different deployment, which can happen only with increased personnel. Although the Feinstein-Hatch bill would also allocate $200 million for prevention and intervention, more than three-quarters of that money would be administered by law enforcement. That is as misguided as having Homeboy Industries — a gang rehab center — enforce a gang injunction.

What's really going on here is politics. Feinstein and Hatch's ill-advised bill will neither prevent nor deter gang-related crime. It's time to stop funding wasteful law enforcement initiatives and listen to those who know what works — and it's not the politicians. This turkey of a bill needs to die a fast death.

problem with going to federal funding agencies is you get little grants for 18 months at most. That's not enough."

Newark's Christie has called for a special, multi-level unit that would target an entire gang operation — much like the Mafia was targeted — not simply the most visible members on the streets. "It is not uncommon for a single gang to be involved in drug dealing, firearms trafficking, murder, robbery, money laundering and, more recently, mortgage fraud," he said. To deal with such broad-based activities, he suggests, the U.S. attorney's office should lead a team consisting of the FBI, DEA, BATFE and the Marshals Service, along with local authorities. [54]

Without such broad-based coordination and information sharing, many investigations and prosecutions languish, authorities say. Investigations are also hindered by the lack of funds to adequately protect witnesses. "For many prosecutors, a witness-protection program simply consists of a bus ticket or a motel room," said McCulloch, of the National District Attorneys Association, who has pleaded for federal funds for such programs. In Denver, he points out, the number of prosecutions has dropped sharply because of the lack of protection while the number of gang crimes "has increased tremendously." [55]

Lately, Congress appears to be listening: In addition to making some gang activities federal offenses, the proposed Gang Prevention and Effective Deterrence Act would provide approximately $100 million of federal assistance for state and local law enforcement and $40 million for prevention programs over five years. In the Senate the bill was scheduled for markup in mid-May and expected to pass largely intact. A House companion bill has yet to be submitted.

Johnson of the National Association of Police Organizations predicts the measure will eventually become law. "Maybe not in this Congress before the [November presidential] election," he says, "but I do think it will pass. It won't be a cure-all but another tool in the box that will marginally and incrementally help bring down gangs and make communities safer."

However, Denver criminal-defense attorney Jeralyn Merritt calls it "a terrible bill" that "panders to irrational fear but resonates politically." In a scathing criticism of the proposal on the Web site *talkleft.com*, she argues: "We already have enough gang- and gun-related sentencing 'enhancements' to send a 17-year-old who has never been in trouble with the law to prison for 35 years to life. And that's without his ever being an actual member of a gang. We need to overhaul these enhancements, not add to them.

"Gangs are not all that mysterious. Reformers know what works with them . . . What works is prevention, intervention and enforcement. You prevent kids from joining gangs by offering after-school programs, sports, mentoring and positive engagement with adults. You intervene with gang members by offering alternatives and employment to help redirect their lives. You deal with areas of high gang-crime activity with real community policing."

OUTLOOK

More Violence?

In Northern Virginia, probation official Rathbun thinks authorities at every level of government have begun to realize the size and scope of the gang threat. As he puts it, "It's kind of the problem *du jour* now."

But whether effective policies will soon emerge is an open question, he says. "There's still lots of crazy things," he says. "We've got a directive from our agency now that says we can't question anybody about their immigration status, which seems stupid."

Moore, of the National Youth Gang Center, expects gang violence to continue its cyclical patterns, with upswings followed by downturns. "Some cities experience a big flare-up in gang violence every year," he says. "They've either never recognized the problem and it bubbles up to the surface, or they think they've dealt with the problem, but it comes back up again."

To U.S. Attorney Christie in Newark, nothing short of a full-scale, coordinated assault by law enforcement agencies at all levels is going to make a difference. Gang crime is, he said, "the new organized crime in the United States, an organized crime that destroys families, corrupts our children and lays waste to neighborhoods in our most vulnerable communities. We must mount a fight comparable to the fight against La Cosa Nostra in past decades if we expect to have the same success." [56]

But the FBI's Riley believes the resources are coming "at a slow pace." Given the FBI's priority on combating terrorism, Riley envisions "probably a 10-year progression to get [anti-gang resources] to the point I'd like to see." Meantime, he expects increasing gang activity as a result of continued immigration and "the phenomenon of the media making the 'gangsta' lifestyle appealing."

But he's also somewhat optimistic. "I see more cooperation between federal agencies — the FBI, the [BATFE] and the DEA and even the Marshals Service."

Although federal legislation may help bring the problem under control, changing demographics and the inherent dangerousness of gang activity may help staunch the growth of gangs over the long-term, says Johnson of the National Association of Police Organizations. "The Baby Boomlet will get older, and as they do, they'll mature and calm down," he says. "As this generation ages, there will be a decrease in the general crime rate. Plus, the really bad ones either get caught or killed. Gang [activity] is a very high-risk business."

McBride of the California Gang Investigators Association doubts that either the proposed legislation or more federal funds will eliminate the problem. "After you get some federal grants, the statistics decrease, and then the politicians walk away saying the problem's solved," he says. "Then, surprise, surprise — the problem's right back."

But if done right, he says, the legislation could help. "If the funding goes for local prosecution and for local gang units, that's going to be a tremendous help. But if it stays federally based, it's not going to have the impact they want it to have."

Rathbun, who deals with juvenile gangs daily, is pessimistic. Some gangs that had seemed to disband in Northern Virginia, such as TRG, are revitalizing, and becoming shrewder.

"The kids are less apt to get the tattoos now, and less apt to dress like gang-bangers," he says, so authorities are less apt to immediately recognize them. Their actions, however, won't be any different than before. Rathbun says the rival 18th Street Gang and the Latin Kings, as well as the new South Side Locos, are beginning to move into MS-13 territory.

"We're expecting turf battles," he says. "Machetes, knives and guns. I think it's going to be a bad summer."

It has already begun with machetes. A 16-year-old boy thought to be a South Side Locals member was walking along a suburban street on May 10 when reputed MS-13 members jumped him and nearly hacked his hands off. His screams woke residents, who called police. Doctors saved both hands, but four fingers were permanently lost, and it is too soon to tell if he will recover use of his hands. [57]

"They were trying to send a message," said Robert Walker, a former Drug Enforcement Administration special agent who runs a gang-identification training program for law enforcement officers. "Gangs deal in what we call the three R's. The first is reputation, and they want to do all they can to build that. The second is respect . . . and the third is retaliation or revenge."

NOTES

1. See Maria Glod, "Man Gets 30 Years in Gang Slaying; Va. Judge Cites Brutal Beating in Sentencing 1 of 4 Charged," *The Washington Post*, Sept. 28, 2002, p. B6. See also Maria Glod, "Gangs Get Public's Attention: Dozen Actively Contributing to Area Crime," *The Washington Post*, Sept. 18, 2003, p. T1.

2. See Maria Glod, "Prosecutors Describe Gang-Style Execution as MS-13 Trial Opens," *The Washington Post*, Nov. 6, 2003, p. B6. See also Maria Glod, "Guardian of Slain Woman Replaces Her as Witness; Authorities Believe Teen was Silenced by Gang," *The Washington Post*, Nov. 7, 2003, p. B4.

3. Sen. Orrin G. Hatch, opening statement before Senate Judiciary Committee hearing on "Combating Gang Violence in America: Examining Effective Federal, State and Local Law Enforcement Strategies," Sept. 17, 2003.

4. Office of Juvenile Justice and Delinquency Prevention, U.S. Department of Justice, "Highlights of the 2001 National Youth Gang Survey," April 2003. See also Neely Tucker, "Gangs Growing in Numbers, Bravado Across Area," *The Washington Post*, Sept. 18, 2003, p. A1.

5. National Alliance of Gang Investigators Associations, "Threat Assessment, 2000."

6. Office of Juvenile Justice and Delinquency Prevention, *op. cit.*

7. Wesley McBride, testimony before Senate Judiciary Committee hearing, Sept. 17, 2003.

8. *Ibid.*

9. Patrick Fitzgerald, testimony before Senate Judiciary Committee hearing, Sept. 17, 2003.

10. National Youth Gang Center, www.iir.com/nygc/faq.htm#q6.

11. *Ibid.*

12. Eddie Jordan, testimony before Senate Judiciary Committee hearing, Sept. 17, 2003.

13. McBride, *op. cit.*

14. Grant D. Ashley, testimony before Senate Judiciary Committee hearing, Sept. 17, 2003.

15. Debra Yang, testimony before Senate Judiciary Committee hearing, Sept. 17, 2003.

16. Robert McCulloch, testimony before Senate Judiciary Committee hearing, Sept. 17, 2003.

17. For background, see William Triplett, "State Budget Crisis," *CQ Researcher*, Oct. 3, 2003, pp. 821-844.

18. See Keith Perine, "Senators Pushing for Increased Federal Role in Fighting Crime Linked to Gangs," *CQ Today*, April 9, 2004.

19. Bureau of Alcohol, Tobacco and Firearms and Explosives (BATFE), "Crime Gun Trace Reports: National Report," June 2002, pp. ix, x.

20. C. Ronald Huff, "Criminal Behavior of Gang Members and At-Risk Youths," presentation to the National Institute of Justice.

21. BATFE, *op. cit.*

22. For background, see Richard L. Worsnop, "Gun Control," *CQ Researcher*, June 10, 1994, pp. 505-528, and Kenneth Jost, "Gun Control Standoff," *CQ Researcher*, Dec. 19, 1997, pp. 1105-1128.

23. Fitzgerald, *op. cit.*

24. See David Heinzmann, "Gangs Run Gun Pipeline from Delta to Chicago; Lenient Laws Make Buying Weapons Easier in South," *Chicago Tribune*, Feb. 5, 2004, p. C1.

25. Jens Ludwig and Phil Cook, "Homicide and Suicide Rates Associated with Implementation of the BHVPA," *Journal of the American Medical Association*, Aug. 2, 2000, Vol. 284, p. 585.

26. Jost, *op. cit.*

27. Heinzmann, *op. cit.*

28. See Carlos Sandovi, "Teen Charged in Humboldt Park Gang Rival's Killing; Police say Suspect also Took Shots at Undercover Cop," *Chicago Tribune*, April 21, 2004, p. C2.

29. For background see Brian Hansen, "Kids in Prison," *CQ Researcher*, April 27, 2001, pp. 345-376.

30. See Lisa Friedman, "Anti-Gang Bill Draws Critics; Juvenile Advocacy Groups Oppose Adult Sentencing," *Los Angeles Daily News*, Nov. 24, 2003, p. N4.

31. *Ibid.*

32. Quoted in Armando Morales and Bradford W. Sheafor, *Social Work: A Profession of Many Faces* (1989), p. 415.

33. For background see Charles S. Clark, "Youth Gangs," *CQ Researcher*, Oct. 11, 1991, pp. 753-776.

34. Anne Campbell, *The Girls in the Gang* (1984), p. 9.

35. Quoted in Irving A. Spergel, *Crime and Justice: A Review of Research*, "Youth Gangs: Continuity and Change," Michael Tonry and Norval Morris, eds., Vol. 12 (1990), p. 172.

36. Quoted in James Haskins, *Street Gangs: Yesterday and Today* (1974), p. 48.

37. *Ibid*, p. 99.

38. *Ibid*, p. 112.

39. See Nicholas Lemann, *The Promised Land* (1991), p. 245.

40. See Michael Abramowitz, "Street Gang Convictions Challenged in Chicago," *The Washington Post*, Dec. 22, 1992, p. A3.

41. See Matt Canham and Tim Sullivan, "Asian Gangs a Scourge: Violent Rivals in the Vietnamese, Lao and Cambodia Communities are Settling Scores at Malls, Amusement Parks; Asian Gangs Target Their Own People," *The Salt Lake Tribune*, April 14, 2003, p. D1.

42. The Associated Press, "U.S. Deportees Cart Crime to Native Lands," *Los Angeles Times*, Jan. 4, 2004, p. A5.

43. Kevin Sullivan, "Spreading Gang Violence Alarms Central Americans," *The Washington Post*, Dec. 1, 2003, p. A1.

44. Steven Wiley, testimony before Senate Judiciary Committee hearing on gang violence, April 23, 1997.

45. Sen. Dianne Feinstein, statement before Senate Judiciary Committee hearing on gang violence, April 23, 1997.

46. For background, see Sarah Glazer, "Boys' Emotional Needs," *CQ Researcher*, June 18, 1999, pp. 521-544 and Kathy Koch, "School Violence," *CQ Researcher*, Oct. 9, 1998, pp. 881-904.

47. National Center for Juvenile Justice, "Juvenile Arrest Rates by Offense, Sex, and Race," May 31, 2003.

48. See Chuck Plunkett, "Gangs' Hidden Fingerprint," *The Denver Post*, Nov. 9, 2003, p. A1.

49. National Alliance of Gang Investigators Associations, *op. cit.*

50. Christopher Christie, testimony before Senate Judiciary Committee hearing, Sept. 17, 2003.

51. National Alliance of Gang Investigators Associations, *op. cit.*

52. See Arian Campo-Flores, "Gangland's New Face," *Newsweek*, Dec. 8, 2003, p. 41.

53. Sen. Patrick Leahy, opening statement before Senate Judiciary Committee hearing, Sept. 17, 2003.

54. Christie, *op. cit.*

55. McCulloch, *op. cit.*

56. Christie, *op. cit.*

57. Maria Glod and Tom Jackman, "Teen's Hands Severed In Northern Va. Machete Attack," *The Washington Post*, May 11, 2004, p. B1.

BIBLIOGRAPHY

Books

Hernandez, Arturo, *Peace in the Streets: Breaking the Cycle of Gang Violence*, Child Welfare League of America, 1998.
Hernandez tells the riveting story of his experience as a young teacher in South Central Los Angeles and the positive effect he had on the gang members who were his students.

Kinnear, Karen L., *Gangs: A Reference Handbook*, ABC-CLIO, 1996.
This compendium on juvenile gangs by a journalist focuses on their activities, membership, motivations and their relation to society and the law.

Lloyd, J.D., ed., *Gangs*, Greenhaven Press, 2002.
A collection of informational essays by a journalist examines why gangs exist, their history, their day-to-day actions and what can be done to lessen the damage they do.

***The Truth about Street Gangs*, Gang Prevention Inc., 2001.**
This publication is designed to help communities identify and understand gangs, focusing on how they operate and how they conceal their activities.

Articles

Campo-Flores, Arian, "Gangland's New Face," *Newsweek*, Dec. 8, 2003, p. 41.
The surge of Latino gangs is reflected in their relatively new and overwhelming presence in Charlotte, N.C.

Canham, Matt, and Tim Sullivan, "Asian Gangs a Scourge; Gunplay: Violent rivals in the Vietnamese, Lao and Cambodian communities are settling scores at malls, amusement parks; Asian Gangs Target Their Own People," *Salt Lake Tribune*, April 14, 2003, p. D1.
Asian gangs wreak havoc in the greater Salt Lake area, mostly within the immigrant community but sometimes outside of it.

Heinzmann, David, "Gangs run pipeline from Delta to Chicago; Lenient laws make buying weapons easier in the South," *Chicago Tribune*, Feb. 5, 2004, p. 1.
To skirt tough gun control laws, Chicago gangs use the proceeds of illegal drug sales to buy weapons in Mississippi.

Jackson, Chriscia, "Asian gangs have reputation for living 'giang ho,' or crazy life," *Associated Press*, May 25, 2000.
A look at the violence and destructiveness of Asian gangs as seen in the story of two juvenile members of Vietnamese gangs in Port Arthur, Texas.

Plunkett, Chuck, "Gangs' Hidden Fingerprint," *The Denver Post*, Nov. 9, 2003, p. A1.
Plunkett details the extensive gang activity throughout the Denver area and the police department's lack of accurate records on gangs.

Tucker, Neely, "Gangs Growing in Numbers, Bravado Across Area," *The Washington Post*, Sept. 18, 2003, p. A1.
Latino gangs are growing rapidly in Washington, D.C., and other areas of the country not previously known for intense gang activity.

"U.S. Deportees Cart Crime to Native Lands; More than 500,000 have been banished under 1996 law," The Associated Press, *Los Angeles Times*, **Jan. 4, 2004, p A5.**
The federal government's tactic of deporting non-U.S. citizens convicted of crimes has sent many gang members back to their homeland, where they resume gang activity.

Reports and Studies

"Highlights of the 2001 National Youth Gang Survey," Office of Juvenile Justice and Delinquency Prevention, Department of Justice, April 2003.
This annual survey documents national trends, activities and developments among youth gangs.

Huff, C. Ronald, "Comparing the Criminal Behavior of Youth Gangs and At-Risk Youths," National Institute of Justice, Department of Justice, October 1998.
A survey shows that criminal activity of youth-gang members is significantly higher than that of at-risk youths.

Moore, Joan, and John Hagedorn, "Female Gangs: A Focus on Research," *Juvenile Justice Bulletin*, **Office of Juvenile Justice and Delinquency Prevention, U.S. Department of Justice, March 2001.**
This summary of research attempts to address the imbalance between research on male and female gangs.

"National Youth Gang Center Bibliography of Gang Literature," Office of Juvenile Justice and Delinquency Prevention, U.S. Department of Justice, 1997.
An exhaustive bibliography of gang literature — dating as far back as the 1940s — reviewed and compiled by the National Youth Gang Center for the Office of Juvenile Justice and Delinquency Prevention.

Reed, Winifred L., and Scott H. Decker, "Responding to Gangs: Evaluation and Research," National Institute of Justice, U.S. Department of Justice, July 2002.
A comprehensive review of recent research about gang behavior as well as anti-gang strategies.

For More Information

Bajito Onda, P.O. Box 270246, Dallas, TX 75227; (214) 275-6632; www.bajitoonda.org/. Foundation dedicated to giving Latino youths positive alternatives to gangs, drugs and violence through education.

Juvenile Justice Clearinghouse, P.O. Box 6000, Rockville, MD 20849-6000; (800) 851-3420; http://ojjdp.ncjrs.org/programs/ProgSummary.asp?pi=2. A component of the National Criminal Justice Reference Service that maintains information and resources on juvenile-justice topics.

National Alliance of Gang Investigators Associations; www.nagia.org. An online coalition of criminal-justice professionals dedicated to promoting a coordinated anti-gang strategy.

National Criminal Justice Reference Service, P.O. Box 6000, Rockville, MD, 20849-6000; (800) 851-3420; http://virlib.ncjrs.org/juv.asp?category=47&subcategory=66. A federally funded service that provides information on jus-

tice and substance abuse to support research, policy and program development worldwide.

National Major Gang Task Force, 338 S. Arlington Ave., Suite 112, Indianapolis, IN 46219; (317) 322-0537; www.nmgtf.org. An independent organization specializing in intervention, management strategies, networking, training and information-sharing regarding gangs.

National Youth Gang Center, P.O. Box 12729, Tallahassee, FL 32317; (850) 385-0600; www.iir.com/nygc. A Department of Justice-funded group that collects and analyzes information on gangs.

Office of Juvenile Justice and Delinquency Prevention, 810 7th St., N.W., Washington, D.C. 20531; (202) 307-5911; http://ojjdp.ncjrs.org. A Justice Department office providing leadership, coordination and resources on preventing juvenile delinquency and victimization.